DATE DUE

GAYLORD   PRINTED IN U.S.A.

HOW TO *Create* SUCCESSFUL CATALOGS

SECOND EDITION

MAXWELL SROGE

NTC Business Books
a division of *NTC Publishing Group* • Lincolnwood, Illinois USA

Printed on recyclable paper

Library of Congress Cataloging-in-Publication Data

Sroge, Maxwell.
    How to create successful catalogs / Maxwell Sroge. — 2nd ed.
      p.   cm.
    Rev. ed. of: How to create successful catalogs. 1985.
    Includes index.
    ISBN 0-8442-3661-6
    1. Commercial catalogs. 2. Advertising, Direct-mail. I. Title.
HF5862.H68   1995
659.13′3—dc20

94-16184
CIP

1995 Printing

Published by NTC Business Books, a division of NTC Publishing Group
4255 West Touhy Avenue
Lincolnwood (Chicago), Illinois 60646-1975, U.S.A.

5 6 7 8 9 ML 0 9 8 7 6 5 4 3 2 1

Contents

Introduction

Welcome to the second edition of the best-selling book ever published on the subject of creating catalogs. We've taken the best of the first edition and enhanced it based on new technologies and the newest catalog strategies.

This book is designed to be *used*, not merely "read." Browse through it, enjoy it, mull it over, learn from it, even argue about it. In these pages you'll find the step-by-step guidance of hands-on catalog experts . . . dissecting, explaining, illustrating every aspect of a catalog's creation. Whether you're a catalog "pro" or a "beginner," you'll find value in the techniques exposed here. This book can be used by *anyone* who wishes to create a catalog and to do so *successfully*.

Each chapter is self-sustaining. Use them as separate guidelines to a particular area of your interest, or use them together. Though there are many approaches to each step in creating a catalog, there also are some basics which must be followed by both experienced cataloger and novice. These are the methods which will produce a *good* catalog: one which attracts the target customer, has appropriate style, and compliments the product line (and the image of the catalog house) with its graphics and copy approach. A "good" catalog is one which *sells*.

The methods presented in this book are proven. The fresh ideas and approaches here are founded on these proven methods and will result in a professional catalog with plenty of selling punch.

To "begin at the beginning," Chapter 1 reflects on the origins of catalogs, and Chapter 2 deals with the all-important technicalities of planning and scheduling (a first step, after all). But those of you *creating* your first catalog should start with Chapter 3, Forming an Approach, and move to Chapter 5, Photography and Art, and Chapter 6, Copy. The excitement and detailing of catalog creation are found in these later chapters and prepare you to tackle the more tedious, but basic and vital elements found in Chapter 2, such as scheduling.

Chapter 3 defines the purpose of the three major catalog sections: front cover, back cover and inside pages. Design approaches are discussed and basic methods are explained. Execution techniques are provided with blueprints (grids) for various styles of page layouts. Chapter 4 leads you through methods of deciding upon the art and copy approaches which are most appropriate for your product line and your target customer. Here is where you discover "product work sessions," the "scientific" basis for your "creative" decisions. Chapter 5 tackles the exciting and awesome task of how to present your visuals. You are guided through the four basic photographic techniques, as well as when to use artwork instead of photography. In Chapter 6, copywriting skills are described. Here you'll find a formula to produce good product copy, clinching the sale and building credibility for your products and your company. Chapter 7 discusses covers, captions, and other catalog copy, and Chapter 8 addresses the guarantee—that element which either can provide credibility for your catalog, or create doubts in the mind of your prospective customers. Closing the sale in the easiest way is described in Chapter 9, The Order Form. Techniques used here practically place the pen in the hand of the customer, encouraging that final step, placing the order. The "how-tos" of print production, from choosing the right paper to communicating with your printer and lettershop, are addressed in Chapter 10. Chapter 11 alerts you to the fact that many of your actions when creating a catalog may have legal ramifications as well.

First, a special thanks to Anne Basye, who researched and edited the entire manuscript for this new edition. Without her dedication this book would not have been possible. In addition, it is a pleasure to acknowledge the following individuals whose thoughts, work and ideas enhance this book.

Richard L. Bencin
Richard L. Bencin & Associates
Brecksville, OH

Gordon F. Bieberle
Bieberle Associates
Des Plaines, IL

Robert W. Bly
Copywriter/Consultant
New Milford, NJ

Jim Coogan
Woodworker's Supply
Albuquerque, NM

Jim Curtis
Curtis Software Corporation
Torrance, California

M. Virginia Daly
Daly Direct Marketing
Potomac, Maryland

Joe Donley
Artemis and Associates
Chicago, Illinois

James M. Doyle
Webcraft
North Brunswick, NJ

Helene W. Eckstein
Spectrum, Inc.
Golden, Colorado

Donna Elias
Windsor Vineyards
Windsor, CA

Mark Favus
Foote & Davies
Atlanta, GA

Frank Gesualdi
Prod. Consultant
Lincroft, NJ

J. T. Gillett
Direct Marketing Copywriter/
    Consultant
Ashland, OR

Rene Gnam
Rene Gnam Consultation Corp.
Holiday, FL

John Hauser
Artemis and Associates
Chicago, Illinois

Erwin J. Keup
Attorney at Law
Newport Beach, CA

Joyce Kole
Webcraft, Inc.
North Brunswick, NY

James E. Lentz
Lehigh Press
Pennsauken, NJ

Steve McInerny
Ovation Marketing
LaCrosse, WI

Maureen Murnane
Minor Miracles
Chicago, Illinois

Jim Osgood
Brilliant Color
Libertyville, IL

Scott Peota
Peota Graphics
Chicago, IL

Dean Powell
Dean Powell Design
New York, NY

Arthur Pryor
Pryorities Advertising, Inc.
Tamarac, FL

Sally Richman Rogers
SR Enterprises
Los Angeles, CA

Ernest H. Schell
The Communications Center
Jenkintown, PA

Mordecai Schiller
Far Rockaway, New York

John Schmid
J. Schmid & Associates
Shawnee Mission, KS

James A. Semsar
The Studio
Baraboo, WI

Henry Spitz
Brodie Advertising Service
Chicago, IL

Russ Sup
Artemis and Associates
Chicago, Illinois

Warren Swanson
Warren K. Swanson Studio, Inc.
Ringwood, IL

Zane Tankel
Collier Graphic Services
New York, NY

Bob Vacko
Direct Marketing Services, Inc.
Chicago, IL 60616

Jim Vogel
The Alden Press
Elk Grove Village, IL

Arthur Winston
Winston & Sherman, P.C.
New York, NY

In addition, numerous industry experts offered insight and assistance; many of their comments appear in sidebar notes throughout this book. Each of these contributions is sincerely appreciated.

Grateful acknowledgement is made of all the catalogs used to illustrate examples of photography, art and copy for the critiques and commentary throughout *How to Create Successful Catalogs*.

Maxwell Sroge
President, Maxwell Sroge Company, Inc.
Chicago, Illinois

MAXWELL H. SROGE

Maxwell H. Sroge is founder and President of Maxwell Sroge Publishing, a leading source and repository of information on the U.S. mail order industry and catalog marketing. He is also a partner in Trans Atlantic Catalogue Corporation, an international catalog development firm specializing in business-to-business and consumer catalogs. As president of Maxwell Sroge Company, he is one of the leading catalog consultants in the country.

Mr. Sroge's business career began in 1950 when he joined Bell & Howell Company as a district salesman. During the 14 years he spent with Bell & Howell, he rose to the positions of director of sales, director of product planning, and president of the mail order subsidiary he established. At the age of twenty-seven, he was the youngest sales manager in Bell & Howell's seventy-year history.

In 1966 he formed his own mail order marketing services firm, but retained his association with Bell & Howell as a marketing consultant. In 1970 he created Maxwell Sroge Company/Consulting Group—a first for the direct marketing industry—to conceive and develop new direct marketing businesses into operational activities.

Sroge compiled and published the first statistical report on the mail order business in 1972. This work, now referred to as the U.S. Mail Order Industry Annual Report, has been quoted by every major business publication in the country.

To serve the industry's growing needs for statistical and other information, he founded Maxwell Sroge Publishing in 1977. Headquartered in Evanston, Illinois, Maxwell Sroge Publishing gathers data and publishes a variety of newsletters and special reports, all directed to the mail order and direct marketing industry. Other books published include *Inside The Leading Mail Order Houses, How to Create Successful Catalogs* and *101 Tips for More Profitable Catalogs.*

Active in industry affairs, Maxwell Sroge assisted in the development of the Direct Marketing Association's Standards of Practice, has organized seminars in financial planning and analysis, and conducts seminars throughout the country on catalog marketing.

Featured speaker for a wide variety of clubs, universities and association conferences in the United States and abroad, he was voted the most outstanding speaker to have appeared before the Chicago Association of Direct Marketing. His articles and speeches have been reprinted in numerous U.S. and foreign publications.

His firm is the winner of the DMA Gold Mailbox Award for Best Direct Mail Campaign and the Gold Carrier Pigeon International Award.

A mid-westerner since 1950, he was born in New York and attended City College of New York and New York University.

Mr. Sroge is listed in Who's Who in America, Who's Who in Industry, Who's Who in the Midwest and Who's Who in Advertising.

CHAPTER 1

The Mail Order Catalog

The word *catalog* is derived from the Greek word *katalogos*, which means *to list*. Even today, when catalogs boast luxurious production values, alluring copy, and hard-to-resist merchandise, most are still essentially lists. They are visual and verbal listings of products for sale. The sophistication of today's design, photography, layout, and printing have transformed the original unadorned list into one that is fully costumed, ready to entertain, educate, and sell with the flip of a page.

The Origins of the Catalog

The first catalog, a listing of books, was produced in Europe during the 15th century. In the United States, the first mail order catalog (also a book catalog) was produced by Ben Franklin in 1744. The catalog was a natural outcome of Franklin's profession as a printer and his appointment as the country's first postmaster. In those days, postmasters could send any type of printed matter through the mail at no charge, so Franklin had a pretty good deal.

But the individual most often recognized for starting the first mail order catalog is Montgomery Ward. In 1872, he put out a single-page flier listing such items as handkerchiefs, coats, and tablecloths at below-retail prices. Low prices were achieved by quantity purchasing and the elimination of the "middle man." The flier quickly grew into one of the two great "big books" of its time.

Catalogs Today and Tomorrow

Today, catalogs are so widely circulated and accepted that more than half the U.S. population makes at least one catalog purchase a year—adding up to almost $40 billion in sales!

But the world of catalogs is changing in ways Montgomery Ward never could have anticipated. Before you start thinking about creating and producing your next catalog, take some time to ponder the implications of today's major trends. If they haven't already affected your business, they will certainly have an impact on you tomorrow.

Catalogs Are Consolidating

Lone wolves are out there, but they're getting rarer. Many catalog companies are actively acquiring smaller companies to take advantage of the efficiencies that come with large-scale merchandising, production, and fulfillment. These strategic alliances let small companies gain access to deep pockets and major fulfillment muscle, and offer large catalogers a way to expand without incurring the heavy costs of starting up a new catalog.

Catalogs Are Growing More Specialized

Catalog conglomerates may be growing, but catalogs themselves are becoming more specialized. Gone is the era of the "big book" offering something for everybody. In its place are thousands of catalogs that offer specialized merchandise to highly targeted groups of consumers. Catalogs offer dental supplies, apparel for wheelchair-bound adults, bird-related accessories, teddy bears, new age merchandise, butcher equipment, and much, much more.

Specialty merchandising has led many catalogers to spin off new catalogs from established books. For example, Current, Inc., which sells greeting cards, gift wrap, and gift items, has created two new catalogs offering printed products for teachers and faith-inspired products. The new catalogs are expected to build new business by offering merchandise that will appeal to a specific segment of the marketplace.

Catalogs Are Finding It Harder to Offer Exclusive Merchandise

This demand for specialized and segmented catalogs has increased the pressure to find new and unusual merchandise that can be offered exclusively by mail. But because the retail trade has also become highly segmented, it's harder to find fresh merchandise unavailable in stores.

But "fresh" merchandise is essential—*especially* in a highly segmented catalog devoted to a narrow category such as energy-efficient light bulbs or high-quality gardening tools. In response, some catalogers have broadened their selection. A gardening tool catalog has added planters, garden furniture, and other garden accessories to widen its customer base beyond its core of master gardeners. Others have advertised services instead of products, like the catalog that added interest and boosted sales by advertising Caribbean golf cruises and tours of Scotland in its winter golf equipment catalog.

The Catalog Marketplace Only Gets More Competitive

It's estimated that there are more than 7,000 catalogs circulating in the United States—and new ones start up every year. More catalogs means greater mailbox glut, stiffer competition for new customers, and higher start-up costs. Yet people persist in launching new kitchen-table enterprises—and many succeed.

Customer Service Can Make or Break a Catalog

You don't put up with shoddy service; why should your customers? Today's most successful catalog companies invest in customer service. They hire good people and give them good tools and training. When times turn tough, companies with stellar customer service operations still flourish. And when catalogs offer similar merchandise at similar prices, great customer service can catapult one to stardom . . . while lousy service holds the other one back.

Customer service is critical because consumers expect more. UPS, Federal Express, and Express Mail have put an end to the old delivery mantra, "four to six weeks." When people know they can order gifts on December 23 and still have them under someone else's tree by Christmas, why should they spend time with a company that offers anything less?

In the best-run companies, all orders are picked and out the door in 48 hours. In the business-to-business sector, office supply catalogs promise overnight delivery. If you can't meet these benchmarks, you might consider holding off investing in creative until your fulfillment operation is on solid ground.

Catalogs Are Achieving New Levels of Production Quality

Desktop publishing, digital photography and color separation, and new printing and binding techniques are leveling the catalog playing field. There is still room for the black-and-white or two-color catalog, but customer expectations have risen along with production standards. A sloppily prepared and produced catalog will be set aside in favor of a catalog that takes its production seriously.

Catalogs Are Becoming More Promotional

Like their retail counterparts, catalogs are seeking new ways to build market share and customer loyalty. Discounts, rebates, early purchase discounts, house credit, free shipping, deferred payment plans, and frequent-buyer programs are growing more common.

Catalogs Are Looking for New Markets

Lines between consumer and business-to-business catalogs are beginning to blur as catalogers cross categories to build new business and smooth out sales cycles. Companies are repackaging consumer gift catalogs for the corporate gift market . . . selling professional art supplies to the creative person at home . . . creating stylish office furniture catalogs for the home office market. Is there consumer demand for your business-to-business products? Could your consumer products work in a business environment?

Catalogs Are Going Global

As the domestic market reaches saturation, many companies are looking overseas for sales growth. Some large companies are setting up overseas operations to reach less-developed markets in Europe—but the investment is high and the risks are significant. Smaller companies are concentrating on selling to other English-speaking companies from their U.S. base.

Since the debut of the North American Free Trade Agreement (NAFTA), interest in sales to Canada and Mexico have increased. Neiman-Marcus and J.C. Penney have developed Spanish-language versions of their catalogs for the Mexican consumer market. Spanish-language catalogs are also going to Hispanic consumers in the United States. Are there opportunities abroad for you?

Catalog Companies Are Exploring Non-print Alternatives

Catalogs are taking up their positions on the information highway, as trend setters experiment with on-line ordering and CD-ROM, disk-based, and video catalogs.

As more consumers go on-line, catalogs and ordering services that use Prodigy, CompuServe, and other on-line companies are growing at a rate of 30 percent a year. But not everyone has an E-mail address—and on-line catalogs face severe format limitations. While photographic quality images of merchandise can be transmitted, the quality isn't good enough to sell a luxury item crying out for a lavish visual presentation—say, the Neiman Marcus His and Hers Christmas gifts.

CD-ROM and computer catalogs are becoming more common in the business-to-business market, especially in computer equipment and accessories. Computerized catalogs can be created and copied on computer, and sent by modem instead of mail. They cost less to produce and mail than a traditional catalog, particularly for companies whose products or prices change often. But even though personal computers are everywhere and CD-ROM disk drives are spreading like wildfire, the cataloger that relies exclusively on CD-ROM and disk-based catalogers will miss the biggest part of the market.

With plans afoot for 24-hour interactive television shopping channels, there's no question about it: we're stepping into a bold new world of interactive media that holds great promise for the catalog industry. But while all of these alternative formats help save energy and attract new customers, they will *supplement* but not replace the traditional catalog. Because the traditional catalog is still the easiest to browse through and easiest to buy from!

So why not master the basics of the print catalog now, and later, when the opportunity arises, transfer your knowledge of what works to a new medium?

What This Book Can Do for You

This book deals with the fundamentals of creating a successful catalog. It starts *after* your company concept has been formed, your products selected, and your business plan made. It does not propose to include every approach to creating a mail order catalog. But it does endeavor to give you successful, workable methods of creating a successful catalog. It will complement and guide your skills so you can create a new catalog or improve methods used before on other catalogs.

Our goal is to help you create a catalog that generates orders because it meets your customer's expectations, is a pleasure to shop, and is easy to use and order from. But before you start, check to make sure you have finished the necessary strategic groundwork.

Catalog Strategy Checklist

Before you can begin creating and producing your catalog . . .

- *Define your product or service, your company, and the marketing niche you intend to occupy.* Think of key words that describe your company . . . and key words that don't describe it. Why is your merchandise unlike other merchandise? What spot in the marketplace can you stake out as your own? What need can you fill that the competition is overlooking? The most successful catalogs occupy clearly definable niches. These are the ones that come to mind instantly when you think of outdoor sporting goods, women's apparel, gardening, office supplies, and other categories. What niche can you "own"?

- *Develop a unique identity that will let you succeed in the marketplace.* Determine your catalog's *unique selling proposition*

(USP). It is the result of a unique blend of your merchandise, your pricing strategy (upscale? discount?), your offer, and your physical presentation, including the trim size, paper stock, design, and photography.

- *Define your competition.* What is its niche? How can you differentiate your company's products from the competition's? If you can differentiate your company's product's from your competitions, you've found a niche.

- *Define your customer.* In today's data-rich environment, there's no excuse for *not* getting to know your customers. Collect and retain information about your prospects and customers so you can track their buying habits, key special offers to highly responsive segments of your market, and personalize your catalogs whenever possible.

- *Choose products carefully.* Choose products and services that fit the image of your catalog niche, have a track record of successful sales and a decent profit margin, are from a company that will ship on time, and will make you money. Look for quality items, and you will reduce returns and headaches later on. Shop the way your customer will. Be thorough. Be assertive. Be picky!

Top 10 Reasons Why Catalogs Fail

10. The company lacks a sound inventory control plan.

9. Inadequate fulfillment/customer service.

8. Financial skills are inadequate to make the catalog profitable.

7. The company underestimates the time it takes to build a customer list.

6. The acquisition of names is haphazard, at best.

5. The company does not understand the creative subtleties of a catalog.

4. The company does not know enough about who its customer is.

3. The catalog fails to establish a clear identity or niche for the company or the merchandise.

2. The company has difficulty getting financing or is under capitalized.

1. The company fails to have a plan for where it is going.

The Players

Producing a catalog is a team effort. If you're new, you may need to be introduced to the members of your team.

- *The merchandiser* plans, develops and purchases merchandise, and gives the creative team essential background on why the product fits the catalog's profile, and what the creative presentation should emphasize.

- *The marketer* crunches the numbers that back up merchandising's "hunches," calculating the profitability of catalog items and pages, and planning strategies to increase average orders and acquire new customers. He or she may have a lot to say about how much space is devoted to each item on a page.

- *The art director/designer* develops the "look" of the overall catalog and draws up a pencil or computer layout of each catalog page. The art director may also art direct photography, by drawing thumbnail sketches of individual product shots, and styling and propping photos.

- *The layout artist* is responsible for executing the art director's overall design on individual pages.

- *The photographer* arranges lighting, determines contrast levels, and chooses backgrounds so each shot shows the product to its best advantage. The best results are achieved when the art director gives specific instructions for each shot, but the photographer can style and prop the photos, if no art director is available.

- *The copywriter* turns the merchandiser's raw product information into copy, headlines, and captions that will inform, tantalize, and *sell* the customer.

- *The production manager* chooses a printer, selects paper and binding styles, and produces and mails a catalog that matches your expectations, stays under budget, and meets your mailing date.

- If yours is a small operation, a *catalog agency* may coordinate the work of the designer, layout artist, writer, and photographer. In some instances, the agency may also handle prepress and print production.

What is your role in creating your successful catalog? Are you the "quarterback" who will manage the process, or just one of the players? If you're in charge, you'll need to become *very* well acquainted with the process outlined in this book. (Even if you're not in charge, it's still a good idea to understand the big picture.) Start by planning and scheduling your catalog—the subject of Chapter 2.

Planning a Catalog

You've got a great new catalog concept and the perfect merchandise for a very well-defined target audience. Now you have to take the first steps toward producing your catalog. What do you do next?

Draw up a catalog plan. The catalog plan can be compared to the rudder of a ship. Without one, you lack control and direction, and will probably not achieve your desired goals. Your basic concept may be diluted, your approach will be weak, your schedule may slip, and your carefully planned mailing date might be missed altogether.

This chapter tells you how to establish a catalog plan that will guide you through the seven major tasks of creating a catalog. Each of these tasks is examined at length in later chapters, so you may find it helpful to review this chapter after you achieve a better understanding of the steps from other areas of the book.

Seven Major Tasks

Creating a catalog can be broken into seven major tasks. Planning and scheduling your catalog must be built around these tasks:

1. Dummying the catalog based on products selected

2. Product review

3. Design and layout

4. Copy

5. Photography

6. Press preparation

7. Printing and lettershop

1. Dummying the Catalog Based on Products Selected

Dummying the catalog means placing products within the catalog pages once the products have been selected. Categories of products must be placed in groupings or in some kind of order according to product popularity and season. Consideration must be given to retail prices and space allocation. The bottom line is that all products must be placed where they justify themselves, *collectively*, with the most sales.

Dummying the catalog is primarily the job of the merchandiser. Because the merchandiser is aware of product sales and seasonality, he or she should be concerned with placement, creating additional sales with specific products, and taking advantage of catalog "Hot Spots" (discussed in Chapter 3) to boost selected product sales.

The merchandiser will dummy the catalog following the overall format established by the art director, who is responsible for the catalog's visual appeal. The art director may decide to follow a format in which products are grouped by category, theme, or function. Once the merchandiser has finished placing the products, the catalog will move into the hands of the art director's staff. An unusually complicated format may require the art director to work alongside the merchandiser in dummying the catalog.

For example, a symmetrical layout with a product or theme/function format is fairly easy for the merchandiser to dummy. Art and copy sizes are balanced proportionately and may be predetermined by the merchandiser. Keeping the products in such categories as stationery, kitchen appliances, office forms, desks, and twine is pretty cut-and-dried. But when an asymmetrical layout is chosen, the knowledge, talent, and guidance of an art director are critical to the outcome. (Symmetrical and asymmetrical layouts are discussed in Chapter 3.)

All of these factors must be considered when you are making up a schedule. A symmetrical layout will take less time and most likely involve fewer people; an asymmetrical layout will take longer to dummy and will involve a number of people and several meetings.

2. Product Review

Product review by the copywriters and artists, along with the merchandiser and other product buyers, is how the selling message to the customer begins. In Product Work Sessions, new products are introduced to the creative staff and the catalog art and copy are planned. Chapter 4 outlines who should attend these sessions, what material should be on hand, and what should be discussed.

Product Work Sessions are vitally important and productive. Adequate time should be devoted to each new product, so that creative staff can learn why it was selected, why the customer will purchase it, which competitors have run it, how the art might be approached, and what should be included in the copy. If you have only a few new products—say nine or ten—you might be able to get by with one long review session. But if you have a hundred, you may have to schedule several sessions.

Do not expect the art director to work on design and layout or the copywriter to produce copy without the benefit of these meetings. Your bottom line will suffer if they are skipped.

3. Design and Layout

Design and layout still take considerable time, despite great advances in desktop publishing and other computer programs that are revolutionizing the way that catalog pages are produced. Even though the products have been assigned to their pages and the basic approach to their presentation has been formed, ample time should be allowed for the artists to wave their creative wand. Chapters 3, 4, and 5 all deal with presentation.

4. Copy

Copy, along with attractive visuals, sells your products. Writing good copy takes time. Copywriters need to assemble the facts, emphasize the benefits, and sell the customer. Rewrite time must be considered, too, especially for revising copy on old products or making seasonal changes. Copywriting for new products can take even longer if legal releases from the manufacturer are needed for copy claim protection. Don't shortchange time spent on copy! Chapters 4 and 6 deal with copy approach and writing.

5. Photography

Photography can be either extremely involved (if done on location in Greece) or less complicated (if done in the studio). But do not think that photographing catalog products is easy just because the photographer often is able to rely on detailed, to-size layout sketches of how the shot should look. (Many times, all the photographer gets is an empty square and instructions to fill it.) The right props have to be found, the models arranged for, the background readied, and the lighting planned. Once the real products are positioned and viewed through the photographic lens, the layout may not work well. Allow plenty of time for reshooting. Chapters 4 and 5 deal with photography and visual presentation.

6. Press Preparation

Press preparation covers all the tasks involved in preparing your catalog for printing. Setting type, preparing final pages, separating color photographs for reproduction—all take a good share of time. The better your work is prepared, the fewer problems you will encounter on press. All time spent at this stage will save time, trouble, and money at press. Chapters 5 and 9 cover prepress planning.

7. Printing and Lettershop

Printing and lettershop are the final stages in the catalog production process. Four-color printing generally takes six weeks from the time the job is received by the printer to the time the first catalog drops in the mail. (If your final art is slick-as-a-whistle and color separations are provided, you may get your catalog in five weeks, but don't count on it.) Chapter 9 on production planning goes into this step more thoroughly.

How to Set Up a Catalog Creative Schedule

To set up and maintain a schedule, you need to assign *and meet* a deadline for each of these seven tasks. If yours is an established catalog company with an established mailing pattern—and you know exactly how many different catalogs will be published during your fiscal year and when they need to be mailed—a schedule for each publication date should be made as soon as the mail date has been set.

If yours is a new catalog venture, setting a schedule is even more important. An overall catalog schedule lets you see the demands for all areas (buyers, copy, art, pricing, printing, and lettershop) and how these demands overlap for each catalog. Everyone involved will be able to adjust their time to make the deadlines. For a new catalog, it's a good idea to add some extra time into your schedule, as a buffer against unexpected delays.

The mail date is the most important date in structuring a catalog creative schedule. It is the one date that cannot be missed. Once it has been established, you can work backwards to establish other deadline dates. Elements with fairly set time frames help you establish other important dates. For example, catalog printers generally take five to six weeks to prepare and print your catalog. Envelope printers need only two weeks if one or two colors are involved, or four weeks if your envelope is four-color. But the envelopes should be on the catalog printer's floor two weeks prior to the catalog press date.

If Christmas, New Year's, or Thanksgiving falls in the scheduling period, build an extra week for each holiday into the schedule.

A Catalog Production Schedule

This twenty-one week schedule would be typical for an average size catalog (up to 100 pages), if enough staff people are involved and if all intermediate deadlines are met.

Desktop publishing systems make it possible to produce a catalog in far less than 21 weeks—but the schedule you follow should depend on your overall needs and environment. Business-to-business catalogers, for example, typically turn around their catalogs in less time. In the fast-moving field of electronics product developers and buyers may scream at a three-month-out closing date for new products.

While merchandisers and creative people must be lenient and understanding where fast-changing products are concerned, they must also be realistic. Mail dates need to be met in order to take advantage of ideal selling periods, and the creative process demands a fair amount of time to produce the vehicle that will sell the products.

How Desktop Publishing Has Changed Catalog Production

The rhythm of catalog production has been changed forever by desktop publishing technologies.

Many tasks that once needed to be performed by hand—such as retouching photos or correcting color—can be quickly handled by computer. And many tasks that were once distinctly separate are now linked together and performed simultaneously. So instead of sending out hard copy for typesetting, a catalog designer is more likely to "pour" copy from the copywriter's disk into a computer-created page template. Instead of merely indicating the position of art on the page, the designer may include a low-resolution version of the final art, which the separation house has separated and digitized and will ultimately provide in high-resolution format.

DTP (desktop publishing) systems let you get a good idea of the final look of a catalog weeks before the catalog goes to press, and allows you to make major art, design, and copy changes with the click of a mouse. Your art department or catalog agency can still receive copy and art changes up until 3 weeks before printing—and make those changes without racking up big film and plate charges. Some companies produce their own color separations and film; others have invested in in-house color printers that let them proof their own work before turning it over to the printer.

Desktop publishing systems are definitely a boon—but they can also be a nightmare if you allow endless alterations to jeopardize your mailing dates. Your catalog schedule must insist on firm dates and full cooperation—or your catalog may never see the light of day.

That's why these 38 steps are important. They let you guide your work flow, and keep tasks *and* people on schedule.

---

38 Steps to Catalog Production

1. Preliminary review of products, old and new.
2. Special promotion products selected.
3. New products finalized.
4. Catalog dummy complete.
5. Art and copy review meeting.
6. Photography and art started.
7. Art and copy review meeting.
8. Old products finalized.
9. Product releases sent.
10. Envelope/order form design started.
11. Late product closing.
12. All art and copy reviewed.
13. Layout finalized.
14. Cover design/art finalized.
15. All products to photographer.
16. Cover complete and to printer.
17. Envelop/order form art to printer.
18. Product changes, final review.
19. Begin setting copy.
20. Begin page layout.
21. Selling prices reviewed and finalized.
22. Copy releases accounted for.
23. All prices and copy changes complete.
24. Final pages pulled.
25. Envelope proof received, returned to printer.
26. Cover press proof received.
27. Color printer spreads viewed.
28. Color spreads to separator.

---

29. Paste-ups corrected.

30. Proofing complete, final art to the printer.

31. Envelopes received by printer.

32. Catalog proof received.

33. Catalog proof returned to printer.

34. Catalog on press.

35. Catalog published.

36. Transparencies returned.

37. Files broken down.

38. Gather bound catalogs.

Week Countdown	Task

Week 21

1. Preliminary review of products, old and new.

The total product needs of the catalog are reviewed. Sales figures for all previously-run products and product categories should be analyzed to determine the final merchandise needs. Decisions on old (carryover) product inclusion and sizing are determined according to performance and season. The number of new products needed is finalized, and their space allotment is indicated. Completing this step will take several weeks.

Week 19

2. Special promotion products selected.

"Special promotion" includes any free gift or incentive-priced merchandise. Also included are products placed on sales-boosting pages (explained in Chapter 3): front cover, back cover, order form. These products will not only influence the design, layout, and copy in the catalog, but they will also need special attention in the purchasing department because of the above-average sales volume that their placement produces.

Week 17

3. New products finalized.

All new products should now be selected. Information on material, availability, and cost should be on file for art and copy use. Production samples should be in-house. Products needing special attention such as copy releases, official test document claims, and warranties should be marked for needed action.

Week Countdown	Task

Week 16   **4. Catalog dummy complete.**
Each product being cataloged should now have an assigned catalog page number. If the catalog is symmetrical in design, sizes may be assigned at this time by the merchandiser. If the catalog is asymmetrical, meetings with the art and copy department will help in assigning final space allotment.

Week 16   **5. Art and copy review meeting.**
This is the first of the Product Work Sessions (Chapter 4) in which you will be thoroughly going over each new product. A minimum of fifteen minutes should be allowed for each product, since competitors' listings must be reviewed, test results combed, and manufacturer's information looked at. A full understanding of the product (why it was selected, its main benefit, and why the customer will purchase it) influences how the art is presented and the copy approached. The product shots requiring models or extensive proofing should have precedence over the straight shots because their photo prep and shooting take longer. These meetings are intense and therefore should not last over three hours. Several may need to be scheduled.

Week 16   **6. Photography and art started.**
If you're working with symmetrical layout, some individual product layouts may be ready to send to the photographer—the sooner the better. Even if your photographer doesn't start shooting until all products for one catalog have been sent, sending some of the products early will allow the photographer to look for props and to have plenty of time for setup.

Week 13   **7. Art and copy review meeting.**
Just the same as step number five. More meetings will need to be scheduled if there are over twenty or so new products.

Week 13   **8. Old products finalized.**
All repeat products should by now have been verified for availability and possible changes from the manufacturers. Shaky products (slow sellers or those with availability problems) will have been dropped, and product specifications that have changed should be reviewed for art and copy changes.

Week Countdown	Task

Week 12   **9. Product releases sent.**
Some catalog companies get a signed release form from the manufacturer for every product they carry. Essentially, the catalog copy is sent for specification review and an accuracy check. Some companies ask for releases only on critical items where copy claims may be subject to doubt, because of the nature of the product. Exercise equipment, ointments, diet pills, bunion pads, ingested items, and electronics products are a few areas considered critical. Getting a signed release stating all claims are true relieves catalog companies from any doubts, as well as any legal problems. Plenty of time must be allowed to ensure that the signed release (or correct copy) is on file when camera-ready art is sent to the printer.

Week 12   **10. Envelope/order form design started.**
Any products appearing on the order form should be verified by now. Design and finished art must be completed so the envelopes can be sent to the printer in plenty of time. Also, actual printed samples must be double-checked for accuracy in gluing, perfing, and folding.

Week 12   **11. Late product closing.**
This is it—the last chance for the buyers and product developers to get products in this catalog. If there are some new products at this date, review them and get the art and copy going.

Week 11   **12. All art and copy reviewed.**
All of the product work sessions should be over and the catalog layout nearly complete. If more than the two scheduled art and copy review sessions are needed, they should have been done before now. Turn final copy over to the designer.

Week 11   **13. Layout finalized.**
The catalog layout and all product layouts must be okayed. Any problems with visual presentation must be worked out *now*; no more time is left.

Week 11   **14. Cover design/art finalized.**
Photographs must be finalized (both front and back cover), original art and design okayed.

Week Countdown	Task

Week 11   **15. All products to photographer.**
The last of the product layouts and products must go to the photographer. Sending anything later will not allow for reshots if they are needed. Many catalogers attend the photo sessions themselves to offer guidance and on-the-spot approval for props and changes.

Week 10   **16. Cover and photography/design complete and to printer.**
The cover needs to go early so a press proof can be pulled, if desired. Many catalog companies request a press proof of the cover because of the cover's critically important function—attracting the customer's attention. Getting the right color tones and combinations becomes vitally important—errors can be caught and corrected now.

Week 10   **17. Envelope/order from art to printer.**
Camera-ready art needs to be sent off. Be sure to review postal charts, special messages, and products.

Week 9   **18. Product changes, final review.**
This is the last go at old or new product changes to be included in copy or art. Double-check your "Change Memo System" (discussed directly after this catalog production schedule) and manufacturer product confirmations.

Week 9   **19. Begin setting copy.**
Send the copywriter's disk of all new and old copy to your typesetter or desktop publisher. Be sure to include clear instructions on width, line length, style, size, and weight of type.

Week 8   **20. Begin page layout.**
Now the process of laying out pages begins. Following the overall catalog design, a desktop publisher or designer or art director will build pages using approved copy and art. Headlines, body copy, and art are positioned and proofed, often with a laser printer. If photos are scanned electronically, low-resolution copies may be included in the sample pages.

Week 8   **21. Selling prices reviewed and finalized.**
All costs and prices need final approval as working pages are proofed. Old products should be cost checked and any new prices established. New products should have all cost workups done and prices set.

Week Countdown	Task

Week 8

22. Copy releases accounted for.
Don't forget to follow up on the requested copy releases. If any changes resulted from them, now is the time to make them.

Week 8

23. All prices and copy changes complete.
Although DTP systems allow you to make changes until virtually the night before your press run, strive to adhere to a definite deadline for copy and price changes. Be sure to make all necessary changes on old items through your "change memo" system.

Week 8

24. Final pages pulled.
Camera-ready pages should be printed and checked before being turned over to your printer.

Week 8

25. Envelope proof received, proofed, returned to printer.
Your final chance to view envelope and order-form art and copy before it's printed and shipped to the catalog printer. Be sure to keep a copy—double-check glue coverage and position, perf-positioning, and type of perforation.

Week 7

26. Cover press proof received.
Check for color, blotches, position—how the art and photographs blend. Is the paper your proof was pulled on the same as what it will be printed on? It makes a difference. (See Chapter 9.)

Week 7

27. Color printer spreads viewed.
All new product photographs—in fact, *all* catalog product photographs—should have been reviewed for correctness and acceptance.

Week 7

28. Color spreads to separator.
If you are using DTP technologies to produce your catalog, you have probably been sending art to your separator in batches all along. By this date, all the separations should be complete.

Week 5

29. Paste-ups corrected.
All changes that have come in due to manufacturer changes in the product, price increases, or the pulling of doubtful products should now be complete. The art should be in perfect shape, ready to be photographed for platemaking.

Week Countdown	Task

Week 5

30. Proofing complete, final art to printer.

A full-blown proofing session should be done on the final art. This is your last chance to make reasonably inexpensive changes. From here on, changes will involve film and plates—major costs compared to changes made now.

Week 5

31. Envelopes received by printer.

Always keep checking on how all production is doing. You should have been in contact with your envelope printer to make sure that the envelope went on press, when the printing was complete, and when the envelopes were shipped to your catalog printer. Your checking samples should have been air freighted to you and approved before the main shipment to the catalog printer was made. If the envelopes have not been received on time (two weeks prior to catalog press date), find out where they are and get them to your printer.

Week 4

32. Catalog proof received.

There are a number of names for a proof—blueline, silverline, brownline—it depends on the process used when making them. You should have two proofs—one to send back to the printer with the corrections marked, and one to be kept by you. This way, you'll both understand what to talk about if questions arise about the changes because at this point you are not at the printshop. (If extensive changes are requested, you may want a second proof copy pulled to check before the presses roll.) At this point, a really hot product can still be included if the art and copy are ready and another product taken out to make room. It can be done, though it will cost you plenty.

Week 4

33. Catalog proof returned to printer.

Make sure all corrections are clearly marked and any material needed to make the corrections has been sent. The best approach is to make a separate list of the corrections wanted, in page order. This acts as a checklist for the printer and better assures that corrections will be made.

Week 3

34. Catalog on press.

Be there! Check the press sheets as they come off the press against any last-minute changes you may have made. See how the color is running once the press is up to speed and the press people have had a chance to balance colors. If colors need adjustment, work with your representative and press operator for the best result. When everything looks good, that sheet will become the control to follow for the rest of the job. Get a handful of press sheets to take back for others to see and use.

Week 1   35. Catalog published.

It's in the mail—at least the first segment. Many high-volume companies have mail patterns that extend over a one-to two-month period before one catalog version mailing is complete. This allows stable order inflow and smoother work handling for fulfillment and operations. It also allows a regional timing factor, boosting sales with more timely delivery in different sections of the country.

Week 1   36. Transparencies returned.

Be sure to get the transparencies back so they can be disassembled and filed for use in the next catalog. (This simple step is very easily forgotten. Then when transparencies are needed, they must be hunted down, if possible, and prepared for use, wasting valuable time and causing unneeded frustrations.)

Week 1   37. Files broken down.

This does not sound very creative, but it too is a chore which—if not done—causes chaos in all departments. Break the files down right away, getting the needed information to the appropriate departments such as bookkeeping, data processing, and warehouse control.

Week 1   38. Gather bound catalogs.

Don't forget to have a few hundred catalogs shipped from the printer to the marketing department for future creative use. Too often *no* catalogs are set aside, and the catalog company ends up not having a copy for its own records or use.

This 38-step countdown is just a skeleton to help guide you along. Additional steps will need to be added for each individual demand. Just be sure to take your schedule seriously, be reasonable in setting the deadline dates, and adhere to the deadlines set!

How to Prevent Errors in Your Catalog When Products Undergo Changes

A *Change Memo System* will help keep track of changes in your catalog production. Details can be uninteresting and no fun—especially when no immediate action is required or when the impact of these details is unknown or not understood. But the importance of a Change Memo System should not be minimized. The detail of recording possible product changes and following through when the changes are needed may seem to have few rewards. Not true! *A Change Memo System collects facts and institutes actions that allow the cataloger to have a "clean" catalog,* a catalog that is *error free.* This must be made clear so the people involved realize the importance of their actions.

Here's the flow of a Change Memo System: the five steps to take, plus the why . . . and the reward.

1. Choose a Vehicle to Record Changes

This might be a wire-bound memo book with two-up or three-up memos, and the ability to make at least one copy from a built-in carbon. A bound upright version can be referred to easily and stored on a shelf or in a desk drawer.

2. Identify Catalog Areas of Change

Four major areas are affected most seriously:

Supply. Product supply may be cut off or may be too small. Sometimes factories really do burn down or other complications arise that temporarily make the product unavailable. The merchandiser may have to omit a product from the catalog until it's available again.

Art. If product style, color, size, function, or raw material changes, the visual of the product also changes . . . and catalog art must reflect the difference.

Changes in more than one area

Copy. If the product style, color, size, or function changes, or the number of components differs, the copy must reflect this. Your customer relies on good, thorough, correct information provided by copy explanation. Reflecting any change is vital.

Selling prices. A cost increase from a supplier generally means a price increase to maintain an acceptable profit margin when the product is run again. Your catalog must reflect the most current and desirable prices.

3. Identify In-House and Out-of-House Departments That Must Know of the Change

Two major areas of concern exist within the cataloging department: active and inactive products. Active are those products running in the current catalog or slated for the catalog being prepared for press. Inactive are those products not presently running, but still viable for future catalogs. Three other departments exist outside the cataloging department: Data Processing, Plant (order entry, warehouse, customer service), and Ad Agency. These departments will need to know any changes affecting them.

4. Record the Change

All changes must be recorded in such a fashion that they are easily implemented. Here are three important facts to be sure to record:

1. Product identifying number and name

2. Nature of change

3. Date change needs to be implemented

And here's an example of a typical Change Memo:

H 50555 Weather Stripping.
Cost increase from J.W. Jones Manufacturing, to
$24.00/dz., effective 10-95. Price change,
effective for Jan. '96 catalog, to $8.95.

Attach the original copy of the memo to the copy used for catalog paste-up (wherever it is stored). Then, when the item is again run, the change will be seen. Also, the cost of making the change will not be incurred if the product is not run again. Keep a duplicate memo in a special file (according to product number) and send other duplicates to departments also affected (such as your ad agency).

5. Make the Change

When a catalog is being assembled, the Change Memo File becomes paramount in importance. All the changes needed for all old products are in one place and therefore easily made. The Art Department needs only to refer to the file to make sure the right art is used. The Copy Department needs only to make the changes these memos record to have accurate, updated copy. The merchandiser can rest easy that products are represented properly and prices meet profit structure requirements.

Memo all departments

Reward

A catalog that is outstanding and complete in product representation for the customer, and with profitable products for the company.

Don't shortchange yourself or your catalog by sidestepping or putting little effort into the planning stages. Allow plenty of time for each step in your plan, and then stay on schedule. You'll be rewarded with happy employees, happy suppliers, a terrific looking catalog, and buying customers.

How to Live Happily Ever After with Your Catalog Agency

In days of yore, catalogs were produced by armies of in-house writers, artists, and photographers. Today it's commonplace for small-and medium-sized catalogs to job out writing, design, photography, and production to a catalog agency or creative services company.

Unfortunately, these alliances can go sour. Many cataloger-agency marriages grow strained not because of creative differences, but because of a breakdown in communications. It's easy to forget that the production of a catalog is a business transaction, not merely a creative process. In any business dealing, effective communication is the cornerstone of success.

Follow these six tips to keep *your* business relationship on the right track.

1. Involve your agency people in key strategy sessions. The better they understand your marketing direction, the more likely they are to hit the mark in their creative work. Most critical is the pagination session, where you decide what products go where and why. Ideally, your account manager, creative director, copywriter, and art director should participate. Later, there will be other important junctures where agency involvement can be valuable, including sessions on circulation, budget, and name acquisition.

2. Establish creative ground rules right away. This is especially critical when working with a new agency. Don't let artists and copywriters rush headlong into their work without knowing what direction they'll take. Too often you'll end up with a pile of layouts or copy that misses the mark. Insist on approving a sample layout with copy at the start. Work with the writer to establish a basic platform that addresses the style, personality, and key components for all product copy.

3. Make sure your creative team has the ammunition it needs. Product information sheets are absolutely essential, both for writer and artist. If you don't have a standard product sheet, let your agency devise one it is comfortable with. A comprehensive product sheet will include the key benefit plus product ingredients, source, size, and price. If possible, send sample products to the writer and artist.

4. Keep the project on schedule. Use the 38 steps of catalog production to develop a realistic, step-by-step schedule with extra time built in for unforeseen time-eaters.

5. Put it in writing! Verbal communication is fine, but your agency contacts should summarize important discussions in conference reports. Make your revisions in writing, not by phone. The agency should confirm key revisions in job diaries. All of this takes time, but it definitely pays off in the long run.

6. Stay informed on the budget. This area sinks more cataloger–agency relationships than anything else. Encourage your account manager to keep you abreast of production costs with weekly reports. Before specifying major creative changes, find out how they'll affect your budget. The agency should warn you if it appears spending will exceed budgetary limits.

And here's a seventh tip:

Understand the catalog production process. Too often, people with expertise in merchandising and management are not acquainted with the process they are asking their agency to execute. This can result in unrealistic expectations and, down the line, needless misunderstandings caused by unexpectedly high invoices and a slipping schedule.

If your background is not in catalog production, reading this book can be the biggest favor you ever do your agency. By understanding just what is involved in each of the 38 steps of production, you can increase the likelihood that your catalog will meet your expectations. You'll also decrease your mental and emotional anguish, and greet the finished product with something approaching peace of mind.

For Great Results, Hire a Quarterback

At every stage in the production process, questions will arise and choices will present themselves. How will you know which option to choose?

For maximum results, put one person in charge of all the plays. Even if you're a great head coach, you need a quarterback. The leader of your creative team—be it an in-house creative director or the creative director at your agency—should oversee all stages of production.

Having a quarterback makes everyone feel more at ease. The photographer has someone who knows the layouts, can answer questions, and keep a shoot on track. The separator can get direction from someone who knows the photography, the printers, and the paper stock. Best of all, you'll have one person to go to for answers. The creative director will work with you to make the inevitable compromises and will keep you informed of choices and developments every step of the way.

CHAPTER 3

Forming an Approach

To succeed, your catalog needs an image—an ambience that pervades the entire book, becomes a setting in which to place your products and messages about them, and quickly tells your customers who you are and what you are all about.

The merchandising and marketing aspects of planning your catalog are vital to its success. But what guarantees your success in the very crowded catalog marketplace is your ability to pull these diverse elements together in the look, the image, and the personality of your catalog. In catalogs, the whole *is* greater than the sum of the parts.

Research indicates that the image your catalog creates has as much to do with your customer making a purchase—and the amount of the purchase—as do the products you offer and the solicitation vehicles you use, the lists you use, and the frequency with which you mail. To gain a truly competitive edge, your catalog's personality must also be positioned in the minds of your customers.

How to Develop a Personality for Your Catalog

When you know your target audience inside and out, you can develop a creative package that presents your products or service in a way that not only meets your customers' perceived needs, but meets them in a way that sets you apart from competitors.

Two catalogs that have created highly successful and distinct catalog personalities are Lands' End and L.L. Bean. Lands' End sells consciously-unselfconscious active clothing and related items to youthful, at least young-at-heart, upper-middle-class customers. Its personality comes through with a design and copy that emphasize quality manufacturing. The visual message is that Lands' End travels the world to find only the best—a point the company incorporates into its catalog photography, illustrations, and product descriptions that reinforce this.

L.L. Bean takes a slightly different approach. It promotes apparel with no-nonsense appeal, reflecting good, conservative—but very stylish—Yankee value. This philosophy is captured perfectly in the catalog's design, with less "glamorous" graphics that emphasize the product and use ordinary people as models. So even though Bean customers may not be great outdoorspeople, they can still have that look in their rubber moccasins and shooting sweaters for rainy-day "hunting trips" to the mall.

Both of these catalogs give customers something to identify with, and something to "buy in to." To be truly successful, you have to create your own winning combination of products, services, and creative approaches, all based upon the most important factor of all: your in-depth knowledge of your customers.

Your catalog's personality is a blend of the look of its photographs, the sound of its copy, and the texture of its merchandise. It is expressed in the way you approach the front and back cover and every page inside.

The Front Cover

The cover of your catalog needs to persuade your customer to pick up the catalog excited (or at least interested in) its contents. It needs to create desire and motivate the customer to read more. Above all, it needs to attract attention from the right customers—the ones who will buy your products. Like the L.L. Bean and Lands' End catalogs, your catalog cover needs to say who it is for and why anyone should read it.

Your cover communicates a number of facts about your company, your products, and your customer, including:

- Cost of merchandise (high-end, middle range, inexpensive, discounted)

- Type of merchandise (clothes, gifts, general merchandise, food, computer accessories, nuts and bolts, stationery, sports gear)

- Attitude and image of catalog house ("serving the customer since 1900" reliability, brand-new-company excitement, political correctness, urbane sociability, down-home neighborliness, sweepstake seduction, banker's reliability)

- Seasonality of merchandise (Christmas gifts, summer fun, spring fix-up)

- Type of customer to whom you are appealing (affluent/middle-class; country/city; intellectual/physical; refined/simple taste; business/homebodies)

If you think of your catalog as a store, then the cover is its "window." If you fail to grab your consumers in your window, they will not wander into your "store" to find out what you are all about. They'll move on to someone else who makes it simple for them.

There are three basic approaches you can use to entice consumers on the front cover:

1. Dramatic impact

2. Product line identification

3. Sales/benefits

Dramatic Impact

The dramatic impact approach grabs the customer's attention with a startling design, commanding photo, or unusual presentation. Most often this approach does not picture products; it is more artistic in effect. Catalog companies often become known for a specific type of dramatic effect which then becomes a trademark for the company. Patagonia is a case in point.

In **Figure 3.1**, a lush photo of sockeye salmon about to spawn in a secluded Alaskan stream is one of a series of stunning portraits Patagonia

Figure 3.1   Patagonia catalog

has used to adorn its covers. This arresting photo tells customers that they are holding the new Patagonia catalog, even though Patagonia's name is almost hidden among the intricate patterns of grass and fish.

A prospect receiving this catalog for the first time will be attracted by this dramatically effective visual. Patagonia knows the cover will qualify the viewer's interest and encourage the potential customer to open the catalog for products related to exploring the outdoor world.

The Smith & Hawken garden catalog in **Figure 3.2** attracts customers and prospects with a beautiful duotone of a lush spring garden. The vine-covered archway that frames the photo invites the viewer to step inside the garden and the catalog to see what delights it holds. This effective cover achieves another goal: it creates desire by depicting an environment that Smith & Hawken's products will help the buyer achieve.

Figure 3.2   Smith & Hawken catalog

Elektek uses dramatically lit and rendered product pictures in a haunting composition that attracts attention and communicates this catalog's product category (**Figure 3.3**). The design is visually commanding, interesting, and creates a high-tech look that is compatible with this supplier of computer hardware and software.

Figure 3.3   Elektek catalog

Advantages
Total aesthetic appeal; possibility of catalog being kept around longer or kept in view, because of attractiveness; possibility of getting customer's attention due to visual impact.

Disadvantages
Catalog being overlooked because of magazine appearance; non-identification of product type; missed opportunity to sell products or verbally direct the customer inside.

Product Line Identification

By far the most common approach to catalog cover design, product-line-identification covers show selected merchandise either alone against a plain background, or in use. Often just one product is presented, but several can be pictured. The products chosen should be top sellers or new products that are very similar to the top sellers. Seasonal aspects should also be emphasized.

A well-executed product line identification cover can be aesthetic, as **Figure 3.4** shows. One look at this chubby, happy toddler and there's no doubt about the products to be found inside the OshKosh B'Gosh catalog: sturdy, colorful children's wear. The total impact neatly identifies the product and defines its appeal. Customers choosing to pick up and open this catalog will not be disappointed when they look inside. The company won't be disappointed, either: orders will come in because of the cover's ability to communicate its product line and its market.

Figure 3.4   Oshkosh B'Gosh catalog

Figure 3.5   Mutiplex catalog

Multiplex's studio shot of slides and a slide viewer visually supplement the copy messages on this catalog (**Figure 3.5**), telling customers that this is indeed a "Visual Communications Sourcebook." Each slide cleverly contains an image of a different product featured in this catalog. The total cover image is appealing and clearly identifies the product category.

Advantages
Product type immediately identified; getting the customer's attention via area of interest and attractive presentation; visual motivation to look inside; verbal reference motivating inside interest; additional sales.

Disadvantages
Possibility of unattractive cover due to poor product selection and awkward and unclear presentation.

Sales/Benefits

In the sales/benefits approach, a product or products are pictured with copy and pricing directly on the cover. Benefits or incentives are directly stated.

Heartland America communicates a message of value by selling three products from its all-business cover (**Figure 3.6**). No pictures, no poses, no dramatic impact gets in the way of this direct sales presentation.

Figure 3.6   Heartland America catalog

Rocky Mountain Computer Outfitter illustrates its name with a whimsical photo of a fly fisherman who has reeled in the catalog's latest product (**Figure 3.7**). Red price tags along the bottom of the cover tell customers where to find each featured product inside the catalog—an approach that will definitely boost sales of these seven programs.

Figure 3.7   Rocky Mountain Computer Outfitter catalog

Advantages	Disadvantages
Product line identification; visual motivation to look inside; verbal reference motivating inside interest; credibility building via benefits; direct or additional sales.	Possibility of unattractive cover due to product selection and presentation; cluttered effect due to too much information; customer confusion due to too much information or cluttered design.

One Product Category—Three Approaches

Catalogers within a single product category often take very disparate approaches to their covers, as this comparison of three outdoor clothing and equipment companies shows. The difference in image created by the chosen approach of each catalog are immediately apparent. So, to a degree, is what each cover says about the cost and appeal of the products inside.

The Territory Ahead chooses a dramatic impact shot, attracting customers with a lovely, muted photo of a Christmas-wreathed barn in a secluded, snowy spot—just the place where customers dream of wearing the rugged, good-looking clothing inside (**Figure 3.8**). This shot appeals more to the outdoor enthusiast in repose than to the outdoor enthusiast in action, as REI chooses to do in **Figure 3.9**.

This in-use shot (also fairly dramatic!) of climbing equipment immediately establishes the product line offered inside this REI catalog and tells the world what kind of customer it is seeking. While the unusual perspective of the photo will capture any eye, the carabiner and rope help qualify the customer by attracting readers who enjoy scaling steep rocks to dizzying heights.

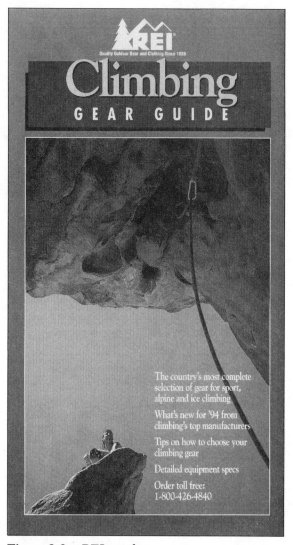

Figure 3.8 Territory Ahead catalog

Figure 3.9 REI catalog

Sierra Trading Post communicates a value message with a sales/benefit approach on the cover shown in **Figure 3.10**. Because the line drawing has been screened back, type is the most prominent element on this cover. It tells readers that phenomenal savings are to be had on brand-name clothing and equipment. Calling this issue of the catalog "Vacation 1994" helps broadcast the message, "Time to stock up on equipment you need for your next trip!"

Though these catalogs share a merchandise category and market to very similar customers, each one chooses a different way of telling the customer what to expect inside. The style and mood set by each catalog is maintained with every catalog that company creates. The customer can quickly recognize the source, and each new catalog mail-

Figure 3.10   Sierra Trading Post catalog

ing reinforces the company's image. Existing customers develop loyalty and confidence through familiarity, and prospects in the same target group become customers because they see a format with which they are comfortable.

Choose carefully, for when you choose your cover approach, you are establishing your image and setting the tone for your entire catalog.

The Multiple Cover Approach

Many catalogers get more life—and more sales—out of their catalogs by using multiple covers. Why?

Multiple covers can help one catalog reach several markets. A telecommunications company marketing its equipment to home workers might produce one cover featuring a woman, another picturing an older executive-turned-consultant, and a third showing a younger male executive or the male proprietor of a design-related business. In each case, the contents of the catalog would be identical—but the customized cover would let the company target its message to three distinct market segments.

Multiple covers also allow a company to develop one cover for its current customers, one for prospects, and one for customers who haven't purchased lately and need an incentive to return to the fold.

Multiple covers are routinely used to extend the life of a catalog during a long season. Some catalog companies mail the same catalog five times during the holiday season, using a different cover on each one.

What Else Can a Catalog Cover Do?

- Announce payment and delivery methods and promote the convenience of ordering from the company;

- Advertise toll-free telephone and facsimile numbers, customer service numbers, or an E-mail address;

- Promote ordering incentives such as a free gift, discounts, and sales;

- Build credibility by mentioning number of years in business, including customer testimonials, or promoting the company guarantee.

Front Cover Checklist:

☐ Establish theme.
☐ Determine approach.
☐ Select merchandise.
☐ Select special message.
☐ Design cover.

Always:
1. Put company name on cover.
2. Show continuity of theme.
3. Indicate seasonality.
4. Motivate the customer to look inside, both visually and verbally.

Strongly Consider:
1. Charge card availability.
2. Toll-free number.
3. Credibility factors like company longevity, customer testimonials, guarantees.
4. Ordering incentives such as free gift, sale, discount, sweepstakes.

The Back Cover

The back cover is the second most visible part of your catalog, and it will probably be the first thing your customer sees. Why? Postal employees need to see the name/address side in order to sort mail, so it is likely to be the side which is "up" when the catalog reaches the customer's mailbox or in-box.

Because the back cover is so visible, it is important that it help maintain your image. But maintaining an image doesn't necessarily preclude making product sales.

While the back cover's primary job is to identify the receiver and the sender, it can also perform three other functions:

1. Image carryover

2. Direct sales promotion

3. Referral sales promotion

Image Carryover

This approach carries the theme or look established on the front cover onto the back cover through artwork, design, or color. This aesthetically-pleasing approach includes little or no product, but may incorporate general information such as a telephone number or a quick index. The spawning salmon on the cover of the Patagonia catalog wend their way onto the back, too, as **Figure 3.11** shows. The illustration fills half of the cover, but a pale green picked up from the photo unites the illustration with lists of retail store locations and a photo credit. Nothing competes with establishing an image and mood for the catalog. A visual, dramatic effect has been given full responsibility for enticing the customer inside to look at Patagonia's array of outdoor apparel.

Advantages	Disadvantages
Aesthetic appeal maintained; little problem created for address panel space; clutter and confusion eliminated.	Loss of valuable sales and reference space; lost additional dollar sales; minimal product line identification.

Direct Sales Promotion

This is the most common approach found on back covers, and certainly the most profitable. The back cover may picture a product or products not shown elsewhere in the catalog, with all information necessary for placing an order, including the retail price. These products will enjoy a healthy sales increase (two to three times more than the same listing inside the catalog) and therefore should be chosen wisely. Products must meet two criteria before they are put in this important position:

1. They must be strong sellers.   Consider not only the staple items in your line, but also items with seasonal pull (toys for Christmas, environmentally-friendly bug killers in the summer).

2. Products should have excellent profit margins.   Extra sales should bring in maximum profits.

Higher-end catalogs tend to minimize the number of products shown on the back cover. Many, like Gardener's Eden, devote the back to one elegantly presented product (**Figure 3.12**). Here, a set of four frosted glass flower vases is shown in a manner thoroughly in keeping with the overall look of this catalog. In contrast, The Lighter Side Company squeezes half a dozen products onto the back cover, in a busy layout that closely resembles interior pages (**Figure 3.13**).

Inmac, a computer supplies, accessories, furniture, cables, and data communications devices catalog (**Figure 3.14**), chooses an exclusive

Figure 3.11 Patagonia back cover

product to sell directly: an adjustable keyboard shelf. The product is illustrated both solo and in use, and a photo silhouette illustrates its versatility. Not a chance is lost to attract the customer for a sale. Approximately one-third of the page is used for illustrating one inside page and referring the customer to four others. This is very smart and should produce some nice additional sales for those referenced products. However, the page numbers are so hard to find and to read that some of the advantage is lost. A startling move is the omission of a phone number, as up to 90 percent of business-to-business orders are placed over the phone.

Sell directly from the back cover

Figure 3.12   Gardner's Eden back cover

Advantages	Disadvantages
Identification of product line; additional direct sales; customer interest qualified; visual motivation for customer to look inside catalog.	Possible clutter in design; chance of confusion.

Figure 3.13   The Lighter Side Co. back cover

Figure 3.14   Inmac back cover

Referral Sales Promotion

Attracting the customer with back-cover visuals and then referencing inside pages is an approach that will move customers inside your catalog. There are several variations on this approach. Descriptive copy can accompany the picture of the product, the product alone can be pictured, or copy can stand alone. Products referenced will enjoy a 25 to 35 percent increase in sales. The important step is to get the customer to open up your catalog, and inside page references help accomplish this.

New England Business Services (**Figure 3.15**) devotes two thirds of this back cover to presenting a strong benefit: getting the right checks for your printer. Instead of discussing individual styles and formats, the copy treats benefits common to all of its checks, and refers customers to the checks section on pages 3 through 9.

It's a good idea to refer to products on several different pages, so that customers will see as many pages as possible. NEBS has done this by highlighting an entire category, so that customers will leaf through sixteen pages as they search for the check model most appropriate for them.

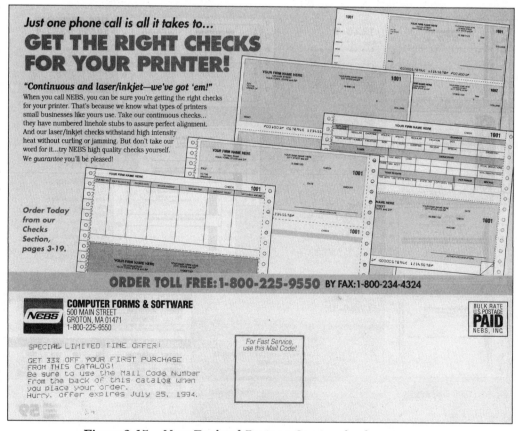

Figure 3.15 New England Business Services back cover

Advantages	**Disadvantages**
Product line identification; direct motivation to get the customer inside the catalog; opportunity to increase sales or products directly referenced and other products on pages referred to.	Possibility of cluttered design; possibility of customer confusion.

Combining Direct Sales and Referral

An effective way to sell products and reference inside pages is to combine the direct sale and referral sale approach. Increased sales will be realized when a picture and complete ordering information are provided for one or two products. When inside pages are referenced, customers are motivated to look inside and the referenced products enjoy increased sales. Surrounding products on the same page also sell better.

Figure 3.16 from the L'Eggs Outlet Catalog combines a direct sales blurb with a panel that refers customers inside. The referral highlights one of the catalog's best offers (and probably one of its most profitable).

Figure 3.16   L'Eggs Outlet catalog back cover

Back Cover Checklist:

☐ Determine method of front cover theme carryover, if used.
☐ Select direct-sale merchandise.
☐ Select referral-sale merchandise.
☐ Determine size of address panel.
☐ Determine address correction message.
☐ Design back cover.

Always:
1. Put company name and address on back cover.
2. Put toll-free or regular telephone number.
3. Show charge card acceptance visually.
4. Refer customer inside the catalog in some way.

Strongly Consider:
1. Credibility factors such as company longevity, customer testimonials, guarantees.
2. Special offer announcements: sale, free gift, contests.
3. Mini-index.
4. Retail store location.
5. Phone specials.
6. Guarantee statement.
7. Customer testimonials.

Inside Pages

Once your "doorway" has lured in customers, the hard work begins. The customer's interest must be carried over eagerly from the cover and held on every page throughout the catalog. Each product must call for attention independently, without overpowering other products. The catalog designer must exercise great skill in creating eye flow while calling attention to special offers and product benefits—and never losing sight of the need for customer convenience.

Like a retailer, you need to design your "store" so that customers find what they need quickly. Products need to be *arranged* in a manner that invites further browsing (a responsibility of the merchandiser), and *portrayed* in a manner than evokes the desire to purchase (the responsibility of your creative staff).

Natural Hot Spots

A handful of "hot spots" produce more sales than a typical catalog page. The most powerful sales pages in the entire catalog are the front and back cover—but three other spreads are also effective.

1. The first spread.   The first spread (inside front cover and page 3) is to a cataloger what the first ten feet of floor space is to a retailer. It's where you show the best you've got and then convince them there is even more. To misuse this spread can be fatal. It can literally turn people back, and right out of your "store."

2. The middle pages.   The middle pages (center spread) produce greater sales because a saddle-stitched catalog tends to fall open here naturally. (This is not a hot spot in a perfectly bound catalog.) Most catalogs insert their order forms here, but some move the order form to a different signature to take advantage of this spread.

3. The last spread.   The last spread (inside back cover and the page opposite) enjoys a moderate increase in sales because some people look at a catalog from the back to the front. Many extra sales opportunities that normally would be gained by this position are actually realized by pages 1 and 2. Once customers are attracted by the back cover, it is their natural inclination to turn the catalog over to see the front cover and start viewing from that point.

Contrived Hot Spots

Contrived hot spots are areas where greater sales are enjoyed because the cataloger has made a special effort to produce them. The three most common are:

1. Front cover referenced pages.   Any products or product categories pictured and referenced on the cover will enjoy greater sales.

2. Back cover referenced pages.   Products both pictured and referenced from the back cover will enjoy more sales than those that are simply referenced. Specific categories whose inside page numbers are referenced will also sell better.

3. Bind-in areas. Your catalog will automatically open to wherever you bind in your order form or other insert. (In business-to-business catalogs, the catalog will open to spots where reply cards have been bound in to generate new leads and inquiries.) Be sure to use the surrounding pages to their most profitable use by spotlighting winning products.

The opportunity to bind in an order form presents itself between every signature. Signatures are generally printed in multiples of 8, 16, or 32 pages, depending on the type of printing and type of press you are using. A 96-page catalog printed in 32-page signatures would have three opportunities to bind in material: between pages 16–17 and 80–81, pages 32–33 and 65–65, and between 48 and 49, the middle of the catalog. If the middle of the book is a natural hot spot, why not bind your order form into other signatures, and create additional sales from these hot spots?

Because all of these spots get extra attention and are likely to be read by your prospective customers, use them to showcase your best-selling merchandise. They are also good positions for popular products with high profit margins.

You will always realize more sales if you strive to make sure that contrived reference areas and natural hot spots do not carry the same products. Let them help you move the customer on to new and different merchandise!

Catalog Formats

Many things influence the way you arrange your catalog, but the price range and type of merchandise will be the governing factors. Once your merchandise is selected, you have already taken a big step toward determining the type of format to use.

Another major determining factor is your market. The general consumer has traditionally approached purchasing by mail in a fairly relaxed manner. Because he or she is able to choose the time and place for shopping and tends to have a broad interest in products, this customer enjoys leisurely browsing through catalogs and discovering impulse items. By contrast, the business customer's time and interests are limited. This person needs a more orderly and expeditious way of selecting merchandise.

The three major ways to organize products in a catalog are:

1. Product category format

2. Theme/Function category format

3. Mixed product format

Product Category Format

A consumer catalog choosing this format will group products according to a category, placing kitchen products, garden products, or toys together. A business-to-business cataloger would put all roof repair supplies together, all paint, all screen doors.

Figure 3.17 is from a J. Crew catalog divided into three (unlabeled) categories: men's apparel, women's apparel, and accessories such as shoes, ties, hats, and belts. The spread shown is the first in the accessory section, which bridges the gap between men's and women's apparel.

Figure 3.17   J. Crew catalog

The Global company divides its products into numerous categories, covering every aspect of office supply products. Figure 3.18 shows a page from the diskette section. The running head in the top left corner helps identify the section and the particular types of diskette sold on this page.

Figure 3.18 Global catalog

Theme/Function Category Format

This format presents products according to function, or groups them according to theme. A food specialty catalog, for example, might devise separate areas for steaks, fowl, sauces, desserts. A business-to-business cataloger might lead off with word processing, then move into accounting and organizers.

Figure 3.19 shows a page from Lillian Vernon, in which holiday novelties and gifts are displayed under the head, "Lilly's Celebration." Appropriately enough, these twelve pages of items open the catalog's 55th anniversary edition. Williams-Sonoma, a catalog for cooks, usually intersperses food items with culinary equipment. But in its holiday edition, it highlights "Holiday Foods" in a multi-page section at the front of the book (Figure 3.20). Both of these catalogs use the theme/function approach to take advantage of seasonal sales patterns and get the most out of the front pages of the book.

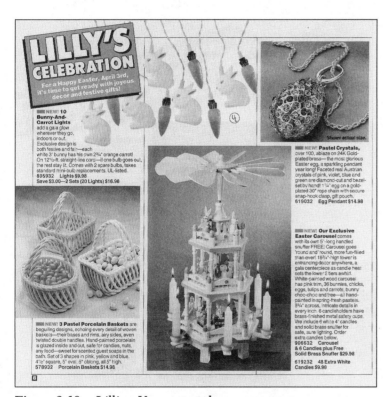

Figure 3.19   Lillian Vernon catalog

Figure 3.20   Williams-Sonoma catalog

Advantages
Requires only the function to be known, not the specific product—makes for fast, easy referencing; easy comparison of products performing the same functions; easy presentation of customer education and specific promotional copy areas.

Disadvantages
Possible sales decline for less popular product styles; boring page layouts; lost product coordinating opportunities; undesirable carryover when there is not enough area for all products in one section.

Mixed Product Format

In a mixed product format, any product type can be dummied on any page with any other product. This is the most popular format in the general consumer area, because it is relatively easy to mix products, and sales are less dependent on product grouping by function or category. (It is inappropriate for business-to-business catalogs.)

At first glance, this approach looks simple—but it is very difficult to execute well. Care must be taken not to mix products whose proximity might offend, such as a cake pan and a kitty litter box. Each product's share of space also needs to be carefully considered. A product with seasonal appeal, such as a shelving storage unit, might demand more space in January than in the fall gift season. High-ticket items, large items, and items with many features will also demand more space. All these factors need to be considered when you dummy a mixed-product-format catalog.

The Paragon, a general gift catalog, uses the mixed product approach (**Figure 3.21**). This page offers a set of glasses, a blue glass straw dis-

Figure 3.21   Paragon catalog

penser, and a checked dhurrie rug. To pull the page together, there are tones of blue in each picture. The rug and the straw dispenser are blue, and a blue band to the left of the glasses pulls the blue to the top of the page. The blue straw dispenser is bordered in red to unite this left-hand page with the merchandise it faces, which has red and yellow highlights. This type of format occurs on page after page in the Paragon catalog.

Advantages
Lively, appealing visual format; product coordination; color coordination; individual product appeal; size flexibility of product presentation; encourages browsing.

Disadvantages
Possible increase in preparation and production costs due to different layout and different product presentation in each issue; scattered customer attention; inability to index easily; no reference ability for product category or product function.

How a Customer "Reads" a Page

Researcher Siegfried Voegele strapped a camera to the heads of thousands of subjects in order to determine their catalog reading patterns. He found that the average reader peruses a spread in this order:

1. He or she looks first at the *upper right* of a catalog spread;

2. Then at the *middle left*;

3. And finally, at the *lower right*.

4. The top and bottom left corners are often ignored altogether.

Take advantage of this flow by placing important products as close as you can to the most-noticed positions.

You can also create contrived "hot spots" within a page spread. Researchers have found that attention is naturally drawn to:

- the largest photo in a spread

- products accompanied by an in-use shot

- products highlighted by graphic "labels" or symbols that provide readers with quick product information

The BT Publix catalog is ordered alphabetically—an A-to-Z of office equipment and supplies (see **Figure 3.22**). This format allows buyers to find their way quickly and easily around this business-to-business catalog of more than 600 pages. Notice in **Figure 3.23**, the clean, easy to read page headings. Each section is color-coded so that buyers can see exactly where it begins and ends.

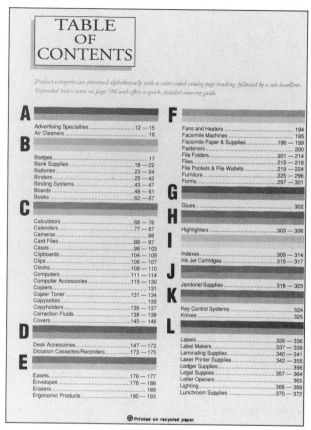

Figure 3.22   BT Publix Catalog

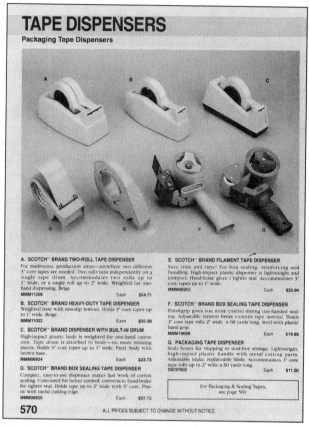

Figure 3.23   BT Publix Catalog

Page Layout

Once you have selected your format, you can choose the style of layout that is best for your products, price level, and image.

The term *layout* simply means the physical arrangement of the design (in the case of catalogs, the products) throughout the catalog. Layouts are affected by how you decide to group your product line (e.g., your format choice), and your product grouping, in turn, is affected by how your customer will respond.

Layout techniques falls into two basic approaches: *symmetrical*, a measured grid format, and *asymmetrical*, a nonproportional grid format. To select the best layout for you, answer these questions:

• What products are you putting in your catalog?

- What method of organization do you wish to use?

- Who is the customer to whom you are trying to appeal, and what is the "tone" that will make them most comfortable?

- Which style can you handle most efficiently, not just for one catalog, but on a regular schedule?

- Will the style you're inclining toward create budgetary problems or problems with your ability to execute it?

One reason to consider the flexibility of the layout you choose is the need to frequently reshuffle the merchandise in your "store." Catalogers who mail continuously throughout the year rearrange their "stores" often to test products in new locations and to keep their buyers interested. The layout you choose will determine how easily you can enlarge, reduce, or replace merchandise.

A catalog, like a retail store, has to use its precious "square footage" wisely. There are many successful configurations for catalogs, and no format or layout is beyond improvement. But the wise cataloger learns the rules before disregarding them for a new idea!

Once you have selected a style of layout, stick with it. It will become an identity for your company—an identity that will help build customer loyalty. When customers are comfortable with your book, they're glad to shop there! If the style is truly successful for your customers, prospecting for new customers will cause similar kinds of people to respond to your book, and the growth of your customer list will fit a logical pattern.

Symmetrical Layouts

In a symmetrical layout, art and copy are generally in balanced proportions, or there is a measured ratio of art to copy (for example, art taking one third of the allotted area and copy taking two thirds). Low-end merchandise generally works well in this type of layout, because a number of low-priced products need to be put on a page for that page to make a profit. The mechanics of layout for each catalog are easy because of the measured space, and economical because the size of the art and copy areas almost never changes, making it easy to pull and replace products as needed.

Figure 3.24 shows a page from the Walter Drake catalog. Here, art and copy share an almost identical space. The layout has a very measured effect. The copy area is always identical in width (flush left and right), and the number of lines is always within a line or two of the same length. The typeface is traditional, readable, and printed in black against a white background for greater clarity. The pages are equally balanced and the art and copy have the same characteristics throughout the catalog. And yet all pages are not identical. Some use this layout vertically; others are changed to horizontal across the top and vertical across the bottom.

A more upscale version of the symmetrical layout is found in the Hold Everything catalog (Figure 3.25). Here, the symmetry relaxes, as art and copy are not exactly equal, and photos are not identical in size. The copy is flush left, ragged right, allowing a freer look. The order found in all symmetrical layouts is retained because of the vertical columnar format of the page. Through this layout, Hold Everything is able to convey a sense of the order that its products create and its customer is seeking to acquire.

A symmetrical layout can be of great help to business-to-business catalogs that must contend with hundreds, sometimes even thousands of listings in one single catalog. **Figure 3.26**, a page from the Rio Grande jeweler's supply catalog, is a perfect example of how clarity need not be boring when a cataloger faces this problem.

Appealing layouts must have clarity

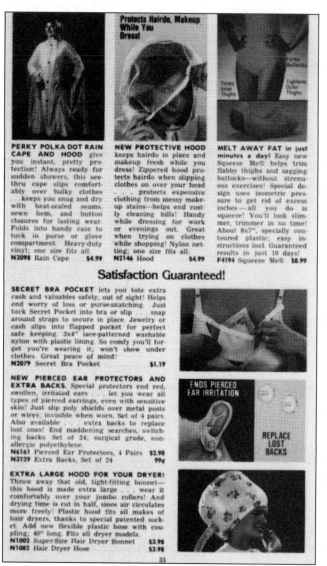

Figure 3.24   Walter Drake catalog

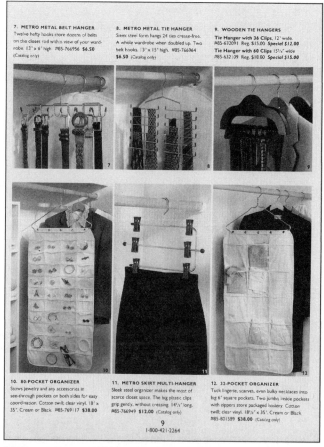

Figure 3.25   Hold Everything catalog

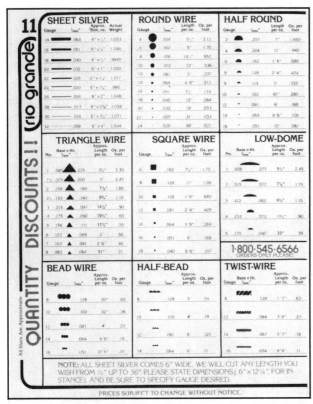

Figure 3.26 Rio Grande catalog

Advantages
Easy matching of copy with artwork; facilitates all products sharing equal prominence; easy interchange of product listings throughout the book because of equality of space allotment; economies from this ability to interchange art and copy; rapid layout because so many of the items use exactly the same amount of copy and art space; minimal creative and production costs, as once the photograph is taken and the copy is written and typeset, it can be used over and over again; customer appreciation of measured neatness and orderliness in a book like this.

Disadvantages
Static and boring style without careful variation of other page layouts throughout the book, from vertical to horizontal; same look for all pages; the inability to easily vary the size of copy and art, hurting adequate treatment of items needing more space for optimum presentation or products needing dramatic presentations; tendency of customers to think they have seen this page before.

Asymmetrical Layouts

Most mid-to-high retail catalogs and many consumer and business catalogs use some form of the asymmetrical layout, which uses a nonproportional approach for individual art and copy sizes. The mechanics of this technique are more difficult and more costly because art and copy need to be changed for each new catalog produced. Generally, this type of layout also requires more experienced creative talent.

The Colonial Garden Kitchens catalog shown in **Figure 3.27** uses silhouette photographs (where the backgrounds have been dropped out—a typical technique in an asymmetrical layout) as well as items placed in windows. One side of the copy block is always flush to the relevant item, making it easy for the customer to match the item's copy to its photograph. The other side of the copy is ragged, allowing the page to retain a graceful, freer look. Air is balanced against occupied space in a way that encourages the eye to flow rhythmically from item

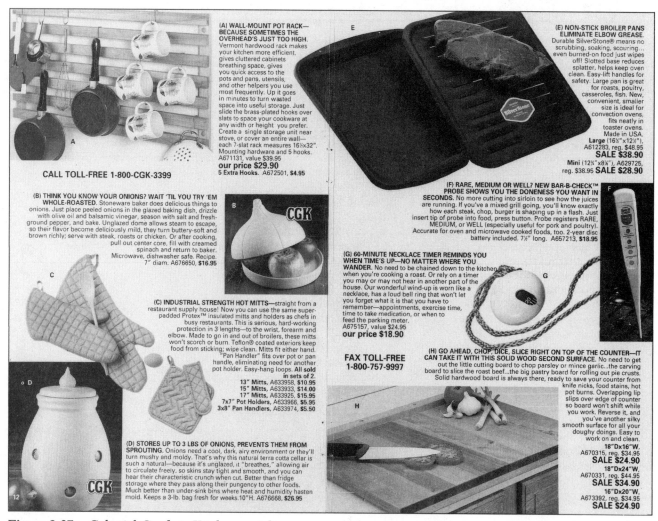

Figure 3.27   Colonial Gardens Kitchens catalog

to item, never having to jump gaps that are too large, or struggle with crammed areas.

   This style of layout is a fine balance between discipline and freedom. It inspires the customer to give equal attention to every item, yet continue to move through the book, viewing each page in turn. In its many

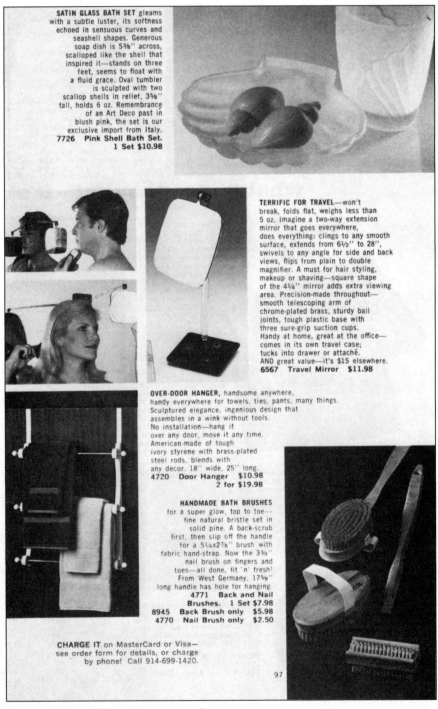

SATIN GLASS BATH SET gleams with a subtle luster, its softness echoed in sensuous curves and seashell shapes. Generous soap dish is 5⅜" across, scalloped like the shell that inspired it—stands on three feet, seems to float with a fluid grace. Oval tumbler is sculpted with two scallop shells in relief, 3⅝" tall, holds 6 oz. Remembrance of an Art Deco past in blush pink, the set is our exclusive import from Italy.
7726   Pink Shell Bath Set.
1 Set $10.98

TERRIFIC FOR TRAVEL—won't break, folds flat, weighs less than 5 oz. Imagine a two-way extension mirror that goes everywhere, does everything: clings to any smooth surface, extends from 6½" to 28", swivels to any angle for side and back views, flips from plain to double magnifier. A must for hair styling, makeup or shaving—square shape of the 4¼" mirror adds extra viewing area. Precision-made throughout—smooth telescoping arm of chrome-plated brass, sturdy ball joints, tough plastic base with three sure-grip suction cups. Handy at home, great at the office—comes in its own travel case; tucks into drawer or attaché. AND great value—it's $15 elsewhere.
6567   Travel Mirror $11.98

OVER-DOOR HANGER, handsome anywhere, handy everywhere for towels, ties, pants, many things. Sculptured elegance, ingenious design that assembles in a wink without tools. No installation—hang it over any door, move it any time. American-made of tough ivory styrene with brass-plated steel rods, blends with any decor. 18" wide, 25" long.
4720   Door Hanger $10.98
2 for $19.98

HANDMADE BATH BRUSHES for a super glow, top to toe—fine natural bristle set in solid pine. A back-scrub first, then slip off the handle for a 5¼x2⅞" brush with fabric hand-strap. Now the 3¾" nail brush on fingers and toes—all done, fit 'n' fresh! From West Germany, 17⅜" long handle has hole for hanging.
4771   Back and Nail
Brushes.   1 Set $7.98
8945   Back Brush only $5.98
4770   Nail Brush only $2.50

CHARGE IT on MasterCard or Visa—see order form for details, or charge by phone! Call 914-699-1420.

97

Figure 3.28   Lillian Vernon catalog

variations, asymmetrical is probably the most frequently seen style of layout in cataloging.

To see how art and copy in a basic asymmetrical layout can be used for another catalog without changing size or reshooting, and yet be different, look at **Figures 3.28** and **3.29** from Lillian Vernon. In the

Figure 3.29   Lillian Vernon catalog

two examples, you can see that the lower portion of each page is identical, but one item in the upper half of the page (the Japanese design bath set in **Figure 3.29**) has been replaced with another item (see **Figure 3.28**). Perhaps for aesthetics, the travel mirror at the top of the page was repositioned when the new item was added. This caused copy to be reset. In the new layout, the body is flush left; in the old layout it was flush right.

Asymmetrical layouts let designers structure pages around the shapes of the products featured on the page. **Figure 3.30** is a case in point. In this spread from Smith & Hawken, the designer has achieved a fascinating three-dimensional affect by silhouetting the umbrella and the terracotta pots over the photo showing vegetables grown from a featured seed collection. Playing off the shapes and angles of these products, the designer has tucked the canvas color swatches under the umbrella itself, and wrapped type around the pots and baskets shown on the page. The final result is a sophisticated, contemporary, and highly engaging page that invites the customer to linger awhile on its contents.

Figure 3.30 Smith & Hawken catalog

Advantages

Easy adjustment of space allotted to individual copy and art areas permits the cataloger to show each item to its best advantage, because every item does not have to fit into the dimensions of a specifically defined "block." The same is true for the copy, which allows the copywriter to write to the demands of the item (longer or shorter); easy interchange of items occur because certain sizes are standard throughout the book, even including the silhouette; permits possible rewriting of copy, or at least re-typesetting, if it is necessary to change the margin from flush left to flush right; rhythmical feel to pages retains the customer's interest, allows the eye's travel from item to item and page to page because of the controlled free-form positioning of the items.

Disadvantages

Greater care needed to size the art and copy so that the air between items is appropriately balanced to retain eye flow (this means that judgments have to be made continually, which requires extra time and money, as well as allowing the possibility of errors in that judgment. This format also requires more attention—again, time and money—to the line-for-line positioning of copy, at least for the graphics accompanying the initial listing, plus additional expense in the resetting of copy when adjustments to an item's positioning are made); longer lead time to put together the catalog, which also adds to cost; possible problems in the copy-to-artwork match-up, creating a risk that the customer cannot easily find the proper product description; possibility that errors in creative judgment will cause layout to appear chaotic, disrupting eye flow and, consequently, sales.

An Exercise in Grid Design: How Layouts Grow from Grids

A grid is any combination of overlapping horizontal and vertical lines that will ultimately aid in the page design of a catalog. A catalog may utilize one grid design or several. Grids may be symmetrical or asymmetrical. Their main function is to act as guides to the designer in identifying margins, space, and columns. The grid design approach is the backbone of the electronic design used in computer graphics and the wave of the future. It can be a catalog designer's best friend.

Symmetrical Grid Layout

In the symmetrical grid layout, the art and copy are perfectly balanced and proportioned; art and copy blocks are placed in exact or logical relation to one another.

Let's look at an example of how a perfectly balanced symmetrical layout was achieved from a four-column grid. **Figure 3.31** is a four column, $8\frac{1}{2}" \times 11"$ page grid. Note how each column is divided into five equal squares, allowing room for ten products to be displayed on the page in a balanced, systematic way. **Figure 3.32** from The Sharper Image shows how the designer easily utilized the grid. The two middle column squares are each used for same-size product photos, just combining the top two middle squares into one photo and dropping in a silhouetted side view of the diamond pendant at the top left of the second photo down. The two outside columns are used for product description copy. Note how the balance of individual copy length and the air around these copy blocks is proportioned (i.e., long, short, short, long, long) so when the copy is positioned with the photos the whole becomes a

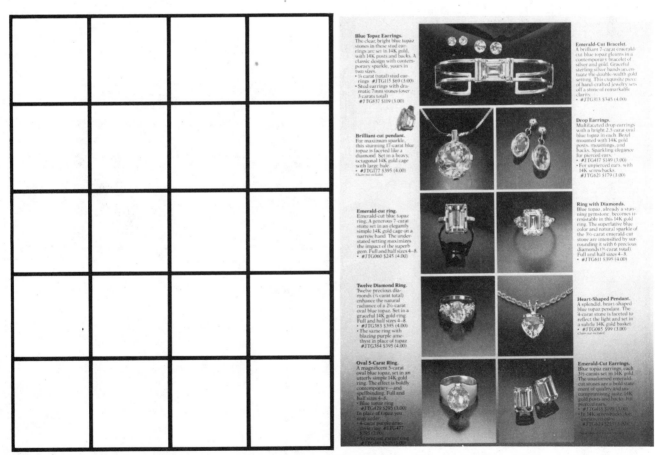

Figure 3.31   Page grid   Figure 3.32   Sharper Image catalog

perfectly balanced visual. Another version of the four-column grid is seen in the same Sharper Image catalog. **Figure 3.33** shows how the symmetrical grid is used to produce a horizontal product presentation that is perfectly balanced in the top 60 percent of the page. The remaining 40 percent of the layout is still guided by the four columns but becomes asymmetrical in design. The orderliness of the symmetrical design is maintained with the balanced placement of the copy blocks.

DRI Industries employs a two-column grid throughout its 96-page catalog with variations that allow the layout to become asymmetrical. **Figure 3.34** shows the basic two-column grid dividing an $8^{1}/_{2}$" × 11" page into eight equal parts. **Figure 3.35** shows how DRI presents four different tool shops. Each copy block is dropped slightly below each picture division, allowing a small and interesting visual element to add variety to the page and encouraging the eye to travel down the page. **Figure 3.36** shows how enlarging the grid areas for one product and utilizing the silhouette technique of dropping out part of the product picture onto the second column area gives the impression of an asymmetrical design. Also, note that part of the copy description is formed around the silhouetted product, further adding to the more relaxed presentation. **Figure 3.37** is yet another page in the same DRI catalog that deals very successfully with multi-item listing. Twenty-two products are picture-listed, all falling nicely into the two-column grid guide.

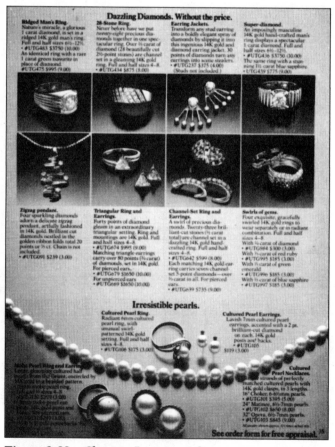

Figure 3.33   Sharper Image catalog

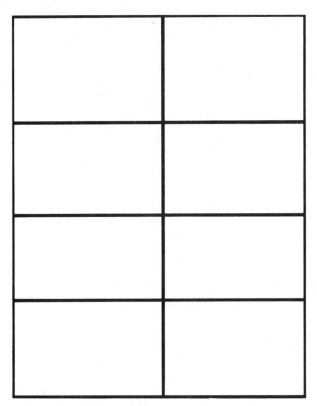

Figure 3.34   DRI catalog

Figure 3.35   DRI catalog

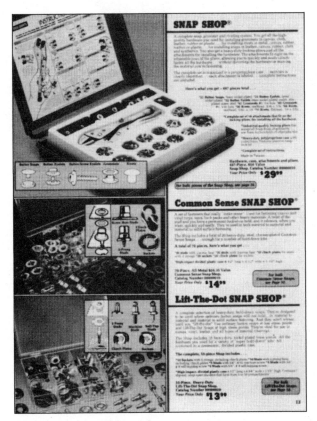

Figure 3.36   DRI catalog

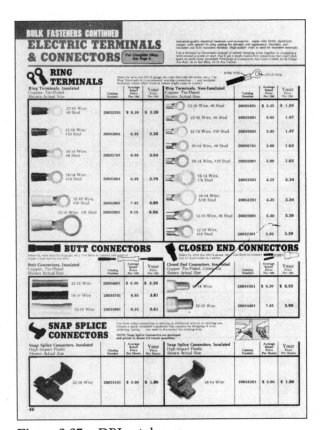

Figure 3.37   DRI catalog

Interest is added to the page with category headers containing a crisp silhouette of general product shape and bold identifying headline classifications.

The symmetrical grid method is an easy and fairly expeditious way of doing proportional page layouts. It offers both the easy art and copy coordination and the orderliness that are often appreciated by the customer.

Asymmetrical Grid Layout

The horizontal and vertical lines forming the asymmetrical grid act mostly as a guide to identification of certain parameters such as column measures, margins, and space possibilities within a page. It is a less stringent format than the symmetrical grid. Designers need to be able to apply the principles of proportion in such a manner that their creative abilities dominate the final design. The layout will result in a seemingly looser, more relaxed page.

Brookstone's Homewares catalog is a joy to view, mainly because of the way the designer laid out the 98-page catalog with a three-column, nine-item grid as a guide. **Figure 3.38** is the basic grid with three $2^{1}/_{2}''$ columns acting as the layout guide for an $8^{1}/_{4}'' \times 9''$ page. **Figures 3.39, 3.40,** and **3.41** illustrate the expert page layout throughout the

Figure 3.38   Brookstone's Homewares catalog

Figure 3.39   Brookstone's Homewares catalog

catalog. In **Figure 3.39** the designer has chosen to highlight an expensive ($300) product with a nice one-half point border, taking up approximately one fourth of the page. Note how the boxed area overlaps the right margin edge and the left column. The designer has completed the page with silhouette drop-outs (top left and middle left) and fully bordered photos with accompanying copy blocks. Secondary vertical lines become prominent layout guides (see our added dotted lines in **Figure 3.39** indicating secondary guides). **Figure 3.40**, another seven-product page, highlights the page's most expensive product by silhouetting the set of bowls (upper right) and overlapping the outer margin and, this time, the right columnar line. In **Figure 3.41**, Brookstone presents a collection of lower-priced kitchen merchandise (ten products in all). Rhythm and eye flow are achieved even on this product-packed page by bordered photos, product silhouetting, and a combination of both. The designer has chosen to use the vertical line columnar grids as part of the design. These lines have created interest and eye flow where without them white space might have let the photos and copy "float" without purpose or direction. The designer has pulled together all the products on each page to present a total viewing occasion, retaining individual product interest.

A good business-to-business catalog with a layout that follows the same three-column grid approach is Inmac, a computer accessories

Easy eyeflow

Figure 3.40   Brookstone's Homewares catalog

Figure 3.41   Brookstone's Homewares catalog

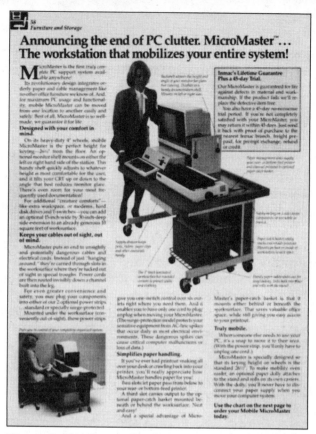

Figure 3.42   Inmac catalog

catalog. Here are three 8½″ × 11″ pages, each illustrating the different look and feel that can be created, depending on the demands of the product being presented. **Figure 3.42** shows how the descriptive copy falls into the three-column format, resulting in what is very near to a magazine page. The main illustration uses two thirds of two columns to show the product, a Mobile Micromaster organizer system, and to highlight the company's guarantee, which is smartly bordered to maintain the single-column approach. A small, one-column photo in the lower left shows how easy the product is to use. **Figure 3.43** shows again how the three-column format is utilized for 16 different products. One-point line rules help divide the page, adding order and interest. The designer has used the upper left one third of the page to sell Inmac's special Line-Links. Interest and asymmetry are achieved with "wandering" or columnar overlapping of silhouetted product photos. **Figure 3.44** shows how the three-column grid can look like a horizontally dominated layout while really being based on a vertical three-column format. Note the top of the page showing the conformity to the three columns. Now follow our added gray dotted lines downward (lines not printed in the actual catalog) to see how the three columns are carried through.

Figure 3.43 Inmac catalog

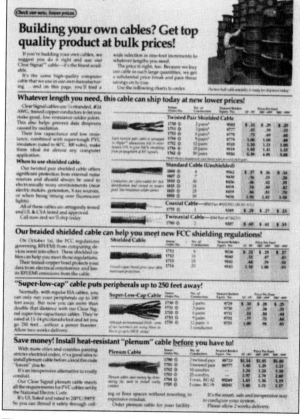

Figure 3.44 Inmac catalog

A Master Grid for a Digest-Size Catalog

The grid actually acts as a blueprint for a catalog page, meant to guide and aid the artist in laying out the catalog pages. **Figure 3.45** is the master grid used to design the 16 grid combinations on the opposite page. The vertical lines on a grid are meant to act as column guides, to designate the space between columns, and to indicate the inner and outer margins. The horizontal lines aid in the depth of type and the placement of visual material and headlines, and they indicate the upper and lower page margins. This grid is designed for a 5½" × 8½" digest-size page.

Good layout requires skillful use of air

Figure 3.45   Master grid

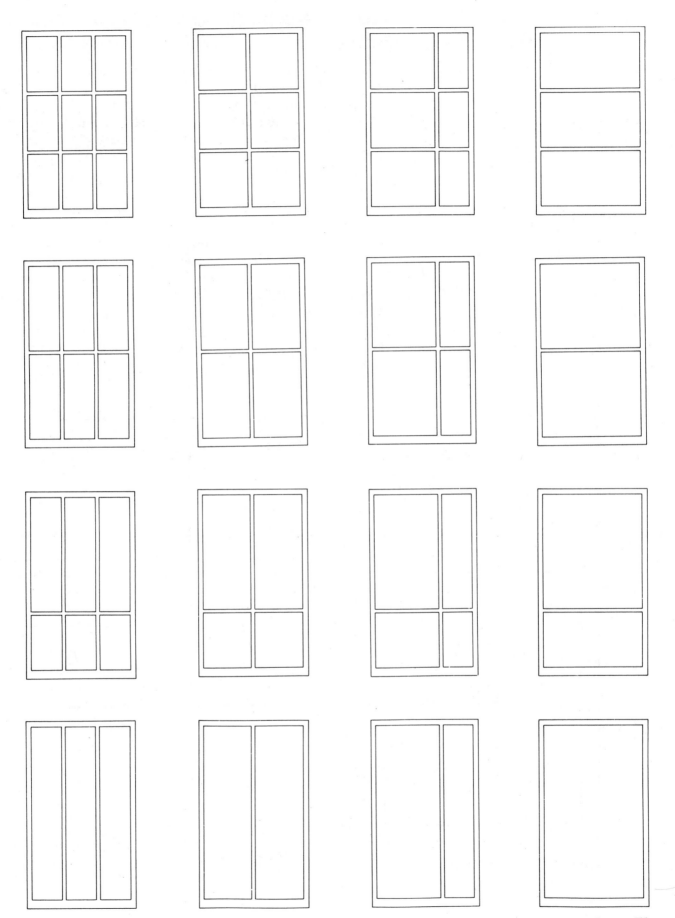

Two Different Layouts from One Grid Design

In **Figure 3.46**, we see a basic three-column, nine-unit grid designed to be used for a horizontal catalog page. **Figure 3.47** illustrates how the artist has applied a symmetrical layout in presenting four basic products. An attractive, full column view of the pivotal and most expensive product, a dress, is seen at the left of the page. The top and bottom margins are indicated by the horizontal lines of the top and bottom grid units. The middle column guides the placement of the headlines and type. Even though the right margins of the type are ragged, they still stay within the perimeters of the middle column vertical guidelines. The three units in the right-hand column of the grid act as exacting guides for the photographs of the three accessory products. **Figure 3.48** shows how the artist has maintained the full left column to present the main product and has still come up with an asymmetrical page design. The artist has created an easy flow starting with the logo and headline, directing the eye over to the photo of the scarves in the upper right. Because of the angle of the scarves, the eye is pointed back into the page and over to the wallet. The corner of the wallet is silhouetted outside of the bottom border to direct the eye down to the copy and

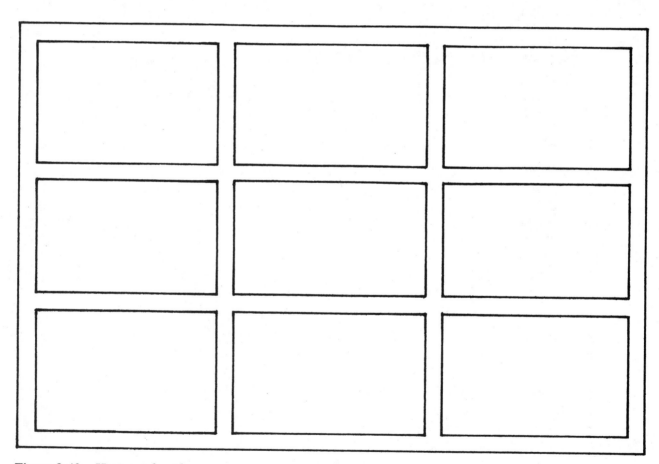

Figure 3.46   Horizontal grid

Figure 3.47   Symmetrical page design

Figure 3.48   Asymmetrical page design

over to the handbag. This is a wonderful job of directing the eye over the entire page. The copy is essentially still in the middle column, but it overlaps onto the right column in the upper part of the page and then falls into the middle column perimeters at the bottom. The art treatment of silhouetting the scarves and handbag loosens up the page and acts as an attractive visual aid to the asymmetrical design. By using the basic grid as a guide, the artist was able to come up with two different and attractive page layouts.

Alternatives to the Grid

Besides symmetrical and asymmetrical layouts, there are three other layout techniques you can put to work in your catalog:

1. Art separated from copy

2. Product grouping

3. One item to a page

Art Separated from Copy

This format is especially interesting because it can retain the orderliness of the symmetrical layout along with the rhythm of the asymmetrical.

Figure 3.49   Crate & Barrel catalog

Individual product shots are grouped on one section of the page or on a separate page entirely, while the accompanying copy is in a separate area or page. Such a format functions well for catalogs appealing to a variety of retail segments, high-ticket to low-ticket, although it must be handled differently for each one, particularly in the use of air.

General Consumer. Examine this example (**Figure 3.49**) from Crate & Barrel. Varying the size of individual photos within a firm, geometrical area keeps the layout interesting. The copywriter is working within the discipline of making the copy for all items fit onto the page, but retaining the advantage of being able to adjust the length of each item's description. If the copy on a right-hand page had been allowed to run to the next page, causing the customer to turn the page to read about an item pictured on the previous page, an inconvenience would have been introduced. Whenever a situation makes things less convenient for the customer, sales are affected negatively.

This technique can also work in low-end catalogs, provided that enough space is provided so that artwork is not cramped and difficult to match with copy. Art needs to be properly sized and cropped, and not be formatted too tightly. Both photos and copy need "air" to relax the eye and keep the art and copy blocks from running together.

Advantages

Specific sizing of art in advance of the shot, to fit into an area the exact dimensions of which are known; eliminates the risk of forcing the eye to jump around the entire page, which sometimes occurs in asymmetrical layouts, since all copy can be found in one area; easy viewing of all products one after another, without interruption.

Disadvantages

Requires greater attention to juxtaposition of items and air within the photographs, and air surrounding them, so the customer's eye is not confused; greater attention to gapping of the photographs; possibility that the page will not retain both a visual blend and a separation if background colors for photographs are not carefully coordinated; possibility of visual "run-together," adding confusion when used in a black and white catalog (black and white creates a solid mass from border to border in the area where the photos are abutted, discouraging visual differentiation introduced by varied colors in a four-color layout); difficulty in readily matching the description to the photo (letters referencing the photo to the copy block must be easily picked out in each area); greater probability of a cluttered layout if copy is not properly gapped.

Product Grouping

A popular technique among high-end home furnishing and table-top catalogs is product grouping, in which a single photograph includes a group of separately sold items. The success of this format depends on how readily the eye can separate the individual products in the grouping. Copy is positioned separately.

Figures 3.50 and **3.51** show two approaches to the product grouping, both from Pottery Barn. Both incorporate half a dozen items into a perfect room, but **Figure 3.50** highlights hard-to-see items by repeating them in individual photographs to the left of the copy, which is set outside the photo. **Figure 3.51** includes product copy and information within the photo spread, but the items are arranged in a manner that lets copy sit almost adjacent to the item it describes.

Figure 3.50   Pottery Barn catalog

Figure 3.51   Pottery Barn catalog

Advantages	Disadvantages
Encourages coordinated purchasing; aesthetically pleasing, although aesthetics are of value only if they encourage the bottom line; more interesting to view when all one category subject; lower production costs, in some cases (only one picture to take, one color separation, one photo to strip up instead of six, for example, if set-up can be kept simple, such as in the B. Dalton layout—however, may be more expensive for the Vernon shot because of photographer's fees for a more complicated photograph, requiring more time and originality).	More difficult for items to retain individual attention from the customer, who often has to search for each one; more difficult art/copy match-ups because it is hard to place reference letters in the main photograph without making them either too prominent, causing a distraction, or too recessive (all of which forces the customer to work, which is a liability in creating an easy sales climate); difficulty of achieving the hoped-for use of association to lend greater appeal to each item in order to create more sales; in practice, possibly disastrous results by not calling proper attention to all of the merchandise available, causing lost sales.

One Product to a Page

This style of layout has many variations and may even extend to two pages in some catalogs. Basically, a full page is devoted to both art and copy in presenting one product. Of all styles, this one is most often dictated by the type of product being presented. It is quite often used when a product line offers many versions of the same product type, such as a "good, better, best" situation, or when one product has many features which need to be pointed out.

Figure 3.52 illustrates how a very high-ticket product can benefit from extra-long copy. Often this technique is used on $8\frac{1}{2}" \times 11"$ pages, but in the Herrington catalog, which is digest size, this copy fits onto a $5\frac{1}{2}" \times 8\frac{1}{2}"$ page. Two-thirds of the page is devoted to long, conversational, benefit-packed copy that offers detailed information about this $4500.00 product. Easy art and copy reference is achieved with this method, of course.

Figure 3.53 shows how the Day-Timer catalog uses the one-item-to-a-page layout to help sell an item that offers multiple benefits and it made up of many components. This wallet/binder product offers loyal users of Day-Timer time management systems to upgrade into a sophisticated "Joint Venture" that combines a traditional desktop organizers with a pocket scheduler. The copy, art, call outs, and photo insets work well together to play up the product's many benefits.

Graphics like the ones employed in this Day-Timer spread can help

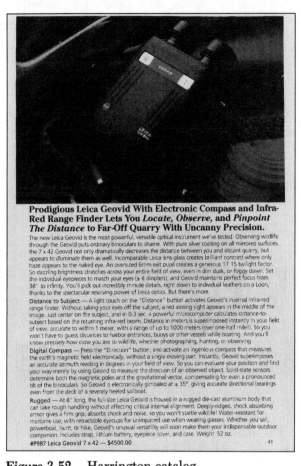

Figure 3.52　Harrington catalog

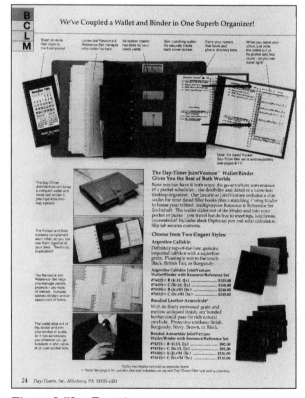

Figure 3.53　Day-timer

keep a one-product-per-page from looking dull. Tinted panels, bulleted copy, subheads, and call outs are all devices that can break up long copy into palatable, readable chunks.

Advantages

Detail easily emphasized in both copy and art, affording the opportunity to relay to the customer all information for a buying decision; minimal "competition" between products; maximum space and attention allowed to each product in the catalog.

Disadvantages

More difficult to achieve cost-effectiveness since one product must bring in enough sales to justify the cost of a full page; greater copy skill needed (long copy sometimes hard to keep lively and interesting).

Inside Page Checklist:

☐ Determine style of format best suited.
☐ Review key sales areas.
☐ Select layout approach.
☐ Determine basic page design.

Always:
1. Consider customer convenience.
2. Consider individuality of product line.
3. Consider advantages of product comparison.
4. Choose the best approach for moving the customer through the catalog.
5. Understand your budget restrictions.

Strongly Consider:
1. Trying several of the basic approaches before making a final decision.
2. Choosing a layout approach you can live with always.

CHAPTER 4

Product Work Sessions

In product work sessions, you and your creative staff decide how to present the new products that will appear in your catalog. You determine why the customer will buy the item, how to present it with photography or artwork, and what to say about it in the copy description.

During the sessions, merchandisers present the reasons each product was selected, so that the artists and copywriters can blend their interpretive and creative skills into a winning sales combination.

All of your creative staff—in-house and freelance alike—and every merchandiser or buyer who has new products must attend product work sessions. Because this is likely to be the first time the artists and copywriters have seen the new products, they will need ample time to make their acquaintance. As Chapter 2 recommended, a minimum of fifteen minutes should be devoted to each new product. If you have only a few products—say nine or ten—you might be able to get by with one long review session. But if you have 100 new products, it's better to schedule several sessions.

Product work sessions focus on *new* products. Products that have succeeded in earlier issues of your catalog can be rerun as is—unless you think that revisiting the copy and art strategy will boost sales in a forthcoming catalog.

What to Bring to the Session

A great deal of groundwork needs to take place before merchandisers and creative staff get together. Most of it is the merchandiser's responsibility.

Good merchandisers select products for specific reasons, not just because they liked them. In order to convey these reasons to the creative staff, merchandisers should gather together materials that help creatives understand the rationale behind each selection. There are five such types of material:

1. Sample product
2. Art clippings showing how competitors depict the same or a similar product
3. Copy clippings that show competing copy strategies for the same or a similar product
4. Testing results
5. Manufacturer's information
6. Merchandiser's notes

Sample Product

Make sure the merchandiser brings a production sample, not a prototype, to the sessions. If a prototype is all you have, watch out! Minor changes in style, function, or material may be made prior to actual manufacturing, and then art and copy will be incorrect and misleading. A number of dangers exist:

- A poorly put together prototype or a prototype that is not fully functional may not photograph well. Art may not fully represent the product benefits, thus depressing sales.

- A prototype that looks better than the ultimate product or is a different color may mislead and ultimately disappoint purchasers.

- An inaccurate prototype means copy cannot capitalize on color assets, product mechanics and benefits, and may mislead consumers on important points such as style, size, or material.

All of these scenarios end with disappointed consumers, lowered sales, and increased returns. Don't risk it—schedule your meeting when actual product samples are available!

If you can't bring the product to the work session because of its size (computer, pool table, boat, etc.), try to schedule the creative people for a visit to the product.

Art Clippings

Most products selected are already being run by someone else (your competitors). Gather competitors' presentations together for the creative people to view. You know the product is selling well by mail. Part of the reason for that is the clarity and purpose of your competitors' presentations. Your staff will want to learn and benefit from others' success. There may be many examples; bring them all. Mount them all on a piece of paper for easy comparison of selling points. Include any magazine or newspaper ads. If the manufacturer has furnished a photo, bring that, too, even though it will most likely not be used.

Copy Clippings

These may or may not be included with the photos. Mounting copy separately will make it easier for everyone to study, and the mounted copy will ultimately be given to the assigned copywriter. Much of the copy will be from competitors' catalogs but may also be from magazine and newspaper ads and from manufacturers.

Testing Results

By the time a product has made it to the work sessions, it should have been fully tested. Merchandisers should have tested it themselves or assigned the testing to someone else to make sure the product is valid. Following are three areas of testing that help generate information your art and copy people need to know:

1. *Will the product do what the manufacturer claims? Example:* The manufacturer of a child's highchair makes specific safety claims. The chair should be tested to prove or disprove the claims. Catalogers can run their own tests or ask a consumer group or parents' organization to test for them. These groups are highly critical and will give the claims a thorough test.

2. *Is the product quality up to your company specifications? Example:* When listing quilted fabrics, test to see if they are washable. Will they bleed or shrink? Test to see if the fabrics are wrinkle resistant. Your customer needs to know.

3. *Packaging . . . Will the item be delivered to your customer in good shape? Example:* You don't want your package to arrive broken open and badly dented with the item crushed. Ship a sample to a person in another state and ask this person to tell you the condition of the package when it arrives. If the item does not arrive intact, you have a quality problem with your packaging. *Note:* Be prepared to eliminate an item or two from your inventory line when you follow this procedure.

Test your own catalog products

Manufacturer's Information

Each product being listed should be accompanied by a product information form filled in by the manufacturer. This form, which your company should originate, tells what the product is made of, its colors and dimensions, and other important information. Additional information sheets may also be supplied by the manufacturer.

Claims documentation should also be provided. For example, a grower claims a dwarf fruit tree will bear full-size fruit. Obviously, you cannot test this claim in time for your next catalog. Ask the grower for documentation of the claim. All legitimate companies offering products such as plants, gas savers, nonallergenic items, and so on must have test documentation to back their claims. State or federal laws generally require this proof. Ask your lawyer!

The completed form can help answer questions for art and copy production and for retail pricing as well as provide information for other areas in the company, such as warehousing and purchasing.

The following checklist includes the information that your form should request of a product's manufacturer.

What to Include on the Product Information Form

1. The Supplier

   - Company name, address, phone, fax

   - Person to contact, title

   - Area marketing rep, phone, fax

   - Credit references

Tip: Large companies have regional, state, or local representatives with whom to deal, but a greater discount may be realized if you purchase directly from the company. However, a rep *can* help with delivery problems.

2. The Product

   - Stock number, name of product

   - Country of origin

   - Dimensions, inches, ounces

   - Materials: wood, metal, etc.

   - Intrinsic details, such as UL listings, battery-operated, etc.

   - Sizes and colors available, percent of sales in each category

   - Is product warranty protection provided to defective merchandise? If so, how much liability is offered?

Tips: The stock number is the key to supplier processing; use it for speedier transactions. An import may need to be ordered early. Such things as materials or components are essential for catalog description. Knowing the mix of percent of sales helps you to protect quantity needs and decide on which colors to list. Drop the low sellers.

Bona fide sources will always tell you the amount of liability they carry to cover defective merchandise. Use this protection if needed; it will keep your own insurance payments down.

3. Pricing and Drop Shipping

   - Recommended price

   - Cost each, quantity cost breaks

- Is product prepriced; if so, for what dollar amount?

- How about a "guaranteed sales" deal?

- Is drop shipping available? At what cost?

Tip: Ask whether the supplier will consider total quantity ordered during the life of your catalog for quantity discounts. Prepricing can be a problem; ask if it can be deleted. You can avoid overstock with "guaranteed sales," but the product will cost more. When the supplier drop ships to your customer, you save costs of warehousing, freight, and overstock.

4. Packaging

- Master shipping carton quantity

- Weight of master carton

- Master shipping carton quantity

- Individual packaging: display, bulk, poly bag, individual mailer

Tip: Suppliers prefer shipping full cartons; if shipping less, costs may be more. Display packaging crushes easily when mailed; a poly bag is less costly and may work as well.

5. Shipping and Terms

- FOB point

- Shipping point

- Payment terms

- Freight allowance

Tip: Who pays the freight? Will terms or allowances help keep your costs down?

6. Availability

- Is the item in stock? If not, when will it be?

- Is supply continuous, or are there seasonal lows?

- What is normal on-hand supply?

- How long will it take to ship after receipt of order?

Tip: Be sure the product is actually manufactured and in stock before cataloging. If you don't, you may find yourself refunding all orders.

7. Advertising and Production

- How many samples do you want?

- How about a glossy photo or transparency?

- Any supplier contributions toward cost of art and copy?

- Any advertising allowances?

Tip: Get enough samples for evaluation, testing, art, copy. If you're cataloging plants or food, the manufacturer often has a transparency you'll want to use. Many will contribute to photography costs. Some will pay an advertising allowance upon proof of publication. Ask!

8. Product Sales Experience

- Any previous sales in mail order, and with whom? (Ask for a clipping.)

- If product is sold in media, ask for a copy of advertisements.

- Ask for company sales literature.

Tip: Never miss a chance to see how the product has been previously presented. Get as much sales history as you can. Art and copy samples will help with your catalog presentation.

9. Other Information

- Ask about other items offered by the company. Don't ever miss a chance to find new products.

- State your mail order status on the form to indicate your need for maximum discounts and price protection once an item is catalogued.

10. Space for Signature

- Ask for the signature of an officer of the course company; it is more binding than the signature of a rep.

Merchandiser's Notes

Merchandiser leads product work sessions

The marriage of merchandise and market occurred the moment the buyer decided a specific product should be listed in your catalog. Why? Because products are selected for specific reasons having to do with customer wants, needs, and previous buying records. All buyers know what it is about any given product that will attract the customer, and therefore they know what must be described clearly. These are the types of facts and feelings that the artist and copywriter will benefit from—and so will sales.

The major individual responsible for this material is not the art director, not the copy chief, and not the creative coordinator. It is the merchandiser. The merchandiser (or buyer) is the one who knows *why the product was selected.* The art director and copy chief are the people who know how to channel the customer's attention in the direction you want *once they know what that direction is.* But do not let them choose the direction (though this does not mean they cannot contribute to it). The merchandiser has chosen the product and bears the ultimate responsibility for its sales.

How to Conduct a Product Work Session

Since nobody knows the product and the reasons for its selection better than the merchandiser, this is the person who leads the product work session.

Armed with all of the materials just listed, the merchandiser should start the session by furnishing everyone with a list of products to be reviewed. As each product sample is passed around and examined, six areas need to be discussed:

1. Why the product was selected

2. The merchandiser's art visualization and copy headline visualization

3. The product's sales history

4. Competitive art and copy clippings

5. Testing results

6. Manufacturer's information

1. Why Was the Product Selected?

The first area to discuss is why the product was selected. The merchandiser should be able to discuss the reasons from notes made when the product was selected. Everyone can help determine the product's benefits by answering these questions.

Discussing these reasons for selection will help the creative staff focus on a main art and copy element: where and how the product is used. Customers will not purchase a product unless they can find a use relating to their own needs. (Don't forget that this use can even be "ego.") Some products may have a specially defined area of use; others may have three or four areas where the product can be placed or several ways it can be used. In this situation, avoid confusing the customer. Present a main area and allow the other areas to be secondary.

2. How Does the Merchandiser Visualize Art and Copy Headlines?

A good merchandiser will have pictured the catalog presentation of the product during the selection process. This vision should be shared now. Even if the image is hazy, discussing the visualized impact will help trigger the artist's creativity and stimulate concepts for the final composition.

Similarly, the merchandiser should also share the words or headline conjured during the selection process. Many times it is easier to imagine headlines than art. The merchandiser's thoughts will be valuable to the copywriter, who will polish and add to that initial thought.

3. What Is the Product's Sales History?

The merchandiser might very well have selected the product because it has run several times in one or more competitors' catalogs or space ads—a clear sign of a good seller. Or perhaps it is similar to other products that sell well in your catalog. Or it may be an old product that is being revived. Some products are cyclical and can be reintroduced when the time is right.

4. What Do Competing Art and Copy Clippings Say about the Product?

Take some time to peruse the clippings gathered by the merchandiser. Discuss the main effect created by the artwork. What main element is emphasized? Is the product clearly shown? Which benefits are visually presented? From what angle was the shot taken?

As you examine copy clippings, pay close attention to the headline, and the reasons and benefits the body copy gives for purchasing the product. Analyze the order in which those reasons are given to the customer. If you are viewing a competitor's copy, discuss how to apply your catalog image to the competitor's copy points.

Your competitors' presentations may serve as a model to you, or they may inspire you to create an entirely new presentation. While there is always room to do it your own way, be cautious if your creative staff wishes to take a different (especially a drastically different) approach. Remember, the product was chosen because of its sales track record, and the art and copy you are viewing helped create that success.

Don't ever decide upon your art and copy presentation before viewing existing presentations. Competitor research is a powerful sales tool. Even the most innovative approach is built upon an accumulation of past knowledge. Thorough observation, inspection, and analysis, your catalog marketing competition gives you a basis upon which to make judgments.

If you're just beginning your first catalog, it's vital to watch others. And if you're already a successful cataloger, watching others will guarantee continuing success. The need for careful observation never ends.

Competitor Analysis Exercise

Here is an example of the way you and your creative staff would use a product work session to analyze presentations created by others. Start with the premise that you want to see the results achieved by their efforts. (A competitor who has repeated a listing no doubt has a successful product, and the art and copy have aided that success.) Let's look at two different presentations of the same product and see what we can discern from them.

Example one This illustration is from the Bruce Bolind catalog (**Figure 4.1**).

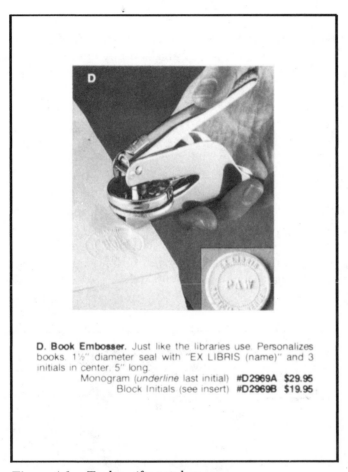

D. Book Embosser. Just like the libraries use. Personalizes books 1½" diameter seal with "EX LIBRIS (name)" and 3 initials in center. 5" long.
Monogram (*underline* last initial) **#D2969A $29.95**
Block Initials (see insert) **#D2969B $19.95**

Figure 4.1   Taylor gifts catalog

Art.

The photo visually implies that the embosser has just completed the operation of embossing, because it shows the item in someone's hand with an embossed page immediately underneath. The dark background allows the light metal to stand out clearly. A small inset shows the actual embossing in detail.

Copy.

The headline "Book Embosser" identifies where the product is to be used and what it does. The copy is minimal but states the diameter of the seal, and the price lines let the customer know that both a monogrammed style and a block initial style are available.

Example two   Pennsylvania Station tries another approach (**Figure 4.2**).

Art.

The vinyl case has been added to the illustration. This catalog house has chosen a side-on view of a hand actually embossing. The seal has been brought up in size to a large inset for easy design identification. Was it necessary to show the product twice, or did doing so only add to presentation clutter?

Copy.

The headline attempts to attract interest with uplifting wording ("Scholarly Seal"), but instead it achieved only vagueness. The size of the embossing is stated plus the reason for purchasing the product: "identifies your books." A full description of what is embossed is given and there is a clear request for information ("Send exact name and up to three initials"), but no letter limitation is given. Delivery delay notification is clear, too, although reversed copy makes it hard to read.

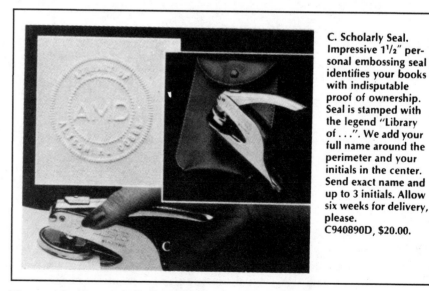

C. Scholarly Seal. Impressive 1½" personal embossing seal identifies your books with indisputable proof of ownership. Seal is stamped with the legend "Library of . . .". We add your full name around the perimeter and your initials in the center. Send exact name and up to 3 initials. Allow six weeks for delivery, please. C940890D, $20.00.

Figure 4.2   Bruce Bolind catalog

After reviewing these examples, what knowledge have we gained for our own presentation?

Art.

- Show contrast between product and background so product will stand out.

- Bring an example of the embossing up close for the customer to view. This is most easily accomplished by an inset.

- Consider showing the product in use so the customer can easily relate.

- Consider having props that are easily identifiable and help explain the product function.

- Consider an art headline that helps to identify product benefit.

Copy.

- Make headline identify product or product benefit.

- Inform the customer of product benefit—personal identification—in body copy.

- Emphasize individual personalization appeal (ego)—"your name" for identification.

- Consider giving letter limitations for full name or initials. However, the actual limitation may be well over the number of letters in an average name, and refunding of the few exceptions may be better than using catalog space and possibly discouraging sales.

- Inform the customer of delayed delivery (for Federal Trade Commission (FTC) compliance, see Chapter 10) due to drop shipping and thus avoid informing after ordering if need arises.

Art/Copy checklist

Pitfalls can be avoided if you look at other art/copy presentations. If you want a product photo background of book pages, you now know that the problem of making the light-colored item stand out from the light-colored background can be handled by photographic lighting. If you're using an inset, you'll realize that the lighting must be appropriate to make the embossing dominant, and the inset must be large enough to serve its purpose. Your copywriters are now alerted to the inclusion of all the facts. This is important. The omission of letter limitations could necessitate refunds, and this means loss of sales, internal processing expense, plus disheartened customers whose long names cannot be accommodated.

This embosser is not a complicated product to show. But many questions have been raised about the optimum presentation. Five catalogers have shown it differently. There's no doubt about it—your competition is one of your best "helpers" for doing a better job. Examined thoroughly, their art and copy will help you decide upon the best presentation for your book. Even if the product has never before been listed in mail order, it is still helpful to view presentations of similar items, both from competitors' books and your own.

There are two important facts always to remember:

1. The easier the product and its benefit are to identify, the greater product sales will be because of customer ease.

2. Competitors have repeated the product listing because of its success, based on proven art and copy presentation.

5. What Do the Testing Results Indicate about the Product?

A product that is faulty, fails to meet quality standards, or is just no good will probably not have gotten to this stage. But during testing, you may have discovered that the product is exceptionally easy to use—an important feature to play up in your catalog presentation. The mobility of an office table, for example, might be outstanding, providing new uses the manufacturer neglected to emphasize.

Testing might reveal areas that need to be clarified or adjusted, such as product sizing. The copywriter should be extremely aggressive in questioning the testing phase, so that all the pluses and minuses are revealed.

6. What Information Did the Manufacturer Supply?

Examine everything the merchandiser asked the manufacturer to send along with the product: promotional sheets, wholesale catalog pages, photographs, clippings, claim documentation, warranties, and field testing results. Most important of all, examine the completed product information form.

Review the main features and benefits that are likely to make your customer purchase, so that the art and copy direction is clear.

Wrapping Up the Session

At the end of each product presentation, recap the main points that art and copy should emphasize. Because it takes energy to absorb new information, limit the number of products to be reviewed at one time. Overload and flagging concentration are enemies of any long meeting, so break up the number of products to be reviewed into groups of 10 to 12 per meeting. You will be rewarded with quality art and copy presentation.

Product work sessions are vital to the success of your mail order catalog. This is where it all comes together: your merchandise, your market, and the creative approach that makes the sale!

Product Work Session Checklist:

Prepare Ahead
☐ Acquire actual product sample.
☐ Gather competitor catalog/media art samples.
☐ Gather competitor catalog/media copy samples.
☐ Gather similar product art and copy samples.
☐ Test product.
☐ Acquire manufacturer information.
☐ Have list of merchandiser/buyer comments.

Actual Meeting
☐ Have merchandiser conduct meeting.
☐ Have all buyers responsible for product selection attend.
☐ Have design and layout artists responsible for presentation attend.
☐ Have copywriter responsible for product copy attend.

Always:
1. Present actual production sample.
2. Review reasons for product selection.
3. Review competitor art presentations.
4. Review competitor copy descriptions.
5. Review merchandiser/buyer's art visualization.
6. Review merchandiser/buyer's copy headline visualization.
7. Review testing results.
8. Review manufacturer's information.

Strongly Consider:
Trying the product yourself or having your artist and copywriter do so to further understand the product.

CHAPTER 5

Photography and Art

Photography and art play a vital role: to attract the customer's attention, and to sell merchandise.

Because ours is a visual world, we learn to depend on "looking" as a major factor in the process of making a decision. That is why a catalog's visual appearance is so important. Your front and back cover need to attract your customer's attention so your catalog will be singled out from all the rest. And every product you feature must also attract attention, so it may vie for its share of the almighty dollar and justify the space it occupies.

By this stage in the catalog production process, you should know what image you want to convey. If your image is value, you may want to avoid elegant settings and presentations because the "value" message may not get across. On the other hand, an elegant and dramatic setting may be just what you want if you are selling high-priced furs, jewels, or cruises.

Almost always, photography is the means by which your image is conveyed. Therefore, it's important to have the right photographer for your specific product line.

How to Find the Photographer for You

You're looking for several important characteristics in one person: know-how, talent, and an ability to carry on a meaningful dialogue with you and your creative staff. If the photographers you're considering are missing any one of these three basics, you won't get the kind of end result you want and need.

Use these guidelines when making your search for a photographer:

1. Look at portfolios. Viewing samples of photographers' work is a fast way to gain an impression of their talents, know-how, and specialties (for example, as photographers of high fashion, kitchen items, or industrial work). The best portfolios will present the original prints and transparencies, as well as the printed end results; and if all these are included, it will tell you much about the photographers' common sense and how much confidence you can place in each candidate's abilities. If the portfolios include sample catalogs, ask which specific photographs you should consider. Frequently, catalogs are shot by more than one photographer. Don't be swayed or dismayed by the total graphic impression of the printed piece you are viewing, since the quality of paper, graphic design, and other elements contribute to the total. Try to confine your analysis to each photographer's work itself.

2. Ask for and *investigate* references. The portfolios will suggest things about the photographers' skills and talent, but references will help you assess on-the-job working relationships. Talk to people who've worked with the photographers. Ask about their speed and ability to meet deadlines. Inquire about their attitudes toward revisions or changes. Try to assess their communication skills and talent for working with others.

3. Question their workload. Will they really have the time to do your job? Ask how much volume each photographer can handle. Do they have a staff who will be helping, perhaps even taking some of your shots under their guidance? You must feel confident that the one you choose will not be too overloaded to accomplish your job in the time period important to you. You may also wish to anticipate their ability to grow with you as your business grows.

4. What support services can they furnish? Do the photographers have access to models, props, and sets? Do they process their own film, furnish retouching or stripping services? Areas such as these will affect the quality of work and your job's outcome.

If you are expecting them to furnish photo layout services (to-size sketches of the desired presentation), be specific. Though you may have a catalog layout, you may not be creating a layout for each item. Discuss how the photographers will expect you to convey the direction you want each shot to take. This will give you a good idea about how they work and will help ensure that the images produced will satisfy you.

5. Assess their ability to communicate with more than a camera. Telling your story on film is vital, but it usually cannot be accomplished if you and your creative staff cannot communicate with your photographer. Ask your candidates if you will be dealing directly with them when giving direction and instructions, or if you will be talking with someone on their staff. Try to look beyond photography into areas such as the style you're trying to achieve. Do the candidate photographers have a "feel" for what you're trying to sell and how you're trying to sell it?

Learn photographers' language

Because photography is a specialized field, it has its own special terminology, with which you may not be familiar. Learning to speak the photographers' language is important to you because it helps you communicate on common ground. Even if you think you know the meaning of some words your photographers are using, ask. A word as simple as "silhouette" can also be defined by the terms "outline," "C.O.B." (crop out background), and "drop out." They all mean an image to be printed without a background. So as you develop a relationship with your photographers, also be aware that it is important to define your terms (and theirs).

6. Are they willing to do a test or "spec" photograph? How far are they willing to go to get your business and show you how they work? Will they test photograph a sample product? Are they willing to photograph an item to the specifications you've furnished in a layout? Most photographers are willing to invest a little time and materials to prove they can produce what you want.

Depending on your needs, you may have to use more than one photographer. If you have a large product line or short schedules, you've got a good reason for more than one photographer. If your product line is extremely diverse in content, you may need one photographer who specializes in food shots and another who works with clothing and models. Photographers tend to be specialists, but a good catalog photographer must have the ability to do all things well. If you use several photographers, you must be sure that their styles are similar so that your catalog has a consistent, uniform look. Background materials and lighting techniques may have to be coordinated, in tonal qualities, among the different photographers shooting your book.

7. Establish charges. This isn't as obvious as it sounds. A simple $100 (or $1,000) per shot may seem straightforward, but can become a real bone of contention between photographer and cataloger. Misunderstandings don't usually arise over creative fees. But photographers charge for other services, and it's important to establish what those charges are.

For example, whose responsibility is it to pick up (or return) products to be photographed? Will review sessions between client and photographer be charged for? Who pays the models? Who assembles products or touches them up in order to make them photograph properly? Suppose the photographer has to wait for products to be altered or delivered. Who pays for the reshot when it occurs because you, the cataloger, have changed your mind? (Photographers should absorb reshot costs when the error is theirs.)

If the photographer you are thinking of engaging is not specific about these areas, ask. If you don't, you risk, receiving less than the job you expect, and paying more for it.

This kind of investigation into photographers' ability and style of working not only lets you assess whether or not they fit into your catalog image, but also defines the role and functions they will be performing in your particular organization. And remember, no matter how well your catalog is printed, nor how good the paper might be, the physical end result never will be better than the excellence of your art and photography.

Be an Effective Communicator

While you may have found the perfect photographer, the responsibility of direction still remains with you. And you will need material at your disposal to help you be effective in your direction. There are two main strategies which will help you know what you want and help you convey what you want to the photographer.

1. Competitor clip files. Back in Chapter 4, Product Work Sessions, we explained how to watch your competitors and the advantages of doing so. Now, all the art which you clipped and saved from your most interesting competitors is going to help you in the photography and art area. Even though product sketches "to-size" (the exact size that will appear in the catalog) should have resulted from the product work session, your competitors' art will be beneficial when you're talking to the photographer. Perhaps the lighting is especially good or maybe the background color compliments the product nicely. Or the product positioning or props could be undesirable. The photographer will want to know! By having something to show your photographer, you can be more certain the desired message will be understood.

2. General clipping file. This file should consist of catalogs, magazines, space ads from newspapers, trade journals, manufacturers' catalogs—anything that you like or dislike in product presentation. The products pictured need not be those in your product line. The importance of this file is to show effect, technique, and approach so you can easily convey your likes and dislikes to the photographer.

Look at successful catalog presentations

Now, when reviewing each product with your photographer, you'll be able to indicate that you want "a background like this," or "an angle like that," or "lighting like this photo, not like that one." It's important, by the way to have a sample of each product available for your photographer to see in advance of the shooting session. An item you may feel is "camera ready" may not fulfill the photographer's criteria. You may think that a prototype product sample with the logo pasted onto it is going to "blend in," but the photographer may know that this prototype status will be very apparent in the final photo. Be sure to listen to what the photographer has to say. This person's a professional and will have suggestions on how to present your merchandise or achieve the look you're after.

When you're putting together a catalog, your thoughts are naturally involved with the products that are going to be housed within the catalog. You are concerned about how to present them, finding the best photographer or artist to make them appear appealing to the customer. But you need to give careful consideration to what is going to happen on the front and back covers.

Chapter 3 should have given you information that helped you to decide what type of cover is best for your catalog. Now you have the job of creating a visually commanding cover that will *get the customer inside* where the action of buying occurs.

Front Cover Art and Photography

In our era of mailbox clutter, it is the front cover that will most likely determine whether your customer rescues your catalog from the mail and sets it aside for careful reading. Choosing the right approach for your cover is important—and so is choosing the right photographer. The front cover is so important, you may want to consider hiring a separate photographer for the cover—one who specializes in the high-impact photographic work a cover requires.

As you plan your front cover, carefully consider the following questions. How can you get the most qualified attention with your cover? What approach will be best? Would the customer be more attracted to an appealing country scene or a high-energy city scene? Can stock photos be successfully used? Would a studio shot work better?

Because your knowledge of your customers will help you answer these questions, they may have been answered long before you get to work on the cover. Generally, your approach to the cover should not be determined until after you know the overall image of your catalog.

As Chapter 3 mentioned, there are three basic approaches to the front cover: the dramatic approach; the product line identification approach; and the sales/benefit approach. Once a direction is chosen, you can decide which method of photographic presentation is best. There are four basic options:

1. Studio shooting
2. Location shooting
3. Stock photos
4. Art illustration

Studio Shooting

Studio shooting is the most commonly used method. That is because a studio gives the photographer the flexibility to shoot a plain, unadorned shot of a product; a dramatically effective shot of products or objects, or to simulate a setting that is indicative of the character of the products.

In studio shots, the photographer has more control over lighting, wind, and rain, and studio shooting is generally less expensive than location and complicated art illustrations or renderings. A photographer or studio specializing in kitchen or other in-the-house room shots will have studio sets built for continual use: a built-in bathtub for shower products, a kitchen for kitchen products, a bedroom for bedroom products, and so on.

The Signals catalog utilizes studio photography. **Figure 5.1** highlights catalog items against a neutral background. The items, for sale inside but not referenced on the cover, are classy, upscale items that appeal to the highbrow public television audience. The depth and feel of the photograph was achieved by a skilled photographer in a controlled studio environment.

Figure 5.2 is the cover of Domestications, a catalog specializing in linens, window coverings, and carpets for the home. The photograph looks like a grand bedroom. It is, of course, a studio shot taken in a special room set built for multi-uses. (The same set is used for another bedroom setting inside the catalog.) This is an example of utilizing studio photography that appears to be photographed in its natural area of use.

Advantages	Disadvantages
Controlled atmosphere allows exacting lighting; weather not a bothersome factor; minimal costs.	Realism sometimes lost, thereby lessening credibility; aesthetic appeal sometimes minimized.

Location Shooting

In location shooting, the most glamorous sounding method of presentation, the photographer, client, and entourage travel to some near or distant place to "shoot" the cover and maybe some inside product shots, too. Needless to say, it is also the most expensive. The cost of travel and accommodations plus time for the photographer and other personnel quickly becomes exorbitant and often breaks the budget. But the results can be effective.

Patagonia uses location shooting to transmit its message that its rugged outdoor clothing is matchless in harsh (but pristine) environments. Product durability, convenience, and enjoyment are all conveyed in the cover shot in **Figure 5.3**, which shows the Aletsch Glacier in Switzerland's Bernese Oberland.

Dozens of shots of Patagonia apparel in use in exotic places fill the interior pages—but because these photographs are solicited from customers, Patagonia keeps costs while still managing to convey the look of the location-shot catalog.

The elegantly attired brunette on the beach in **Figure 5.4** is sure to appeal to the upscale working women who are Spiegel's customers. Besides providing a dramatic background that brings out the colors and lines of the cover outfit, this alluring beach scene helps associate Spiegel products with glamour, romance, and excitement.

Figure 5.1 Signals catalog

Figure 5.2 Domestications catalog

Figure 5.3 Patagonia catalog

Figure 5.4 Spiegel catalog

Twelve Hints for Location Shooting

1. Does a location's atmosphere *compliment the merchandise?* Will the product setting have an *important* effect on the customer's *perception of the merchandise quantity?*

2. *Does the setting suggest what the merchandise will look like when used by the customer? Does the setting enhance the believability* of the item or product?

3. *Stay as close to home as possible.* Plan the location to fit the seasons. Shoot summer shots in the south or southwest when it is winter in the north.

4. Consider cost and *plan every shot in as much detail as possible BEFORE you leave.*

5. *Shoot studio shots* concurrently with location shooting. Location photography is not an "add-on" to your schedule, but should "mesh" with it.

6. Know the ability of the photographer and *how many shots he or she can shoot in one day.* An expensive photographer who can shoot faster may be cheaper than one who appears less expensive but is slower.

7. Take along the support people (stylists, makeup artists and assistants) who are needed *so shots can be set up and broken down in a reasonable time frame.*

8. Hire local models. They go home at night and save on hotel bills and transportation costs.

9. Scout locations and finalize layouts before the day of shooting. Schedule in detail *so everything needed is possible in the time it takes to set up and shoot.* Nothing is worse than having to hunt for locations as models stand around, or send for items that are not on location when needed.

10. Work with travel agencies that can give you a *package deal.*

11. *Consider the weather* and anticipate problems that could arise from it.

12. *Negotiate cancel dates* with your photographers before you hire them. Allowances must be made for possible sickness, bad weather, or accidents; non-penalty cancel-dates must be understood.

Stock Photos

If you don't have an on-staff photographer and if you don't use your own products on your cover, using stock photos can be economical as well as satisfying.

Say you want to introduce your early-fall apparel catalog with an appealing cover shot of a family hiking on a forest trail. To convey an autumn palette, you want the foliage to be at its peak, and you want a setting sun to cast its glow on the trail and the family. You could dispatch a photographer and models to a national forest a whole year in advance of your catalog, and have them bide their time waiting for perfect lighting conditions—or you could use a stock photo, and benefit from someone else's perfect timing.

The quality of stock photos can be very high, especially if they are acquired from stock houses, companies whose business is shooting pictures of different subjects for use by individuals and companies for a fee.

If you want a certain subject—say a wholesome young woman meant to represent your typical customer, or hot air balloons that imply a spirit of adventure and discover—stock companies may offer the best choice. To find the scene you want, request a selection from several stock companies. (Some companies charge for this service, but the cost will be minimal.) Ask your art director to help you review the candidates and choose the photo that best suits your needs.

Figure 5.5   America's Catalog. Reprinted courtesy of Direct Marketing Services, Inc.

If you become a regular customer of stock photo companies, they will tell you when they are going on shooting assignments pertaining to the subject you are interested in and will shoot some spec shots for you.

Stock photos are also a useful source of inspiration. Thumbing through a stock catalog can help you brainstorm photo and layout ideas for future covers or inside page shots.

In **Figure 5.5,** America's Catalog has used a stock photo to capture its target market: young families seeking furniture and accessories to decorate and improve their (probably older) homes. The picture communicates its message for a fraction of the cost of a location shot, but it wasn't cheap. A photo of this quality will probably cost at least $500.00.

Advantages	**Disadvantages**
Large choice of subject matter; consistently good quality of photographs; low costs.	Individual catalog personality sometimes lost; commercial and stilted appearance likely if selection process not carefully done.

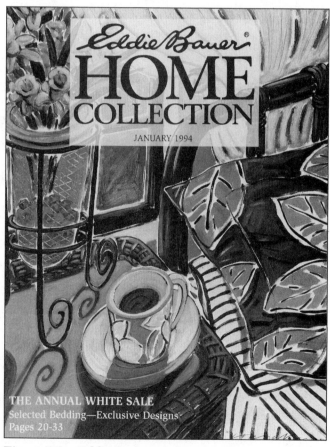

Figure 5.6   Eddie Bauer catalog

Figure 5.7   Flax Art and Design catalog

Art Illustration

While most catalogers show photographs of products on the cover, art illustration can add impact to a catalog and make it stand out from the crowd. It can project a desired image, create a mood, and identify a product category, as well as illustrate products realistically and in a desirable fashion.

Figure 5.6 uses a striking and sophisticated scene that recalls the bold lines and colors of Matisse. Commissioned by Eddie Bauer and painted by a Texas artist, this painting depicts a bed, linen, bedside table, vase, and cup and saucer that are sold inside the catalog.

Through an amusing cartoon/painting, the Flax Art & Design catalog cover tells customers that it is an artist supply catalog (**Figure 5.7**). At a glance, the illustration stylishly conveys the catalog's position and image: a catalog of traditional and innovative tools for hardworking creative artists.

Business-to-business catalogs make use of original art illustrations, too. The Power Up! Direct catalog cover uses the famous Mona Lisa to illustrate the tag line, "Create *your* masterpiece" and help sell the benefits associated with the high-productivity software it sells (**Figure 5.8**). Office supply cataloger B.A. Pargh uses a series of colorful, imaginary, computer-generated postage stamps to illustrate the range of brands it carries without using actual product photos—a dramatically different technique in this product category (**Figure 5.9**). As computers continue to influence art and design, it's likely that more catalogers will turn to computer-generated art and illustration to convey a contemporary image to their audience.

To create a good attention-getting cover illustration, meet with your artist early on. Involve your copy people, too. It's important to have a good cover, so spend some time considering your options.

Figure 5.8   Power Up! Direct catalog. Clip art used with permission of Softkey, © 1994.

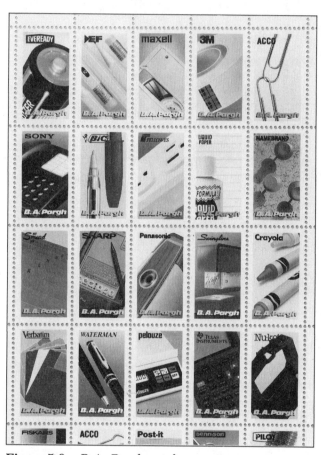

Figure 5.9   B.A. Pargh catalog

Advantages	**Disadvantages**
A different look for greater attention; easier emphasis on a desired area or mood; sometimes lower costs than photography; possibility of using cover design for product design, too.	Possible loss of realistic look; possible questioning of credibility if product or image carelessly distorted.

Front Cover Checklist:

☐ Define approach to take.
☐ Review clip files for ideas.
☐ Decide method of creative execution.
☐ Select photographer.
☐ Select artist.
☐ Consider budget.

Always:
1. Consider your customers' tastes.
2. Consider using stock photos.
3. Consider going with an approach you can stay with and become recognized for.

Strongly Consider:
A separate and specialized photographer for cover shots.

Back Cover Photography

The back cover plays many important roles. It carries the customer's name and address, the required postal indicia, and your name and address. It also sells products and directs the customer inside. Finally, the back cover, like the front cover, must attract the customer's attention—especially if the mail carrier has tossed it on the floor with the front cover down. That's a tall order—but photography and art can help it fulfill its varied roles.

Once the approach has been determined, the layout artist must carefully consider how to successfully execute an attention-getting back cover that meets address panel requirements.

If a dramatically inviting setting is shown on the front cover, the artist may wish to carry the feeling and visual image over onto the back cover. Garnet Hill wraps front cover photos onto the back cover in a manner that unites front and back cover and makes the recipient want to turn the catalog over to see more of the vivid blue and green shots (**Figure 5.10**).

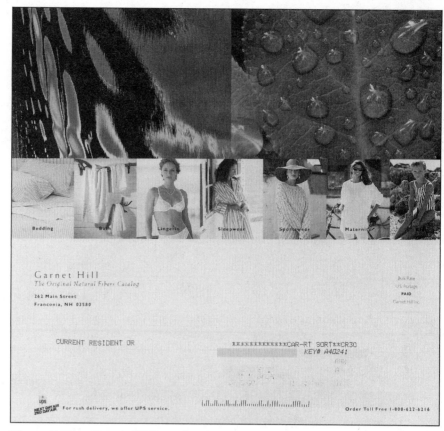

Figure 5.10   Garnet Hill catalog

A business-to-business catalog utilizing a similar approach is C&H Distributors. The yellow-peach background color used on the cover is carried over onto the back cover, and the semi-truck illustrated on the front is repeated in the upper left-hand corner (**Figure 5.11**).

The most common way to approach the back cover is to treat it as a separate page whose job it is to bear the customer's name and address and to sell products and promote company services and policies. Typical back covers are seen in **Figures 5.12, 5.13, 5.14,** and **5.15.**

Figure 5.12 is the back cover of L.L. Bean, featuring a polo shirt sold only on the back cover. The product is photographed in a manner similar to interior pages.

In **Figure 5.13**, Brooks Brothers' short sleeve pullover shirts were photographed especially for the back cover. Even though the general feeling and approach is the same as for inside product photos, this photograph is a horizontal shot, while all of the inside pages are presented vertically. Notice how the shirts are positioned in order to show the product well and provide the desired room for the company name and address and the customer name and address.

Semantodontics, a business-to-business catalog whose customers are dentists, uses a combination of product photos (See **Figure 5.14**). Some photos are the same as used inside, like the dental book and blood pressure unit. Others are croppings of a larger inside photograph ("Ev-

Figure 5.11   C and H Distributors catalog

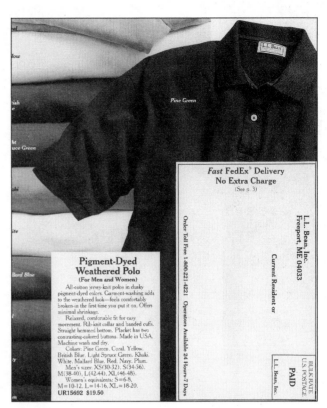

Figure 5.12   L.L. Bean catalog

Figure 5.13   Brooks Brothers' catalog

Figure 5.14   Semantodontics catalog

Figure 5.15   Becone Uniforms catalog

erything for your walls"), some are appliques, while still others are original photographs (learning cassettes and prevention supplies).

The back cover from Bencome Uniforms (**Figure 5.15**) uses photographs that are typical of inside product photos. Yet the products on the back cover are not sold inside this catalog issue.

Back Cover Photography Checklist:

☐ First decide approach.
☐ Double check address panel requirements.

Always:
1. Clearly represent catalog image.
2. Use a product that is exemplary of your product line.

Strongly Consider:
1. Selling products directly on the back cover.
2. Continuing the mood of the front cover.

Inside Product Photography

The first goal of any product illustration is to attract the attention of your customer. You can illustrate a product with a photograph or an artist's rendering, such as a line drawing, a watercolor, a computer-generated illustration, or another form of mechanical illustration. The photograph is by far the most common choice, mainly because it performs one function a drawing cannot: it encourages credibility. The customer trusts a photograph, and knows subliminally that an illustration can always "cheat."

But getting the kind of photographs you want takes some work.

How to Direct Your Photographer

A key ingredient of getting good photography is giving clear directions to your photographer. You must be able to convey exactly what you're looking for. Simply issuing a vague direction like "make this desk set look classy" is not enough.

There are two ways to communicate your ideas to the photographer. You an supply samples from a clip file, or use a layout sketch.

If you have no art staff to furnish sketches of layouts, you're going to need to start a "clip file" of layouts gathered from other catalogs.

Professionals can look at a photo and know how to achieve the same results. They can tell you how the subject was lit, the kind of camera used for the shot, and how much time and expense was involved.

The clippings you gathered for the Product Work Sessions described in Chapter 4 will be of great help in communicating your wishes to the photographer. The background color, the effect, and the total creative visual approach you desire can be easily communicated by a sample or two. Your photographer will be happy to have concrete instructions, and you will be happy with the outcome—because you both know what you want to achieve.

An even more effective way to direct your photographer is to furnish clippings with an artist's sketch of the layout you desire. This sketch is exactly the size the shot will run. It shows the exact placement of the item, the angle from which it is to be shot, the kind and color of background, the props to be used, and so on. Guidance for these layouts will have been given during the Product Work Sessions, when your art director reviewed competitor clippings and noted the features and benefits that motivated the merchandiser's purchase.

In almost all cases, products are shot to the size that the photos appear in the catalog. A 35 mm or $2\frac{1}{4} \times 2\frac{1}{4}$ camera is not used for this purpose, but rather a 4×5, 8×10, or even larger camera. The photographer must stage the photographs carefully, because they have to fit a given space and size. When you develop your layouts, think of them as the frame for your product. The layout becomes the "frame" that the photographer uses as a guide.

Figure 5.16 is an example of a to-size layout sketch and the final photograph taken using it. Notice the art director's directions to the photographer.

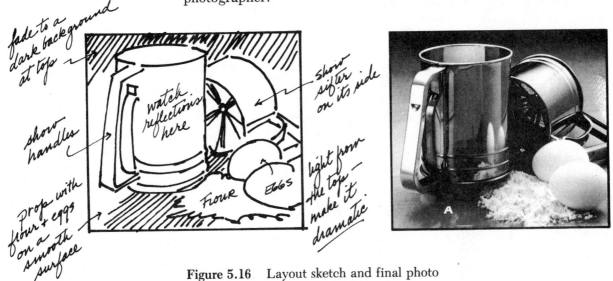

Figure 5.16   Layout sketch and final photo

Lighted instructions: "Fade to a dark background at top," "Light from top—make it dramatic," and "Watch reflection here." These are detailed instructions that ensure the end result of a good photograph with the mood and effect wanted.

Product positioning: "Show handles" and "Show sifter on its side." The important feature of the product is the ease-of-use that the handles allow. Therefore, the photo must visually show the customer the handles and the inner workings, thus telling the product's story and benefit.

Propping instructions: "Prop with flour and eggs on a smooth surface" further ensures the desired end result of a professional presentation by adding interest to the photo without detracting attention. This type of instruction is done by a talented and knowledgeable artist. The cataloger who does not have this kind of talent available must sit down with the photographer and carefully go over the product and the desired end result.

Once the customer's attention has been captured, the primary intent is to picture the product clearly and truthfully. In any discussion on product presentation, there is always a battle between reality and enhancement. Where you stand on this issue must be clearly understood by your photographer for each item you wish photographed. It's the photographer's job not to misrepresent the merchandise, but still to give it all the appeal it needs to attract the prospective buyer. Also, don't forget that the more truthfully you present the merchandise, the greater the customer's satisfaction. If "what you see is what you get," a bond of loyalty and trust is established between cataloger and customer—a great incentive for future order placement. In the long run, your internal systems benefit from this approach as well, because there are fewer returns and fewer complaints.

Basic Photographic Techniques

Being aware of photographic techniques helps you to convey your desires to the photographer, both verbally and in the layout form we've just seen. For instance, an art director who doesn't have some knowledge of what photographic lighting techniques can achieve (as well as the problems lighting could cause) will be hard pressed to issue the directions in the layout/photo example just given. There are technical aspects of photographic technique that you will want to be aware of. What techniques and elements help convey the product image you desire?

The style of photography you choose for your catalog contributes in two vital ways: it suggests your *image* (who you are and to whom you wish to appeal), and it presents your products effectively. From the cataloger's point of view, there are three photographic techniques and three elements of photography through which both image and products are interpreted. The basic techniques are:

1. background

2. lighting

3. camera type and focal length

These techniques are used to highlight the three basic elements teased out of your product: shape and form, detail and clarity, and texture. These are areas that you can use to judge a photographer's skill, or to determine whether a photo is good or bad.

Background

Imagine a simple seamless sweep in a standard, straightforward background usually lighted for even, shadowless illumination across its width and depth to produce a "nonbackground." This is particularly suited to utilitarian images. But that same seamless sweep can become very dramatic when shadows and highlights are intentionally cast upon it, becoming quite appropriate for upscale images.

Backgrounds can be used to suggest mood and use of items, as well. High-tech images, for example, are often produced on "high-tech" backgrounds such as black slate-textured Formica, black Plexiglas, narrow-slatted metal window blinds, striped or checkered mirror, and black industrial floor matting with various textured surfaces. Wood-graining as a background can create many moods, from old-fashioned elegance to a business-office environment.

Complementary background vital to product sales

The important area of concern in the use of backgrounds is two-fold: don't let it overpower the item, but at the same time make sure it enhances the item. One of the major errors in the use of backgrounds is to choose a color or intensity that does not properly promote the item. A dark background with a dark item upon it attracts the eye less than a light background featuring a dark item. This is not a hard-and-fast rule, however, because many of these choices are affected by the style of the catalog.

In any catalog, backgrounds should be coordinated in range of color to give the catalog a coordinated, tied-together appeal. For example, the first choice you make in deciding upon your backgrounds is actually just like that of an artist who selects a specific color palette from which he will create a specific painting. No matter how many colors are chosen, they are all clear and bright (clear yellow, bright blue). Or perhaps they will be muted shades (grayish blue, pale lavender). If your catalog has various sections that are sharply defined in content, you can change this palette from section to section. But generally, each section retains the same mood/palette of background. Occasionally a surprise color can be interjected for effect, but this must be done with care so it does not look like a mistake.

Within the background palette, you can use several kinds and textures of backgrounds to avoid visual boredom, repeating the same backgrounds every few pages to add necessary continuity. *The background style must be planned in advance to visually pace the customer.* Backgrounds are crucial because they help move through the book by adding color flow without interjecting distraction.

A consistent palette ensures that all of your new items match previously photographed products. The new products intermingle with the older ones, maintaining a coordinated look as you publish each catalog edition. If you create each one of your catalogs with an entirely new group of backgrounds, you can of course change your palette for each book. But this is the exceptional situation, rather than the rule. In a case such as this, or in a brand-new catalog, you would develop thumbnail layouts (at least) of the finished total catalog to maintain continuity in the printed piece.

Catalogs can also achieve "nonbackgrounds" by using silhouetted products instead of photographs in "frames." This can open up the look of the catalog, especially a book with many dark backgrounds. The silhouetted products seem larger than they would when within a frame, and a light, airy look is achieved because a great deal of white space has been injected into the catalog.

Backgrounds are affected tremendously by the style and quality of light that is cast upon them, either directly or indirectly, which brings us to our next basic technique.

Lighting

The variables that can be achieved with studio or outdoor lighting are almost infinite. The quality of light (hard or soft) and color temperature of light (warm, cool, neutral) affect the catalog's continuity as much as the backgrounds do. *For continuity and a look of cohesiveness, both quality and color temperature of lighting should remain the same on all products in the catalog.* Again, if a catalog is broken into obviously different sections, each section should be filled with images that reflect lighting continuity, but in this case not necessarily the entire catalog. Exceptions to the continuity can be quite effective, but they must be carefully orchestrated by an art director. Each divergence must be planned to create a specific effect (and surprise alone is an acceptable reason) at a specific spot in the finished catalog.

Many effects are controlled by how your photographer lights the subjects for your catalog shots. The choices are natural daylight, strobe or electronic flash, and tungsten lights. Don't let anyone trap you into judging which is best, because each has its application and produces different results.

The most important decision you will have to make is not what kind of light your photographer uses, but what kind of *result* you want. Light has a lot to do with how your customer reacts to the product. As an example, a soft light with open shadows or streaking sunlight can communicate a romantic feeling, great for fashion or nostalgic looks. Hard lighting with deep shadows can be very dramatic—appropriate for high-tech decorator items or for a business-to-business catalog selling computer hardware.

But the main concern should be how your *product* looks under the lighting used by your photographer, and whether or not the lighting helps delineate those important elements we mentioned earlier: shape, detail, and texture. Because your three-dimensional product is being translated to the two-dimensional printed page, these elements are vitally important.

Your product must be lighted so it has *shape, dimension, and form.* It should look real enough to lift off the page, with three distinct planes: top, side, and front. Flat lighting often fosters an unreal look, which subconsciously builds doubt in the viewer's eye. Often a photographer will use lighting to darken the background of a photograph to give the product more depth and dimension. This roundness, or form, is very important to the impact your product makes on the customer.

In addition, your product must be lighted so that it has detail. Don't let shadows hide important product details like switches or dials, engravings, or important lines of product design. Even on the dark, shadowed side of a subject, all the important details of the product still should be visible for scrutiny by your customer.

Light your product so its texture is properly represented. Chrome must look like chrome and gold like gold. You should be able to see—and have the illusion of feeling—the texture of leather, suede, plastic, wood, or corduroy. The lighting is the primary medium in showing texture. The *direction and intensity of light* usually are best determined on set to suit each product's unique demands. To a degree, this also is true of light quality. A broad, soft source is essential to make chrome or brass shine, while a hard, small source is a must to bring out texture in fur or high-pile fabrics. A cross light can bring out a rough texture, and the proper reflector can accent a smooth, shiny surface. The visual effect of these textures upon the viewer can make the difference between sale or no sale.

The underlying goal of all lighting is to make your product look as real and believable as possible by representing it as true-to-life as possible. Secondary lighting techniques can give the photo drama, excitement, or romance, but they must never steal the show from the product. Lighting, even dramatic lighting, should not be the obvious factor in the finished photo.

If through proper lighting of your product you can convey to the customer exactly what you are selling, you have eliminated one of the largest stumbling blocks of mail-order resistance: disbelief in that product. Subconsciously your customer says: "I know what I'm getting. I saw it clearly, realistically, honestly—as it is and will be when it arrives."

Lighting ratio (the difference between brightness of highlights and shadows on a subject) *should remain the same, or nearly so throughout a catalog for consistency.* If this is not done, a catalog can have a choppy effect, and the customer senses the jarring note and does not wish to continue moving through the book.

Camera Type and Focal Length

Whether strict perspective control will be observed or abandoned throughout a catalog should be determined before the first image is recorded on film. Images with converging parallel lines now show up often. This technique was once a definite no-no in professional photography, and it still is frowned upon by many conventional catalog marketers. But this break from the traditional can be effective, particularly for catalogs that feature high-tech merchandise or that appeal to the avant garde customer. Though perspective-controlled images and those with obvious distortion may be mixed in a catalog, the use of just one or two photos with mildly distorted perspective will look like a mistake or afterthought.

Telephoto lenses from normal to short are used for more traditional photos because they "see" products with minimal distortion, just as the eye normally sees them. In more upscale catalogs, wide-angle lenses frequently are used to purposely and dramatically distort perspective. This again reflects a contemporary acceptance on the part of catalog marketers and consumers alike. Not long ago, the product shape was sacred and could not be distorted either within itself or in relation to other subjects. Consumers just weren't sophisticated enough to realize that distortion was due to optics and not to a strangely-shaped product. Today, that is not so.

The two-drawer file in the center of this layout from The Sharper Image catalog (**Figure 5.17**) reveals how distorted perspective is ac-

Figure 5.17   The Sharper Image catalog

cepted today. The image was probably made with a medium-format camera that does not control converging vertical parallel lines. The distortion in the file cabinet is subtly but effectively offset by the outline halftone of the briefcase. The tilt of the left angle directly counters the tilt of the cabinet side closest to the briefcase.

Focus is another area that is often thought to make the difference between a good photo and a bad one. Almost everyone thinks that all good photographs must be *sharp*. But every rule is made to be broken, as each situation is unique and those rules cannot solve every problem. Creative focusing can be a strong force in the presentation of your offering.

A sharp photograph inspires a subliminal sense that what is portrayed is technically correct. This is good to keep in mind if you are photographing a highly mechanical or technical product. In contrast, a soft-focus subject suggests romance—an excellent technique to use for lingerie. A deliberate soft-focus or misty technique can add immeasurably to the mood of the item.

Because a photographer can usually control focus within a composition, varying the focus can be a dramatic product presentation tool. For example, when it is felt that the background will interfere with the presentation of a product, the composition can become stronger if the photographer puts the background out of focus. In **Figure 5.18** from Brookstone, note how the broom and drain in the background are clear enough to suggest the function of the submersible pump, yet are not so distinct that they compete with or distract from it.

A soft focus or blur can also add the dimension of motion or speed to your product or service. For example, a slow shutter speed that allows the movement of an item to be seen in a soft blur, can indicate speed of delivery.

Even if you have a photograph you like, ask yourself if it could be improved if certain areas—the foreground, background, subject—were

Use of focus strengthens presentations

Figure 5.18   Brookstone catalog

to be refocused. Focus is an interesting tool, and one that truly can be exploited by "breaking the rules."

Four Basic Layouts

All of the techniques just discussed can be used in four basic layouts or photographic styles of product presentation:

1. The straight shot

2. The propped shot

3. The in-use shot

4. The end-benefit shot

While each one can clearly and appealingly illustrate a product, which type best *matches* your products will become clear in the thinking and planning stages that precede the photo shoot. As you make your selection, consider the tone and image you want to convey in your catalog. Keep two factors in mind: the product itself, and the customer. Ask yourself two questions:

• What benefit does this product provide the customer?

• How can the benefit best be shown while maintaining the catalog image and customer appeal?

Select the presentation that best meets both the product's and the customer's needs.

The responsibility to execute each presentation effectively rests with the creative director and the photographer. They must have the skills to convey the desired effect in each photograph and evoke the desire to purchase in the customer.

The Straight Shot

If an item does not need any "editorial comment" or enhancement to show what it is or what it does, then a straight shot can be used.

Items that have no complications and are readily identifiable fall into this category. So do higher-ticket items, because a catalog must look very clean to fulfill the aesthetics demanded by high price tags. Upscale customers may feel patronized if, for example, in-use photos are used when not necessary.

Items that require close-up views to maximize their details or importance also benefit from straight shots. For instance, a necklace worn as an accessory to a dress is difficult to sell from the same photo because the details that enhance the necklace cannot be seen.

A straight shot does not have to be boring. Lighting techniques and backgrounds can enhance the product and create a mood.

Computer disks, car seat frames, or a professional butcher knife would employ a straight shot when they are sold into the markets that use them: offices, auto repair companies, and meat packers. A valuable piece of art such as a collector's art print or a pre-Columbian vase would use a straight shot to place it in a "museum" setting that would allow the upscale customer to view it without undue interference from props, people, and other competing factors.

Ask yourself these questions when you decide whether or not to use a straight shot:

1. Is the product perfectly identifiable on its own?

2. Can it be enhanced to evoke the purchasing emotion merely through use of lighting, background, and positioning of the item?

3. Are there any advantages that might result in greater sales by propping the item or showing it in use?

Figure 5.19, the Gemstones and Jewelry catalog by The Sharper Image, is a straight-on shot of a ladies' ring. A dramatic air has been achieved by careful lighting that casts a heavy shadow, presenting a dimensional side view while still allowing the front of the ring to be seen.

Figure 5.19   The Sharper Image Catalog

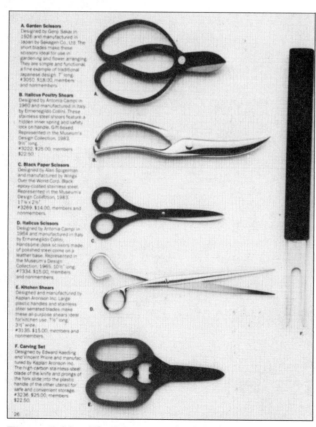

Figure 5.20   The Museum of Modern Art catalog

Figure 5.21   The Museum of Modern Art catalog

Figure 5.20 is a page from The Museum of Modern Art catalog. Six products are shot straight. All pertain to an act of cutting. The shapes, textures, and colors make them attractive designs, but would subtle props have helped identify their use and therefore attracted more potential buyers? Another typical straight-shot subject matter seen in this catalog is greeting cards. **Figure 5.21** is a page illustrating seven Christmas cards. Other common straight shots are seen in the home furnishings field. **Figure 5.22** from the Scatters catalog shows four rugs spread out on the page, with three pillow designs inset in the lower right-hand corner. The products (rugs and pillows) could have been glamorized and put in an actual room setting, but the size of the product would have to be smaller and attention would have been diverted to objects other than the products themselves. This type of presentation is also less expensive.

Most business and industrial catalogs have, in the past, used the straight shot approach almost exclusively—often because it is the best approach to showing business products. Reliable illustrates most of its products with the straight shot approach. **Figure 5.23** features three calculators and calculator rolls in straight solo shots—a clean approach to products whose uses hardly need to be illustrated. **Figure 5.24** is from the Arrow Star catalog, which relies on photos and copy to suggest

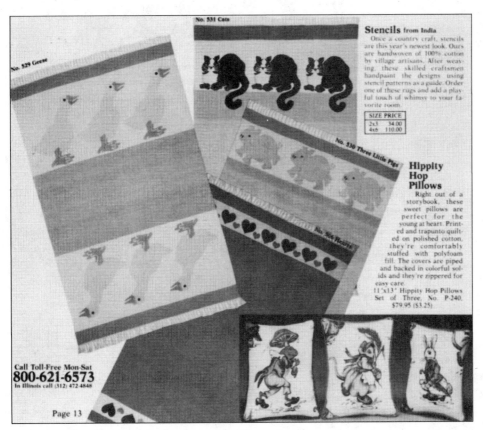

Figure 5.22　Scatters catalog

use. Since this catalog goes to a select audience of business and plant equipment purchasing agents, this may be all that is needed.

Figure 5.25 shows how background material with a high-tech look can suggest the personality and interests of the end-user of the product through variation, texture, and depth. Though this is a straight shot, the way the photographer has placed the item ("standing" and at an angle) gives it animation and vitality.

Figure 5.26 from LaShack shows the problems of using straight shots to sell jewelry and other accessories. The middle model is wearing a necklace color-coordinated with the outfit she has on. The necklace is for sale, but it is barely distinguishable in style or color. Because of its small size, the detail needed to sell it simply is not there.

Figure 5.27 from an Esplanade catalog solves this problem by including a necklace and earring as accessories in the upper-left corner illustration—but actually selling them in straight shots elsewhere on

Figure 5.23   Straight shot approach

the page. Product size has been increased so the customer can see the detail and color of these items. The page is made visually interesting, too. This approach lets all six products on the page command their share of interest, and provide the customer with enough individual detail to show the product benefit.

The Propped Shot

Catalogs use props because they can clarify product characteristics, suggest product use, imply a benefit, dramatize scale, create a mood, or help call attention to the product.

Props can also complement an item, catching the customer's eye or subliminally appealing to the shopper's hidden desires. And they are

Figure 5.24   Arrow Star catalog

particularly useful when they explain an item at a single glance, or when they add "sizzle" to an item which might otherwise be commonplace.

Don't leave the choice of props to the photographer. Merchandisers can be most helpful and should work closely with the layout artist or photographer to assure that props add appropriate definition of product benefit or purpose. There can be important, subtle differences in the intended use of a product: an enameled cash box intended as a "stowaway" spot for teenagers (and pitched that way in the copy) could easily be misunderstood by an unguided photographer and propped with a man's pocketknife and a hundred dollar bill.

Ask yourself these questions when trying to decide whether or not to prop the product:

1. Will the identity, function, or benefit of the product be clearer with a prop?

2. Is the item so visually dull that a prop will add appeal or draw the eye of the customer to the photograph?

3. Will it help the product sell by appealing to subliminal desires on the part of the customer?

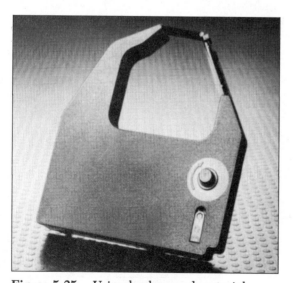

Figure 5.25   Using background material

Figure 5.26   LeShack catalog

Figure 5.28 from The Paragon catalog is an excellent example of declaring the product function. The frog bank would look merely like a ceramic decoration if it were not for the coins grouped around and balanced on it. Using these as props shows the product function at a single glance.

Figure 5.29 from an American Express catalog subliminally suggests a benefit that the consumer may derive from the product. The briefcase is propped with the Wall Street Journal and a pipe, implying that it is carried by a successful, upper-class individual. The viewer need only make a small leap to conclude that by carrying this briefcase, the viewer will also appear (or become) successful. Stated baldly in the copy, this claim would be laughable. But the subtlety of this visual message can be accepted by anyone.

A macho, carefree message is related in **Figure 5.30.** The Sharper Image is selling a leather flight vest. To get the message across and to appeal to the most likely customer, the photograph has shown a silk scarf casually draped over the front side of the vest. The scarf's light color attracts attention, and it suggests a carefree approach to life. An

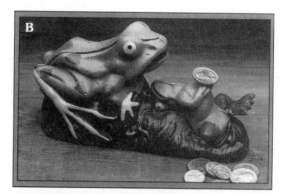

Figure 5.28   Paragon catalog

Figure 5.27   Esplanade catalog

Figure 5.29   American Express catalog

Figure 5.30   The Sharper Image catalog

Figure 5.31   Horchow catalog

Figure 5.32   Chris-Craft Catalog

old black leather flight cap is barely seen in the upper right of the photo with a strap carefully hanging down on a Varga pin-up girl calendar.

Romance and popularity are subtly suggested by this excellent use of props. The lighting adds to the effect, too, allowing highlights to play on the leather vest. The props have set a mood that implies a style of life that can be had by anyone who purchases the vest.

This not only suggests a carefree approach reminiscent of World War II, but also acts as an attractant because of its light color. An old black leather flight cap is barely seen in the upper right of the photo with a strap carefully hanging down on an old Varga pin-up-girl calendar. A romantic life of popularity is subtly suggested by this excellent use of props. The lighting adds to the effect, too, allowing highlights to play on the leather vest. The props have set a mood that implies a style of life that can be yours if you own the vest.

In **Figure 5.31** we see how propping can make a presentation in the Horchow catalog more interesting in form or color, thereby helping call attention to the product as well as helping clarify the size of the product. Three oranges are placed around the two Chinese plates that are being sold. The plates are blue and white and would have been far less noticeable if it weren't for the lovely bright-orange oranges. Two cigarettes alongside suggest use. This small (approximately $2^3/8''$ × $1^7/8''$) presentation could have gone unnoticed on the large 9″ × 11″ page if it were not for the colorful orange props calling attention to it.

A small analog quartz alarm clock (**Figure 5.32**) from the Chris-Craft catalog is nicely scaled by the placement of a cloisonne pen alongside. Such scaling as this is especially effective when the product being photographed must be brought up in size to be noticed on the page. With propping to bring scale to the product, the customer will not be misled, and still the photograph of a small product is as large as those of other truly larger products on the page.

Business-to-business catalogs tend to use fewer props. In many cases, photography is more or less treated like a visual listing. But business customers are people, too. They respond to mood and benefit, and they identify with a product and its setting as well as the general consumer.

In **Figure 5.33**, Quill has created a busy but personable desk scene as a backdrop to a leather portfolio. The setting is more attractive than a straight shot, shows off the features of the portfolio, and helps make the sale by encouraging the customer to imagine what it would be like to use the portfolio.

Figure 5.34 is more elaborately propped. In this shot, the Reliable Home Office catalog places its rolltop desk and file in what looks like a living room. Because this catalog's customers are professionals who work from a home office, they want to see how the desk-and-file combination can enhance their productivity while still blending into a home environment—a key concern for those seeking to balance space for work and leisure.

C.M. Almy and Sons, a religious-products supply company, warms up a silver chalice and paten by placing it on an altar propped with

Figure 5.33   Quill catalog

Figure 5.34   Reliable Office catalog

Figure 5.35   C.M. Almy and Sons catalog

plants in a soft-focus background (**Figure 5.35**). This treatment also helps buyers imagine how beautiful these objects will look when put to use in their own church.

There is some danger that props will overpower the product, which should always be the photo's main focus. **Figure 5.36** from Leichtung's tool catalog props a woodburning kit with a carved wooden duck. While the prop helps clarify the product benefit—the ability to burn feathers on the duck—it is almost more prominent than the product. Cropping the photo so that part of the decoy is missing keeps this from happening. Including an entire prop might confuse customers if they can't tell which item is being sold. Cutting into props concentrates customer attention on the product and creates mystery, which increases customer interest.

Props don't always add buyer motivation or interest to a photograph. In **Figure 5.37** from the Neiman-Marcus catalog, a plate, fruit, and coffee cup have been used to prop a set of folding tables. But the props do not illustrate a use that was otherwise unclear, nor do they add subliminal desire to make the purchase. Artistically they are too small to affect the composition of the photograph. Though this is not a bad photo, it is not an effective use of props.

Figure 5.36   Leichtung's catalog

Figure 5.37   Neiman-Marcus catalog

The In-Use Shot

This technique can describe an otherwise unidentifiable product, show how to use the product or how the product functions, and indicate all the benefits of owning the product (easy or fun to use, elegant to wear). An in-use shot makes the benefits offered by the product seem readily within the customer's reach. Any type of product can be presented this way, but categories that particularly benefit are clothing, sporting goods or exercise equipment, office equipment, factory and plant equipment, and gardening items.

The use of colorful accessories in a propped shot, or dramatic lighting and backgrounds in a straight shot, have caused a gradual movement away from in-use catalog shots. But showing a product actually being used can make the illustration more interesting and compelling for the customer. And it is almost demanded when the product is complicated in function or when the resulting benefit is the major selling point.

Ask yourself these questions before deciding whether or not to choose an in-use shot:

1. Is the product function too complicated or indeterminate for a straight shot?

2. Is the product benefit or use the major selling point?

3. Will sales benefit from an in-use illustration?

Figure 5.38 from the Chris-Craft catalog shows how an in-use shot instantly clarifies that a pair of binoculars is actually a flask. Though the eyepieces are actually shot glasses, using them to catch the liquid would have added nothing to the photograph and might have been extremely confusing. This point is covered in copy, and rightfully so. Note, too, that in the background at the top of the photo, a pennant has been used as a prop. Perhaps it is supposed to suggest that the flask can be used at ball games, but its message is unclear. In this photo, the pennant only adds clutter.

A standard in-use shot for containers such as vases, dishes, or glasses is to show something in them. **Figure 5.39** from Pottery Barn illustrates how effective two glass vases can be when shown in use. The sunflowers not only show how to use the product but also add color to the photo, helping attract attention. Another clever in-use example from the former Chris-Craft catalog shows designer rubber gloves being used to suds a dish (**Figure 5.40**). They would not have been nearly as attractive without this approach.

Some products need to be shown in use in order to be identified. **Figure 5.41** from an American Express catalog uses a model's foot to tell the shopper that the item being sold is a foot product. Without the foot, viewers would have passed the photo by, but it is still not clear just what the product is. **Figure 5.42** shows how The Sharper Image showed the same product in use. By adjusting the camera to a slow shutter speed and picking up the vibration movement in the photo-

Figure 5.38   Chris-Craft catalog

Figure 5.39 Pottery Barn catalog

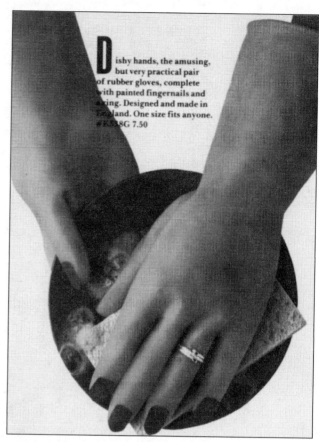

Figure 5.40 Chris-Craft catalog

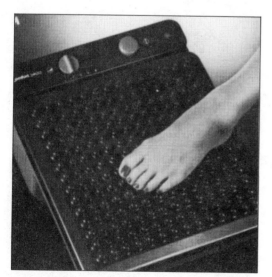

Figure 5.41 American Express catalog

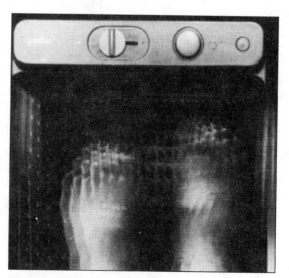

Figure 5.42 The Sharper Image catalog

graph, the photographer has shown how the product—a foot massager—actually works. A small straight shot of the product to one side allows the customer to see it in an unobstructed way. Together, the two shots clearly identify the product as well as its use.

There are many opportunities for in-use shots in business-to-business catalogs. **Figure 5.43** is a typical in-use application drawn from the Chiswick catalog of packaging, shipping, and warehouse supplies. A model representing a factory worker is using Chiswick equipment to make and seal custom poly-tubing bags. The picture shows three products in action—the poly tubing, the dispenser, and the sealer trimmer. Straight shots of each product accompany this presentation, but the in-use shot draws the customer's eye.

Figure 5.43   Chiswick catalog

A three-step photo series shows how easy Garon's Instant Concrete is to use (**Figure 5.44**). In just an hour's time (note the clock in each photo), this product easily solves a common and irritating problem. This is an exceptionally fine solution of how to present a difficult and uninteresting product in an attention-getting way. The visual presentation has told the story and sold the product too!

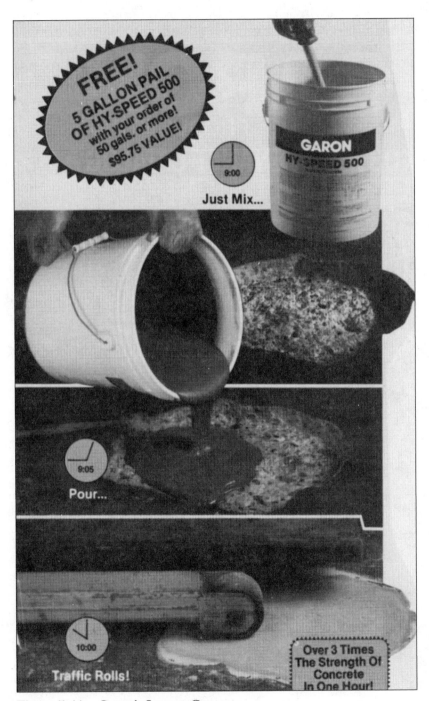

Figure 5.44   Garon's Instant Concrete

The product category that relies on the in-use technique most often is apparel.

Neiman-Marcus (**Figure 5.45**) shows three elegant partygoers walking down city streets in furs ranging in price from $8,000 to $30,000. The casualness of the scene reflects the mood only moneyed people will create in such apparel. The very casualness of presentation will attract those who can afford the product.

J. Crew uses casual, unstaged shots to market its clothes and a very distinctive lifestyle of relaxed, upscale adventure. In **Figure 5.46**, a male model is wearing an unconstructed jacket as he leaves a rugged vehicle and a set of fishing gear. At $98.00, the jacket doesn't shout "wealth" the same way a full-length fur coat does—but the rural fishing lodge conjures up visions of a life full of challenges and leisure time.

J. Crew also uses nontraditional poses and crops like the one shown in **Figure 5.47** to convey a feeling of spontaneity. Instead of saying,

Figure 5.45   Neiman-Marcus catalog

Figure 5.46   J. Crew catalog

Figure 5.47   J. Crew catalog

Figure 5.48   Eddie Bauer catalog

Figure 5.49   Hanna Andersson catalog

"that's a model," the viewer sees what looks like a real person caught in a real gesture—in this case, retrieving something from a car at the beach.

Eddie Bauer's All Week Long catalog takes a more conservative, posed approach in an outside setting. **Figure 5.48** shows the garment well and minimizes the photograph's cost because action shots, when done well, take more time to get just right and also demand more skill from the model and the photographer.

In children's clothing catalogs, there's nothing like an in-use shot to really clinch the sale. What parent or grandparent could resist the cherub in **Figure 5.49** from the Hanna Andersson catalog?

The End-Benefit Shot

A product that has no visual attraction on its own, but has a splendid visual when used by the customer, needs to be illustrated with an end-benefit shot. Use it when you are selling an item not for its look but for the benefits received by the customer when using it. Craft kits, seeds and bulbs, fruit and nut trees, diet and slimming aids, and training courses can use this technique with effective results.

To determine whether you should use an end-benefit shot, ask yourself these questions:

1. Is the product form merely a means to an end, with the end-result the reason for purchase?

2. Is the product dull or unidentifiable without showing it in its final form?

3. Will the end-benefit shot be a better road to sales?

A perfect example of the end-benefit technique is seen in **Figure 5.50** from the Park Seed Flower and Vegetable catalog. Over half a page is devoted to tantalizing photographs presenting Park's Sugar Snap pea. Not one photo shows the pack of seeds the customer receives, or

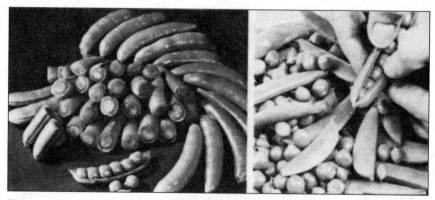

Figure 5.50   Park Seed Flower and Vegetable catalog

even the plants that result! Instead, they illustrate the "picked" peas as they are opened and cut, and as they might be served when harvested and ready for the table.

Williams-Sonoma's Catalog for Cooks (**Figure 5.51**) makes a full production of presenting a vertical poultry roaster. The product empty and in use helps show the steps involved in using it, but the most important element is the end benefit: the sumptuous roasted chickens that result from this unusual roasting method. Without this part of the presentation, the purpose of the product could not visually be identified.

A-C Poultry cooks up to 50% faster on a **Spanek Vertical Poultry Roaster**, plus meat self-bastes to stay juicy and exceptionally flavorful. To use, simply set the bird upright on the tempered steel frame. A 4 to 7-lb. chicken will need about 10" vertical space in an average oven, a 9 to 18-lb. turkey will need approximately 11" to 12" of vertical space. In the oven the frame conducts heat into the bird, so that it roasts faster, cooking from both inside and out. There is no need to baste or turn and fat simply drains away — a healthy bonus! Made in the USA. Recipes included.
A Chicken/Duck Rack, 7 3/4" high. #46-362566 Each **$20.00**
B Cornish Hen Racks, 5 1/2" high. *Set of two* #46-584631 **$17.00** *Catalog only*
C Turkey Rack, 9 3/4" high. #46-584649 Each **$25.00**
Special Set, one Turkey, one Chicken and

two Hen Racks, Instructional Video plus a Shish-Kebob Holder with 8 skewers that fits on the chicken rack. #46-570192 **Special Price $63.00** *Catalog only*

D Carve a chicken, duck, cornish hen or turkey directly on its vertical roasting rack with the specially designed **Spanek Carving Board**. The board has three concentric ring-shaped wells, one for each size of Spanek vertical roaster, to hold rack and bird stable and steady as you carve. Both sides of the board are grooved to collect juices, plus each has a pouring lip (the reverse side is flat in the center for all-purpose slicing). The ash board is specially treated to resist moisture and knife damage. 22" x 14". #46-721886 **$39.00**

Figure 5.51   Williams-Sonoma's Catalog for Cooks

Figure 5.52 HearthSong catalog

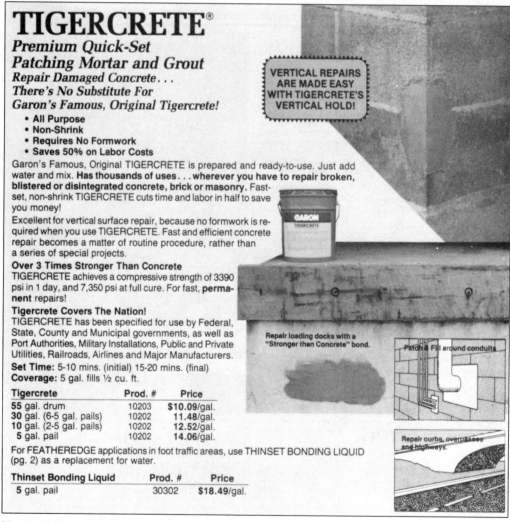

TIGERCRETE®

Premium Quick-Set Patching Mortar and Grout

Repair Damaged Concrete...
There's No Substitute For
Garon's Famous, Original Tigercrete!

- All Purpose
- Non-Shrink
- Requires No Formwork
- Saves 50% on Labor Costs

VERTICAL REPAIRS ARE MADE EASY WITH TIGERCRETE'S VERTICAL HOLD!

Garon's Famous, Original TIGERCRETE is prepared and ready-to-use. Just add water and mix. **Has thousands of uses. . . wherever you have to repair broken, blistered or disintegrated concrete, brick or masonry.** Fast-set, non-shrink TIGERCRETE cuts time and labor in half to save you money!

Excellent for vertical surface repair, because no formwork is required when you use TIGERCRETE. Fast and efficient concrete repair becomes a matter of routine procedure, rather than a series of special projects.

Over 3 Times Stronger Than Concrete
TIGERCRETE achieves a compressive strength of 3390 psi in 1 day, and 7,350 psi at full cure. For fast, **permanent** repairs!

Tigercrete Covers The Nation!
TIGERCRETE has been specified for use by Federal, State, County and Municipal governments, as well as Port Authorities, Military Installations, Public and Private Utilities, Railroads, Airlines and Major Manufacturers.

Set Time: 5-10 mins. (initial) 15-20 mins. (final)
Coverage: 5 gal. fills ½ cu. ft.

Repair loading docks with a "Stronger than Concrete" bond.

Patch & Fill around conduits.

Repair curbs, overpasses and highways.

Tigercrete	Prod. #	Price
55 gal. drum	10203	**$10.09**/gal.
30 gal. (6-5 gal. pails)	10202	**11.48**/gal.
10 gal. (2-5 gal. pails)	10202	**12.52**/gal.
5 gal. pail	10202	**14.06**/gal.

For FEATHEREDGE applications in foot traffic areas, use THINSET BONDING LIQUID (pg. 2) as a replacement for water.

Thinset Bonding Liquid	Prod. #	Price
5 gal. pail	30302	**$18.49**/gal.

Figure 5.53 Garon Products

Craft catalogs that sell kits, not finished products, show all their products in their completed form. **Figure 5.52** from the HearthSong catalog for children shows a boy wearing a tie-dyed teeshirt and holding up a pair of tie-dyed pants. The squirt bottles, dye powder and fixer, rubber gloves, instructions, and other materials used to create these items are not shown, although the attractive package that contains them is illustrated next to the copy block. (What a cluttered, unappealing, and uninteresting photograph that would make—a real deterrence to purchase.) Customers want to see the benefit derived—not the work to be done. Because this photo shows a child admiring the finished product, parents know children will enjoy the end benefits and the process, too.

Business-to-business catalogers have many ways to take advantage of the end-benefit technique. How-to or self-help books and programs can picture the benefit derived from using the product. A leadership program could picture a confident-looking person standing happily in front of a group of people, with the book or tapes overlaid in the foreground. Any problem-solving product can show the "after" treatment or application, as Garon Products does in **Figure 5.53**. This spread shows how a quick-set patching mortar and grout mix has patched difficult areas. Line drawings show other suggested areas it will repair. The actual product as it will be received occupies very little of the photo in its position on top of the loading dock.

Unix Central uses before and after shots to illustrate the end benefits of a business-graphics software program (**Figure 5.54**). Instead of illustrating complex product features, the photo shows that the program can help a harassed executive pull together a credible presentation in minutes flat. This is virtually saying, "You too can be successful because of the power of this new software."

Figure 5.54   Unix Central catalog

How Photography and Layouts Work Together to Sell Products

Every effective photograph needs a focal point . . . *and it must be your product.* While the techniques used by your photographer can help to focus the customer's attention on the product, the *placement* of the item within the frame of the photograph is vital. Prospects who view your catalog are not devoting themselves to intimate examination of every detail on every page. Most of the time the customer is browsing. Any impression you wish your product to make must be made *quickly.* And in a fast impression (which is probably all the time the customer will give you), *the product should be the first thing seen.* The first area of interest in the photograph should *not* be the color of the background, the location of the shot, or the props. It should *not* be the aesthetics of the photograph. It's the *product* you're selling.

Making sure the customer's eye focuses on the merchandise is easier said than done. Many subtle occurrences can cause the customer's eye flow to be disrupted or your viewer to focus on the wrong area. But a proper blend of the photographic techniques of background, lighting, and focus, along with the graphic technique of layout, can prevent these errors.

The major layout elements used to focus the customer's eye properly on the product are:

1. The *size* of the item in relationship to the photographic frame. Problems arise in this area when the product is shown either too large or too small within the photograph.

2. The *position* of the item within the photographic frame. Errors commonly occur here when the item is not placed in proper balance with other elements that might be present in the photo, such as models or props.

3. The *physical balance* between the item and its surroundings. This is a matter of how much "air" surrounds the item. Too much or too little will cause the viewer's eye to be bored.

4. The *color balance* (if a color photograph) or *tonal balance* (if a black and white photograph) between the item and background or other elements. The wrong balance between the item's color or tone and that of the background will cause either boredom or distraction.

You might think that layout is rather simple. The camera is aimed at the product, the photographic frame is filled with the product, and the shutter is clicked. Unfortunately, too much can go wrong.

For example, a simple product such as a coffee cup, shown against a simple background such as a sweep of color, seems as though it should be immediately apparent in a photograph. But if the coffee cup is yellow and the background is gold, there may not be enough contrast between the two to make the cup "snap" out of its background. Lighting must then be used to make highlights play upon the cup to catch the viewer's eye. Would a navy background work instead? Yes, but maybe you don't want a high-contrast look. In that case, the way your photographer lights the item is the answer. And this must be indicated to your photographer by the layout. If that same cup is photographed quite tightly within the borders of the picture, there may not be enough air around the cup to help the viewer's eye rest upon it. Or if the cup is photographed with a great deal of background showing, there may be so much air that the item doesn't demand focus and the photograph is boring. Again, the viewer's eye skips right over the presentation.

Figure 5.55 shows (a) not enough air around the cup, (b) too much air around the cup, and then (c) the right amount of air around the cup to attract the viewer's eye.

There are other elements that can cause this simple cup in this simple photograph to be poorly presented. If the camera angle is too high, the cup will appear foreshortened and its proportions will not be represented realistically. If the angle is too "head on" the cup will not look interesting. So even with an item as straightforward as a coffee cup, shot without a complicated background or even a prop, *the elements of size, positioning, physical balance, and color balance all play an important role.*

Figure 5.55   Cup and background

How to Determine if a Layout Demands Focus for a Product

When your customers are moving through your catalog, their eyes are moving fast and their minds are absorbing information rapidly. Anything that is not immediately apparent is either misunderstood or ignored. *After* you create your product layout and *before* it is executed, ask yourself these questions:

1. Does this layout *leave no doubt as to the identity of the product and its function?*

2. Does this layout make sure that the *customer's eye is drawn to the product*—and not focused on a less important element?

If you can't answer yes to both of these questions, go back to the drawing board and start over. If there can be any confusion on the customer's part about these two issues, then your product sales will suffer.

Products with many elements or functions can be even more difficult to deal with, simply because the multiple elements can cause confusion about the product's main function. Products that resemble something they are not—such as an item that looks like a pistol but is really a cigarette lighter—can fall into the difficult-to-present category. These kinds of products require extra thought in presentation.

Perhaps props will help make the product's function clear. A cigarette and an ashtray might explain the purpose of the pistol lighter, or perhaps a pack of cigarettes or even a single cigarette would work better. Determine which props provide the clearest enhancement and the least distraction to the main focus, and indicate them to the photographer in your layout.

It's up to you and your art director to direct the photographer toward the most effective presentation. This direction always begins with a decision about what the final photograph is expected to accomplish, and ends with conveying those demands to the photographer to carry out.

There is no "right" or "wrong" style, but what may be effective for one catalog may not work for you. Knowing which approach to use is half the battle. Accomplishing it effectively is the other half.

Let's examine the elements of layout with some products and photographs that are more complicated than the coffee cup just mentioned.

Figure 5.56 shows a page out of The Sharper Image catalog from a few years ago, when the cordless telephone was not as ubiquitous as it is today. The phone could have been photographed propless and with minimal background, but here is an excellent example of how the product remains the first thing seen, even with a complicated background, a model, and several props.

The focus remains on the product because the product is "sized" properly in relationship to the other items. It is positioned forward and toward the center of the page it is on, which is the main focal area in almost any photograph. Its immediate background (the car hood) does not fight with the item in terms of overall balance, or by making the photo too busy. And the physical balance of the house in the background and the hands in the foreground keep leading the eye to the product.

This item was photographed in this manner because the background and the props add subliminal feelings of distinction and elegance to the cordless phone. The photo helps convey the status of possessing this model. Features are not the only thing being sold. Benefits are also sold here. The small inset showing how the base station converts it to a wall phone is simply an added benefit.

Figure 5.56   The Sharper Image catalog

Figure 5.57, from Bloomingdale's "Taste of France" catalog, also tries to sell benefits. But it ends up puzzling the customer, who isn't sure which of the many items depicted is actually being sold. It isn't the lace table cloth, the most prominent item here; it is a group of products appearing on top of the table, including a bottle of mineral water, cherries, and coffee.

In this photograph, the size and position of products are dwarfed by the background and props. The physical balance of the photo is disrupted by incorrect placement of all items. This negates orderly eye flow and positions a non-product, the block of lace, in the most prominent area. And the color balance is upset because the white lace draws the eye. Though this photograph attempts to sell benefits, it is not successful because the benefits do not relate clearly to the specific products being sold.

Figure 5.57   Bloomingdale's "Taste of France" catalog

Basic product presentation rule

For any given product in any given catalog, take the *elements of layout* (size, positioning, physical balance, and color balance) *and combine them with the photographic techniques* of lighting and focus to control and illustrate your product's features and benefits. Do this after you consider how best to present these benefits to your specific audience.

An Exercise Comparing Two Product Presentations

These two photographs of jewelry present a study in contrast. The first illustration (**Figure 5.58**) is from The Sharper Image Gemstones and Jewelry catalog. An abundance of subtleties focuses the customer's eye on the merchandise. The photograph uses a model and prop (the fur) to sell benefits by adding glamour and image to possession of the jewelry. (These elements effectively size the product, as well.) But the addition of these elements does not prevent the jewelry from remaining the focal point, even though the amount of space occupied in the photo by the merchandise is small compared to the amount occupied by the model.

Figure 5.58   The Sharper Image Gemstones and Jewelry catalog

This has been achieved by using the photographic techniques of lighting and focus in combination with elements of layout.

1. Lighting. The model's face does not demand the attention it would have if it had been lit with the same intensity as the rest of the photograph. Instead, it is "shadowed," which controls the balance of this area of the photograph. Because the jewelry is the most brightly lit area, it remains the focal point. This style of lighting also adds drama to the products.

2. Focus. The depth of field is shallow, making the jewelry the sharpest area of the photograph, giving a subdued feeling of soft-focus to the rest of the photo. Some photographs could exaggerate this technique even more strongly. They could use a filter to soft-focus the background, or conversely to make a "star" appear where a facet of the gemstone reflects the light.

Four important techniques

3. Positioning. The merchandise is in the center of the photo with the arm angled toward the center and the fur framing the center point. Everything leads the eye to the grouping of neckpiece, rings and bracelet, which are in close juxtaposition. The eye does not jump across the photo trying to locate the items in different areas. No distractions occur because there are no jarring angles.

4. Color. Though you cannot see it in this black and white rendition, the blue topaz stones command attention within the neutrals of skin tone and white fur. Color balance has been effectively used to attract the viewer's eye to the product.

The next illustration (**Figure 5.59**) from an American Express catalog shows that bigger is not necessarily better. The original of this photo is a bit larger than the Gemstones example, but the merchandise featured here has been overwhelmed by the rest of the photograph. Its layout has destroyed the viewer's ability to focus on the products, and the photographic elements have not helped this situation. The photo could just as well be a skin cream ad. Let's take a look at the same elements used in the preceding photograph to see what happened.

1. Lighting. The lighting is soft, flat, even. No shadows, no highlights—nothing to force a glint or gleam from the diamonds, or to add drama, impact or mood—nothing to direct eye flow. Lighting does not help the eye focus on any area of the photograph.

2. Focus. Because the photo is a tight close-up, conflicting elements are in the identical plane (and identical focus), such as the model's eye and the ring. The techniques is almost clinical—as though every inch of the photograph has to show subject matter with equal clarity.

3. Positioning. Here, the actual span between ring and pendant covers about the same area as on the model in the Gemstones photograph, but this layout forces the eye to jump a much greater distance, with nothing guiding it along a *travel* route. The background dwarfs

Figure 5.59   American Express catalog

the items, making them appear insignificant in relationship to the expanse of skin and hand. The total diamond weight of the ring is one carat, but it appears unimpressive. Though the hand leads into the photograph, it points toward the eye. Both pieces of merchandise remain on the fringes of interest.

4. Color. This photo is completely composed of neutrals, since diamonds are also colorless. But here is where the addition of "black" *via shadows* would have helped add contrast. The merchandise would have stood out with emphasis from a shadowy background, even if the items had remained on skin-toned hand and neck.

The customer must never be confused about where to focus (on the merchandise) and how the eye should travel (never at random, never jumping, always flowing). Good layout is not merely "position." It is control of the viewer's eye flow via all elements and techniques of photograph. It is forcing the viewer's eye where you want it—on your product!

If the Main Focus Is the Item . . . Then What Is the Item's Main Focus?

Poor focus and layout often occur because techniques are badly used. But in addition, an ineffective presentation is frequently caused by confusion on the part of the catalog marketer about the main point of the product.

No matter what your product is—no matter how many features it offers the customer and no matter how complicated it is visually—any product has a certain area that offers a major advantage to the customer. Perhaps even a couple of areas. But never *all* the areas.

A frequent error in art and copy presentations is the *inability of the creative staff to choose (or decide upon) the main thrust of the product.* And every time a product is presented with all thrusts given equal weight (or almost equal weight), the presentation is diluted. This weakening usually occurs because the eye of the viewer is confused and has to work harder to draw conclusions about the item, and about whether or not to purchase it. There is no logical reason why you want to make your customers have any more difficulty making a purchasing decision than absolutely necessary. This problem of equally weighting all of the assets of a product is a concrete example of the old saw: "More is less." You'll often see this problem of presentation in catalogs geared to businesses, because the products offered for sale frequently have many features.

In layouts presenting products with many features, the copy often is as intrinsic to the visual presentation as the photograph. The copy not only tells about the item, but works in immediate juxtaposition to the artwork.

The example below from a Day-Timer catalog (**Figure 5.60**) indicates confusion between the main feature of the item and its subsidiary advantages. To determine what the item is and does, the customer must do a lot of scattered looking. The main feature, 5 Books in 1, is tucked into a small space to the right of the item photo. This main feature is printed in type that asks for the same attention as that asked by the auxiliary features below it, which occupy a great deal more space. The fact that a wallet is also involved (which can be personalized) is a confusing element sandwiched in between the main and the auxiliary features. If a customer is not familiar with the physical make up

Complicated presentations must be made easy for the customer

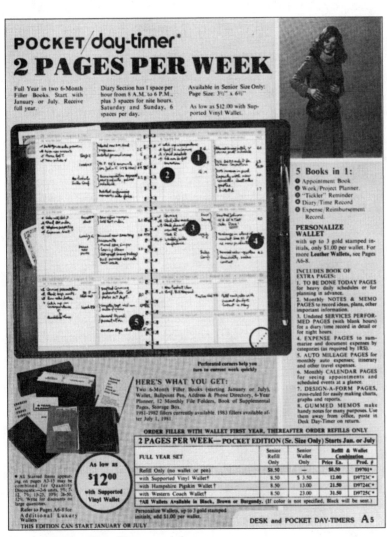

Figure 5.60   Day-Timer catalog

of a Day-Timer, the logical question would be: "What wallet?" since none is apparent from the photograph.

The copy below the main headline does not clarify any of the main features of the item. It begins, "Full year in two 6-Month Filler Books," but it could have clarified the product by saying, "Full year diary/ planner in its own wallet."

Random copy points are placed within the layout anywhere that space is available, rather than with forethought regarding size, position, and balance. The comment squeezed into the lower left of the ad is an example: "This edition can start January or July." Another example is the copy block immediately above that talks about quantity discounts available for "starred items" in the ads. But it's hard to reference the starred items to this copy. (You'll find them in the right-hand column of the order information chart.)

And if a customer wanted to purchase a dozen of any of these products, the discount incentive isn't apparent in the chart (which is where it normally would appear and be noticed). This chart of ordering information is also confusing. There are product numbers in the right-hand column that seem to refer to the refill and wallet combination. But if the customer wants to order the refill or the wallet only, what product number should be specified? Yet at the top of the order chart, bold capitals instruct repeat customers to order refills, if they already own the wallet from a prior purchase.

This presentation is a plethora of confusion, not only in the lack of isolation of main product features, but also in the confusing placement of vital ordering incentives and information. And, incidentally, quite a bit of valuable space is used at the upper right to show a woman placing the item in her purse. Ostensibly this is shown to imply female usage, as well as male (because preceding ads for other Day-Timers picture men only).

Obviously the product is chock-full of features. Though it may not be too difficult to determine which are the main item points, it is certainly quite a project for the cataloger to decide how to emphasize and promote the features in a way which is orderly to the customer's eye . . . and which allows the eye to pick up and mentally absorb those points one by one. Compounding the problem are such things as quantity discount incentives. In the Day-Timer example, could this idea have been presented in a larger format in one main place in the catalog, instead of in the fine print used here (and in other individual ads)? Then the individual ads could have said: "Quantity discounts—see order form." Some people argue the sensibility of making the customer flip elsewhere in the catalog. If this is a problem, then place the information in the chart, where it belongs.

As you can see, solving the problem of promoting the product's main point takes thorough analysis.

Artwork versus Photos

Nothing is as believable to the viewer as a photograph of an item. That is why photos are invariably the first choice for presenting a product. Subconsciously, a person viewing artwork may wonder why he or she is not seeing the "real thing," and conclude that it is because the item doesn't look very good in real life. This is a definitive negative, and a reason why most catalogs avoid artwork unless absolutely necessary.

But there are times when photos simply will not work, or are too impractical to consider. Three situations generally call for art. They are:

1. When the item's size is so large or long that only a long shot will fit all the elements into the frame—causing the photograph to lose perspective and the item to lose details.

2. When the item is made of material that can not be picked up by the camera lens, or actually obscures the main function of the item or destroys its shape.

3. When the product would look more interesting in an illustration than in a photograph.

Let's look at these one at a time.

Using Artwork to Depict Size

In creating **Figure 5.61** from Walter Drake and Sons, the artist has decided that two issues are important: the length of the washer, and its ability to pulsate. The artwork warps the perspective of a two-story house to show the length, and uses an inset to show the head of the washer with a headline indicating the pulsating action. The copy headline, "Wash Second-Story Windows Easily," underlines the thrust of the artwork by clearly stating its main function.

But this presentation does not illustrate the washer's components and functions. Presumably, these were overlooked in an effort to avoid diluting the main selling point of the washer with secondary sales points. On the whole, this is an entirely satisfactory presentation, which a photograph could never have accomplished.

Figure 5.62 from Miles Kimball also uses full-color artwork to exaggerate the length of the washer and its ability to wash second-floor windows. But this presentation also includes an inset showing an additional attachment, a gutter cleaner. This is not easy to show in the space allotted, mainly because the gutter cleaner has a mirror attached to it which confuses the artwork (though the copy explains it clearly). The mirror attachment is too unfamiliar a device to be instantly absorbed by the mind in such a small piece of art. In this situation, perhaps an art headline would have been a greater aid ("Gutter cleaner available too!").

Figure 5.63 from Taylor Gifts photographs the item but uses artwork to illustrate the functions. But not enough space is given to these drawings, which show the tool being used to wash a car, a screen, a boat, and an upper window. Everything is crowded, making the functions hard to isolate.

Line art works best when it relies on only a few simple lines, rather than the shading and dimension that regular artwork would need. But often too much is included in the line drawing and some of the clarity of the technique is lost, as it is here. In the upper drawing, the male figure could have been eliminated, along with the rear end of the car. This would have allowed the rest of the drawing to be larger, and the function would have been more isolated and consequently clearer for the mind to absorb.

The moral? If you choose to use line drawings, be sure you don't negate their function by including too much. Whenever you illustrate an item, you need to consider the restrictions you have to work in.

Figure 5.61 Walter Drake & Sons catalog

Figure 5.62 Miles Kimball catalog

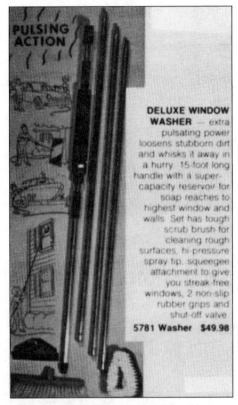

PULSING ACTION

DELUXE WINDOW WASHER — extra pulsating power loosens stubborn dirt and whisks it away in a hurry. 15-foot long handle with a super-capacity reservoir for soap reaches to highest window and walls. Set has tough scrub brush for cleaning rough surfaces, hi-pressure spray tip, squeegee attachment to give you streak-free windows, 2 non-slip rubber grips and shut-off valve.

5781 Washer $49.98

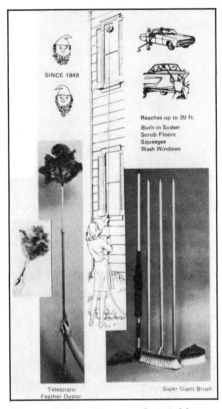

SINCE 1848

Reaches up to 20 ft.
Built-in Sudser
Scrub Floors
Squeegee
Wash Windows

Telescopic Feather Duster

Super Giant Brush

Figure 5.63 Taylor Gifts catalog

Figure 5.64 Hammacher Schlemmer catalog

There is nothing wrong with trying to show the versatility of this washing system, but not in the space that Taylor Gifts has to work with.

Figure 5.64 from Hammacher Schlemmer shows not only the pulsating washer, but also a portion of another piece of artwork, a telescoping feather duster. This is an error in page layout that hurts both items. Although both items are long handled, their physical juxtaposition confuses rather than enhances each item. In addition, this layout allowed some air to remain in the upper left section, and filled it with two little line drawings (presumably Hammacher and Schlemmer?) and a date—further cluttering the main presentation.

Here the washer components have been shown in a photograph. The second-story function is shown in a well-done line drawing. But two more line drawings have lost their effectiveness because of the lack of cohesiveness in the layout. The headlines in the artwork are also barely noticed for the same reasons. The hodgepodge quality of the layout has affected the clarity of the individual presentation. Remember, the blending of the elements which you determine to be necessary is as important as the decision on which elements to include.

Using Artwork to Depict Unusual or Hard to Shoot Materials

Sometimes an artist's brush can show an item better than the camera can—especially if the item is made of materials that obscure its function or appearance. Occasionally these problems can be solved by retouching a photographic print to add details to the photo, but more often the solution is to turn to artwork.

Figure 5.65 from Joan Cook shows a hummingbird feeder that presents several problems from a photographic point of view. The window glass is hard to photograph, whatever is behind the glass will be a distraction (and if the glass is backed with a sheet of colored paper, it won't look like glass any more), clear plastic is hard to photograph, see-through suction cups do not photograph well, and hummingbirds are not very cooperative subjects.

Figure 5.65   Joan Cook catalog

All of these obstacles make artwork a logical solution. The drawing clearly shows the plastic's see-through quality, demonstrates how the product attaches to the window, and shows the feeder's size and how much liquid it holds. Best of all, it shows the product in use. The illustration successfully captures these elements in a very appealing way.

Figures **5.66** and **5.67** show water heater blankets as depicted by Bruce Bolind and the Old Village Shop.

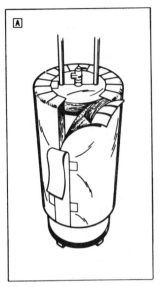

Figure 5.66   Bruce Bolind catalog

Figure 5.67   Old Village Shop catalog

Figure **5.68** from Harriet Carter portrays hard-to-convey qualities while enlivening a dull subject. The woodpile cover is black—a hard color to photograph and achieve detail, especially when the camera has to back away from the subject to fit everything in. The cover is also vinyl, creating a reflective sheen that discourages detail. It is reinforced with fiberglass, another detail that is hard to show in a photo but easily captured here by crosshatching.

Assembling the logs for a shot would be heavy and difficult work for a studio photographer, and there is nothing about real logs that is more believable than a drawing of logs. All of these add up to the logical choice: art instead of photography.

Figure **5.69**, also from Harriet Carter, uses color art to capture glow-in-the-dark Christmas tree icicles, a subject guaranteed to drive

Figure 5.68   Harriet Carter catalog

Figure 5.69   Harriet Carter catalog

any photographer crazy. Here, the luminous quality has been represented by little glow lines emanating from each icicle. To convey the quantity, the drawing shows many distinct icicles in a large group—an impossible task for the camera, which would have captured a colorful mass. Other details, such as the small molded hooks, would also have been difficult to capture. The result is a drawing that presents the item with far greater glamour than a photograph would have achieved.

Figure 5.70, 5.71, and 5.72, all from Walter Drake and Sons, illustrate three additional challenges better handled by artwork than photography. A photograph of the over-the-door bookrack in **Figure 5.70** would have been plagued by the challenge of lighting three separate surfaces—the door, the bookrack, and the books. Each need a different lighting approach to look good. A photo of the sensor night light in **Figure 5.71** would not have captured details like the plastic faceted cover, especially if it attempted to create a "night" shot. And the clear vinyl pockets of the purse and shoe caddies in **Figure 5.72** might have created glare, wrinkles, and indistinct pocket contents.

In all three cases, artwork has let the art director capture important qualities and materials and let the customer instantly understand the function of each item.

Figure 5.70 Walter Drake and Sons catalog

Figure 5.71 Walter Drake and Sons catalog

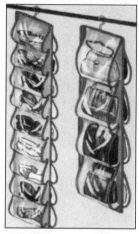

Figure 5.72 Walter Drake and Sons catalog

Using Artwork to Enhance a Product

Sometimes an illustration can make a boring or predictable product much more interesting—or contribute so much that the product would look boring if photographed in the same manner as the artwork presents it.

A case in point comes from the Foodways catalog shown in **Figure 5.73**. A whimsical approach to layout and lovely, childlike illustrations make the bean soups shown on this page appealing beyond words.

Figure 5.73 Foodways catalog

Presenting these same products in photographs would have been challenging, possibly a great deal more expensive, and certainly less imaginative than the alternative chosen for this 16-page catalog.

Like the Foodways catalog, J. Peterman completely eschews photography in favor of illustration. **Figure 5.74** shows a typical spread, in which watercolors and line drawings help evoke the places, times, and emotions elaborated upon in Peterman's long copy blocks. Without a model (and finding models to match the story told in Peterman's copy would be difficult), a photograph would have made this caftan look flat. Instead, this illustration uses flowing lines to capture the garment's lines and details.

In these cases and others in which artwork is elegantly and appropriately used, the potentially negative aspects of art are turned into positives. Thanks to the overall blend of art and copy in these catalogs, customers don't need to be reassured by seeing "the real thing." The products they see, enhanced by talented artists, are real enough.

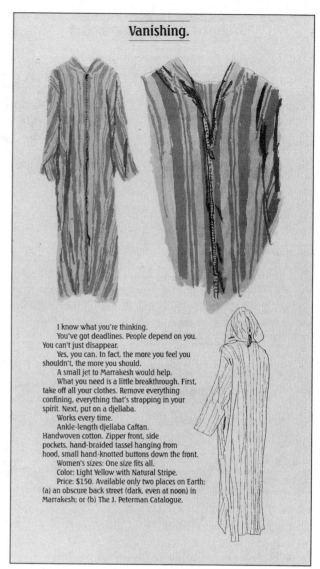

Vanishing.

I know what you're thinking.
You've got deadlines. People depend on you. You can't just disappear.
Yes, you can. In fact, the more you feel you shouldn't, the more you should.
A small jet to Marrakesh would help.
What you need is a little breakthrough. First, take off all your clothes. Remove everything confining, everything that's strapping in your spirit. Next, put on a djellaba.
Works every time.
Ankle-length djellaba Caftan. Handwoven cotton. Zipper front, side pockets, hand-braided tassel hanging from hood, small hand-knotted buttons down the front.
Women's sizes: One size fits all.
Color: Light Yellow with Natural Stripe.
Price: $150. Available only two places on Earth: (a) an obscure back street (dark, even at noon) in Marrakesh; or (b) The J. Peterman Catalogue.

Figure 5.74   The J. Peterman Company catalog

Combining Art with Photography

Occasionally, artwork can be very effectively combined with photography, as the Coach Leatherware catalog in **Figures 5.75** and **5.76** show. In one catalog featuring 28 handbags and totes, only two are photographed, both in full-page color shots. All the others are presented with drawings, usually two or three to a page.

The photograph shows customers the bag's soft sheen, leather grain, lovely tan color, and detailed stitching. The drawings present an aesthetic "feel," a sheen created by the artist's highlighting and shadowing (much more intense than could be achieved with a camera lens), and

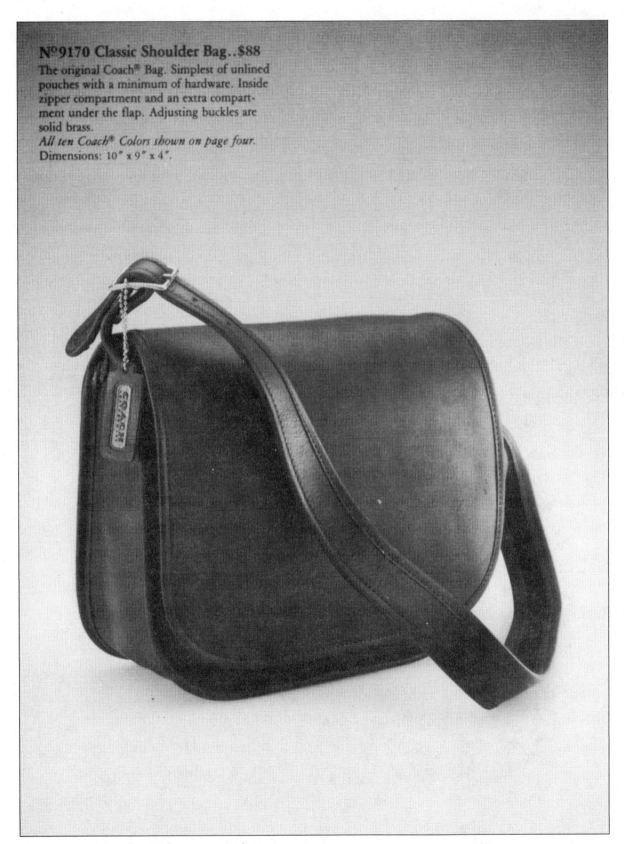

N⁰9170 Classic Shoulder Bag..$88
The original Coach® Bag. Simplest of unlined
pouches with a minimum of hardware. Inside
zipper compartment and an extra compartment under the flap. Adjusting buckles are
solid brass.
All ten Coach® Colors shown on page four.
Dimensions: 10″ x 9″ x 4″.

Figure 5.75   Coach Leatherware catalog

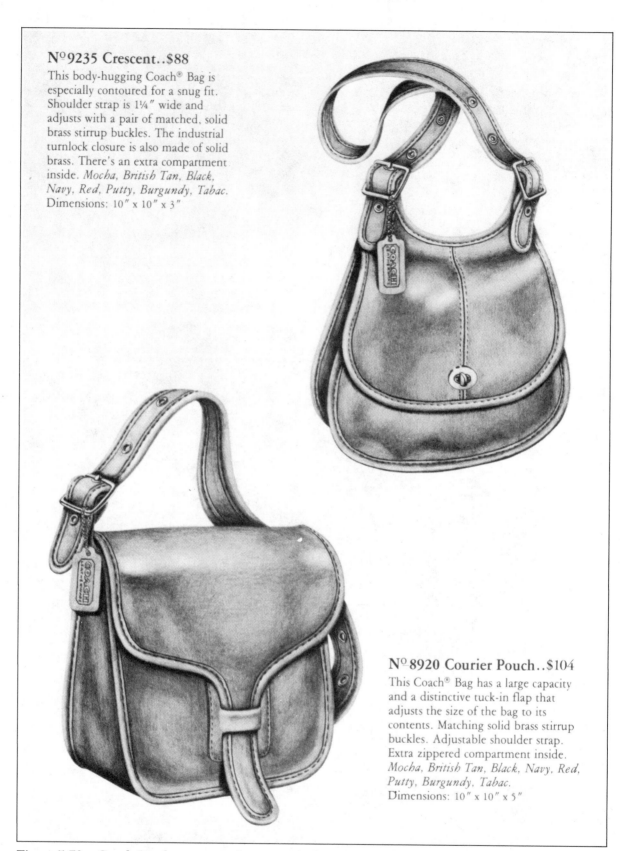

Nº 9235 Crescent..$88

This body-hugging Coach® Bag is especially contoured for a snug fit. Shoulder strap is 1¼″ wide and adjusts with a pair of matched, solid brass stirrup buckles. The industrial turnlock closure is also made of solid brass. There's an extra compartment inside. *Mocha, British Tan, Black, Navy, Red, Putty, Burgundy, Tabac.* Dimensions: 10″ x 10″ x 3″

Nº 8920 Courier Pouch..$104

This Coach® Bag has a large capacity and a distinctive tuck-in flap that adjusts the size of the bag to its contents. Matching solid brass stirrup buckles. Adjustable shoulder strap. Extra zippered compartment inside. *Mocha, British Tan, Black, Navy, Red, Putty, Burgundy, Tabac.* Dimensions: 10″ x 10″ x 5″

Figure 5.76   Coach Leatherware catalog

an excitement developed by the way the illustrations exaggerate these features. In addition, the customer "sees" in each drawing the memory of the photograph, with all its reality. The photograph serves as a realistic support to the aesthetics of the artwork.

These handbags might seem boring if photograph after photograph were viewed. Extra props would have been required to keep boredom at bay. By using artwork, the customer remains engaged in the products, and actually feels that the illustrations give a better vision of the products than the camera could possibly do.

Coach saved plenty of money by eliminating color separations and four-color printing—and the fee paid for the artwork probably is much less than a comparably talented photographer would charge. Yet the catalog quality was not compromised or sacrificed. To show customers the ten colors in which these bags are available, Coach uses page three of the catalog to show ten color swatches in the Coach Tag that hangs from each bag. The copy presents the colors and also tells why the Coach Tag stands for a very special product.

This example confirms that in certain cases, the combination of artwork and photography works better than either medium used alone. This technique is particularly advantageous when a cataloger has a product line with many similar items and certain difficulties in photographing them effectively. It's worth considering if this problem arises in your book.

Photography

Advantages	Disadvantages
Greater believability due to picture of actual product; heightened credibility because of seeing the "real" thing; greater customer association with product.	Possible misunderstanding of product function; lost product detail; possibility of uninteresting visual.

Art

Advantages	Disadvantages
Emphasis on product function for greater customer understanding; easier emphasis on product detail; easy addition of seasonal aspects when preparing catalog in off-season; easy illustration of end-benefit such as bearing fruit trees.	Lost realism, lessened credibility; product distorted.

Advantages	Disadvantages
Emphasis on product detail with art while realism is retained by photography; emphasis on function.	Visual clutter highly possible; more costly production due to double charges (art plus photography) and film stripping in printing pre-stage.

Ensuring Good Photo Reproduction

Sometimes catalog photos look great at the transparency stage, but end up looking ho-hum in the printed catalog. This happens when a photographer or a photo studio produces transparencies that are beautiful by photographic standards, but have too great a range of contrast for the printing press to handle. As a result, catalog photos lose detail in the very dark or very light areas—perhaps obscuring important product features.

To overcome this, encourage your photographer to limit the *f-stop* range of your transparencies to four or fewer f-stops. (F-stop is a term used in photography to denote the size of the aperture, or lens opening, of a camera; for example, an f-stop of 5.6 lets in more light than an f-stop of 8.) Research has shown that most printing presses are able to handle a range of four f-stops, or if you use the measuring system used by separators, 2.05 density units. This doesn't mean the entire transparency needs to be within a four-stop range, just the critical elements that show the product and details essential to showing its use.

Ask your photographer to show, either with a Polaroid or transparency overlay, exactly where meter readings were made. He or she must indicate the brightest highlight, the darkest shade, and the midpoint. By bracketing exposures this way, you will end up with better catalog photos and lower production costs. The separator can program the scanner more quickly and precisely and make fewer corrections during the scanning process.

Besides an overly wide range of contrast, a number of other areas present a challenge to accurate color production. A good color prepress house will be able to work with many of these difficult subjects, but you should allow enough time for them to work on them and expect to pay a higher price:

- Subjects with built-in moires, such as checks or plaids

- White-on-white or black-on-black detail

- Dropouts of hair, bicycle wheel spokes, or other intricate parts

- Grainy subjects requiring enlargements of more than 1,000 percent

- Subjects requiring outlines with no clear definition between subject and background, such as black object on black background

- Metallic colors, such as jewelry, gold lamé fabric, and so on

- Flourescent colors

- Subjects with many subtle pastels

- Subjects with flat lighting or a lack of internal contrast

- Subjects with excessive contrast in key areas (Overcome this with the f-stop approach just outlined.)

CHAPTER 6

How to Write Product Copy

Photography is important—but copy is king.

That's because copy alone can sell a product, while a photograph *always* needs copy to complete the sale. Thus, while great pictures capture the customer's attention, it is copy's responsibility to take that attention and *sell* that customer the product or service offered.

Copy's multifaceted role includes grabbing the customer's attention, then directing, educating, informing, entertaining, referring, describing, even trying the product on for the customer before stroking, befriending, assuring, and guaranteeing that customer! Copy also builds company credibility and consumer confidence. And it does all of this while maintaining a level of truthfulness that will result in repeat business.

Copy is by far the most powerful selling tool available to the cataloger. It is mail order's secret weapon, because it provides information that educates, informs, and sells the customer. Retail stores are unable to equal this feat because clerks cannot know everything about each product in the store. They are also often unavailable, and frequently less friendly and accommodating than desired. Well-written copy does not discriminate: it is always friendly and helpful to all customers.

The subject of this chapter is *product body copy*, the copy which immediately follows the copy headline. It is often referred to as descriptive copy, selling copy, the copy block, or product copy. How to write headlines and price lines is also covered here. Front and back cover copy, photo captions, the catalog letter, and other catalog copy will be covered in Chapter 7. Advice on using type effectively can be found in Appendix 1.

Gearing Up to Write Product Copy

Before you put pen to paper—or fingers to keyboard—you (or the copy-writer, if you aren't writing copy yourself) need to cover three essential steps:

1. Get to know your customer.
2. Get to know your company.
3. Get to know each product.

1. Get to know your customer   You cannot write good selling copy unless you know to whom you are writing. Are you appealing to corporate executives, proprietors of small businesses, retired people, collectors, home chefs, or college attendees? You need to know so you can determine the tone and approach of your copy. Use your customer list to tell you who the catalog is being mailed to and what the buyer is like. Find out:

- Whether the typical buyer lives in the city or the country

- Whether the list is predominately male or female

- The average dollar order

This kind of demographic information will help you write copy that really speaks to your customer. You wouldn't address a Madison Avenue matron the same way you would a beach bum in Hawaii. And you won't make that mistake if you know exactly whom you are addressing.

2. Get to know your company   In order to write convincing copy, you also need to know what your company is all about. Has your company been in the business for years, or is it just starting out? Is it considered an expert in its product field? Does it specialize in value-priced merchandise, high-end specialties, customer service?

These factors will help you build the image of your catalog and create its persona—a critical factor in an age of "me too" catalogs. The most successful catalogs have readily identifiable *personalities* that their copy works hard to convey.

Secure in your knowledge of who you are and who you are addressing, you can choose the tone that is best for your catalog and product line. A colloquial, conversational style might be just right for a food line from the hill country of Tennessee, whereas a shorter, clipped approach would be better for steaks sold as executive gifts. The right kind of copy, paired with the right kind of design and photography, can establish an ambience for your entire book.

3. Get to know each product In the Product Work Session, your copywriter was introduced to critical information about the products in your line. But the copywriter shouldn't stop when all of these materials—competing catalogs and copy, manufacturer's information and testing results, and merchandiser's reasons for selecting the product—have been assimilated. Before pen meets paper or fingers meet keyboard, more questions should be asked.

What are the product's major benefits? Its secondary benefits? What are all the jobs the product can be used for? Is it an exclusive? Does it have a warranty? Has it been used by professionals or by business prior to public release? Does it solve a particular problem? The answers to these questions and many more will help the copywriter gain as much knowledge as possible about the product to be sold.

For best results, follow this five-step process.

Step 1: Consult the merchandiser or buyer who selected the product.

This is by far the most important step because the person who selected the product knows why the target customer will purchase the product. The merchandiser is the one who ultimately answers for its success or failure and so has very definite reasons why the product will appeal to the customer.

The merchandiser should be able to tell the writer why the product was selected: what the main benefit is, what problem the product will solve, what service it will render, how it is like past or current successful products, and whether it has been successfully run by competitors in their catalogs or in space advertising.

The writer should ask a lot of questions and expect answers that will become the informational backbone of the copy. Information derived from the merchandiser should be given every consideration when the writer is structuring the copy because the merchandiser, not the writer, best knows the appeal of the product.

Step 2: Collect background information.

Writing catalog copy seldom requires original research. Usually, the products to be included in the catalog have already been described in previous brochures, flyers, ads, and data sheets. Collecting and organizing this printed material is a crucial step in getting ready to write the catalog copy. The writer should get all pertinent product literature received from the manufacturer. (And if the catalog house doesn't have this literature, it must be solicited.) For an existing product, this information can include ad tear sheets, brochures, old catalogs, article reprints, technical papers, press kits, audio-visual scripts, direct mail promotions, and spec sheets.

If the product is new or manufactured by the catalog company itself, these publications may not exist. But the birth of any new product is accompanied by mounds of helpful paperwork, including internal memos, letters of technical information, product specifications, engineering drawings, photos of prototypes, business and marketing plans, reports, and sales proposals.

If the catalog house is supplying the copywriter with information on many products, file folders should be used to separate source material by product. Include a brief with each folder indicating whether the enclosed background material is complete and up-to-date and, if not, names of persons the writer can call to fill the gaps.

Be sure to mark the source material to indicate what information should be included in the catalog and what should not. Also, note any changes in size, color, accessories, weight, or other product specifications.

Step 3: Study the previous catalogs, previous ads, and promotional pieces.
The writer will have to study all promotional information disseminated over the past few years to decide which ideas, formats, and techniques work, and to discard those that don't.

The writer should know about any *mandatory* format or stylistic requirements. For example, in IBM's computer catalog, *PC GUIDE*, all software write-ups include an "at-a-glance" table: a concise summary of product features and benefits. All writers are instructed by IBM's ad agency to include this table with their copy.

Step 4: Set a direction.
The writer must be aware of any instructions or suggestions the catalog house wants followed. (These should be written down.) The catalogers might have definite ideas on how they want their catalogs arranged and organized. Or they may prefer one style of copy to another. But copywriters can't read anyone's mind; they must know the catalogers' preferences.

Some writers contend that it's the writer's job to set the tone, style, content and organization. Experience shows that catalogers have their preferred ways of doing things. And rarely does a staff writer (let alone a freelancer or agency) make revolutionary changes from one year's catalog to the next.

Step 5: The catalog merchandiser must be available.
Once the background material is ready and the merchandiser's information is supplied, the writer is ready to write the copy. At this point, the merchandiser must be available to answer questions, gather additional information, and review rough drafts, outlines or concepts. If the merchandiser is *not* available, the project will be held up until the writer gets the information, feedback, or approval that is needed.

All merchandisers should make sure their people support the copywriter's efforts. A good bet, if an outside agency or individual is used, is to appoint one employee to act as liaison between catalog company and writer. It's inefficient for a writer to have to track down the many people in a company who are involved with the catalog and its creation.

In addition to these five steps, there is a crucial sixth step that every writer must take: **Use the product!** The best copy comes when you have a firsthand, intimate knowledge of a product's benefits and features.

Copy written from secondhand materials only will lack the personal dimension of copy written out of experience.

Starting to Write

Now, you are ready to sit down and start writing product copy.

Every writer has a "creative" side and an "analytical' or "editing" side. The creative side comes up with the ideas; the editing side holds the ideas up to the cold light of day and judges their effectiveness. Both sides are needed in copywriting, but they should be used in separate and distinct phases of the writing process.

When you try to be creative and analytical at the same time, your editing facilities inhibit your creative facilities, and writer's block may result. To ensure that the words flow smoothly, give your creative side free rein by following this three-stage process.

Stage One.   Ignore the constraints of space, format, and style, and simply WRITE. Let the words flow. Write whatever comes naturally. Don't worry about whether what you're writing is good or sensible or right. You can go back and fix it later. For now, just let the words pour out.

Some writers like to keep two pads (or a computer and a pad) in front of them as they write. The first pad or the computer is used for composing the copy. Any stray thoughts or phrases that come to mind but don't yet fit in with the copy are jotted down on the second pad for use in future drafts.

Stage Two.   In this phase, edit your rough draft to make it better. Try to:

- Delete unnecessary words and phrases
- Adjust the copy to the exact word length the specs call for
- Rewrite awkward phrases
- Make sure all necessary facts are included
- Reorder copy points to make the organization more logical
- Make copy conform to catalog format and style, adding tables, call-outs, charts, or special sections as needed
- Rewrite to fit the overall "tone" of the catalog

Stage Three.   Polish your copy. Proofread it, checking for errors in spelling, punctuation, grammar, capitalization, or abbreviations. (The word processor's Spell Check program is essential at this step.) Don't forget to check details such as patent numbers, product numbers, product specifications, registration marks, trademarks, and technical accuracy.

The "User-Friendly" Approach to Copy

The user-friendly approach uses copy to *inform the customer* so he or she knows enough about the product to order it.

Some of the most successful examples of product copy in the mail order business are found in The Sharper Image. Each piece of copy in its catalog is like a finely tuned machine operating specifically to inform and sell the customer. Each is an authoritative dissertation that easily engages customers' attention and supplies them with information.

Space age crossbow fits in your hand.

The most powerful crossbow pistol ever made, Magnum Force Trident sends its arrows (called bolts) at speeds up to 45 miles per hour. It's accurate up to 60 feet and penetration at close range is amazing. At 25 feet, our bolts went through the Yellow Pages to page 339.

Frame is heavy gauge die-cast aluminum. Contoured hard plastic grips. The laminated fiberglass bow is strung with 45 lbs. of tension. Aluminum bolts are perfectly balanced for pistol shooting. Weighs 24 oz. 18" long with a 16" bow span. Safety mechanism locks with a flick of a thumb.

Use the precision micro-adjustable sights or the 1.5 × 15 power scope (optional). Comes with two target bolts. Package of 5 more bolts available below. *Target bolts should under no circumstances be used for hunting.* (Game arrows are available directly from Barnett.) One year warranty.

Trident is the newest design from Barnett, the world's largest crossbow-maker (featured in the James Bond film "For Your Eyes Only"). Trident is easy, accurate, and completely free of "kick." Test-fire yours with the security of our 30 day home trial. *Must be 18 or older to purchase.*
• Trident Crossbow #ZBN544 $99 (5.50)
• 1.5 × 15 Scope #ZBN546 $69 (2.50)
• Set of 5 Arrows #ZBN545 $9.75 (1.00)

A15

Figure 6.1   The Sharper Image catalog

Figure 6.1 shows an outstanding example of copy that *informs* the customer about the product, *validates* the product and its benefits, and *builds strong credibility.* This particular example even calls attention to product dangers and legal ordering requirements and does so in a way that strengthens product credibility.

This "user-friendly" formula can be applied to almost any catalog copy:

1. Identify the product by name and/or benefit. (In this example, the product is identified and a benefit is announced immediately with a few short, well-chosen words.)

2. Establish product credibility. (Performance test results do this capably.)

3. Give product specifications concerning the material of which it's made, its components, size, etc. (This example supplies exacting specifications.)

4. Build in authority if possible. (The vital caution information and the product warranty make product validity very strong and eases the customer's mind about placing an order. Credibility is highlighted by associating the product with a James Bond film.)

5. Encourage the customer to buy. (A confidence-building guarantee, "30-day home trial," subtly commands the customer to buy.)

This outline shows the general style used for every single piece of copy in the entire catalog. It is a successful format that makes customers want to read—and thoroughly informs them as they do.

A catalog which is almost completely opposite in appeal would seem to need a completely different copy approach (**Figure 6.2**). This copy illustration is from Annie's Attic, a friendly catalog appealing mostly to women from middle America interested in needlework. But, really, how different is their basic copy approach? Not very:

1. The headline *identifies* the product, announcing a *benefit* ("Luscious").

2. *Credibility* is established through a friendly, colloquial description that unveils the true product use.

3. Specific *method of using* the product is given, along with the *material* of which it's made.

4. The ending features a friendly command to buy.

Entertain!

LUSCIOUS FRUIT POTHOLDERS™

IT'S A BUMPER CROP! What an appealing batch of colorful fruit! And, believe it or not, they're really potholders that make a beautiful decorative table centerpiece. Or hang them as singles anywhere. Each luscious fruit is designed to open in back for gripping handles, lids, etc. Each is realistic in size and detail and made from washable acrylic yarn. Simple to crochet from detailed instructions and diagrams. Harvest this collection—they're ripe for the pickin'! Strawberries, Watermelon, Banana, Grapes, Pineapple, Lemon/Lime, Orange and Apple, only **$1.50** each or **all 8 for only $6.60.** Kits only **$3.89** each or **all 8 for only $21.95.**

Figure 6.2   Annie's Attic catalog

Both of these catalog companies inform their customers through a copy approach that fits their individual customer profile. With The Sharper Image this is a macho, fairly affluent 30- to 45-year-old male. With Annie's Attic the profile is a salt-of-the-earth but young-at-heart female, 35 to 50 years old, from the "heartland" of America.

The "User-Friendly" Formula

1. *Identify the product* by name and/or benefit.

2. Establish product *credibility*.

3. Give product *specifications* concerning the material of which it's made, its components, size, etc.

4. Build in *authority* if you can.

5. *Encourage the customer to buy.*

Above all—inform the customer!

The Elements of Good Copy

Good copywriting stresses benefits, not features.

Features do not move people; it is what those features can achieve—their benefits—that make the sale. Only by translating the features of your products into the human benefits they deliver can you create a selling motivation that is almost guaranteed not to fail.

Don't tell facts, sell benefits. A fact is not a benefit. Create a sense of fantasy and desire about the product as you convey facts. Imagine a storyline about the product. Talk about why it was chosen to grace the pages of your catalog. Describe the unique problem it solved. To catalyze yourself to think up benefits, ask yourself why anyone would want your product. Draw up a checklist of benefits that come to mind, and structure your copy around them.

Good copy is not necessarily short or long. Although some people believe copy should be stripped to the bare bones, it takes more than three lines to inform the customer about benefits, attributes, basic specifications, and materials, *and* make the customer want to buy. Some products, especially complex ones, may require a great deal of explaining.

Let's take a look at how nine lines of copy can say it better than twelve. In the following examples, copy A is packed with unnecessary words that only discourage the customer from reading. Copy B, although shorter, says everything necessary and says it better. Notice how headline B immediately draws attention by announcing the product benefit.

Copy "A": BRIGHT, CLOSE-UP VIEWS WITH THE ILLUMINATING 30X MAGNIFIER. This convenient pocket magnifier is designed to be a valued companion for work, hobby or recreation. Its diminutive size ($5^1/_2$ × $1^3/_4$ × $3/_4$") allows it to slip easily into pocket or purse; its 30X makes it ideal for detailed examination of plants, gems, stamps, photos. It features a center focus wheel for precise one-hand operation; retractable condenser lens pinpoints light so you can zero in on your subject. Light source is built in; batteries not included. A really handy tool. 30X MAGNIFIER NO. 31,291 $12.95

Copy "B": ILLUMINATING 30X MAGNIFIER IS POCKET-SIZED. Ideal for a detailed inspection of plants, gems, stamps or photos. It features a center focus wheel for precise one-hand operation, a retractable condenser lens to pinpoint light and a built-in light source. Batteries not included. $5^1/_2$ × $1^3/_4$ × $3/_4$". 30X MAGNIFIER No. 31,291 $12.95

A good guideline for writing strong, solid, tight copy is to first write as much as you like. Imagine you have twice the space the artist has given you. Then edit. Take a pencil and remove all the "that's." Next, remove any non-selling statements. Next, double check to see if you included (or the photography makes clear) all necessary facts: color, size, weight, function, use, etc. And last but not least—*avoid words beyond the reader's reading level.* Now, rewrite. Finally, repeat the above steps. Look at what you have left. You'll have reduced the copy by half and ended up saying everything necessary. So don't worry about the length of your copy. Instead, worry about *what it says* and *how well it sells.*

Another good way to approach writing catalog copy is to *write copy to solve reader problems.* Your customer doesn't realize it, but actually he or she thinks: "If the catalog copy identifies my major personal or on-the-job problems, it has a better chance of convincing me to buy."

Before writing, review target mailing lists so you can *identify clusters of names for similar life or job problems.* Then make a *Problem Checklist,* and next to each situation note how the particular product or service you're promoting will solve the problems.

You might accumulate the following list in an attempt to sell a special watch to a target group of entrepreneurial managers:

Product Copy

One key thing to keep in mind is making the catalog enjoyable for the reader. Make it logical, visually appealing, and make the copy interesting. The longer you keep them in the "store" the more likely they are to buy.

Patrick D. Smith, Jr.
Production Manager
California Polytechnic
University

PROBLEMS:	SOLUTIONS:
■ Managers work late, have difficulty waking each day.	■ You can set multiple wake-up alarms with this watch.
■ They must budget their time for each job they tackle.	■ You get an hourly chime to keep you on schedule.
■ They must know how long each job took.	■ Because this watch functions as a stopwatch, you can time your productivity.

Notice that the "solution" copy did not state the problem. Rather, when you identify the problem, you should be able to create copy that implies the solution. Allow the readers to *read in* what their problem may be. You state the solution.

Also notice that in each solution example, the copy is presented with *clear reader benefits*. "Hourly chime" is insufficient. "Hourly chime to keep you on schedule" tells prospective purchasers why the chime is important and what it can do for them. The concept is *identify a problem; then write copy that lets the reader see how your product or service solves that problem.* This concept works for every audience, product, or service. By examining your lists before writing, you can find the readers' problems. But in doing this, you'll be flustered when you discover different clusters of readers who have different problems. Then your problem will be how to include all salient points for each cluster.

Solve problems

Your solution is easy: *write more than one benefit* for each product or service feature. Now your copy might read:

Soft hourly chime, which only you can hear, keeps you on schedule, and you can switch it to alert you at half-hour intervals, quarter-hour periods, or any minute in any hour.

Give solutions

Now you can see how problem-solving benefit copy appeals to more segments of your list audience.

Good copy says just enough, and no more. Telling your customers more than they want to know is an easy trap to fall into. Worse yet is telling them things that are interesting only to you, not them.

Good copy *does* use exciting words for products that might otherwise seem boring. To find better words, put yourself in the reader's shoes. Say you're selling pipefitting tools to plumbers. You don't find anything exciting about these tools, but plumbers do. Pretend you are a plumber, and ask yourself detailed questions about how the product will help you.

- Which problems will the tool solve?

- How will it cut my workload?

- Does it fit in my tool kit?

- Can I make more money with it?

- Can it be used in combination with my other tools?

- What accessories does it have?

- How will the product make my life easier?

- What can I do with the extra time I'll have due to the new tool's performance?

Add your answers to these questions to your checklist of benefits the plumber will find exciting. Just write your copy to address those benefits, and you'll automatically use more exciting words. Always put yourself in the position of the product user in order to write exciting copy. (And don't forget to *try* the product!)

Good copy uses colorful, descriptive language. Product specs and tech-talk don't move buyers to action. Persuasive language does. If its' colorful and descriptive, it paints a picture of what the product can do for each customer. For example:

Tech-talk:	**Persuasive language:**
"The XYZ mixer is devoid of pinch-points or dead spots where viscous material might accumulate."	"Our mixer is free of sharp edges, nooks, and crannies where gunk might get stuck and clog up your pipeline."

Good copy uses precise language. Beware of language that is either overly colloquial or general. You want your writing to be conversational enough to win the reader over, but not so vague that it doesn't communicate your meaning.

Good copy has a seasonal flavor. Christmas copy sounds like Christmas, Easter copy sounds like Easter, and winter is so aptly described that the copy makes you feel the chill—even though the copywriter may have written the copy camped in a chaise lounge by the ocean. Adding seasonal flavor always boost sales. You'll sell more down jackets if you can convey an impression of winter in your copy.

Above all, good copy is enthusiastic about the product and remembers the customer by giving complete and accurate information. Everything you can do to make your message clearer will be reflected in your bottom line.

Should copy be humorous?

For decades copy experts such as Claude Hopkins and John Caples strongly advised against writing humorous copy. While it is safest to avoid humor in catalog copy, humor can sell. A light, humorous touch can add an element of humanity that engages and involves the reader.

In general, use humor if—and only if:

1. You use it to reinforce and support your basic premise.

2. You use it to be friendly, not funny.

3. You use it to attract, not to distract.

4. You *never* lose sight of what you're really doing—selling.

5. Your humor is appropriate to your product line and your catalog's particular tone or style.

A Few Words about Truth

In your eagerness to create copy that sells, it is natural to want to describe every product in the most glowing terms you can devise. *Be careful.* Readers search your copy to find points with which they can disagree, unbelievable points, or obviously false claims. When they find those stretched truths, they don't buy. If your claims are so extravagant that an unsuspecting reader is convinced, buys, and then is disappointed because the product didn't live up to your claims, refund requests go up.

School yourself with this credo: you are creating copy to get long-term customers who will try you once, like you, and then have faith that they can continue to deal with you. That means writing copy that is *true.*

Victoria's Secret very skillfully combines both the essential facts (which a customer needs to make a buying decision) and the beautiful benefits (enthusiastically expressed) received by purchasing the product—and disciplines itself into never overwhelming or overstating. Its copy might tell the reader to "slip into another world where nights are glamorous and romance is in the air." It might say the gown is "bias-cut to flatter your figure" or that the fashions are "sensuous." But it does not say that your figure will look magnificent in the gown or that you will be sensuous. It merely implies—and does so in a gentle and genteel manner—and consequently remains credible in the mind of the customer.

Of course, your copy may be 100 percent truthful—but the reader's perception of your wording may lead to an impression of falsity or exaggeration. This problem is licked by switching to short words and phrases, often in a staccato presentation minus complete sentences.

Example:
From the very first moment that you start using this handsome executive calendar, you'll discover how marvelous it is to have the ultimate convenience of high-lighted, easily-accessed, color-coded separate sections for important appointments, personal notations, expense memorandums, things-to-do listings, and staff schedules. And it's all yours in a modern, spring-loaded loose-leaf binder so you can insert special company memos at key reminder dates.

Edited:
Instant ring-binder convenience is yours. Add memos at key dates. Use color-coded separate sections for appointments, personal notes, expenses, reminders, schedules. Modern. Handsome, executive styling.

The edited version contains every sales point from the longer version but is less argumentative, and the staccato copy implies enthusiasm—a much more convincing approach than using enthusiastic wording.

---

10 Tips for Truthful Copy

1. Do not use the word *best* for every item.

2. Avoid superlatives when possible.

3. Avoid strings of adjectives.

4. Do not exaggerate . . . eliminate puffery.

5. Avoid imprecise copy.

6. Do not mislead to get a sale.

7. Do not use subtleties or nuances that may not be understood quickly by fast readers.

8. Avoid disorganized copy that confuses the reader.

9. Do not overly stress the legitimacy of your company.

10. Avoid excessive enthusiasm.

How to Use the Five Copy Styles

Selecting a copy style is important, because the tone of the copy should fit the character of your catalog and the market to which you are appealing. If your customer reacts favorably to a bare-facts approach, then that is what you will want to use. However, most customers appreciate copy that is friendlier, more informative. Some customer groups want and need to know in detail about the product or product category being offered.

There are five successful copy styles:

1. **Conversational,** the friendly approach that suggests familiarity—even to the point of being vernacular—to fit the products being offered.

2. **General category,** where one copy presentation explains and provides information pertaining to a group of related products, allowing shorter copy for individual products.

3. **Involved,** in which copy will go into the aspects of the product more deeply than normal. Benefits and attributes are fully explained.

4. **Bare facts,** where copy is short and crisp, relating the minimal amount of information. This approach relies heavily on the knowledge or familiarity of the customer.

5. **Benefit highlighting,** when a single product has several benefits that need to be highlighted.

Conversational Copy

Eddie Bauer is a master at conversational copy that exudes authority, builds credibility, and informs the customer in a friendly way. And it is done in a convincing manner, selling with every word. **Figure 6.3** shows how well the copy is done. After the product-identifying headline, the copy states the main product benefit (attractive wearability), which is further explained in the second sentence. The next three sentences artfully explain the many product attributes such as epaulets, pockets, cuffs. However, what makes these attributes special is the manner in which they are described: *functional* shoulder epaulets, *expandable* cargo pockets with *security* flaps and *buttoned* cuffs. This is wonderful descriptive writing that is *selling copy!*

The copy block ends with a terrific credibility builder: "We have sold these fine jackets to big-name sportsmen, television correspondents, diplomats and many others who, like you, require comfortable sportswear with definitive style." That is almost a celebrity testimonial. It is convincing, informative first-person copy that sells! Specific product specifications are given in brief but complete form, handily above the identifying number and pricing. The conversational style in first person reads well, encouraging the customer to order.

Moore Business Center sells modular furniture in much the same conversational way. An easy, businesslike conversational copy style tells you about the product being offered. **Figure 6.4** shows how the headline immediately identifies the product and the product benefits. The second paragraph tells about product attributes, ending with a credibility-building sentence reinforced with a problem-solving statement. The conversational tone is achieved by letting the customer know that "The Modular Concept isn't new, but Marvel has executed the concept with flair . . ." and that "Those advantages wouldn't matter very much, however, without durability." This approach has promoted believability in a friendly manner, yet on a business level.

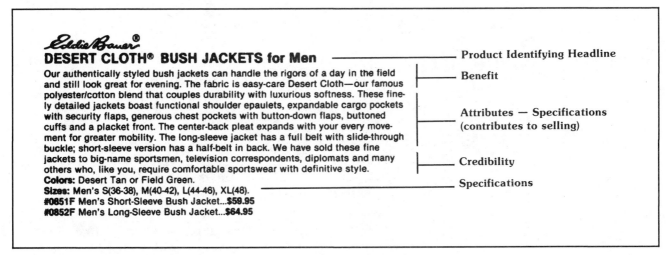

Figure 6.3   Eddie Bauer catalog

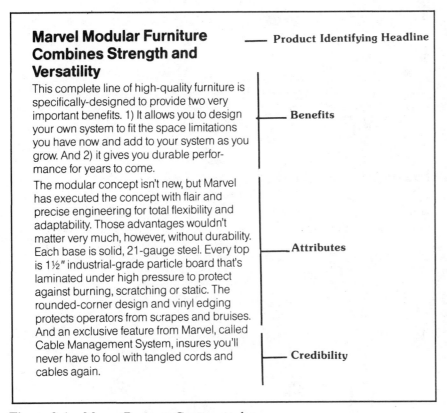

Figure 6.4   Moore Business Center catalog

General Category

L.H. Selman Ltd. produces a Collectors' Paperweights catalog that is also a price guide for collectors and dealers. The products, collectors' paperweights, are classified into two categories (Contemporary and Antique) and then broken down within these categories by individual artisans and studio artists.

It is very important that the market to which Selman appeals be informed of many aspects not normally utilized in more common product lines.

Figure 6.5 is one of the two introductory pages for the Contemporary paperweights being offered in this catalog. An explanation of Contemporary paperweight production is given, plus the note of excitement in the recreation of nearly lost techniques and the "renaissance" of new designers whose fancy has been taken by this 200-year-old art form. Note the interest created by providing a photograph showing a stage of actual production, telling us that these are genuine techniques and skills recovered and newly dedicated to this art form. Elements such as these are very important to collectors. The more they know and understand about production, artists, and the history of skills, the more legitimate the offer appears. Allotting space to this subject is making use of a subtle selling tool. And the ease with which the art and copy can be referenced is a customer plus.

Figure 6.6 is an example of the pages preceding the presentation of actual paperweights by father and son artist contributors, Ray and Bob Banford. The introduction tells when they started making paperweights, the style they produce, where their work has been displayed, and how their work is signed (so that authenticity can be established). Background information on how each became interested in this type of work is given, too. The writing style throughout the catalog is casual and personal, and yet it also seems disciplined and reliable—just the right combination to make customers feel at ease, inform them, and let them know this is information that can be trusted. The style and manner in which this education is approached is that of a friendly professor holding class on the lawn at a college campus. The introduction on the Banford artist team says, "Ray's interest in glass began . . ."; with others there is information such as "surrounded by Debbie's rose garden and Del's vegetable garden . . ." and a gentle suggestion of service: "We look forward to helping you, too, build an outstanding collection." This copy informs and introduces 12 different products.

The actual product copy is always short, briefly stating attributes of design and color. The headline consists of the catalog number and the artist's name. A typical product copy block is: "25. BOB BANFORD. A brilliant, well-designed lampwork bouquet centers around a traditional purple and yellow pansy in this stunning weight set on a clear waffle-cut base. Signed with a 'B' cane at the base of stems. $1440." This softly informative copy is all that is needed because of the prior copy concerning the classification and artist.

Create interest

Copy Copy

If space permits, a brief description of product background and suggested use make for interesting reading and may increase sales.

Frank Merritt

Colonial Williamsburg
Foundation
Williamsburg, VA

CONTEMPORARY FACTORIES AND STUDIO ARTISTS

Arranging lampwork petals on a template.

In the 1950s, Paul Jokelson, an importer and avid paperweight enthusiast, approached the glass factories of Baccarat and Saint Louis and urged them to revive the classic art of paperweight production.

Paperweights had not been produced in significant numbers for more than 80 years, and glass artisans at the two factories were faced with the difficult and challenging task of rediscovering the almost lost techniques of paperweight making. Once they succeeded, interest in the contemporary weights led to further production and experimentation.

Since then, a number of glass factories have joined Baccarat and Saint Louis in producing modern paperweights. Cristal D'Albret of France, "J" Glass, Perthshire and Caithness of Scotland, and others utilize traditional techniques and classical motifs while exploring exciting new possibilities in design and technology.

With the renewed interest in paperweights, a number of individual glass workers have also been encouraged to experiment with designs and techniques and produce paperweights on their own.

8   COLLECTORS' PAPERWEIGHTS

6-33

Figure 6.5   L.H. Selman Ltd. Collectors' Paperweights catalog

RAY AND BOB BANFORD

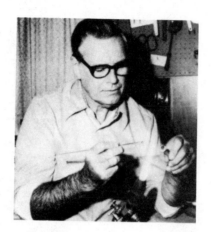

Glass artists Ray and Bob Banford, father and son, have been making French-style paperweights since 1971. The two, who share a workshop behind their home in Hammonton, New Jersey, draw upon each other's expertise but work independently, creating their own designs and functioning as individual craftsmen.

Ray's interest in glass began when he and his wife visited the Corning Museum of Glass and the workshop of an elderly Czechoslovakian glassmaker, Adolph Macho. Ray became fascinated with glass and the glassmaking process, and when Adolph Macho retired, he bought the glassmaker's equipment and began a new career. In addition to paperweights, Ray creates glass buttons and pendants and tends to the business of his and Bob's production.

Bob's glass career began when he received a torch from his parents as a high school graduation gift. With it he began experimenting, first by making ships and carousels of spun glass, then with the challenge of lampwork and paperweight production. Bob's complex lampwork motifs, which include flowers, insects, and reptiles, are realistic and consistently well-designed. His work is displayed at Wheaton Village, the Corning Museum of Glass, and the Smithsonian Institution.

Bob signs his weights with a red, white, and blue "B" initial cane. Ray uses the same initial cane, but in black and white.

20   COLLECTORS' PAPERWEIGHTS

Figure 6.6   Collectors' Paperweights catalog

Day-Timer takes one full page to illustrate and inform the customer of the types of Day-Timer systems that appear in the catalog (**Figure 6.7**). Under the benefit head, "Pick the System That's Right for You," four categories of Day-Timers are depicted, each one the solution to someone's time management problems. By answering the questions surrounding the photos, the consumer can quickly determine which of the myriad Day-Timer systems best meets his or her needs.

Copy does not need to dwell on the virtues of using a Day-Timer system to manage one's time, because the provocative questions themselves elicit benefits—simple systems for keeping track of people and projects or meetings and appointments. The pages that follow hone in on individual product benefits, information, and specifications.

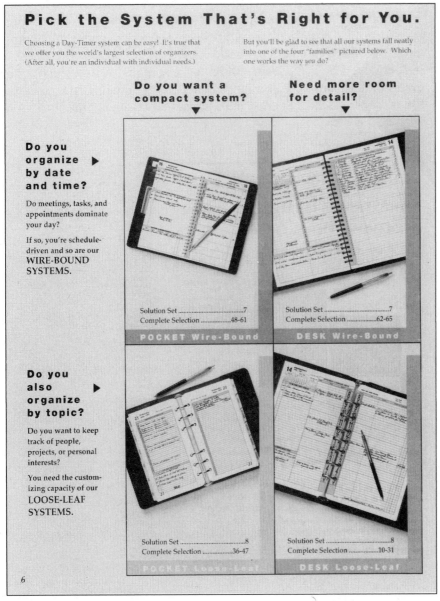

Figure 6.7 Day-Timer catalog

Involved Copy

Figure 6.8 from the now-defunct Early Winters catalog is an outstanding example of the involved copy approach. This fine example of "tight" copy leaves nothing to the customer's imagination except the joy of ownership.

The headline identifies the product, the benefit ("neat, light, convertible"), and makes a promise: "does it all." By suggesting product use in the first paragraph, the body copy tells the customer why this Fanny Pack is much more versatile than other packs. The next four paragraphs describe at length the product makeup, benefits, and attributes. Not a detail is missed, because this type of information is vital to the prospective buyer, who wants to know every bit of information pertaining to the product's function and the customer's agility wearing it.

Phrases like "Buckle on our Expedition Fanny Pack . . . Two zippers transform . . . a pair of wing pockets keep your snacks and map at hand . . ." help the reader practically try on the pack without leaving the catalog! The last paragraph invites the reader to test the product, gives comparisons with similar products, and manages to suggest that the reader is discerning enough to participate in the great outdoor adventure.

Fanny sack to daypack, our neat, light convertible does it all.

Buckle on our Expedition Fanny Pack and you're ready for ski tour, day hike, or summit assault.

Two zippers transform this 650-cu.-in. fanny pack into a *2050-cu.-in.* hip-suspension pack, with adjustable shoulder straps and a pouch roomy enough to hold a sleeping bag!

Made of Weatherlite,™ a strong, waterproof nylon ripstop, the Fanny Pack has a main pouch & deck pocket that hold a day's supplies.

A pair of wing pockets keep your snacks and map at hand. Two bottle pockets detach for quick refreshment. Pull up the zippered top pack to store layers as you shed them.

A Technolite™ urethane/foam internal frame molds to your back and keeps the load solidly and comfortably on your hips.

Abrasion-resistant nylon ballistics cloth against your back takes the rub with less wear. Seams are bound and reinforced at stress points for years of use.

Order your Expedition Fanny Pack. Test it and see if this 18-oz. "convertible" doesn't admirably fill the gap between mere fanny pack and full-bore backpack.
Fits waists 28-43"

Expedition Fanny Pack, No. 2131 . . . $74.95

Figure 6.8   Early Winters catalog

In the hands of this copywriter, every pocket and cranny of the fanny pack fills a need for the expert hiker. This copy gives information and makes the sale even as it retains a wonderful, invitingly casual writing approach—an ideal for any involved copy!

In **Figure 6.9,** Day-Timer uses an involved copy approach for its most popular planner, the 2-page-per-day calendar. Two full pages are devoted to copy and illustrations, and they work hand in hand. The product-identifying headline spans two pages at the top of the presentation. The major benefit ("The 2-Page-Per-day Regular Edition offers the Day-Timer 5-in-1 System with Maximum Space for Keeping a Detailed Record of Your Day . . .") lets the busy individual know that there is plenty of room to track even the fullest days.

The copy then expands on the five functions that make up this benefit. Each is explained and identified by number for easy visual reference. Needed specifications are given about size, extra sheets, and a seven-ring binder sold on other pages. End-use benefits such as "Ideal for Working at Your Desk . . . indispensable for planning . . . easy to carry" are all what a busy person needs and wants.

These 46 lines of copy are devoted to functional information that is beneficial for the customer to know and essential for the ultimate close of the sale. In this successful involved copy, Day-Timer assures the customer that its product will organize even the busiest day.

Bare Facts Copy

The OshKosh B'Gosh catalog sells the same sturdy children's clothes it distributes through retail stores. Presumably because OshKosh B'Gosh clothes are so well known and well thought of, its catalog product copy leaves out the flourishes and focuses on the bare facts. (Every product is illustrated, though, with appealing shots of toddlers and young children.) The headline in **Figure 6.10** identifies the product ("Red T-Shirt"), while the body copy identifies attributes (100% cotton jersey, OshKosh logo on sleeve), sizes, and price. This bare-bones copy gives the customer all the information needed to make a decision. Little else is included because OshKosh feels the quality of its product is a given to the parents purchasing from the catalog.

Harneds' catalog reaches the butcher supply market. Because its audience is so narrow and the application of its products so specific, the catalog copy can be especially short, containing only the minimal facts, as this example shows.

Chicken Dolly

Heavy duty, chrome plated, tubular steel construction. Poly drip pan slides out for easy cleaning. Four swivel casters, 22-1/2" W × 28-1/2" L. 13" H. 849–1015. Chicken dolly complete, ship wgt 34 lbs.—$101.51

Product Identifying Headline

Desk Day-Timer® System

Major Benefit

Benefit Components

The 2-Page-Per-Day Regular Edition Offers the Day-Timer 5-in-1 System with Maximum Space for Keeping a Detailed Record of Your Day...

With this edition, each day of the week is covered on two full pages, so you have plenty of space for scheduling your appointments and planning your day for maximum effectiveness... then recording your results as your day progresses.

This edition offers Day-Timers' five functions in one as described below, with the location of each of these functions numbered 1 thru 5 on the Day-Timer sample page shown here.

These Five Functions Include...

① **APPOINTMENTS** Hours range from 8 am to 6 pm with four lines per hour, so there's plenty of space for entering all your daily appointments.

② **TO BE DONE TODAY** Use this section to keep a running list of items to be done. Check off items as completed. Reassign unfinished tasks to future dates.

③ **TICKLER REMINDER** Use this same section to enter any items that may require some review or follow-up in the future. List the items on the day action will be taken.

④ **DIARY RECORD** Hours range from 8 am to 6 pm with four lines per hour. This becomes your permanent record of work accomplished during the day. It's a great progress checker.

⑤ **EXPENSE RECORD** This section is combined with the Diary Record, so your expenses are tied-in directly with your daily activities. Can also be used for time-billing.

This edition is available in two sizes: Sr. Size with 8½" x 11" pages, or Jr. Size with 5½" x 8½" pages.

Twelve tabbed monthly calendar sheets help you quickly find the current date.

This full-year loose-leaf edition will fit in a Day-Timer 7-ring binder with 1½" ring size, however other ring sizes are available to suit individual needs. See our complete binder selection on pages 32 and 33.

28 DAY-TIMERS, Inc., Allentown, PA 18001

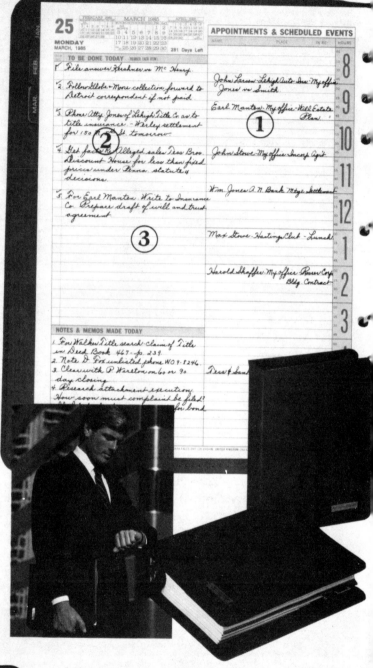

Quantity Discounts: 2-6 units, 5%; 7-12, 7%; 13-25, 10%; 26-50, 12%; 51 or more, 15%.
Orders for all Day-Timer Fillers that are identified by a closed star (★) may be combined for

Figure 6.9 Day-Timer Catalog

2-Page-Per-Day Regular Edition

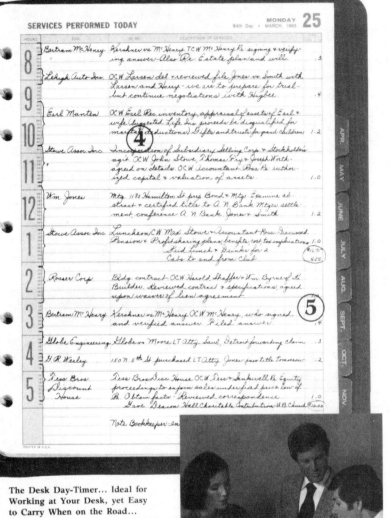

Functional Information

The 2-Page-Per-Day Regular Edition Desk Day-Timer... Our Most Popular Desk Diary!

This is the original Desk Day-Timer... preferred by most busy desk-oriented executives who normally work regular business hours and need maximum space for detailed records. In this 2-Page-Per-Day edition, the left page tells what you must do, while the right page becomes a permanent record of all your activities and work accomplished.

Regular daily coverage is from 8 am until 6 pm, with reduced space for evening hours. Hours for Saturdays are from 8 am until noon, plus ten additional line spaces. Sundays have open hours only, with 16 line spaces. There are four line spaces per hour, with the hourly column notched every tenth of an hour for keeping a decimal time record.

This 2-Page-Per-Day loose-leaf edition is available in two page sizes. Choose Sr. Size with 8½" x 11" pages, or Jr. Size with 5½" x 8½" pages. The full-year edition is designed to fit in a Day-Timer 7-ring binder with 1½" ring size. However, depending on your personal needs, you may prefer to carry only a partial year's supply of pages in either a 1" or ½" 7-ring binder.

As with all Day-Timer loose-leaf editions, you also receive...

- 12 Monthly Calendar/Divider Pages
- Address and Phone Directory
- 6-Year Planning Pages
- 12 Monthly Expense Record Pages
- Extra Pages for Notes and Memos

This edition can start with any month, and includes a full-year set of pages. Specify starting month and year when ordering. Filler pages thru Dec. 31, 1986 are currently available. Prices shown below are for Desk Day-Timer filler pages only. See pages 32 and 33 to order a Day-Timer binder to hold your filler pages.

Sr. Desk 2-Pg-Day Fillers - Regular
#G94010★ $14.95
Jr. Desk 2-Pg-Day Fillers - Regular
#G92010★ $11.95

The Desk Day-Timer... Ideal for Working at Your Desk, yet Easy to Carry When on the Road...

The Desk Day-Timer makes a beautiful desk accessory, indispensable for planning your busy day, yet easy to carry to meetings and on business trips.

When presented in one of our deluxe 7-ring leather binders, it makes an elegant "Gift of Success"... one that can help anyone to become more effective in managing all their daily activities.

And, when personalized with name or initials on the front cover, it becomes a very special gift for your friends and business associates.

End Use Benefits and Attributes

quantity discounts. All accessory items, identified with an open star (☆), that are ordered at the same time will receive this same quantity discount.

Figure 6.10   OshKosh B'Gosh catalog

Benefit-Highlighting Copy

Figure 6.11 from an old Sharper Image catalog shows how benefit-highlighting copy can acclaim several benefits offered by a single product. Here, the overall benefit ("Ride in the lap of luxury") becomes the headline, while the paragraph that follows backs up the luxury claim by telling why sheepskin wool "has become the *ultimate* material for high-quality car and airplane seat covers." The careful word-smithing used to describe sheepskin's desirability builds credibility for the product.

Ride in the lap of luxury.

From the steepest alpine crags where the ice never melts, to the hot, arid outback of Australia, sheep thrive in some of the most brutal climates in the world. Sheepskin wool is nature's own perfect temperature regulator—the one material that can keep you cool through a long, hot summer and warm in the middle of winter. Which is why sheepskin wool has become the *ultimate* material for high-quality car and airplane seat covers.

The finest pelts for the softest covers.

One company—RamsHead—is known for seat covers of unparalleled softness, fit and construction. Run your fingers through one of these covers, and enjoy the plush feeling of pure, silken wool against your skin. RamsHead works with only the prime, 2–3" thick Australian pelts—the softest, finest wool in the world. Each pelt is combed and sheared numerous times, to an even 1" depth of fleece—a luxurious cushioning between you and your car seat.

On humid summer days, RamsHead seat covers absorb *up to 30%* of their own weight in moisture—without feeling wet. You're protected from scorching seats and your clothes stay fresher, less wrinkled. In winter, snuggle into the warmth of 1" deep pile, instead of icy cold vinyl or leather.

Custom made to order for years of perfect fit.

RamsHead earned its reputation custom-fitting covers for cars like Rolls Royce, Jaguar, and Lamborghini. Now, with a repertoire of over *1500 different seat patterns*, RamsHead can fit virtually any make or model of automobile, truck, RV—even airplane (see chart).

Every RamsHead cover is designed and fashioned with the same precision and workmanship as a fine sheepskin coat. Pelts are matched, then sewn with industrial nylon thread which won't fray or break like cotton thread. Every edge is then finished with the heaviest stretch binding available, so your seat covers stay firmly in place with no wrinkles or bunching. The snug, full fit looks as good from the back as from the front. And because RamsHead uses only the largest, prime pelts available there are fewer stress points than other covers—for improved strength and durability.

RamsHead even replaces the naturally soil-repellant lan-

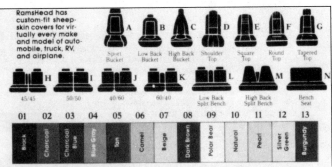

stains are easily removed, and your sheepskin only gets softer after each cleaning.

Colors to match any interior.

Select the cover designed and hand-made especially for your car, then choose from 13 rich colors (see chart). RamsHead uses an advanced chrome tanning process, so every color stays fast—as vivid after years of use as on the day you first sink down into it. And every cover is backed up by a *3 year warranty*.

You spend countless hours in your car. Experience what a difference 1" of soft, silken RamsHead sheepskin can make to your driving comfort. Originally created for sports and luxury cars—the finest sheepskin seat covers you can buy are also surprisingly affordable. Order your own custom seat covers now, and turn your next commute into a pleasurable excursion. *How to order:* Please specify seat style and color (from charts, above) and the make, model and year of your vehicle. Custom fitting requires 4–6 weeks for delivery.

• Pair of Seatcovers #URS493 $370 (12.50)
• Pair of Headrest Covers #URS700 $95 (4.50)
• Car Wash Mitt #URS600 $15 (3.50)

With every order receive a Rams Head sheepskin wool wash mitt ($15 value) for a no-scratch professional car washing and polishing.

Figure 6.11   Sharper Image catalog

Boldface subheads call the customer's attention to three different benefits, each one fully explained in copy that follows. Not by coincidence, these three benefits happen to be the ones that matter most to the type of customer to whom this product appeals.

The Rand McNally catalog shown in **Figure 6.12** highlights benefits in bulleted copy that quickly conveys three benefits that can be derived from three product features. Each bulleted item introduces a main benefit first ("Find answers to city/county questions *fast!*" and then identifies the feature that delivers it. This approach leaves no guesswork as to what the product does and why the customer should buy it. Only brief explanatory copy is needed to make the sale with this type of copy approach.

Rand McNally
1990 CITY/COUNTY FINDER *NEW!*
20141-7   UPC 70609 16358 $14.95
624 Pages   Paperback   6 × 9¼″

The tables and indexes in this authoritative reference provide information on every U.S. county and every city of 100 or more population – a total of 45,000 places! Especially helpful for businesses with offices, plants, or customers in multiple locations who need ready access to city/county data.

- **Find answers to city/county questions** *fast!* The Finder's three indexes allow you to look up information by state, by county, or by city.
- **Quickly identify the county seat, FIPS County Code, and principal city for every county** using index of counties by state.
- **Match any U.S. city with its corresponding county** using index of cities by state.

Figure 6.12   Rand McNally catalog. (Products shown may not be available.)

Make Room for Customer Education

Educating the customer is a never-ending job that can pay off in added catalog profits. The more difficult the product is to sell, the greater the payoff that comes from educating the customer.

To educate the customer, you may talk about the way the product is manufactured, or mention the material from which it is made—especially if it performs a special function, or is the main benefit of the product. You might also talk about how to identify and use a specialized product such as fasteners and wood screws, or describe the proper way to care for areas with special problems, such as a septic tank.

There are two ways to approach product education:

1. Education presented within the product body copy.

2. Education highlighted separately elsewhere in the catalog.

Education Presented within the Product Body Copy

One sure way to enliven dull copy is to educate customers while informing and selling them. Educating the customer will increase sales, because people are naturally inquisitive and respond when information is provided. Not everyone can write good educational copy, however. Find a writer who is up to the job, and allow enough space to let the writer adequately educate the customer.

The Eddie Bauer catalog contains very skilled educational copy. **Figure 6.13** is a portion of product copy about Fleece Seat Covers. Because Eddie Bauer customers expect to order items of the best, most efficient material, over half of the copy is devoted to education about

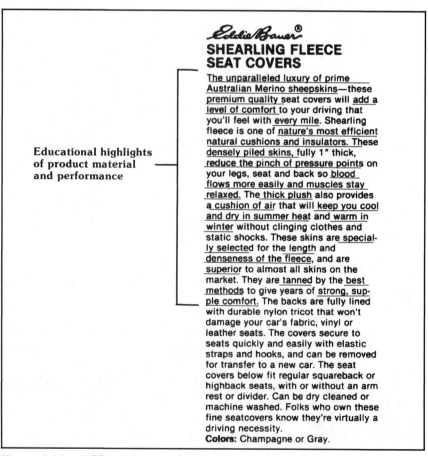

Figure 6.13   Eddie Bauer catalog

the performance of the sheepskin that composes the product. Thus, what sheepskin is and does is a prime selling point—well worth devoting the space to describe.

The copy in **Figure 6.14**, from a Lee Maynard catalog, devotes three quarters of its space to the history of "flint knapping" and the materials and technique that make up the Obsidian Dagger. This copywriter knows that customers can buy useful, high-quality knives anywhere. In this presentation, the product's history, crafting technique, and multiple presentation styles become a benefit that lifts the Obsidian Dagger out of the realm of mere knives and into the realm of museum-quality artifacts.

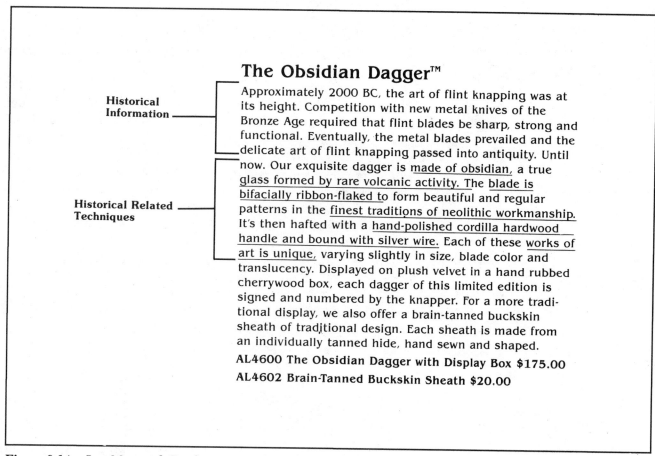

Figure 6.14   Lee Maynard Catalog

Education Separately Highlighted Within the Catalog

Another effective technique involves highlighting short educational facts in one-liners or bordered comments throughout the catalog. Some catalogs devote more copy to education, running sidebars, or actual articles on topics related to the products they feature. Short or long, these editorial entries add interest and help sell products.

Figure 6.15 from the Self Care catalog shows how sales of one category of products—hats—can be boosted with a short essay on skin cancer. By using a sidebar to point out both the dangers of not wearing a hat and benefits of wearing one, the individual product copy blocks are free to concentrate on the benefits of each individual model. Similarly, the Seventh Generation copy shown in Figure 6.16 educates the consumer about the need for vegetable-based cleaners—a helpful but strong way to add interest to the environmentally friendly cleaners sold on the facing pages.

Figure 6.17 shows a marvelous little education blurb that Burpee's seed catalog includes in four different places in its catalog. These few words educate the customer about seed planting while selling a product line and referring the customer to another part of the catalog. Burpee also uses a two-page chart to guide the customer in selecting plants of various heights for short borders, tall backgrounds, or rock gardens. Like many other garden and seed catalogs, it also helps customers determine the time of year to sow, and tells whether plants need sun or shade. The customer cannot help but feel that Burpee offers the easiest possible way to plant a garden. And this has been accomplished through product education, something not available with "rack" seeds.

Separate highlighting is nicely done in Hewlett-Packard's Computer User's Catalog (Figure 6.18). HP educates the customer on the cause and effect of static as a preamble to introducing its anti-static devices. The customer learns how electricity is generated and also learns about some common static-preventing features before being told that electromagnetic waves can still be generated and cause circuitry problems.

To substantiate this problem, "Static Facts" are featured in a bordered box. The solution—"prevent the damaging charge from reaching the equipment"—comes under the section headed "HP's answer to static." All of this customer education precedes a page and a half of static-preventing products. This "cause and effect" story is well-founded copy, designed to educate the customer into making a purchase.

Brown Deer Company devotes an entire page of its concentrated chemical catalog to septic tank care. Figure 6.19 shows how art and copy are combined to educate customers. This diagram shows how liquid passes through a septic tank system. Extensive copy explains this flow, identifies some typical problems, and explains how to prevent them. The opposite page is devoted to a product sold in the catalog that solves septic tank problems. Customer education continues on the next page, where related products are illustrated and sold.

DRI Industries's half-page Guide to Selection and Use of Fasteners skillfully educates the customer into buying. Figure 6.20 shows how various styles are identified with line drawings matched to copy describing appropriate use. This is an outstanding example of how educational copy can assist products that are difficult to sell. But this technique is still useful even in a simpler catalog. Nearly every product can benefit from product education!

Hats and the sun.

Here's one overwhelming fact: More than 80 percent of all skin cancers occur on the scalp, face, neck, and ears. It is very important to wear a hat for sun protection, even on overcast days when, surprisingly, up to 85 percent of the sun's UV rays can reach you through the clouds.

Figure 6.15   Self Care catalog

What's wrong with regular cleaners?

EPA studies show that air pollution inside many homes is far worse than outdoor pollution, because of fumes from common items like synthetic rugs and household cleaners! Not too surprising when you consider that many common cleaners contain ingredients like chlorine, ammonia, and synthetic solvents, which can pollute air and water during manufacture, use *and* disposal.

Are there other problems?

Yes. Many water treatment facilities are overloaded and sometimes release wastewater without treating it. Therefore, it's important to use cleaners that biodegrade quickly and are as gentle as possible on the environment.

Tell me about vegetable-based cleaners.

Before World War II, coconut oil was used in household detergents. When coconuts became difficult to import during the war, we switched to petroleum. While petroleum is a less expensive ingredient (by 25-40%), it takes a real toll on the environment. Cleaners made with renewable ingredients that biodegrade easily have a far lower impact on the environment.

How do I learn more?

To learn more about household chemicals, send $9.95 for *The Guide to Hazardous Products Around the Home* to:

Household Hazardous Waste
1031 E. Battlefield, Suite 214
Springfield, MO 65807

Figure 6.16   Seventh Generation catalog

Use **Burpee's Easy-Sow Straight-Row Seed Tapes.** Easier to plant, precisely spaced seeds reduce thinning, encourage uniform growth. (See page 76.)

Figure 6.17   Burpee Catalog

Anti-static accessories
Facts about static protection

If your work area contains electronic circuitry, such as computers and measurement devices, protection against damaging static electricity is a must. HP's static-control products come in a variety of shapes and sizes. To help you make the right choice, we have collected some important facts about static.

Cause and effect

Static electricity is generated when two different materials come into contact and then are separated. Common actions such as walking (shoes leaving floor), sitting (clothes rubbing against upholstery), and standing (clothes rubbing against the body), cause static energy buildup.

When you consider that modern electronic circuitry can operate using levels of 5 volts or less, you can easily see how static discharge through the circuitry can be extremely damaging. (For typical static buildup levels see box on right.)

Nature tends to balance itself. Just as hot and cold water blend to become lukewarm, static charges must become equalized. Therefore, built-up energy continuously seeks a path to ground (neutral charge).

This is one of many reasons HP designs its computers with a ground connection from the chassis to the wall socket. The charge will then have an easy path to balance itself. We suggest you check the building wiring, especially in older buildings, to ascertain that the ground path really exists.

However, even if the discharge path bypasses all the sensitive circuitry, electromagnetic waves (similar to radio or TV waves) will still be generated by the discharge. Because these waves travel through the air, they are able to reach the circuitry with a very high charge.

HP's answer to static

The solution is simple: prevent the damaging charge from reaching the equipment. Hewlett-Packard offers a complete line of products to do just that. The static control mats drain the charge via a ground cord within fractions of a second after you step on the mat; the anti-static carpet mats distribute the charge over a large area, reducing built-up static in any one area (use only where conditions for static buildup are unfavorable); the tabletop mat affords the same protection as the static control mats, but is more convenient and aesthetically pleasing (operator *must* touch the mat before touching the equipment); the Staticide spray and wipes are for use on areas not protected by anti-static carpets and mats.

Static facts

Static damage is described in two ways:
- Catastrophic—when the component is dead; the board/unit will not work.
- Degrading—when a discharge weakens a component, possibly causing premature failures within days, weeks or months after the incident, or characteristic changes such as intermittent failures (usually with temperature shifts, vibrations, or load variations).

	Most common static reading	Highest static reading
Walking across carpet	12,000 volts	39,000 volts
Walking across vinyl tile floor	4,000 volts	13,000 volts
Working at desk	500 volts	3,000 volts

*Institute of Electrical and Electronics Engineers Inc. (IEEE) from 12th Annual Proceedings of IEEE Reliability Physics.

The static charge level is:	When you:
3,500 volts	feel
15,000 volts	see

Figure 6.18 Hewlett-Packard Computer User's catalog

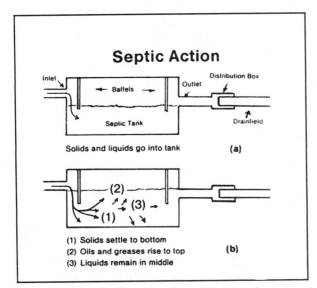

Figure 6.19 Brown Deer Comapny Catalog

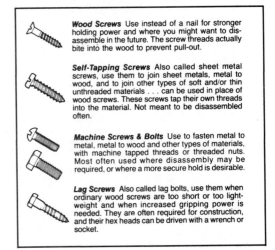

Figure 6.20 DRI Industries catalog

Eight Questions You Should Ask and Answer About Your Copy Before You Print It

1. Is your copy in the right order?   Is there a logical order to the presentation of copy points about your merchandise? And have you been faithful to this organizational principle throughout? Is this the best way to organize the items in your catalog? Or would another method make more sense?

2. Is it persuasive?   Does your copy begin with a strong selling message? Do individual headlines promise solutions to reader problems and draw readers into the product descriptions? Does the body copy stress user benefits as well as technical features?

3. Is it complete?   Does your copy include all the information the reader needs to make a buying decision? Does it anticipate and answer all the customer's questions in advance? Have you fully described products and their features? Have you included all important details such as size, color, dimensions, or material of which the products are constructed? Does the copy make it easy for the customer to find the price line, to specify and order the product?

Know your product before you write

4. Is it clear?   Is the copy understandable and easy to read? Are all terms defined? Don't assume all readers know slang or regional expressions. Is the copy written at the reader's level of understanding?

5. Is it consistent?   Have you been consistent in your use of logos, trademarks, spellings, abbreviations, punctuation, grammar, capitalization, units of measure, layouts, copy style, visuals?

6. Is it accurate?   Is the copy technically accurate? Has the copywriter made sure the item functions exactly as described? Has the merchandiser carefully proofread all copy and "fine print" for accuracy (no one knows details about the product better than the merchandiser)? Do the photos show the current models or versions of your product? Have you matched the right photo to each item description?

7. Is it interesting?   Is the copy lively and informative to read? Or is it boring? Do both the typeface you have chosen for your copy and the style of layout encourage the viewer to read the copy?

8. Is it believable?   Is the copy sincere or is it full of ballyhoo? Have you used photos, test results, testimonials, and statistics to back up your product claims, especially those that seem "incredible"?

Product Copy Checklist:

☐ Review customer list.
☐ Review company image.
☐ Attend Product Work Session.
☐ Determine copy style.

Always
1. Review competitors' copy.
2. Consult merchandiser or buyer.
3. Review manufacturer's material.
4. Clarify product's main benefit.
5. Have the product tested.
6. Identify the product.
7. Inform—include the product specifications needed to make a buying decision.
8. Make every word count.
9. Remember the customer does not have the product in hand.
10. Be truthful.

Strongly consider
1. Testing the product yourself (writer).
2. Hiring a professional writer.

Product Headlines

Picture a newspaper without headlines. How would you determine the items of interest, the ones you want to read? How would you find a particular item you might be searching for?

It's the same in your catalog. A headline that pops out of the page calls attention to the item, lets the customer know instantly what it is, and, if it is a well-crafted benefit headline, tells the customer whether the item is something he or she wants or needs or has been looking for forever.

Headlines save time for your customers and make it easy for them to purchase. Their importance cannot be overemphasized! A potential customer looks first at the picture, reads the headline, glances at the price line, and finally reads the copy. If the artwork catches the eye, the headline should start the juices flowing by identifying the item and assuring customers they are reading the copy that matches it. A benefit headline that pulls the customer into the first main selling point will work even better.

There are two kinds of catalog headlines:

1. Product benefit

2. Product name/identity

Product Benefit Headlines

In an age of skeptical consumers, a product benefit headline can do a lot to reassure a potential customer that a product truly solves a problem.

To construct a compelling benefit headline, ask yourself:

- What will make customers feel they need this product?

- What is the product's greatest asset?

- Why was the product chosen for the catalog?

Take a look at the benefit checklist you drafted while writing body copy. The strongest selling point probably helped you shape your copy. How can you convey that same benefit, choosing words other than the ones that lead off the body copy?

Sometimes a benefit head can include the name of the product plus a descriptive word or two to suggest its benefit. Ask yourself what would further clarify the product's use. What words could help convey the product's primary attribute, or give it strong appeal?

The old adage, "people buy benefits, not features" holds true for headlines as well as body copy. Slightly heavy and out-of-shape people don't want a regular home exerciser, but one that will help them be trim quickly. Hikers don't want ordinary socks; they want socks that prevent blisters.

The Sharper Image headlines its Nautilus Abdominal Machine this way:

Nautilus brings home the fastest way to a trim, tight stomach

This headline attracts both the fitness-conscious person and the couch potato who has been meaning to shape up. Someone desiring a firm, flat tummy will stop and read more, thanks to the hoped-for benefit ("a trim, tight stomach") that can be realized in the privacy of one's home ("brings home") and the promise of a speedy result ("fastest way"). If the headline had used only the product name, Nautilus Abdominal Machine, not as many customers would have been attracted.

Here are some examples of other hard-working product benefit headlines:

Salad Spinner Washes and Dries All in One! (Lillian Vernon)

Keep a Full Two Acres Bug-Free With This Powerful Light (Brookstone)

Detect Ear Infections Before Your Child Feels Any Pain (Self-Care)

You Don't Have to Draw a Single Line to Produce Exciting Art with Print Artist! (Egghead Software)

Trim Trees With Your Feet Safely Planted on the Ground (Plow & Hearth)

You'll Spray Fence Rows, Ditch Banks, Barns and Livestock Faster and Easier! (Modern Farm)

Business-to-business catalogs can reap enormous value from the benefit headline approach. The Sycom Forms and Supplies Catalog, whose market is the health professional, first relates to the customer's problem and then solves it, which is the best of all benefits.

Problem: *Patients forget appointment?*
Benefit solution: *Reminder cards can help you.*

Moore Business Center headlines a word processor workstation like this:

Data-Leggett Work Station Increases Productivity

The benefit, "increases productivity," is but one of the benefits the product has, but it is the main benefit and therefore the one benefit to headline so the customer is attracted but not confused.

Product Name/Identity Headlines

As its name implies, a product/name identity headline usually tells little more than the name or identity of the product. But a few choice adjectives can help a lot. A Pulse Meter designed to be worn while exercising can become a "Freestyle Pulse Meter" to indicate freedom of motion and activity, thereby attracting the jogger and exercise buff. A ladies silk shirt can become a "Sophisticated Silk Shirt," and a doormat can become a "Half-Round Reversible Doormat." In each case, the additional words add allure.

Unfortunately, many business-to-business catalogs still use only the product name, such as "Bookkeeping Machine Forms" and "Statement and Ledger Card."

Nine Points to Consider

1. Type Size. Avoid eye-straining, tiny type. *Your headline is a bridge from photo to copy block* and thus should not be in type that's smaller than the copy block. (The copywriter needs to communicate with the artist.)

2. Lead-Ins.   When layouts restrict space, it often is intriguing to start a headline in the photo display area and have it wind up as the opening for the copy block. This *draws the reader from headline to selling points.*

3. Numbers.   When using several headlines for a single photo, consider *numbering them so your reader tackles them in the sequence you prefer* to move that customer into the copy block. Readers subconsciously follow direction, and wind up getting your most potent copy points.

4. Price.   Price can be presented in the headline if you offer a compelling bargain, an exclusive item, or items priced way under competitive products.

5. Value.   You can also mention price in your headline if you simultaneously refer to the immense value the product gives. Example: "Just under $25 brings you a full wardrobe."

6. Color.   Headlines should be printed in the same color as the body copy and that usually means black. *Headlines are not decorative items.* They are part of copy and are meant to draw the reader into the copy. Do not allow a well-meaning artist to display captions in alternate colors.

7. Sameness.   Headlines begin to train readers how to read body copy. Resist temptations to use alternate italic and roman captions or to use varying typefaces. *Use the same typefaces as used in body copy.*

8. Anticipation.   Try to make your readers anticipate the great joys, conveniences, and status they will gain with your product or service.

9. Quiet Excitement.   Usually, when reading headlines, readers are curiously examining your presentation, not making buying decisions. Try to weave the product's excitement into your headlines so your readers will quietly make decisions on their own. Eliminate the exclamation points, which frequently block continued readership anyway. Use extremely strong copy that lets readers provide their own mental exclamations—exclamations of joy, discovery, and desire.

But remember, let your headline *tell the story.* Let your headline *jump out* at the customer. Let it scream with excitement. Use large, bold, black type so it's easy for the customer to read. Use a headline that *stands alone:* "KEEP FLIES OFF YOUR PICNIC." Or use one that *leads into your copy:* "*WATER RESISTANT FASHION WATCH* to wear at the beach." Make good use of your headlines. They make the customer sit up and take notice. They sell merchandise.

Headlines grab the customers attention

Headline Checklist:

☐ Determine thrust of product.
☐ Determine headline technique(s).
☐ Establish type standards.
☐ Establish style.

Always
1. Be enthusiastic.
2. Be truthful.
3. Inform the customer.
4. Announce benefit or name.
5. Use prime selling points.
6. Edit judiciously.
7. Work with artist.

Strongly Consider
1. Using short words.
2. Using fewest possible words.
3. Using few adjectives and adverbs.

Five Tips for Writing Headlines that Sell

1. Attract your prospects' attention. A headline should offer a solution to a specific problem, tell a story that will engage customers, or tease them with a question. Whatever approach you choose, you must speak directly to your customers to hold their interest.

2. Each headline should stress your strongest sales point. If your products or services are terrific values, exclusive, one-of-a-kind, or brand new, say it in the headline.

3. Highlight your company's unique benefits. There's no better way to advertise your exceptional service, unconditional guarantee, or award-winning quality than with a strong headline that your customer's won't miss.

4. Long headlines that sell your products are better than short, cute or clever headlines that say nothing.

5. Give customers a reason to order soon. Think of your catalog as a showroom and your headline as your opportunity to invite buyers in and give them a good reason to shop around. Once your customers have your showroom in their hands, you should try to close the deal before you lose their attention.

Product Cluster Headlines

Product cluster headlines refer to the offer being made, the category of products being offered, or the function a group of products perform. This headline approach can be used for a page containing an average number of products (generally five) or for pages loaded with second-level (sale or smaller volume) items.

The pages should be designed so products with an affinity to each other are adjacent. This aids the customer's search when scanning for a category of interest, and it increases sales by encouraging more desire or need for products in a particular category.

Do not make the common error of simply displaying a photo, some tight copy, and pricing data on each item. Instead, create an enticing headline for each product cluster to lead the customer into the individual products in that cluster.

Following these four rules will help you create an effective cluster headline:

1. Clearly identify the nature of the cluster. Is it a specific area of interest? Do the products perform a special function? Are the products a special value?

2. Present an "umbrella" user benefit for all items in your cluster, like increased productivity, reduced costs, greater enjoyment of an avocation. Ideally this will suggest the need to purchase more than one or two items from the cluster.

Figure 6.21   Williams-Sonoma catalog

3. Use action typography, such as italics and ellipses, to guide the reader into the cluster.
4. Ask the copywriter and the designer to meet before the page is designed, so ample space is allowed for the cluster headline.

In **Figure 6.21**, Williams-Sonoma follows rule number one by using the simple banner headline "Stocking Stuffers" to declare the subject matter of this two-page spread. It is a low-key, attractive way to suggest that customers can purchase several for last-minute Christmas gifts. Hanna Andersson uses the clever headline, "The pitter-patter of little feet" to organize a myriad of socks and shoes for babies and toddlers (**Figure 6.22**).

Sturbridge Yankee Workshop says "Bath Sale" to call attention to the specially priced items on this page from its sale catalog (**Figure 6.23**). **Figure 6.24** shows how Spencer Gifts uses a double-page spread to tell the customer about special pricing when a specific number of the products are purchased. The left-page headline, "Mix or Match Sale!" tells customers they can choose any products they wish at a special

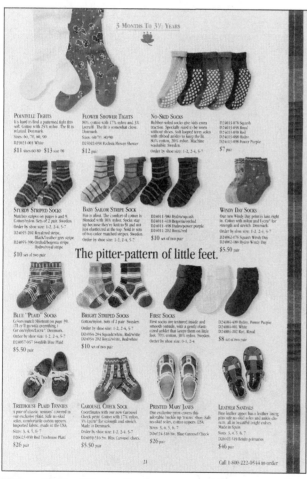

Figure 6.22   Hanna Andersson catalog

Figure 6.23   Sturbridge Yankee Workshop catalog

Figure 6.24   Spencer Gifts catalog

Figure 6.25   Plow & Hearth catalog

price. "Any 6 items on pages 8 through 33" clarifies what the customer must do to take part in the sale. The right page clarifies again how many products must be purchased, and "Sale! Only 88¢ each!" states the bargain price. This is a common example of a second-level product offer with an abundant number of products on a page.

Plow & Hearth follows rule number two in **Figure 6.25,** which shows a good example of an umbrella benefit headline. "Composting Made Easy" gives a logical and appealing benefit to all of the composting products shown on this page and the one following. Grouping products that have a general common benefit can help a presentation and allow a headline to be stated in such a way that it attracts customers. Just a descriptive word or two can convey the benefit and promote the category.

Tips for Preparing a Cluster Page or Headline

1. Include the total number of all items in the cluster to encourage the reader to review all of them. ("6 gifts under $25!" is a good example.) This suggests to the customer that a large choice is available, or that great value can be had once the choice is made.

2. Hint at urgency to get the customer to review the cluster *now*.

Price Lines

Price lines are part of the body copy but should not be treated as a stepchild or just a product number and pricing identifier. Too often this offhand treatment occurs when a more beneficial solution could be used. The wording used in your price lines can have many psychological effects upon the customer. Changing a word or two can add emphasis, punch, and pizazz to a normally straightforward merchandise action—that of telling your customers what the merchandise is going to cost them. Here are five different pricing strategies (**Figure 6.26**), each of which has its own special wording and function.

1. Regular pricing   This is the normal retail that reflects the cataloger's required or desired profit. Example 1(a) shows a price line from the Brookstone catalog using the traditional method of product number identification, product name, and retail price—no extras added. Example 1(b) from Annie's Attic identifies the product by reference to "pattern" and "complete kit" and states the retails. The addition of the word "only" by Annie's Attic indicates a value, even though pricing is actually full retail. This is good merchandising.

2. Sale pricing of original merchandise   This shows a markdown from the regular price, usually due to overstock or desire to move seasonal merchandise. Example 2(a) from the Lands' End catalog uses the very effective method of "X"ing out the regular price and printing the sale price in a bright color. The word "OVERSTOCK" tells the customer the merchandise is of normal high quality and "cut to" emphasizes the bargain being passed on. Bergdorf Goodman, 2(b), tells the customer what the regular price is, "Orig.," and what the sale price is "Now." The message to buyers: "This is original, fine-quality merchandise being offered at a special price."

3. Special purchase pricing

This results from a special quantity purchase, close-out merchandise, discontinued production, or some other type of purchasing at lesser cost to the cataloger. Example 3(a) from the Williams-Sonoma catalog states the price "regularly," followed by the "Special Price." "Regularly" represents the recommended or normal price these goods might sell at, with the actual price being lower. To have used "Sale" or "Now" instead of "Special" would imply previously-carried merchandise, which would be inaccurate. The use of "Special" lets the customer feel that the item, as well as the price, is an unusual value. Austad's in 3(b) goes one step further. Not only is their regular price ("your cost") below the manufacturer's recommended retail because of quantity buying, but they also offer a sale price. This indicates a really exceptional bargain.

Price Line Importance

Make your price line a benefit. Substantiate a low price with actual price comparisons.

Larry Lefavor
Catalog Director
DRI Industries
Bloomington, MN

---

1. Regular

a. aluminum blower tube. 10" long, weighs only 4¾ ozs.
J-10613 Flame starter **$9.95**

b. finishing touch. **Pattern $2.25** or complete **kit only $5.95.**

2. Sale

a. Men's 819474 Women's 814654 ~~$16.00~~
OVERSTOCK Price Cut to $9.00

b. A. ORIG. **$90** NOW **$64** (3.25) L18-2A
B. ORIG. **$37.50** NOW **$24** (2.65) L18-2B
C. ORIG. **$75** NOW **$59** (3.25) L18-2C

3. Special Purchase

a. SMALL FOLDING TOWEL RACK is 27½" wide and has 5 rods. #17-13516, Regularly $32.00 **Special Price $27.00**

b.
MEN'S RIGHT HAND REG. LENGTH REGULAR FLEX	MEN'S RIGHT HAND REG. LENGTH STIFF FLEX	MEN'S LEFT HAND REG. LENGTH REGULAR FLEX	DESCRIPTION	YOUR COST	SALE
SC0813	SC1813	SC2813	Set 8 Irons (3-9, PW), Set 3 Woods (1,3,5) $579.00	~~$353.40~~	$279.95

4. Membership

a. Mother: 6829 $33.00 (Members $29.70) (s/h 2.20).
Baby: 6834 $15.00 (Members $13.50) (s/h 1.60).

b. *Publisher's Edition $14.95*
Members' Edition $11.29 ②

5. Value

210-Piece, Oil Coated Steel $57.60 Value
Half-Moon Key Shop,
Catalog Number 80000029
Your Price Only **$19⁹⁹**

Figure 6.26 Pricing Strategies

4. Membership pricing This is a special retail offered to customers who become members by paying a fee or who participate in a membership offer that obligates them to a specific amount of purchases. Example 4(a) from the Smithsonian catalog states regular pricing, immediately followed by the "member price." A reader soon realizes that a subscription to the Smithsonian magazine (qualifying one as a member) is paid for by the savings received with just a purchase or two. Literary Guild's pricing, 4(b), reflects the reward that a membership commitment brings. The word "member" associated with a lower price is an obvious benefit and merchandising point.

5. Value pricing This often results from customer packaging of several same or coordinated products. Example 5 from the DRI catalog refers to the regular price as "Value" because of the savings reaped by purchasing the package instead of the individual components. "Your Price Only" reflects the price resulting from the cataloger's custom packaging efforts. The words imply that the product is priced especially for you, and with DRI's method of merchandising, indeed it is.

Other words and ways of utilizing the price line for subtle merchandising are yours to create. Don't neglect this small but potentially profitable selling opportunity.

Price Line Checklist:

☐ Verify retail price with management.
☐ Confirm reason for pricing.
☐ Verify product number.
☐ Set price line style.

Always:
1. Use cent sign (¢) for price line if less than $1.00.
2. Write $1.00, not $1.

Strongly Consider:
1. Putting salesmanship into the price line.
2. Separating product number from retail price for easy visual.

CHAPTER 7

Covers, Captions, and Other Catalog Copy

Catalog copy has a great deal more to do than describe products. Even front and back covers—the two most viable parts of a catalog—often receive far less attention than they deserve. Captions, catalog letters, testimonials, order forms, and guarantees also play essential roles, as this chapter and the next will demonstrate.

Front Cover Copy

While the cover art or photography plays a primary role in attracting a customer's attention, copy shares some of the responsibility. Just as a dramatic cover design can grab attention by sheer beauty, arresting layout, marvelous colors, or high subject interest, so too can copy get attention. For starters, it announces the catalog name—an important role by itself.

A new catalog company should give a great deal of thought to its title. Your intended market and your new catalog's personality will help you decide whether your catalog should have a person's name to denote friendly dependability, have a more formal title, or take a whimsical approach. Don't take your catalog's name for granted!

Catalog cover copy can accomplish six functions. It can:

- Include a catalog subhead

- Refer to products or special offers inside the catalog

- Send a personal message to the customer

- Sell directly off the cover

- Promote credibility

- Promote convenience

However you decide to use your cover, the artist and copywriter must work carefully together so the final outcome will be desirable and attract the customer.

Including a Catalog Subhead on the Cover

Adding a subhead to the catalog name is practicing the old adage, "Never leave a stone unturned." Many companies very successfully use subheads to tell the prospective customer what products are offered.

Figure 7.1 shows the cover of the Frontgate catalog. The subtitle, "Enhancing Your Life at Home," tells the customer what kind of products are inside—especially useful given the abstract treatment of the poolside chaise lounge shown on the cover. The message is further

Figure 7.1   Frontage catalog

clarified by the messages "Father's Day Gifts Wrapped and Delivered" and "Pool and Patio Products for Leisure."

Figure 7.2 is the cover of the Reliable Home Office catalog. It sells office equipment, furniture, and accessories to people who work from home. The catalog name is very prominent, overprinted in red on a white background. The subhead, "Superior Design and Function for Your Home Office Environment," clarifies and helps to identify the category of products to be found inside. The cover photo montage illustrates some of those catalogs and motivates the customer to open the catalog. Four other benefits—50 percent off, money-back guarantee, quick shipping, and a 24-hour 800-number—also capture attention. Their vertical arrangement and the line formed by the black squares lead the eye up and down from the title and subtitle to the sophisticated office scene depicted underneath.

Both of these covers have nicely blended art and copy to the maximum advantage. The artist and copywriter have worked closely to achieve covers that visually and verbally attract the customer.

Figure 7.2   Reliable Home Office catalog

Referring to Inside Pages on the Cover

Pages that feature products that are pictured or referenced on the front cover become "contrived hot spots," or pages that enjoy greater sales because of the extra promotional attention. Both products and pages referred to on a cover will sell more because the cover directs the customer to open to them.

Three things can be referenced on the front cover:

1. Product category (a grouping of products with the same function or that pertain to a specific area, such as stationery or gardening equipment)

2. Special offer (sale, free gift, free trial, sweepstakes)

3. Specific product or products

You may choose to use only one of these points, or all three.

In **Figure 7.3**, The Sharper Image references a category (bicycling products) and four individual products, leading the customer to five different pages in the catalog. The Improvements catalog shown in

Figure 7.3   The Sharper Image catalog

Figure 7.4   Improvements catalog

Figure 7.5   Breck's catalog

Figure 7.4 references four products, positioning the first as the answer to an attention-getting question, "What's 0.25″ thick, inexpensive to operate, and GLOWS to light your way forever?" Sales of the products referenced on these two covers undoubtedly received a boost from this tactic.

In **Figure 7.5,** Breck's bulb catalog attracts the customer with a lovely and colorful garden shot (from Holland, to play up its "Bulbs from Holland" subhead) and then references a special free offer. Most of the cover type is white, reversed out of the green background, but the free offer burst is printed in yellow and red. (No page directions are given to help the reader locate the offer, however.)

Garon Products, a maintenance supply catalog, very neatly references three products that are pictured on the cover and identifies a product category for each, thus broadening the subject of interest. **Figure 7.6** shows how well this direction was accomplished. A bullet with the product name and page number ("Aluma-Grip, Pg. 29") appears at the top left of the product photo insert. At the bottom of the photo insert, the product category is identified. In the top left corner of the cover photo, four benefits are stated to build credibility and provide customer information.

Figure 7.6   Garon Products catalog

Figure 7.7   Signals catalog

A more subdued approach is found in **Figure 7.7**, in which the Signals catalog of products for public television viewers quietly highlights the arrival of the video of Howards' End in a footline across the bottom of the cover, printed in the same blue-over-salmon as the catalog name block.

Sending a Personal Message on the Cover

Personalization boosts response rates. And with today's segmentation techniques and inkjet technology, including a personal message on the cover is easier than ever.

Many catalogers send a special "wrap" or cover to customers who haven't ordered for some time. Hanna Andersson adds a post-it note element to the cover shown in **Figure 7.8**, which tells these customers "We've missed you." A customer change of address inspires Lillian Vernon to send a special "Welcome" catalog of "beautiful items for your new home" (**Figure 7.9**). Besides including copy directed to the new homeowner or tenant, this special cover shows items associated with home—a door knocker, mail box, and keys—and includes a free housewarming gift. This is a great example of a cataloger using customer information in a way that the customer will welcome.

Figure 7.8   Hanna Andersson catalog

Figure 7.9   Lillian Vernon catalog

In **Figure 7.10**, Viking is a little more forward. A special message area lets Viking's president tell an individual customer about an overlooked offer. Viking not only includes the name of the customer, but also the date the customer first ordered.

Figure 7.10 Viking Office Products catalog

Selling Directly off the Cover

Because the front cover is so powerful, it should be used to the best, most profitable advantage. Some catalogers feel strongly that the most profitable option is to sell a product or products directly off the cover.

Before you choose this approach, consider carefully whether selling off the cover will misrepresent your catalog's tone and product line. Also, take care not to destroy the mood of the cover with a cluttered sales presentation. To sell off the cover, copy must play a big role because the customer must have enough information to make a buying decision. Generally this means descriptive copy and can require size, color, and style information.

There are three approaches to selling products on the front cover:

1. Include full-length product copy just as it would appear inside if the item were for sale.

2. Shorten regular copy to include only bare-bones facts, but still maintain copy block style.

3. Use facts in short-statement form and list them in bullet fashion.

All these approaches perform better with a strong benefit headline that draws attention to an outstanding product feature, or a special offer or price.

Service Merchandise references three products and sells two products off the cover of its Memorial Day mini-catalog, which directs consumers to place an order by phone or by visiting a store. **Figure 7.11** shows how a resin chair and an iced tea pot are sold in brief blocks that convey all the information—specifications, benefits ("freshly brewed iced tea in less than 10 minutes") and price—needed to make a purchase decision. The very busy presentation suits Service Merchandise's value-oriented approach.

The Modern Farm catalog shown in **Figure 7.12** fills every inch of the catalog with selling copy. Product headlines and descriptive copy are just as they would appear inside. Headlines identify the product and convey a benefit; body copy tells of other product benefits and specifications and gives price information. A special premium for orders

Figure 7.11 Service Merchandise mini-catalog

Figure 7.12 Modern Farm mini-catalog

over $100 is highlighted in the lower-right corner. The top and bottom panels also promote the 24-hour toll-free number and the company guarantee, while the credit card logos testify to the convenience of credit card shopping. A lot of information and products for sale are provided here, but distracting clutter is avoided with clean lines and direct, informative copy.

Credibility

Nothing builds confidence and encourages ordering quite like credibility. It is what gives strength and depth to your company, and makes a customer want to purchase again and again.

Customers need to feel that a company is trustworthy, reliable, and dependable. While these elements of credibility need to be reinforced throughout the catalog, the cover is a key place to reinforce this quality. Copy *can* reinforce credibility on the cover in very few words. To convey *trustworthy* in two words, try "Satisfaction Guaranteed." To convey *reliable* in one word, try *since* plus a year—"Since 1935." *Dependable* can be instantly conveyed by "Our 62-year commitment."

There are three very strong ways to establish credibility on the front cover:

1. Promote longevity.

2. Present your guarantee.

3. Include testimonials.

Longevity.   Nothing makes a customer more secure than dealing with a company known or perceived to have been in business for a long time. In the mind of the consumer, a company that has served the public for many years is seen as smart, dependable, and reliable. The longer a company has been in business, the more secure the customer feels about ordering. Credibility is established!

A company may choose to promote its mail-order longevity, or it may promote the cumulative number of years it has been in the retail or wholesale business. Although the Whale Gift catalog is a relatively new offering from the Center for Marine Conservation, the Center itself has been operating much longer (**Figure 7.13**). "Twenty-two years

SUMMER 1 9 9 4
CENTER FOR MARINE CONSERVATION
TWENTY-TWO YEARS OF PROTECTING
MARINE WILDLIFE AND THEIR HABITATS

Figure 7.13   Whale Gift catalog

of protecting marine wildlife and their habitats" speaks to the group's dedication and implies that the commitment has been carried over to the new catalog. Country Curtains (**Figure 7.15**) weaves reference to its impressive longevity into a well-crafted letter that emphasizes the personal character of its business operations, which is a perfect complement to the kinds of products it sells: "You know, it's hard to believe that my husband, Jack, and I started Country Curtains in 1956. . . ."

Two other catalogs use their retail roots to boost credibility. In **Figure 7.14**, Cuddledown of Maine uses the tag line "Manufacturing Quality Since 1973." In **Figure 7.16**, Hammacher Schlemmer cites its even more impressive age: "Established 1848."

Longevity of business is always a powerful credibility builder!

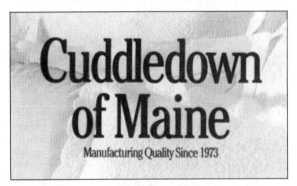

Figure 7.14 Cuddledown of Maine catalog

Figure 7.16 Hammacher Schlemmer catalog

Dear Friend,

I'm so happy to be sending you a copy of our latest catalog. It's always such a pleasure to welcome a new friend!

You know, it's hard to believe that my husband, Jack, and I started Country Curtains in 1956 in Whitman, Massachusetts, with only one style of curtain. It was Jack's idea back then to sell unbleached muslin curtains, and many of our styles are still made with this wonderful, pure cotton material.

All of our curtains fit in the back of our station wagon when we moved to Stockbridge two years later. We soon outgrew the dining room of our new home, and in 1968 we purchased the famous old Red Lion Inn. We moved our blossoming mail order company to the Inn, where we planned to stay forever. It wasn't long before we realized that we needed more space, and after a few expansions, we've settled into our present building a few miles down the road.

Although we've grown by leaps and bounds, Jack and I still pay attention to the many details of Country Curtains and always will. Our daughters and a marvelous staff help us keep pace with a growing company and the extraordinary age we live in.

So, again, welcome to Country Curtains. I hope you enjoy shopping in our catalog as much as we enjoyed creating it for you. I'll look forward to hearing from you soon!

Most Sincerely,

P.S. May all of your decorating projects turn out just as you hoped they would!

Figure 7.15 Country Curtains catalog

Guarantee. "Satisfaction Guaranteed" will suffice but some companies choose to fully state their guarantee on the cover—usually new companies that need to project a strong and convincing image in order to compete with existing companies. (But this approach should not be restricted to new companies, though, as all companies must try as hard as they can to maintain their position and build trust.)

The front cover guarantee is also used by companies whose products lines are difficult to sell by mail, such as shoes and wigs. A good example is the Wright Arch Preserver Shoes catalog. Because proper shoe fit is critical for comfort, the full guarantee is reproduced prominently on the front cover to reassure customers that a purchase can be exchanged or refunded if problems are encountered (**Figure 7.17**).

Figure 7.17   Wright Arch Preserver Shoes catalog

Testimonials.   Hardly anything is more persuasive than a recommendation from a friend or the knowledge that people who have previously dealt with a company are satisfied. While the use of customer testimonials directly on the cover is rare, there are variations on this theme that are not always recognized as testimonials.

Lands' End (**Figure 7.18**) uses a company pricing policy right on the front cover as a testimonial. "We are able to sell at lower prices because we support no fancy emporiums with their high overhead." Office Depot (**Figure 7.19**) couples pictures of employees with benefit statements about its ability to deliver the office products the customer needs when the customer wants. And The Safety Zone (**Figure 7.20**) takes the unique step of quoting a *New York Times* review on its cover. A better testimonial than this one could hardly be imagined: "For every hazard, Safety Zone has an antidote."

The full use of the traditional testimonial is seen in **Figure 7.21**. On one cover, New England Business Services pictured three customers

Figure 7.18 Lands' End catalog

Figure 7.19 Office Depot catalog

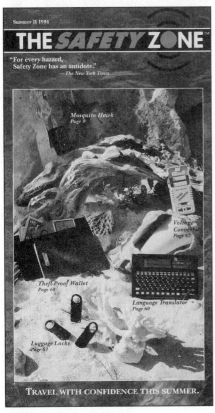

Figure 7.20 The Safety Zone catalog

Figure 7.21 New England Business Services catalog

along with their personal testimonials, each of which reinforced the guarantee and the company's dependability. "When we had a minor error, NEBS replaced the order quickly, and at no charge," said one customer. "We enjoy the quick service" says another. A third stated, "I have been using NEBS products for over 4 years, and find them of excellent quality and even more important—delivered on time."

This is excellent reinforcement of a company's credibility. It shouts, "We are a real company that can be depended on, one which you want to deal with."

Convenience

Even though the convenience of catalog shopping is almost a given, it's still an important benefit to promote on your cover. Stressing the convenience of catalog shopping—especially in those busy pre-Christmas days that constitute a cataloger's "fifth season"—might be just the nudge a customer needs to place an order.

If it fits the tone of your catalog, promote your toll-free ordering service right on the cover. If you glance back at the covers shown in this chapter, you will find 800-numbers prominently displayed in **Figures 7.2, 7.3, 7.4, 7.9, 7.11, 7.12, 7.19,** and **7.21.** Many catalogers also choose to identify the credit cards they accept on the cover as well. **Figures 7.4** and **7.12** are good examples. A company that strongly promotes convenient ordering and payment is Spiegel, whose catalogs are shown in **Figure 7.22.**

Figure 7.22   Spiegel's Christmas Guaranteed and Fall 1994 catalogs

Prompt shipment is another ingredient of convenience that many catalogers stress, especially during holiday seasons. The Eddie Bauer Home Collection catalog shown in **Figure 7.23** promotes convenience by stating, "Our Quick-Shipping Choices Make Shopping With Us The Right Choice." In its late holiday edition, Tweeds (**Figure 7.24**) adds a line "All orders received by December 22 are guaranteed for holiday delivery." Exposures adds the UPS emblem to its cover and the magic word *Free* to tell customers that Valentine's Day gifts will be shipped promptly and at no charge (**Figure 7.25**).

Figure 7.23   Eddie Bauer Home Collection catalog

by mail

All orders received by December 22 are guaranteed for holiday delivery.

Figure 7.24   Tweeds catalog

Figure 7.25   Exposures catalog

Other convenience messages that are appropriate for the cover include quick or mini indexes, a routing list, seasonal identification, new product announcements, or retail store locations.

The front cover can easily become cluttered and out-of-character if not given careful consideration. But consumers are a fickle lot. If you don't tell them or remind them about the convenience of shopping by catalog, they will purchase from someone who does.

Covers, Captions, and Other Catalog Copy   **221**

Front Cover Checklist:

☐ Review the character of the mailing list.
☐ Understanding the catalog company's positioning.
☐ Identify company's strongest point.
☐ Review special offers.

Always
1. Make catalog name prominent.
2. Direct the customer inside.

Strongly Consider
1. Using a subhead to catalog name for product clarification.
2. Stating company longevity.
3. Selling products directly.
4. Announcing special offers.
5. Listing toll-free or regular telephone numbers.
6. Telling of charge card acceptance.
7. Using customer or company testimonials.
8. Offering benefits such as fast service, custom design.

Back Cover Copy

The products and messages placed on your back cover will have a great deal of impact on the total catalog. Next to the front cover, the back cover is the most volatile hot spot you have—so you should take every opportunity to use it well. It is also the carrier of your customer's name and address. The post office uses it as a directional vehicle for delivery to the desired individual, and your customer uses it to order or to be directed inside to special pages.

A back cover *must* include an address panel. But like the front cover, it can also refer customers to products or pages inside the catalog, or directly sell merchandise. There are many different ways to balance this blend of functionality and promotion.

Address Panel

The United States Postal Service has specific requirements you need to follow to assure that addresses can be quickly identified and sorted by zip code, carrier route, and address. For complete specifications, see the U.S. Government publication *Domestic Mail Manual* and quarterly issues of the Postal Bulletin. Contact the Superintendent of Documents, U.S. Government Printing Office, Washington, D.C. 20036.

Although the address panel is generally no smaller than 2-¹/₂″ × 4″, the shape—rectangle or square—is up to you. You must have the postal permit indicia with specific wording, "Bulk Rate, U.S. Postage Paid," and then the company name or permit number. You also need to leave enough space so that the address label or inkjetted address will not interfere with the return address or indicia. A request for address correction or other delivery message goes in the same area.

Figure 7.26   Plow & Hearth catalog

Figure 7.26 shows a traditional address panel from Plow & Hearth. A 4-¹/₂″ × 5″ rectangle in the lower-right corner of the back cover includes the bulk rate indicia, company name and address, a boxed guarantee, and complete telephone and fax information. Ample white space is left for the inkjetted address and key code numbers. In **Figure 7.27**, Hanna Andersson uses different colored arrows to highlight the

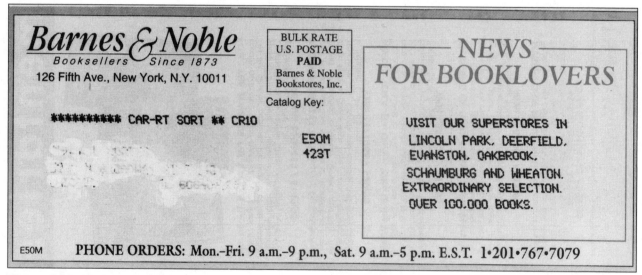

DOWNTOWN STORE 327 NW TENTH AVENUE, PORTLAND, OREGON 97209
OUTLET STORE 9 MONROE PARKWAY AT BOONES FERRY ROAD, LAKE OSWEGO, OREGON 97034

ORDERS AND SERVICES, CALL TOLL-FREE: 1·800·222·0544, 5 AM TO 8 PM PT, EVERY DAY

hanna Andersson

1010 NW FLANDERS, PORTLAND, OR 97209

BULK RATE
U.S. Postage
P A I D
Hanna Andersson
Corporation

Source Code #
A30322   137671
        INSIDE!
SEE OUR NEW AND EXCLUSIVE
    SUMMER COLLECTION
     FOR MOMS, BABIES,
        AND KIDS!

*********** CAR-RT-SORT **CR30
#A30322   U137671   50

Figure 7.27   Hanna Andersson catalog

Barnes & Noble
Booksellers Since 1873
126 Fifth Ave., New York, N.Y. 10011

BULK RATE
U.S. POSTAGE
PAID
Barnes & Noble
Bookstores, Inc.

Catalog Key:

********** CAR-RT SORT ** CR10

E50M
423T

NEWS
FOR BOOKLOVERS

VISIT OUR SUPERSTORES IN
LINCOLN PARK, DEERFIELD,
EVANSTON, OAKBROOK,
SCHAUMBURG AND WHEATON.
EXTRAORDINARY SELECTION.
OVER 100,000 BOOKS.

E50M   PHONE ORDERS: Mon.–Fri. 9 a.m.–9 p.m., Sat. 9 a.m.–5 p.m. E.S.T. 1·201·767·7079

Figure 7.28   Barnes & Noble catalog

source code number and the customer number—a helpful aid to the customer asked to provide this information to a telephone sales representative.

More frequently, the address panel is used to send a personalized message to the customer, thanks to the marriage of inkjet technology and sophisticated list segmentation techniques. In **Figure 7.28**, Barnes & Noble has designed a sort of bulletin board to draw the recipient's attention to special messages. This cover promotes nearby Barnes & Noble Superstores, but the space could just as easily be used for a special offer or news about a bestseller.

The Right Start Catalog in **Figure 7.29** addresses new customers who have a keen interest in this catalog's products: brand new parents. "We've heard there is a new addition to the Coleman Family," is a personal and highly engaging way to draw attention to the catalog and its contents. Jackson & Perkins (**Figure 7.30**) tells the customer which zone his or her garden is in and reassures the customer that Jackson & Perkins roses "grow well in all zones."

Before releasing your back cover design for production, check to make sure that your company's name and return address are legible. Always ask yourself, "Can the customer see my company name easily?" If the answer is no, maybe you'd better go back to the drawing board.

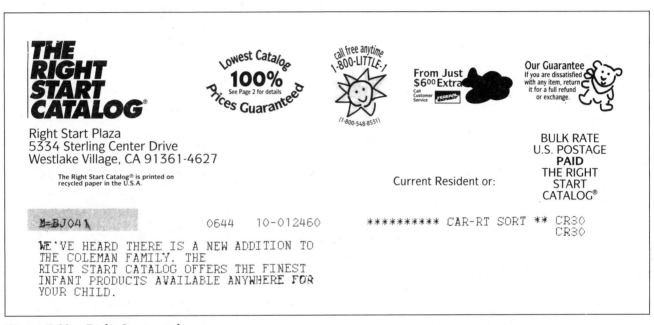

Figure 7.29 Right Start catalog

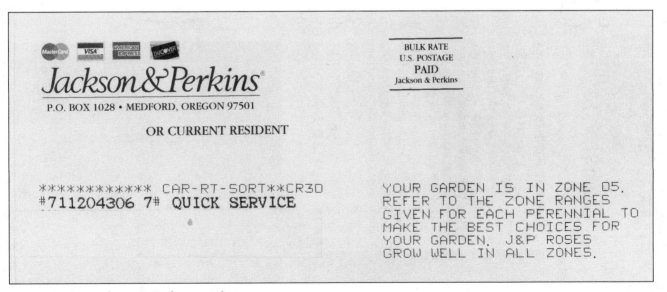

Figure 7.30 Jackson & Perkins catalog

Referring to Products and Pages Inside the Catalog

The back cover is one of the two most-looked-at places in your catalog. What better chance to direct the customer inside to a specific product or product category! Adding a few words with an inside page number takes little space and adds to dollar sales.

In **Figure 7.31**, PaperDirect devotes the top half of its back cover to a business presentation set that includes brochures, letterhead, envelopes, business cards, presentation labels, folders, and other paper goods. Because the complete set has so many components, its back cover presentation is limited to two attractive photographs and a short copy block that directs the customer to pages inside.

Figure 7.31 PaperDirect catalog

Inkjet technology has made it easy to refer specific categories of customers (or even specific customers) to merchandise of interest to them. Wild Wings, a wildlife gift catalog, directs customers to specific pages in its catalog (**Figure 7.32**).

Figure 7.33 shows one of six individual category references sent to the matching customer counterpart. Sycom directs the customer to specific pages bearing products for chiropractors, dentists, optometric professionals, veterinarians, physicians, and podiatrists, and also to

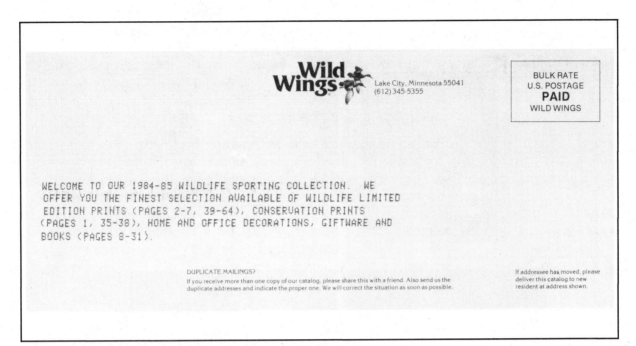

Figure 7.32 Wild Wings Catalog

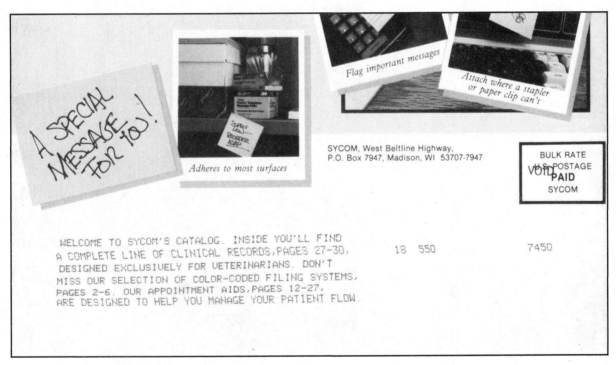

Figure 7.33 Sycom Catalog

other pages and products. One catalog is turned into seven specialized catalogs just by changing the wording and page references. This fine tuning immediately directs the customers to the areas in which they are interested. Catalogs can be customized according to the customer's buying preference. Note how the handwritten post-it note draws attention to the message.

Ink jetting offers a breathtaking array of opportunities: individual personalization, regional product referencing, and category highlighting are just a few. Put this powerful technique to work for you, and you'll reap the benefits in increased sales!

Selling Off the Back Cover

Picturing a product along with selling copy is the most common and successful treatment of a catalog back cover. Products chosen for the back cover should be your best sellers for that season. Full product information must be given in order for the customer to make a buying decision without having to refer to another part of the catalog. You may present only one product or a number of products. Your decision on the number of products may be somewhat controlled by the aesthetic feeling desired. But don't let design and aesthetics obscure the fact that selling products is your catalog's job.

Figure 7.34   Newport News catalog

The Newport News women's apparel catalog takes the full back cover to present one product, a lovely and attractively priced summer dress (**Figure 7.34**). Four photographs showing the dress in each of its color are accompanied by short, straightforward copy promoting its "easy-going, fuss-free" nature. Complete product information is provided so the customer can immediately decide to purchase. The Newport News guarantee, credit card icons, and all three telephone and fax numbers provide a further inducement to order.

Figure 7.35 shows how Inmac directly sells only one product, an adjustable keyboard shelf. The benefit headline and medium-length copy block are typical of what is found inside the catalog. A boxed blurb tells the customer that the product is "An Inmac Exclusive"—a good sales motivator. Seven product benefits, each one solving a problem, are called out from the art presentation. This type of copy treatment allows easy product benefit selling and shortens the length of the main copy block.

Colorifics, a drill-team clothing supplies catalog, sells four products on the back cover (**Figure 7.36**). Again, the copy is the exact style and length it would be if the product were presented inside.

Figure 7.35   Inmac catalog

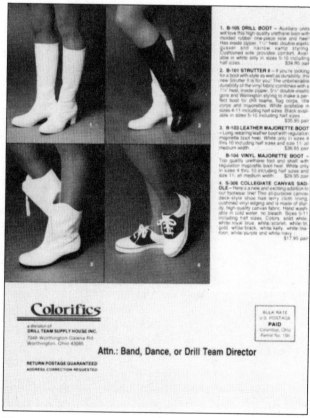

Figure 7.36   Colorifics catalog

Back Cover Checklist:

☐ Review character of front cover.
☐ Choose back cover approach.
☐ Check USPS requirements.
☐ Review special offers.

Always
1. Include company name and address.
2. Include telephone number.
3. Direct the customer inside.

Strongly Consider
1. Selling product(s) directly off the cover.
2. Indicating charge cards accepted.
3. Stating your guarantee.
4. Utilizing inkjet printing for personalized messages.
5. Using customer testimonials.
6. Using a routing directive.
7. Using a mini-index.
8. Stating special company benefits.
9. Directing customer to order form.
10. Using color or headings to clarify the source code, customer number, and other important codes.

Meanwhile, Inside the Catalog . . .

Although product body copy is your most reliable and most important sales tool, several other kinds of copy play a role inside your catalog:

- A catalog letter can help you build credibility and add personality to your catalog.

- Testimonials can also help build credibility, and are often even more effective than a letter.

- Photo headlines and captions can increase readership of essential benefit copy.

- Footlines can enhance a catalog's readability and use.

- Blurbs and insets can catch attention, build credibility, and direct the customer to place an order.

Using the Catalog Letter to Build Credibility

A catalog's credibility and creative presentation can be enhanced by a "message" or catalog letter. A letter plays many important roles.

1. It sets the stage.   The letter is to a catalog what the staging or setting is to a theatrical presentation. It helps introduce your company and its product line.

2. It reinforces your niche.   Segmented, targeted catalogs are clearly the wave of the future. The letter can help drive home your unique identity (niche) to customers or prospects.

3. It highlights important benefits.   Every catalog needs to work harder to emphasize how and why it is different from the competition. What are the benefits your products or services offer? Do you have a special offer to motivate the customer to action? The letter is a great way to point these things out.

4. It builds credibility.   Not every catalog is a household name or a Fortune 500 company with instant brand recognition. The catalog letter can help build your product line's authority and credibility. It can be used to point out the length of time you've been in business, the type of customers you serve, your product's uniqueness, or other pertinent corporate facts.

There are only two logical places to put your letter. Each one is a hot spot where the letter will get high readership and visibility.

The inside opening spread (inside front cover and opposite page) is the most common place, because most people read catalogs front to back and will see it as soon as they start. The centerfold of the catalog is also acceptable if your catalog is center stitched and falls open to this hot spot. Center placement does not work as well in a perfect-bound catalog. Since the letter hardly needs four-color treatment, it makes sense to put it on the front panel of the order form.

Your letter can fill an entire page or just a portion of it. Make sure the letter is easy and quick to read and that it *really* helps you make a sale.

How to Write an Effective Catalog Letter

What you say and how you say it depends on the philosophy behind your company image—the impression you want your company to make. Strive to make your greeting believable and sincere, and make sure it matches the perceptions you want your customer to have about your business.

Consider including the following elements in your letter.

☐ Use an opening salutation such as "Dear Friend" or "Dear Customer" or just "Hi!" A headline saying "President's Message" may also be appropriate.

☐ Follow your greeting with the words "Thank you." In the context of catalog letters, these words are the counterpart to "free" in advertising—powerful words that every customer will appreciate hearing. Thank your customers for their business, their loyalty, their comments. Consider saying thank you in prospecting catalogs that reach new inquiries. In these days of catalog glut, a letter like this can conspicuously announce, "Here's one you actually asked for."

☐ Mention your guarantee, and tell your customers how long you've been in business. If you are a new catalog, trace your heritage back as far as you can. Like the Vermont Country Store and Hammacher Schlemmer catalogs shown earlier in this chapter, boost your history by mentioning the date your *business* began, not your catalog.

☐ If this is your first catalog, consider telling about your special, unique merchandising and service philosophies, and assure your customer of your intent to be around forever. If your existing catalog is changing direction, tell your customers why.

☐ Mention specific products of interest to the reader.

☐ Have a real person sign the letter. In smaller companies, the president or general manager makes sense. In larger companies, the catalog manager, marketing vice president, or other person responsible for the catalog is ideal.

☐ If your target customer is female, have a woman sign the letter. If your target customer is male, you'll probably want a man to be the signer.

☐ Include a photograph of the signer to enhance the "real person" approach. When you use the same picture in every catalog, the face becomes a familiar old friend and creates an atmosphere of trust. If you use a photograph, you'll probably want to change it once in a while. Hair styles and clothing change, and can easily give a dated appearance.

☐ Add a postscript calling attention to new products, a special section or a limited-time offer premium. Combined with "Hurry . . . Limited Quantities," your p.s. will demand immediate action. Because a postscript is darn near irresistible, it lets you use a captive situation and a personal communication to give the recipient the inside scoop on the best values.

A perfect example of what a catalog letter should and can do is found in **Figure 7.37**. Read this Burpee Seed letter carefully, and you can see how each paragraph builds credibility. Paragraph one speaks of the company's longevity; paragraph two mentions the scope of Burpee's market; paragraph three explains its nationwide testing program. Even the map serves its purpose by showing where Burpee seeds are sold. Paragraph four calls attention to a product weakness that it cleverly turns into a benefit—customized order fulfillment. The last paragraph and single sentence wish the customer well.

This is hard-sell credibility at its best. This letter was not together haphazardly. A copywriter spent a great deal of time building the credibility elements and capitalizing on the well-known Burpee name.

Another letter that artfully blends company history, philosophy, and a testimonial comes from the Hearth Song catalog for families (**Figure 7.38**). The first paragraph of the letter reminisces about the early days of the company's mail order experience, when every trip to the mailbox was an adventure for the founder and her family members. After reflecting on company origins, the founder confirms that the growth and change of the intervening ten years have only reinforced the company's philosophy—letting children be children.

This well-written letter reassures customers of the company's credibility and commitment—and strokes parents by offering them "toys you'll feel good about giving" in our stressful times. Parents are further reassured by the Parents' Choice Seal of Approval and the company guarantee, both included in smaller type under the letter. Displayed on a page of its own and printed over a lovely under-the-Christmas-tree scene filled with simple, well-constructed toys, this letter delivers a welcome message that parents will be glad to read.

In the long letter in **Figure 7.39**, Patagonia informs its customers of an important change in policy. After an internal environmental audit revealed the impact of the clothing they manufacture, Yvon Chouinard writes, Patagonia has decided to limit company growth with "the eventual goal of halting growth altogether." Customers learn that 30 percent of the clothing line has been dropped, that the catalog is smaller, and that, effective immediately they can choose from *fewer* color and style choices than ever before.

This is not a message found in many catalogs, and not one likely to appeal to many customers. But this thoughtful essay/letter is *still* a credibility builder. It presents this remarkable decision as evidence of the company's commitment to satisfying its customers now and in the

Dear Friends and Fellow Gardeners:

My grandfather, W. Atlee Burpee, first trumpeted the famous slogan "Burpee's Seeds Grow" more than 80 years ago. Since then the phrase has been recognized and trusted by four generations of gardeners all over America.

From Maine to Texas, from New York to California, Burpee's seeds grow!

To be sure our flowers and vegetables do well under varied soil conditions and climates, we conduct extensive annual field trials on the East and West Coasts, and in several locations in between. We send advance samples of new Burpee varieties to thousands

Wherever
Mails Go,—
BURPEE'S
SEEDS
GROW!

of county agents, horticulturists and garden writers in every state of the union. We work closely with agricultural departments of universities throughout the U.S. We keep up-to-date with world-wide developments of new varieties useful to American home gardeners. In addition, thousands of Burpee customers help our research team by writing us about their experiences with our products.

Of course, not every Burpee variety grows equally well all over. In fact, all plants have specific needs and preferences. For example, marigolds and most other annuals bloom better in sun than shade...carrots grow best in porous or sandy soil...Tropic tomato feels most at home in the South. The information we get from our trials, our customers and our country-wide associates helps us recommend the best varieties for your area, with your climate and soil. Our catalogs are filled with many hints for the home gardener.

By choosing varieties carefully and giving them the care they need -- and by using only Burpee's "seeds that grow" -- you'll have a garden to be proud of.

Best wishes for your most satisfying, productive and joyful year of gardening ever!

Jonathan Burpee

Figure 7.37   Burpee Seed Catalog

long run. ("When we decided to limit our growth, we also committed ourselves to a life-span of a hundred years.") Finally, it builds Patagonia's environmental credentials to near-impeccability—a definite plus in the minds of Patagonia's earth-minded, adventuresome customers.

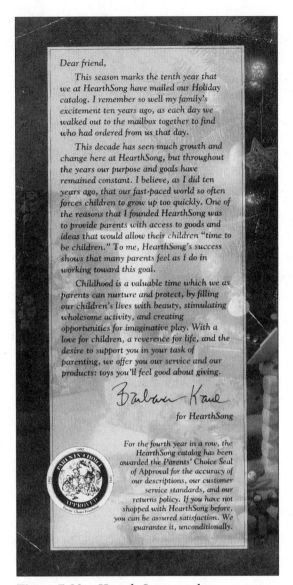

Figure 7.38   Hearth Song catalog

Figure 7.39   Patagonia catalog

The short and simple letter from the Vice President of Monarch Marking explains how the company has met customer needs by adding new products and new delivery options and shortening order turn-around times (**Figure 7.40**). This good news leads into a company aim ("make Monarch Marking the customer's first choice") and a personal guarantee ("We'll put you and your needs first . . . every time!").

This short and effective letter is nicely placed on the inside front cover, where it is grouped with helpful information about ordering, shipping, rush delivery, quantity discounts, and payment options.

Another short but effective letter introduces new titles featured in the Public Brand Software catalog (**Figure 7.41**). This letter is also part of an informative page that includes a table of contents, a definition of shareware, a guarantee, and a special free gift offer—all elements that convey a commitment to serving the customer.

Dear Valued Customer,

Thank you for shopping with us! Inside our 1994 catalog you'll see that in addition to our regular quality products, we've included many *new* items that you've requested. We've also added two rush delivery options and *shortened* order turnaround times for *even faster* shipments!

All this for you! Our aim is to make Monarch Marking YOUR VERY FIRST CHOICE! When you need quality marking equipment, supplies, bags, forms, signage and more...think of us *first!* I guarantee that we'll put YOU and YOUR NEEDS first...*every time!*

Howard Witzel
Howard Witzel
Vice President

Figure 7.40   Monarch Marking Systems catalog

Dear Friend,

If this new Public Brand Software catalog is any indication, 1994 looks as if it will be a banner year for shareware. The ink on our list of New Year's resolutions is barely dry, and we already have some exciting new titles to start the year off.

From Apogee Software — the company that brought you such now-legendary graphic adventure games as Wolfenstein 3-D, Commander Keen and Major Stryker — comes not one, but two great games: **Blake Stone: Aliens of Gold** and the long-awaited sequel to **Duke Nukum**.

And it would be a glaring oversight not to mention **Doom**, a groundbreaking new game from Id Software. This is one of the best games we've ever played!

We're proud to be the leaders in the shareware business, and we owe our success in large part to customers like you. We hope you'll continue letting us know what you like about PBS, what you want more of — and yes, even things you don't like — so we can serve you better and continue being the best in the industry.

Terry Ramstetter
General Manager

Figure 7.41   Public Brand Software catalog

Watch Out for the Ego Letter!

A long, boring, full-page letter from the head of a company might forget to address customer needs and instead run on and on about topics only the company is interested in. An "ego letter" like this is usually an overkill in copy and, therefore, an overkill in space allocated to an important hotspot.

To prevent your catalog letter from becoming an ego letter, keep it short and to the point. Don't try to emphasize too many things—and make sure that what you *do* emphasize interests your customer!

Testimonials

Nothing is more believable or reassuring to a prospective customer than knowing that prior customers have been satisfied with your products and service. Testimonials skillfully placed throughout your catalog and order form are strong ways to merchandise your credibility. (Many times they are highlighted in blurbs and insets, discussed later in this chapter.)

The best testimonials come from your own customers in your daily mail or through phone conversations. Celebrity testimonials and expert testimonials have a place in catalogs, but the word of your customers is the most powerful. To use testimonials effectively:

1. Use specific testimonials. The more specific, the better, because they are more believable. "We saved a lot of money using your book" is not as credible as "We saved $45,600 last month alone using the techniques in chapter six of your book."

2. Avoid anonymous testimonials. Your credibility suffers, because the customer may suspect you made them up. Whenever possible, use a name and city.

3. Get written permission to use testimonials and consult with your attorney on the matter. You cannot use someone's name for commercial purposes without permission. An attorney can help you understand privacy laws and make sure all releases are proper and legal.

Photo Headlines and Captions

A photo on its own can create great desire. But used effectively, headlines and captions can boost product sales.

Photo headlines are especially popular among low-end or sale catalogs. Used sparingly, photo headlines can support benefits, attract attention, and motivate. But using copy within photos does make specific demands on the copywriter. Technically, the copy sits within the photo in one of two ways:

1. Overprint copy is printed directly on the photo.

2. Reverse copy is reversed out of the photo, so that the type appears white.

In both cases, writers face one of the toughest copy jobs imaginable, because they must think of typography as they write. It is a good idea to work closely with the artist before starting overprint and reverse copy in order to:

1. Establish type standards

2. Establish character counts

3. Set standard style policy

4. Decide on ornamentation

The first three goals exist because they determine copy length. The fourth is where the artist rules, deciding on bursts, flags, and other eye-catching devices to spotlight the copy. After establishing these standards, it often is necessary and desirable to create copy to specific character counts per line to aid the reader with a uniform presentation. The writer must trim all phraseology to the bone, so each word communicates, but in the shortest fashion. A typical example of a selling point you might want to communicate in an art or photo headline would be a legend like this: "You get a second beautiful tote bag FREE each time you buy one at our low price!"

That's fine for body copy but *too long* for an art or photo headline. Remember, an art headline is beneficial only when it calls attention to a feature or offer in a short way. Ask yourself the following questions when trying to shorten the wording:

1. Which words are better communicated by the photo? (The reader can see you are selling tote bags.)

Make headline simple

2. Which words are duplicated, and in fact are the reader's perception? (The reader can see they are beautiful.)

3. How can it have greater power? (The reader doesn't need so many words.)

Now the copy becomes: "Buy one, get one FREE" or "TWO for the price of ONE."

This is much stronger copy, communicating the thought more rapidly and clearly. It lends itself much more readily to the disciplines needed for overprint and reverse headlines.

Talk about benefit

What benefits have occurred through rewriting the original version? And what specific benefits lend themselves directly to the situation of overprint and reverse headlines? The rewritten versions:

1. Lend themselves to *larger, bolder type*

2. Are *easier to understand*

3. Imply *urgency*

4. Stress the *bargain aspect*

5. Employ a *command*, letting readers know they *should* do what you suggest

Those are the Five Commandments of writing overprint or reverse copy for use with photos. Always use them to create greater pull and try these additional techniques when appropriate:

6. *Begin with all caps*, for a word or two.

7. Use all caps for the entire legend of overprinted and reversed copy *only when you have very short copy*.

8. Present just a *single thought or benefit* in each reverse or overprint . . . though you can use more than one of these graphic insets, or one of each, with a single photo.

9. Start and end with *commands*, as in: "Buy one, get one FREE now."

10. Use the *shortest possible words*. John Caples says he once increased response by 20 percent when he changed "repair" to "fix."

11. Use *primary selling points*, never secondary.

12. *Reinforce copy statements* from your descriptive copy block.

13. Imagine each photo overprint or reverse as a headline. It is! The reader looks at the photo before reading your body copy.

14. *Target for the reader's perception*, rather than for fact. "Two for the price of one" really means 50 percent off. But "50 percent off" isn't perceived as quickly. And "50 percent off" forces the reader to do math.

15. *Eliminate most adjectives and adverbs*. They belong in copy blocks where you can support them; they're less believable in headlines.

View your photo inset copy, overprints, and reverses as supportive, punchy phrasing. Complete sentences aren't needed here. Motivation is! But don't use a headline in a product photo unless it is beneficial to product sales. Too often, catalogers add headlines that result only in photo and page clutter. If every photo had a headline, *all* would become ineffectual. Before you decide to add a photo headline, ask whether the photograph needs a headline to help attract the customer's attention. The answer may be no.

Figure 7.42 shows how two low-end catalogs use a headline to explain product function. On the right, Harriet Carter simply states "Keep paint fresh!" to let the customer know that this is no ordinary artist's palette. The type style creates an effect of hand lettering and is reversed out of a blue background. The white type shows more prominently than black would.

On the left, Taylor Gifts identifies the product "Insulated Wetsuit" and states the benefit, "Keeps Drink Frosty!" The art treatment, a flag design to hold the headline, makes a clearer, crisper presentation as it calls attention to the message.

Figure 7.43 is from Chadwick's of Boston. This slightly longer headline identifies the products on the page (silk clothing for summer) and pulls out two benefits: the cool luxury of silk, and the great price for the blazer pictured. Because the photo headline helps pull together the page of products, it also functions as a product cluster headline.

Figure 7.42 Harriet Carter/Taylor Gifts Catalog

Figure 7.43 Chadwick's of Boston catalog

Figure 7.44   The Sharper Image catalog

Photo Captions

A variety of studies have shown that captions get two to three times the readership of body copy. So why not use them to sell your product? Your captions should give your prospects a reason to buy the products shown in the photos. Don't simply label a photo, "Winter Coat." Instead, say, "Our goose-down winter coat will keep you warm in even the most extreme weather."

One reason caption readership is so high is that people like to read captions first. Some will read no further, but a well-worded caption will compel most readers to read on. The Sharper Image caption in **Figure 7.44** hooks readers by singling out a benefit that is important to anyone who duplicates videos. After reading "No matter how many duplications you make, each new tape is as crisp as the original—thanks to advanced AmeriChrome copying circuitry," the reader will return to the body copy to find out more about the product.

"Unlike most birds, wrens like houses that swing back and forth" reads the Gardens Alive caption in **Figure 7.45.** This characteristic will intrigue anyone choosing a bird house, and send them to the body copy to find out more about wrens.

Rocky Mountain Computer Outfitters highlights the ease of use of Harvard Graphics software in the caption shown in **Figure 7.46.** Like the best captions, this one—"Create a special pie chart like this in only

Unlike most birds, wrens like houses that swing back and forth

Wren House

Wrens eat lots of insects, and almost nothing else, so they won't visit feeders except for an occasional nibble of suet. But they love these rough cedar houses, which offer safe haven from aggressive birds. Includes hanging rod; hang from a tree, 6'-10' above ground. Cavity is 3-1/2" x 3" x 4-1/2".

#2144 $9.50

Figure 7.45   Garden's Alive catalog

seconds"—is simple, direct, and effective. It hooks the customer by selling a powerful benefit that is reinforced by the headline and the body copy.

Create a special pie chart like this in only seconds.

Figure 7.46   Rocky Mountain Computer Outfitters catalog

Footlines

Footlines—lines of copy at the bottom of a page or spread in a catalog—are copy and design elements that can greatly enhance a catalog's readability and use.

This tiny line of copy can inform and direct the customer, or even help close the sale. Footlines remind the user of service benefits and the ease of ordering.

A simple footline technique is to repeat the name of your catalog on the left-hand page, and your 800-number or fax number on the right-hand page. The military supply catalog U.S. Cavalry includes toll-free, customer service, and fax numbers after phrases like "Attention Government Purchasing Agents" and "Contract Sales." Reliable Office Supply runs its telephone and fax numbers on right-hand pages, and *twelve* different messages—such as "Order by 4 p.m. Your Time, and We'll Ship In-Stock Items That Day!" and "Toll-Free Customer Service Gives You Fast, Free Assistance" on the left-hand pages.

The Comfortably Yours catalog uses footlines to highlight cases in which gift wrap is not available. Brookstone uses footlines to indicate when a catalog item is also available in its retail stores. Sun Television and Appliances uses them to provide instructions on how to call about additional shipping charges for ordering outside the continental United States.

The possibilities are endless!

Blurbs and Insets

Blurbs and insets are copy that is not part of the headline or the product copy block. A blurb can be just a word or two, a copy line, or a visual and verbal message combined. An inset is most often a combination of a visual and verbal message clarifying product components or use.

Not to utilize one or both of these techniques is to miss an opportunity to catch the customer's attention, instill customer confidence, build credibility, or direct the customer to place an order.

Blurbs and insets are typically used to highlight:

- Service and ordering information
- Testimonials
- Guarantees
- Customer education
- Information about products or the company

Service and ordering information. Service and ordering information can generally be conveyed in short messages inserted prolifically throughout the catalog. A telephone number or charge card information can tell the customer that your catalog is a convenient place to shop and that ordering is easy. A Federal Express or UPS emblem will remind the customer that delivery is fast. Many expert catalogers feel that constant reminders like these can subliminally act as a directive to order.

In **Figure 7.47**, WinterSilks promotes toll-free ordering in a blurb that is reproduced throughout the catalog. Smith & Hawken (**Figure 7.48**) decorates its two-color blurb with a botanical emblem that changes with each season—a leaf in the fall, a poppy in the spring, and so on. Museum Collections also uses an icon—this one reminiscent of a museum facade—to draw attention to its toll-free number and to subtly remind customers of the distinction and quality of the museum reproductions, replicas, and adaptations it sells (**Figure 7.49**). Lillian Vernon couples its phone number with the very directive message, "Charge it!" This blurb alternates with another one featuring the Federal Express emblem (**Figure 7.50**).

ORDER TOLL-FREE
24 HOURS A DAY
1-800-648-7455

Figure 7.47   Wintersilks catalog

Figure 7.48   Smith & Hawken catalog

Figure 7.49   Museum Collections catalog

Figure 7.48   Lillian Vernon catalog

Testimonials. Blurbs do a fine job of highlighting short testimonials. A comment or two will do, although sometimes an entire letter can be used effectively.

Customer comments will have more impact if you combine them with a design and sprinkle them judiciously throughout the catalog. This method not only calls attention to supportive remarks about your company and products, it also makes efficient use of catalog space. A small blurb can almost always fit into an area that otherwise would be wasted.

Figure 7.51 from Jackson & Perkins grabs the reader's attention because the actual letter and envelope accompany this testimonial and others like it. This particular testimonial comments on a product being sold on the same page. **Figure 7.52** is from the Walter Drake and Sons catalog. The headline ("Our Customers Say:") calls attention to the comments wherever they are placed throughout the catalog. Because this comment is general in nature, it could be used on any page in the book.

Figure 7.51   Jackson & Perkins catalog

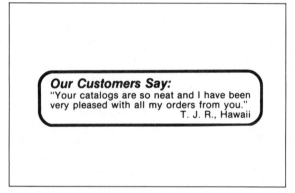

Figure 7.52   Walker Drake and Sons catalog

Guarantees. Guarantees are very effective because they say, "Don't worry, it's okay to order from us." They should be stated often! Simply stating "Satisfaction Guaranteed" throughout the catalog in one-line blurbs is beneficial. But you can do more.

One way is to couple your catalog guarantee with guarantees for specific products. Real Goods uses an inset to highlight the "Infinity Guarantee" for its batteries (**Figure 7.53**). This strongly-worded guarantee includes phrases like "Batteries that Last Forever. . . . You will never have to buy batteries again. . . . These batteries will outlast you." Real Goods is so sure of these batteries that it wraps up the guarantee with "Replacement privileges may not be transferred to your heirs." This art/copy inset has added credibility to the product as well as to the company. It has become a full-fledged promotional tool.

Customer education. Customer education is another primary use for short blurb-type copy, often in conjunction with art or graphic

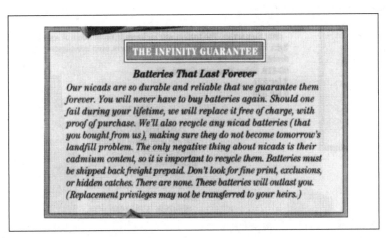

Figure 7.53   Real Goods catalog

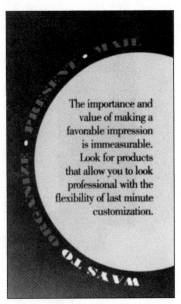

Figure 7.54   "Wow! What a Great Presentation!" catalog

highlighting. All companies can use small space available throughout the catalog for customer education about either the product or the catalog company. The "Wow! What a Great Presentation!" puts educational material in blurbs called "Ways to Organize • Present • Mail." **(Figure 7.54)** Highly visible because they are printed in yellow and bleed off the page, these hints provide general tips that reinforce the catalog's overall theme and subtly support the products shown on the page.

Jackson & Perkins boxes its "Easy Rose Tips" and highlights them with a line drawing of a watering can **(Figure 7.55)**. The number alerts readers that more tips are to come, and encourages them to keep an eye out for them as they thumb through the catalog.

J&P Easy Rose Tip
Moisten the canes of newly planted roses by misting them with a hose and nozzle several times a day until new growth has started.

Figure 7.55   Jackson & Perkins Catalog

Inmac not only includes educational material, it provides an index to its "Helpful Hints." **Figure 7.56** shows the index, which runs on page two. The clever index-card design draws the customer's attention to the twelve pages that offer educational hints on topics such as avoiding common floppy disk dangers. Educational insets that help the customer use a product correctly will encourage orders because the customer can

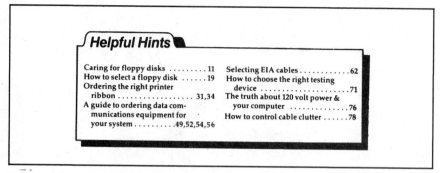

Figure 7.56   Inmac Catalog

more clearly understand the product and associate it with his or her own needs.

The Dickson Company, which markets recording and testing instruments, uses an inset to educate the customer on the vitally important construction of the capillary tube found in sensing bulbs for distant-reading temperature recorders. **Figure 7.57** illustrates how art and copy, as a team, educate the customer concerning the construction and quality of the tube.

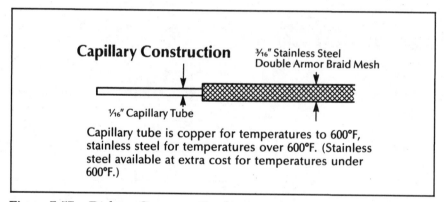

Figure 7.57   Dickson Company Catalog

Information.   Information is another prime use for blurbs and insets. Telling the customer about different product features, company practices, and related product material can help add to sales. Specific product information can be worked in nicely on the same page with a product to which it pertains; general information can be placed anywhere in the catalog. When a standard product is changed, it is a good idea to let the customer know before ordering.

For example, L.L. Bean (**Figure 7.58**) uses an informational blurb to let the customer know about a color and design change in a standard product the company expects to continue to carry. This allows the customer currently ordering to match merchandise previously ordered: "If you purchased a piece prior to 1984 and would like to match an 'old' color, we will continue to offer the luggage in the 'old' colors, and designs. Please direct orders. . . ." This information keeps customer service work down, refunds down, and customers happy. DRI (**Figure 7.59**) uses a blurb informing the customer where to find component parts of workshops offered in bulk form in another part of the catalog. This is a sharp technique as it also gets the customer through the catalog.

The Sportsman's Luggage underwent changes in color and design in 1984. If you purchased a piece prior to 1984 and would like to match an "old" color, we will continue to offer the luggage in the "old" colors, and designs. Please direct orders to attention of the Special Order Department. Specify "old" Green, "old" Navy, "old" Tan, or "old" Gray.

Figure 7.58   L.L. Bean Catalog   **Figure 7.59**   DRI Catalog

Williams-Sonoma, a kitchen and housewares catalog, cleverly uses blurbs for informing the customer about pricing and about policies referred to in the product copy, as well as giving the customer full recipes that match a product on the same page. **Figure 7.60**:

- Explains that favorable foreign exchange rates mean better prices for the customer. On the same page, two products have reduced special prices.

- Clarifies a point made in the copy throughout the catalog: "NOTE" When we say 'recipe included' we will enclose with your order a complimentary 3″ × 5″ printed recipe card. . . ." All informational blurbs originated by Williams-Sonoma are "signed" with a special company logo.

Other beneficial aspects of product quality or company policies can be highlighted in blurbs and insets. Using them not only serves customers with information and attracts their attention, but it also adds a finishing touch that makes a catalog a polished presentation.

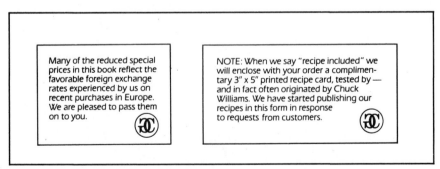

Figure 7.60   Williams-Sonoma Catalog

CHAPTER 8

The Guarantee

A strong, well-worded guarantee is a major persuasive element in giving your customer confidence to place the order.

Your guarantee builds company credibility, symbolizes trustworthiness, and reflects your company's attitudes toward your customers and your products. It tells your customers that they can order with confidence because you have a real stake in every customer's satisfaction. It helps break down resistance due to concerns about fit, quality, workability, color, or a simple change of mind. And it tells your customers that what they receive will live up to their expectations, and that if any problems do happen to surface, they can return merchandise for a refund, a credit, or an exchange.

Your guarantee policies and the way you present them can mean the difference between a catalog that inspires an order and a catalog that is tossed aside. Don't be leery about offering a strong, full money-back guarantee. The stronger your guarantee, the more your customer will trust you and order from you. And a strong guarantee won't lead to a flood of returns or an epidemic of people trying to take advantage of your goodwill. It's a lot of trouble to return goods and complain about problems. If you represent your products fairly, your customer will treat you fairly, too. Simply put, there's no word like *guaranteed*.

Three elements of a customer confidence-building guarantee

1. It offers the strongest guarantee possible.

2. It is worded in a way that is appropriate for the products sold, and builds confidence.

3. It is strategically placed so the customer can easily see it.

What to Guarantee

A guarantee can cover five major elements. If you include all five, your guarantee will be strong and effective tool for building customer confidence.

The Product

The product is your customer's major concern, and it should be yours, too. Because your customer can't inspect it when he or she is making the purchase, there's always a risk that it may not prove satisfactory. It may not fit, not work properly, or just not be what the customer had in mind. Take pains to guarantee your product and to promote your return policy, especially if you accept returns no matter what.

Service

Service separates the wheat from the chaff in the catalog industry. An excellent service operation begins with an honest and complete product presentation in your catalog. Once an order is placed, it offers convenient, round-the-clock 800-number service and helpful, well-trained customer service reps who do their best to meet every customer request, be it an order, a complaint, a query, or a special gift order. (Many companies also offer separate 24-hour numbers for hearing-impaired customers who rely on Telecommunications Device for the Deaf equipment; others have separate telephone numbers for speakers of Spanish.) If you have a strong customer service operation, make sure your guarantee says so. Follow the example of Tiger Software, which uses its cover to promise "the most knowledgeable telephone staff in the business." On the other hand, if you're a little weak in customer service, it will behoove you to correct the problems before you make any claims in your guarantee.

Delivery

Delivery is a terribly important mail order factor. Customers value efficient, prompt delivery. Guaranteeing a specific delivery time is a real plus. In some of its catalogs, Quill ink jets a message telling the customer how late in the day an order can be placed for "lightning fast" overnight delivery. If you guarantee that all orders will arrive in five working days . . . in 48 hours . . . by Christmas morning, tell your customers!

Packaging

Packaging is intrinsic to the safe arrival of your merchandise. Nothing is more disappointing or more irritating to a customer than receiving a damaged product due to inadequate packaging. On the other hand, in today's environmentally conscious marketplace, an over-protected product can be just as irritating. What can you guarantee about your packaging? That your products will arrive damage free? That your packaging is "green" and won't harm the environment?

Price

Price is of vital importance and interest to the customer. Guaranteeing prices for a specific period of time can reassure your customers and act as an incentive for them to place orders quickly. You can also guarantee lowest prices, and offer to refund the difference when customers find identical products available for less elsewhere. Catalogs that offer this option find that very few customers actually request a refund—but that customers feel more secure in ordering from a company that makes such a dramatic guarantee.

Other Areas to Guarantee

What matters to your customers? Can you guarantee it? Home Health Products for Life, The Body Shop, and other natural products catalogs guarantee that their products are not tested on animals. Non-profit catalogs like Save the Children, Co-op America, and The Company of Women guarantee that a portion of their profits will be channeled to the charities and social change groups they support. Hammacher Schlemmer guarantees that all products labeled "best" or "only" have been judged so after thorough research. What tangible or intangible characteristics of your catalog, your products, or your service can be promoted through your guarantee?

Two Approaches to the Basic Guarantee

Every guarantee is modeled on one of two basic structures: the unconditional guarantee and the conditional guarantee. Which base you choose to build on depends on your confidence in your products and your operation, and the limitations you choose to impose. Sometimes these limitations are imposed by someone else. Federal law prohibits the return of animal vaccine, for example, so if that's what you sell by mail, there's no point asking a customer to return it in order to receive a refund.

The Unconditional, Unlimited Time Guarantee

This is the guarantee that built the catalog industry. Today's consumers are willing to shop from catalogs because yesterday's mail order pioneers were willing to take back merchandise no matter what the reason.

This "no questions asked" unconditional guarantee places no conditions on the customer's satisfaction. The customer may return the product for any reason, no matter whether it is defective, not the right color or size, or simply unwanted. A truly unconditional guarantee will also offer the choice of a cash refund, charge card credit, or an exchange for the same or a different product.

The unconditional guarantee offers several advantages. It builds strong customer confidence; builds company credibility; establishes product credibility; and promotes ordering. It also presents no negatives that might subconsciously influence the customer.

On the downside, an unconditional guarantee subjects a company and its products to very high expectations. If you're prepared to meet them, then the unconditional guarantee is for you. But if you're afraid you might fall short, you're better off promising *less* instead of *more* than you can deliver.

Spiegel calls upon its company history to add drama to its strong, simple, unconditional guarantee (**Figure 8.1**), which appears on the inside of its front cover. The fact that Spiegel had been in business for 125 years when this catalog was released tells new customers that this is no fly-by-night operation! The strong sentence, "no questions asked" reassures customers that no lengthy explanations will be required, and spelling out the options—credit, refund, or replacement—lets them know that Spiegel can accommodate any request.

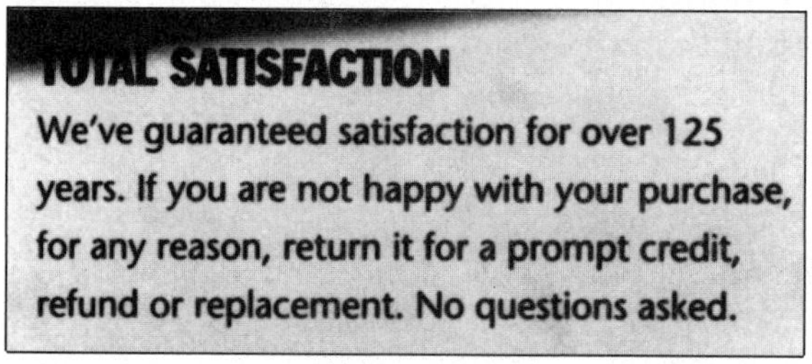

TOTAL SATISFACTION

We've guaranteed satisfaction for over 125 years. If you are not happy with your purchase, for any reason, return it for a prompt credit, refund or replacement. No questions asked.

Figure 8.1   Spiegel catalog

Country Curtains uses its guarantee to back its products and to sell the convenience of mail order shopping (**Figure 8.2**). It positions its friendly, family-oriented, small-town service against the impersonal treatment one risks suffering in a big-city company: "You can depend on us to give your order special attention and to go out of our way to be fair in refunding or exchanging anything that isn't exactly what you want. Simply return any item within 60 days, in its original condition, and your refund will be on its way to you . . . no questions asked! . . ." This guarantee appears above ordering information and a picture of three generations of Jane Fitzpatrick's family. It is next to a letter to the buyer that gives the personal history of the company and ends with a P.S.: "May all of your decorating projects turn out just as you hoped they would!" This guarantee, with the accompanying messages, is an excellent way to dispel *generic* fears about catalog returns and to provide another reason to do business with this *specific* company. A section below the guarantee— "Jane's Answers to Common Questions"—reinforces this image and message.

Military and adventure equipment cataloger U.S. Cavalry words its "Four Star Guarantee" in a way that expresses its overall personality (**Figure 8.3**). *"At U.S. Cavalry, you wear the highest rank. You give the orders"* is a great version of the old saw, "the customer is always right." For maximum visibility, the four-star guarantee is highlighted twice on the order form, once in two colors, and is mentioned in a president's letter that lists reasons why customers can shop U.S. Cavalry with confidence.

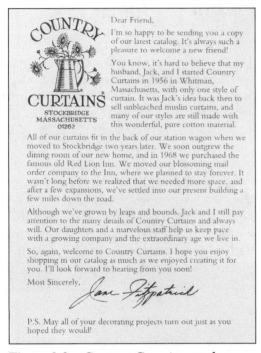

Figure 8.2   Country Curtains catalog

★★★☆

──────── **FOUR STAR GUARANTEE** ────────

At U.S. Cavalry, you wear the highest rank. You give the orders. If you are not 100% satisfied with your purchase, return the merchandise to us, and you'll get a speedy replacement or refund.

GUARANTEED!

Figure 8.3   U.S. Cavalry catalog

Shoes can be difficult to sell by mail—but the California Best athletic shoes catalog keeps orders flowing by placing no restrictions on its guarantee, found on the order form information panel (**Figure 8.4**). *"For any reason, at any time"* tells shoe buyers that a wide range of problems can be resolved whenever they occur.

THE CALIFORNIA BEST GUARANTEE
We are extremely proud of the products in our catalog. If for any reason, at any time, you are not totally satisfied, return any item for refund, credit or exchange.

Figure 8.4   California Best catalog

J. Peterman pares down the unconditional, unlimited time guarantee to its essentials: *"Absolute Satisfaction. Anything less, and you get your money back. Period"* (**Figure 8.5**). It's almost the first thing customers see when they open the catalog, as the guarantee is set off by nearly half a page of white space. The message is repeated again on the order form just under the purchase total box.

> # Absolute Satisfaction.
>
> Anything less, and you get your money back. Period.

Figure 8.5   J. Peterman catalog

The Unconditional, Limited Time Guarantee

Many catalogers stipulate a time period within which a customer must express dissatisfaction in order to receive a refund, credit, or exchange. The time requirements can be anything the cataloger wishes, as long as they are stated clearly and in a reasonably conspicuous place for the customer to see. Ten days, two weeks, 30 days, 60 days, and one year are all common time periods imposed in guarantees.

All product types can be successfully guaranteed within a specific time limit—even products such as seeds and plants that need an extended time period to allow the customer to test them.

Figure 8.6 shows Renovator's Supply's guarantee. The headline, *"Buy with Confidence,"* sets a strong, positive tone for the straightforward message that follows, and the generous one-year time limit is mentioned at the end of the guarantee—*after* the company has established its willingness to be flexible about refunds, replacements, or credits.

Figure 8.6   Renovator's Supply catalog

Country Curtains (**Figure 8.7**) also leads off with positive statements that reinforce how much the company values its customers. *"You can depend on us to give your order special attention and to go out of our* *way to be fair in refunding or exchanging anything that isn't exactly what you wanted.*" The time limit—60 days to return for a refund, more than 60 days for an exchange—is softened by the promise to refund or exchange merchandise that falls short of "your quality expectations." This gracious language tells customers that the company will do what it can to retain and please its customers.

Our Guarantee

Your complete satisfaction is very important to us! You can depend on us to give your order special attention and to go out of our way to be fair in refunding or exchanging anything that isn't exactly what you wanted. Simply return any item within 60 days, in its original condition, and your refund will be on its way to you . . . no questions asked! After 60 days, we'll be happy to exchange any item returned in its original condition. And, of course, at any time, we'll gladly accept, for refund or exchange, any item that, for any reason, falls short of your quality expectations.

Figure 8.7   Country Curtains catalog

Careful wording can make a regular time-limit guarantee sound like a free-trial period. True free-trial guarantees give the customer a stated period of time in which to examine the product. During this time, no monies need be paid. Only after the declared period of time must the customer pay, if the product is satisfactory. If it is not satisfactory, the product may be returned. An example of how simply a regular 30-day guarantee is turned into a free-trial period is seen in **Figure 8.8** from a Sharper Image catalog issued some years back. "*You have 30 days to make up your mind*" can be very easily interpreted as a period of trying out at no charge. The fact is, the customer has already paid, even though money will be refunded if the product is not satisfactory.

1. You have 30 days to make up your mind.
     If not satisfied, simply return the item (in new condition, please) within 30 days for a prompt, courteous refund, whatever the reason. Your satisfaction is the only judge.

Figure 8.8   The Sharper Image catalog

Viking office products lets customers return merchandise for a full credit or refund during a 30-day trial period—but the time limit is only mentioned in the small print. **Figure 8.9** plays up Viking's prompt delivery and willingness to actually pick up unsatisfactory merchandise—a real boon in a busy office. The boxed map reinforces Viking's guarantee that all merchandise will arrive promptly and safely. The smaller box headed "*The Famous Viking Guarantee*" mentions the 30-day time return policy. Yet another guarantee is mentioned on the cover, but not explained inside: "One Year Guarantee on Everything." All these guarantees build consumer confidence in Viking's ability to ship merchandise, but may leave customers scratching their heads over exactly how long the company can keep Viking merchandise.

Figure 8.9   Viking Office Products catalog

The Conditional Guarantee

The conditional guarantee promises to completely satisfy the customer by refunding, crediting, or exchanging *if*: if the personalizing mistake was the catalog company's error; if you have not used the product; and so on.

The most common conditional guarantee is the one excluding personalized products. That's a definite plus for the cataloger, but a minus for the customer, who may hesitate to order products that are restricted in any way.

If there are strings attached to your guarantee, try to state them in the nicest way possible. Ballard Designs (**Figure 8.10**) uses apologetic language to soft pedal its conditional guarantee. "*We regret that person-*

alized items, special orders, cut fabrics and glass tops are not returnable"
is much kinder than the bald phrase, *"Personalized items may not be
returned."*

OUR GUARANTEE

IF FOR ANY REASON YOU ARE LESS THAN
DELIGHTED WITH AN ITEM FROM BALLARD
DESIGNS, PLEASE RETURN IT (PREPAID IN THE
ORIGINAL PACKING) WITHIN 60 DAYS FOR
AN EXCHANGE OR REFUND. WE REGRET
THAT PERSONALIZED ITEMS, SPECIAL
ORDERS, CUT FABRICS AND GLASS TOPS ARE
NOT RETURNABLE.

Figure 8.10 Ballard Designs catalog

Reliable Home Office's guarantee applies to "every item—no exceptions" (**Figure 8.11**). Except that personalized items can not be returned
for a cash refund! But Reliable introduces its policy with a congenial
phrase (*"While we can't offer refund on personalized items . . ."*), provides an honest rationale for the policy (*"because they can't be resold"*),
and offers three other alternatives for handling personalized items.

**THE BEST GUARANTEE
IN THE BUSINESS.**
**Not just on selected items—every item,
no exceptions.** You must be completely
satisfied with the product, the service and
the delivery or we'll quickly issue a
replacement, full credit or a complete
refund. No questions asked, even on
personalized items. While we can't offer a
refund on personalized items, since they
can't be resold, we will make them right,
exchange them or give you a credit coupon
toward your next purchase. No one offers a
better guarantee. And that helps make
Reliable HomeOffice™ products the best
values around.

Figure 8.11 Reliable Home Office catalog

A conditional guarantee can also be useful when a product can be
damaged or destroyed by a neglectful customer or an act of God. **Figure
8.12** shows how White Flower Farm guarantees that its plants are true
to variety and will arrive at the right time, in good condition, and
with instructions on how to plant or care for every item offered. The
guarantee's one condition is that the plant must be properly cared for.

Part two of this guarantee elaborates on the conditions under which
White Flower Farm will not refund or replace a product. The headline,
"Our Shared Responsibility," avoids an it's-your-fault tone by engaging
the gardener in a serious, almost philosophical essay on how plants

flourish. The closing sentence, *"We promise to do our job to the highest standards we know and count on you to do the same"* turns this conditional guarantee into a shared struggle that White Flower Farm's serious gardeners are willing to undertake.

OUR GUARANTEE

We guarantee to ship plants that are true to variety and in prime condition for growing, to deliver at the proper time for planting (presuming timely receipt of orders), and to provide clear and reliable information regarding the proper use and care of every item offered. We will cheerfully refund or replace, one time, any plant that has been properly cared for but has failed to grow. Please notify our Customer Service Department immediately if you find a problem upon receipt of your shipment. Adjustments against selections from this catalogue made must be made before September 30, 1994.

OUR SHARED RESPONSIBILITY

The relationship between you, the gardener, and us, the growers, is important to understand because we are dealing with living things that will occasionally fail despite our mutual best efforts. Our job is to provide vigorous, healthy plants and to get them to you in top shape. Your job is to plant them promptly in an appropriate site, paying attention to the cultural advice that we provide. If our plants get proper care and do not grow, it is our responsibility and we will make good. But if they arrive in good health and are lost to extreme weather or neglect, that is your responsibility and while we may share your disappointment, we cannot share your loss. We promise to do our job to the highest standards we know and count on you to do the same.

Figure 8.12   White Flower Farms catalog

Guaranteeing Price

More and more catalogs are stating a time period during which catalog prices are valid. This approach protects the cataloger from supplier cost increases, allowing a legitimate period of time after which prices may be raised. And it subtly reminds customers that they can keep the catalog a while before ordering—but not too long. If they order after the stated date, they may have to pay more!

Quill, Viking, and many other office products catalogs run price expiration dates on every catalog. Spiegel implies that products or prices will change in its back-cover statement, *"Order from this catalog through. . . ."* To encourage customers to order as soon as possible, sale catalogs almost always promote sale dates on the front or back cover, often repeating the expiration date on the order form and information panel.

Another technique is the comparison pricing guarantee, which challenges customers to find a better price if they can. It sounds risky, but most companies that extend this guarantee end up refunding very little money. Plow & Hearth, whose price guarantee is shown in **Figure 8.13**, is a case in point. The few hundred dollars the company refunds each year are a small price to pay for the confidence this message gives to their customers.

100% Satisfaction Guaranteed
If for any reason, at any time, you are less than 100% satisfied with a product you have purchased from us, you may return it for exchange or a full refund.
Guaranteed Lowest Price
If you find a product identical to the one you have purchased from us at a lower price, we will promptly refund you the difference.

Figure 8.13   Plow & Hearth catalog

This kind of price guarantee works especially well in competitive markets where lowest price is an issue. It can also work for catalogs that carry unusual merchandise the consumer is unlikely to find in a store. But no matter how it is used, the competitive price guarantee is very strong and motivating. It will stimulate an increase in orders that will easily make up for the few "takers" of the offer.

Guaranteeing Delivery

The faster you ship, the happier your customers will be—especially during time-sensitive periods like the last two weeks before Christmas.

As we said earlier in this chapter, if you can take an order on December 22 and guarantee delivery on December 24, say so. If you can take an order this afternoon and have it there by tomorrow, tell your customers!

Figure 8.14 shows how Real Goods, a catalog of energy-efficient items, promotes guaranteed Christmas delivery on its order form. The shaded box stands out on the information panel, and tells customers exactly when they should order to send orders by overnight or regular delivery. Dozens of "fifth season" gift catalogs mailed in early or mid-

December promote delivery guarantees on their front or back covers. The Williams-Sonoma catalog in **Figure 8.15** sticks to a fairly understated back-cover treatment; but in the busy and competitive weeks before Christmas, a high-profile front-cover message is perfectly appropriate.

Guaranteed Christmas Delivery
Orders placed by 8pm Pacific Time
on December 22 can be shipped
overnight for guaranteed delivery
before Christmas.
(Available for in-stock items only.)
To guarantee delivery by standard
shipping, please place your order by
December 14.

For Christmas Delivery
order anytime until noon (PST), Dec. 23.
1 800 541 2233

Figure 8.14   Real Goods catalog   **Figure 8.15**   Williams-Sonoma catalog

Figure 8.16   California Best catalog

Athletic shoe catalog California Best offers guaranteed delivery on four shoe styles in the cover shown in **Figure 8.16.** The guarantee is worded almost like a bet: if the company can't deliver the shoes in 48 hours, the customer gets them free! The customer will be about $60 ahead if the company doesn't come through in 48 hours.

Figure 8.17   Quill catalog

Quill devotes its cover to guaranteeing prices *and* fast delivery—both important points in the highly competitive office supply business (**Figure 8.17**). The image of the clock hand inching toward 6:00 P.M. lets customers know that even an order placed a few minutes before the deadline will be in their hands the next day.

Touting your company's reliable service and excellent on-time delivery record is a great way to make your customers happy and build your credibility.

Where Should You Place Your Guarantee?

A strong guarantee won't mean a thing if your customer can't see it.

Two of the most powerful places to put a guarantee are the front and back cover. Products that are especially hard to sell by mail, such as shoes, benefit enormously from guarantees in this position. California Best runs its price guarantee in a banner right under the catalog name on the cover (take a second look at **Figure 8.16**). Modern Farm also runs a guaranteed banner across the top of its catalog (**Figure 8.18**).

24 HOUR ORDERING • EVERY ITEM 100% GUARANTEED

Figure 8.18   Modern Farm catalog

Figure 8.19   Wintersilks catalog

WinterSilks mentions its guarantee in a bulleted list on the back cover of its catalog—but the small type is overwhelmed by the other elements on the page, including the ink-jetted address and message (**Figure 8.19**). The Paragon solves this problem by using the ink-jet message area to highlight its backcover guarantee (**Figure 8.20**).

The two most common places to promote the guarantee are the company or president's letter and the order form/envelope. The catalog letter is an obvious choice, because it addresses the customer and can help build company credibility. You can do it in the text of the letter, or even make the guarantee itself into a personalized letter, as Plow & Hearth does in **Figure 8.21**, which appears on the inside front cover of the catalog. Coupled with the pictures and signatures of the owners, and a friendly *"We look forward to serving you,"* this is an effective way to make sure customers see and read the company's unconditional and competitive price guarantees.

ROTTWEILER MAT. They'll look twice before entering when this Rottweiler guards your door! He's so real, the only thing missing is the growl. Indoor/outdoor polyester carpeting, non-skid latex backing, hose clean. 20" x 30". USA-made.
#3224 29.00 ⚠

The Paragon

89 Tom Harvey Road
Westerly. Rhode Island 02891
(401) 596-0134

CALL TOLL FREE
1-800-343-3095

CAR-RT SORT **CR 30
CODE 4FTH

AT THE PARAGON, CUSTOMER
SATISFACTION IS #1: IF ANY
ITEM, FOR ANY REASON, DOES
NOT MEET YOUR EXPECTATIONS,
ANYTIME, YOU MAY RETURN IT
FOR A FULL, PROMPT REFUND.

Figure 8.20 The Paragon catalog

Our Guarantee to You

If for any reason, at any time, you are less than 100% satisfied with a product you have purchased from us, you may return it for exchange or a full refund.

If you find a product you have purchased from us at a lower price from another source, we will promptly refund you the difference in price.

We look forward to serving you!

Sincerely,

Peggy & Peter Rice

Figure 8.21 Plow & Hearth catalog

Philosophy.

"People want things that are hard to find. Things that have romance. but a factual romance, about them.

I had this proven to me all over again when people actually stopped me in the street (in New York, in Tokyo, in London) to ask me where I got the <u>coat</u> I was wearing.

So many people tried to buy my coat off my back that I've started a small company to make them available. It seems like everybody (well, not <u>everybody</u>) has always wanted a classic horseman's duster but never knew exactly where to get one.

I ran a little ad in the New Yorker and the Wall Street Journal and in a few months sold this wonderful coat in cities all over the country and to celebrities and to a mysterious gentleman in Japan who ordered <u>two thousand</u> of them.

Well, the coat <u>is</u> magnificent. Simple, functional, handsome, extremely well made, affordable and, yes, romantic.

I think that giant American corporations should start asking themselves if the things they make are really, I mean really, better than the ordinary.

Clearly, people want things that make their lives the way they wish they were."

J. Peterman

Absolute Satisfaction.

Anything less, and you get your money back. Period.

© 1994 The J. Peterman Company   Prices in Owner's Manual No. 32 guaranteed through December 31. 1994.

Figure 8.22   J. Peterman catalog

Figure 8.22 shows how J. Peterman promotes his guarantee under his letter on the inside front cover. Here, great type and plenty of white space make this arresting guarantee hard to miss.

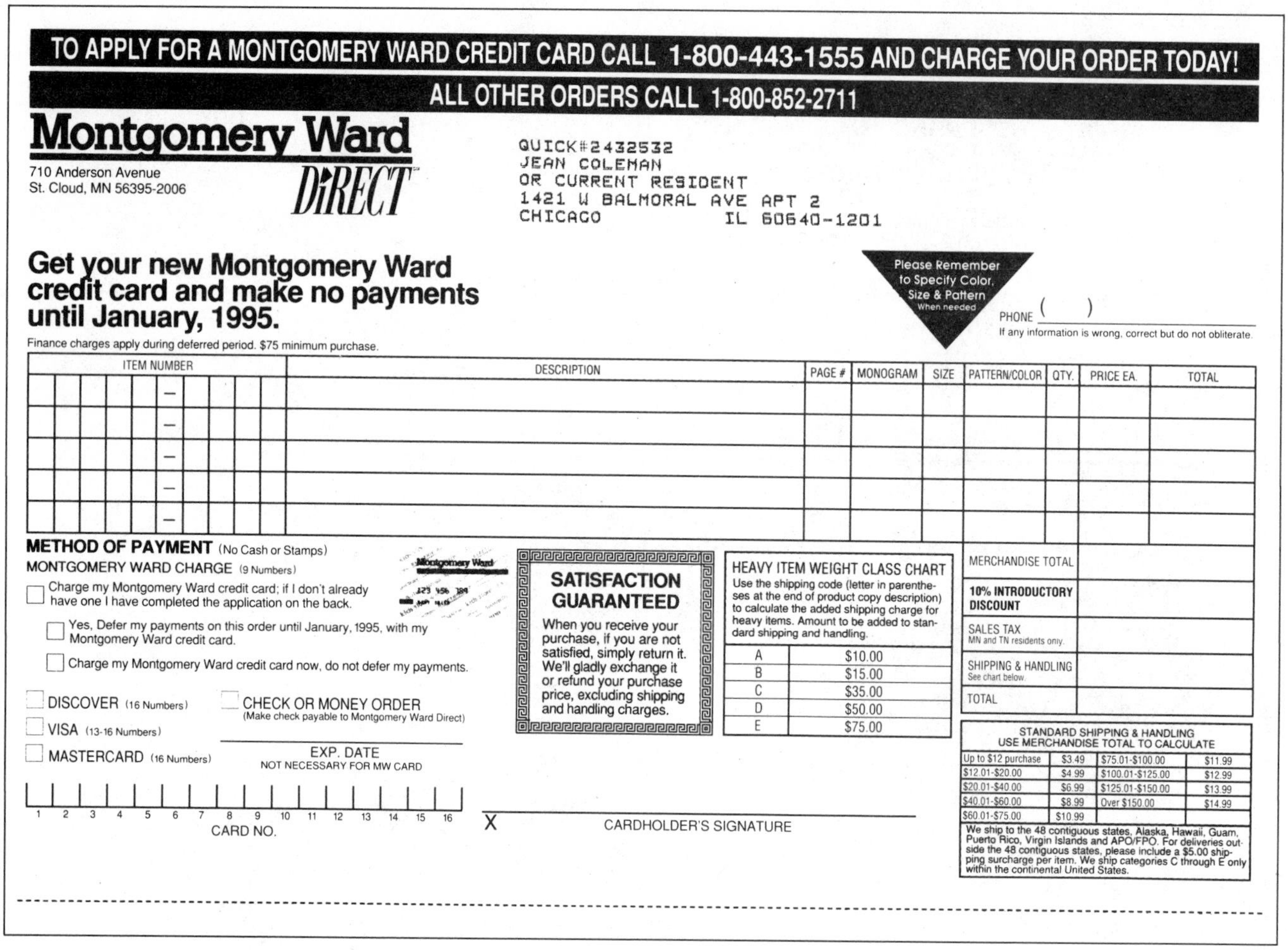

TO APPLY FOR A MONTGOMERY WARD CREDIT CARD CALL 1-800-443-1555 AND CHARGE YOUR ORDER TODAY!

ALL OTHER ORDERS CALL 1-800-852-2711

Montgomery Ward DIRECT

710 Anderson Avenue
St. Cloud, MN 56395-2006

QUICK#2432532
JEAN COLEMAN
OR CURRENT RESIDENT
1421 W BALMORAL AVE APT 2
CHICAGO IL 60640-1201

Get your new Montgomery Ward credit card and make no payments until January, 1995.

Finance charges apply during deferred period. $75 minimum purchase.

Please Remember to Specify Color, Size & Pattern When needed

PHONE ( )

If any information is wrong, correct but do not obliterate.

ITEM NUMBER	DESCRIPTION	PAGE #	MONOGRAM	SIZE	PATTERN/COLOR	QTY.	PRICE EA.	TOTAL
–								
–								
–								
–								
–								

METHOD OF PAYMENT (No Cash or Stamps)

MONTGOMERY WARD CHARGE (9 Numbers)

☐ Charge my Montgomery Ward credit card; if I don't already have one I have completed the application on the back.

☐ Yes, Defer my payments on this order until January, 1995, with my Montgomery Ward credit card.

☐ Charge my Montgomery Ward credit card now, do not defer my payments.

☐ DISCOVER (16 Numbers)

☐ VISA (13-16 Numbers)

☐ MASTERCARD (16 Numbers)

☐ CHECK OR MONEY ORDER (Make check payable to Montgomery Ward Direct)

EXP. DATE
NOT NECESSARY FOR MW CARD

1 2 3 4 5 6 7 8 9 10 11 12 13 14 15 16
CARD NO.

X CARDHOLDER'S SIGNATURE

SATISFACTION GUARANTEED

When you receive your purchase, if you are not satisfied, simply return it. We'll gladly exchange it or refund your purchase price, excluding shipping and handling charges.

HEAVY ITEM WEIGHT CLASS CHART

Use the shipping code (letter in parentheses at the end of product copy description) to calculate the added shipping charge for heavy items. Amount to be added to standard shipping and handling.

A	$10.00
B	$15.00
C	$35.00
D	$50.00
E	$75.00

MERCHANDISE TOTAL	
10% INTRODUCTORY DISCOUNT	
SALES TAX MN and TN residents only.	
SHIPPING & HANDLING See chart below.	
TOTAL	

STANDARD SHIPPING & HANDLING
USE MERCHANDISE TOTAL TO CALCULATE

Up to $12 purchase	$3.49	$75.01-$100.00	$11.99
$12.01-$20.00	$4.99	$100.01-$125.00	$12.99
$20.01-$40.00	$6.99	$125.01-$150.00	$13.99
$40.01-$60.00	$8.99	Over $150.00	$14.99
$60.01-$75.00	$10.99		

We ship to the 48 contiguous states, Alaska, Hawaii, Guam, Puerto Rico, Virgin Islands and APO/FPO. For deliveries outside the 48 contiguous states, please include a $5.00 shipping surcharge per item. We ship categories C through E only within the continental United States.

Figure 8.23 Montgomery Ward catalog

Typical order form/envelope positioning is seen in **Figures 8.23** and **8.24**. Montgomery Ward and Tiger Software both use boxes and two-color printing to highlight guarantees on the order form. In **Figure 8.25**, Exposures highlights its guarantee in a "Pledge of Allegiance" that appears on the back of the order form.

These are good positions because they reassure the customer when placing an order, and may even be a deciding element in placing or deciding to increase an order. Some catalogers feel that many potential customers get as far as the order form and yet do not place an order, from lack of confidence either in ordering by mail or in the company itself. A strong guarantee is a positive element and therefore should be beneficially placed in strategic areas such as these.

☐ **Here's my order.**

ORDERED BY: *Note: We cannot deliver to a P.O. Box.*

CUST#AC07799307   CODE XBJ-171
.MARIE AGUILAR
OR CURRENT RESIDENT   01
5250 N BROADWAY
CHICAGO IL   60640-2304

If your credit card billing address is different than above, please make appropriate changes.

PLEASE! To provide you with better customer service, include your FAX number (optional): (___)_____

METHOD OF PAYMENT *Purchase orders under $100 add $10 processing fee.*

☐ MasterCard ☐ VISA ☐ DISCOVER ☐ DINERS CLUB ☐   ☐ Check Enclosed
                                                      ☐ Money Order

(Please make checks payable to TigerSoftware. Orders shipped subject to clearance of checks.)

☐ **YES!** I have ordered the Miracle Piano and/or any specially marked products featured in this catalog and would like to have my purchase billed in 3 convenient monthly installments on my credit card (VISA, MasterCard, Discover only). *See envelope back for details.*

Account Number—please include all digits.

Month   Year

Expiration Date   Print exact name appearing on credit card

Signature_____

RISK-FREE RETURN GUARANTEE!
We proudly stand behind every product we sell with our ironclad, 30-day return guarantee. If for any reason, you're not 100% delighted with the product, just return it insured within 30 days. We only ask that you return ALL material in new, resalable condition (packing materials, registration cards, etc.) and the original invoice. We will then immediately exchange the program or issue a TigerSoftware credit, less shipping costs, for any future TigerSoftware purchase.

PHONE!
MAC: (800) 666-2562
PC: (800) 888-4437

FAX!
Fax completed order form to (305) 529-2990
(24-hours a day, 7 days)

MAIL!
9100 S Dadeland Blvd
Suite 1200
Miami, FL 33156-7816

INTERNATIONAL ORDERS CALL: (305) 443-8212

SHIP TO: *(if different from address at left)*

Name _____

Company _____

Address _____

City _____ State _____ Zip _____

Day Phone (___) _____ Night Phone (___)_____

ITEMS ORDERED   *(Required to process order)*

Qty	Item No.	Item Description	DOS-WIN MPC-MAC	Disk Size 5¼" or 3½"	Amount
		Total Amount for Items			
Florida and North Carolina Residents Add Applicable Sales Tax					
*Federal Express Shipping and Handling					
TOTAL					

Standard Federal Express Shipping

Merchandise Total:	Add:
Up to $99.99	$5.95
$100. to $199.99	$6.95
$200. to $399.99	$8.95
$400. to $599.99	$12.95
$600. to $999.99	$14.95
$1000. +	$16.95

*Computers, Monitors, Printers, CD-ROM, Scanners, Miracle Keyboards and other large hardware items are charged additional shipping cost. Call for details. For shipping outside the contiguous U.S., please add an additional $10.

Figure 8.24   Tiger Software catalog

"MY PLEDGE OF ALLEGIANCE TO EXPOSURES® CUSTOMERS"

Ronly Bourne

I'll Help Your Photos Live To Be Heirlooms.

I choose EXPOSURES® products not only for their distinctive styling, but for their archival quality – that is, their ability to preserve photos from one generation to the next. That's why my album pages contain none of the harmful PVC (polyvinylchloride) plastics that eat away at pictures. My scrapbook pages and picture mats are 100% acid free.

Exposures Shopping Tips.

Note I've quoted sizes for picture windows, not overall frames, so you can be sure of a proper fit. H/V indicates frames and cards for horizontal or vertical pictures. Look for exclusive items marked . These are designed, manufactured, or commissioned exclusively for EXPOSURES.

I'll Make Last Minute Gift Shopping A Cinch.

For only $2.95 per item, I'll wrap each item (except those noted) in white tissue, tuck it into a box, wrap it in hunter green paper with a white ribbon, and adorn it with a distinctive gold seal. I'll also enclose a gift card with your personal message. Choose our UPS Air Express 2-3 day service for your last minute shopping. Just add $4.95 to our normal shipping charge. ($15 to Alaska and Hawaii.) For shipments to the Caribbean and abroad call 1-800-572-5750. (Sorry, not available to P.O. boxes.)

UPS AIR

I'll Guarantee Your Purchase, No Strings Attached.

If you're not 100% satisfied with your selection at any time, simply return it for a refund or exchange.

Order Toll Free 1-800-222-4947

Figure 8.25 Exposures catalog

What Your Guarantee Should Say

Your guarantee can be short and direct, or long and colloquial. It may be businesslike or personal, simple or complex. Unfortunately, a guarantee can be too long or too confusing—especially when a company is trying to get around a condition it has chosen.

A guarantee should always be worded to sell. A quick look back at some of the guarantees reviewed in this chapter reveals several that turned their guarantee into opportunities to make sales, including Vermont Country Store, Viking, and Quill.

Food is especially hard to sell by mail to a first-time customer. Why? Because food is very personal. People tend to be especially particular about what they eat and what they serve their guests. And oftentimes food-by-mail seems quite expensive. Strong customer confidence must be built. Let's see how two food catalogs meet four very important confidence-building criteria through the guarantees they choose and the *wording* of their guarantees.

Harry and David have sold fruit by mail for decades, with the same guarantee from the start:

> "Our *guarantee since 1936,* Harry and I have *promised to* always please you—*no matter what. Our lawyer,* who used to be *a good pear-picker, says farmers can't guarantee anything* because of hailstorms, wind, drought, crop failures, freezes, mistakes, hazards of farming, birds and bees and everything else. You'll find his fine print on our order blank—but *remember—we guarantee your complete satisfaction or your money back.*"

This is a 100 percent guarantee. The wording is warm and intimate; hard, solid confidence is instilled with a soft, personal touch. The cozy, social approach that relates to the whole psychology of food is used. The guarantees appear on page two and on the back of the order form. Every word sells! Those underlined caress the customer into ordering.

Mary of Puddin' Hill offers a guarantee that psychologically encompasses the feelings Americans have toward food:

> "MARY'S PROOF OF THE PUDDIN' GUARANTEE. We're *proud* of our *products* and also proud of our *customer's confidence.* We will *not knowingly permit a dissatisfied customer.* If you aren't 100% satisfied with any item from Mary of Puddin' Hill, we *will send your money back immediately!* This *includes products, packaging, delivery and service.*"

Again we have a 100 percent guarantee. Friendliness, honesty, and warmth glow throughout the wording. Guarantees appear prominently in Mary's letter to the customer, on a page in the catalog, and on the upper left corner of the order form. Mary comes right out and says that her customers are confident of her products, packaging, delivery, and service; there is no need for customers to interpret confidence. Words underlined are selling hard.

Prism Optical, Inc. Eyeglasses must be one of the hardest products to sell by mail. People's lives—their enjoyment and livelihood—depending on eye care. Convincing people of a company's credibility and dependability, plus product quality, is an enormous job. Prism Optical's catalog has a wonderfully full, complete guarantee!

> Prism Optical, Inc. hereby guarantees that your eye glasses will: 1) look right on your face 2) fit right over your ears, eyes and nose bridge 3) have the right prescription, just as your doctor ordered it for you. You have

30 days from the time you receive your glasses to examine them. If you are not fully satisfied, you can return them to us for a full, prompt refund.

Acknowledge customer doubts

The three major points guaranteed are: (1) *appearance*—relieving the customer of obligation if a wrong style choice is made; (2) *fit*—assuring proper fit and comfort; (3) *accuracy*—guaranteeing a perfect match to the doctor's instructions. In addition to these reassuring, confidence-building points, the customer gets to wear the glasses on a trial basis for up to 30 days. This guarantee is placed on page nine (the back of the lens-choosing guide); it is shortened and printed in red within the "owner's letter," and it is again shortened and critically placed at the bottom of the order form. *Prism Optical does an exceptional job of forming an extra strong guarantee in simple words that inspire customer confidence.*

Master Vaccine, vaccines, plus health and grooming supplies for animals, is serious business and is approached exactly that way. Master Vaccine has a money-back satisfaction guarantee and must deal with more issues than the normal cataloger does because of the product carried. **Figure 8.26** shows how a formal point-by-point approach is successfully executed. The first sentence acknowledges many people's negative thoughts and proposes to alleviate these thoughts. "To buy sight unseen, by mail or phone, is an act of confidence. We understand that and we want to be worthy of it. Our guarantee is simple . . . it has no 'fine print'." That's a pretty good way to counteract a customer's negative thoughts—by being straightforward and using simple lan-

---

**SATISFACTION GUARANTEED
OR YOUR MONEY BACK**

To buy sight unseen, by mail or by phone, is an act of confidence. We understand that, and we want to be worthy of it. Our GUARANTEE is simple . . . it has no "fine print".

1. You must be satisfied -- you are the only judge.
2. Federal law prohibits the return of vaccine.
3. If anything else you order is not to your liking, for any reason or for no reason at all, or if anything arrives in less than perfect condition, you may return it within one month of receipt.
4. You may request exchange, replacement or refund for the full amount of purchase, except shipping charges.
5. Please include your Order Number with any product returned

So, browse through the following pages and order with the complete confidence that every single product will perform to YOUR expectations...OR WE TAKE IT BACK.

Wayne W Nurmi

Wayne W Nurmi
President, Master Vaccine

Figure 8.26   Master Vaccine catalog

guage that cannot be misunderstood. Point number one declares an unqualified requirement of satisfaction: ". . . you are the only judge." Point number two meets and states a federal requirement by stating, "Federal law prohibits the return of Vaccine." Points three, four, and five state other stipulations: return of merchandise, amount refunded or credited, and order number included with the return. These are all worded simply and softly—not in a dictatorial way. The genuine concern of the owner and president, Wayne W. Nurmi, shows through.

Checklist for a Successful Guarantee

- Keep your guarantee direct and to the point. Be specific, and avoid generalizations and "legalese." Let your lawyer read your guarantee . . . but don't let your lawyer write it!

- Establish rapport. Be nice in print, and make your company your customer's ally. Don't draw a line in the sand between "us" and "them."

- Be sincere and be positive. The guarantee is not the place to hem and haw or express your doubts and reservations.

- Make sure your guarantee is believable.

- Use thoughtful, considerate language. Offset negatives with a genuine, considerate tone, or state them in a manner that is not negative at all. Try "*Do anything you like except break it*" instead of "*we will only accept merchandise in saleable condition.*"

- If you must include limitations and conditions, use soft phrases like "*We're sorry, but. . . .*" Consider explaining your policies. Why won't you accept returns and special orders? Your honesty may win orders that a less direct explanation might lose.

- Keep the "small print" out of your guarantee. Let your guarantee simply say that returns are fine. Put the return procedure and any specific information into a separate, order form information panel section on Returns, Refunds, Exchanges, Freight Damage, and Adjustments.

Guarantee Checklist:

☐ Choose strongest guarantee possible.
☐ Investigate manufacturer's guarantees.

Always:
1. Display guarantee prominently.
2. Be careful in the wording and claims—be prepared to follow through with them.
3. Use guarantee as selling element.

Strongly Consider:
1. Placing your guarantee on front and/or back cover.
2. Utilizing your guarantee in headlines, copy, punch lines, blurbs.
3. Placing your guarantee on the order form.
4. Using manufacturer's guarantee as yours.

CHAPTER 9

The Order Form

Traditionally, the order form's role has been to close the sale with ease. Its job has been to get the customer to take the final step in ordering by filling out and mailing the form.

Today, the order form's role is changing. It still captures information about the customer and the order, and it still offers information about the company and its policies. But because telephone orders far outstrip orders received by mail, fewer order forms are actually completed and returned. Of those that are returned, an increasing number of the forms arrive by facsimile machine instead of the U.S. mail.

The order form is now often used to *organize* a purchase prior to placing an order by telephone. So while your ordering staff may not see as many as they once did, the order form is still the best tool for helping the customer—and your order staff—capture and organize essential information.

Order forms can make or break a sale. A complicated order form that is hard to understand may discourage a customer from placing an order. In fact, one of the easiest ways to unknowingly reduce order response is to unnecessarily complicate and confuse your order form.

Internal company battles have raged over what the order form should do, not for the customer, but for the data entry department. But if there are few or no orders coming in, your data entry department won't have anything to do. While the layout for information needed by company departments is important, customers are the important factor. Always, always design your form around *their* needs.

Consumers do not like to wrestle with details. When they must, they want a simple way of doing it. Keep in mind that the easier it is for your customer to understand and use your order form, the better your response will be.

You can use your order form (or "bind in") for much more than a mere ordering device. The basic order form offers four separate areas you can use for various selling and customer service functions. They are:

1. Order form panel

2. Information panel

3. Product panel

4. Ordering envelope

Order Form Panel

The order form panel must make it easy for the customer to place an order. Whether an order is placed by telephone or by mail, this form is the final step in closing the sale. Make it your business to prevent or eliminate roadblocks and visual and mechanical turnoffs that may confuse the customer.

Your order form needs to capture some basic information about your customers and the products they wish to order. The absolutely essential information includes:

1. Customer full name and address

2. Product identity number

3. Quantity desired

4. Name of product

5. Size, color, and personalization requirements

6. Retail price

7. Shipping, handling, insurance charges

8. State tax requirements

9. Method of payment

10. Company name and address

11. Company telephone number (regular and toll-free)

12. Source code number (if inkjetting is not used)

13. Total dollar column

Other beneficial information you may want to capture includes:

1. "Ship to" name and address

2. Customer's day and evening telephone numbers

3. Page number product appears on

4. Request for change of address

5. Minimum order information

6. Company guarantee

7. Special shipping information

8. Mr., Mrs., or Ms. designation

9. Quantity discount or free gift information
10. Thank you

The Reliable Home Office order form shows how a company doing a large volume of business can keep order form demands to a minimum and the design simple for the customer (**Figure 9.1**). The order form covers all the bases in a clean, spare layout that uses two ink colors to highlight Reliable's telephone and fax numbers and to draw attention to its "thank you" note in the lower-right corner of the form. Customers can easily indicate their payment method using the boxes at the top of the form, and the express delivery promise is clearly stated. Black arrows draw the eye to the request for the customer's telephone number and the line where it is to be indicated.

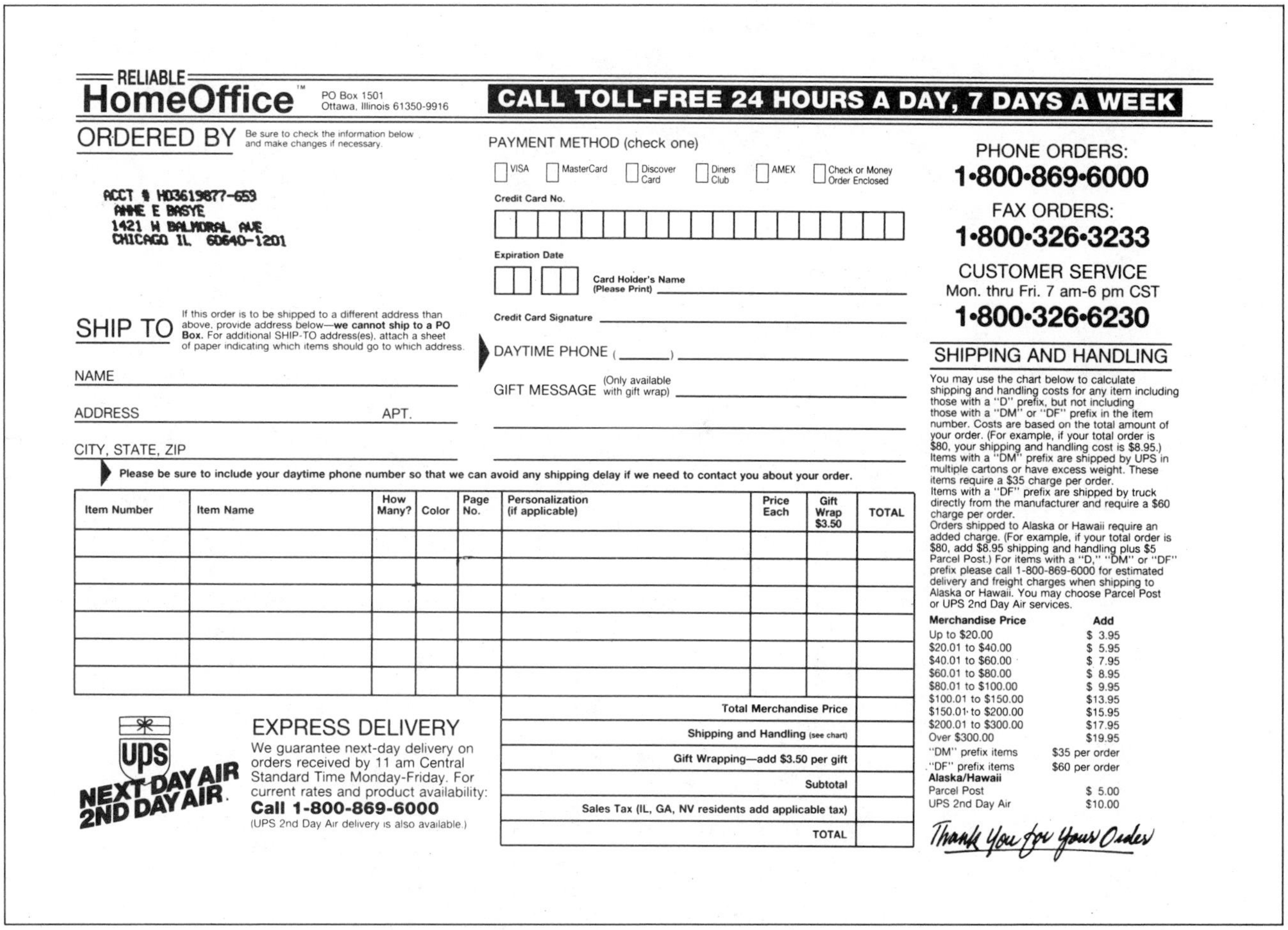

RELIABLE HomeOffice™ PO Box 1501 Ottawa, Illinois 61350-9916

CALL TOLL-FREE 24 HOURS A DAY, 7 DAYS A WEEK

ORDERED BY Be sure to check the information below and make changes if necessary.

ACCT # H03619877-659
ANNE E BASYE
1421 W BALMORAL AVE
CHICAGO IL 60640-1201

PAYMENT METHOD (check one)

☐ VISA ☐ MasterCard ☐ Discover Card ☐ Diners Club ☐ AMEX ☐ Check or Money Order Enclosed

Credit Card No.

Expiration Date

Card Holder's Name (Please Print) ____

Credit Card Signature ____

SHIP TO If this order is to be shipped to a different address than above, provide address below—**we cannot ship to a PO Box.** For additional SHIP-TO address(es), attach a sheet of paper indicating which items should go to which address.

DAYTIME PHONE (____) ____

NAME ____

GIFT MESSAGE (Only available with gift wrap) ____

ADDRESS ____ APT. ____

CITY, STATE, ZIP ____

Please be sure to include your daytime phone number so that we can avoid any shipping delay if we need to contact you about your order.

Item Number	Item Name	How Many?	Color	Page No.	Personalization (if applicable)	Price Each	Gift Wrap $3.50	TOTAL

Total Merchandise Price	
Shipping and Handling (see chart)	
Gift Wrapping—add $3.50 per gift	
Subtotal	
Sales Tax (IL, GA, NV residents add applicable tax)	
TOTAL	

UPS NEXT DAY AIR 2ND DAY AIR

EXPRESS DELIVERY
We guarantee next-day delivery on orders received by 11 am Central Standard Time Monday-Friday. For current rates and product availability:
Call 1-800-869-6000
(UPS 2nd Day Air delivery is also available.)

PHONE ORDERS:
1•800•869•6000
FAX ORDERS:
1•800•326•3233
CUSTOMER SERVICE
Mon. thru Fri. 7 am-6 pm CST
1•800•326•6230

SHIPPING AND HANDLING

You may use the chart below to calculate shipping and handling costs for any item including those with a "D" prefix, but not including those with a "DM" or "DF" prefix in the item number. Costs are based on the total amount of your order. (For example, if your total order is $80, your shipping and handling cost is $8.95.)
Items with a "DM" prefix are shipped by UPS in multiple cartons or have excess weight. These items require a $35 charge per order.
Items with a "DF" prefix are shipped by truck directly from the manufacturer and require a $60 charge per order.
Orders shipped to Alaska or Hawaii require an added charge. (For example, if your total order is $80, add $8.95 shipping and handling plus $5 Parcel Post.) For items with a "D," "DM" or "DF" prefix please call 1-800-869-6000 for estimated delivery and freight charges when shipping to Alaska or Hawaii. You may choose Parcel Post or UPS 2nd Day Air services.

Merchandise Price	Add
Up to $20.00	$ 3.95
$20.01 to $40.00	$ 5.95
$40.01 to $60.00	$ 7.95
$60.01 to $80.00	$ 8.95
$80.01 to $100.00	$ 9.95
$100.01 to $150.00	$13.95
$150.01 to $200.00	$15.95
$200.01 to $300.00	$17.95
Over $300.00	$19.95
"DM" prefix items	$35 per order
"DF" prefix items	$60 per order
Alaska/Hawaii	
Parcel Post	$ 5.00
UPS 2nd Day Air	$10.00

Thank You for Your Order

Figure 9.1 Reliable Home Office order form

The sidebar on shipping and handling charges is the only confusing part of this order form, as it asks customers to check for a prefix to determine whether additional shipping charges are required.

Lillian Vernon's order form (**Figure 9.2**) includes all twelve of the basics and five of the other beneficial information points. The box on personalization plays up the fact that personalization is free, and shows how easy it is to personalize an item. To complete the sale, the company provides a special column where the desired initials can be listed. But the company hasn't included a "thank you" anywhere!

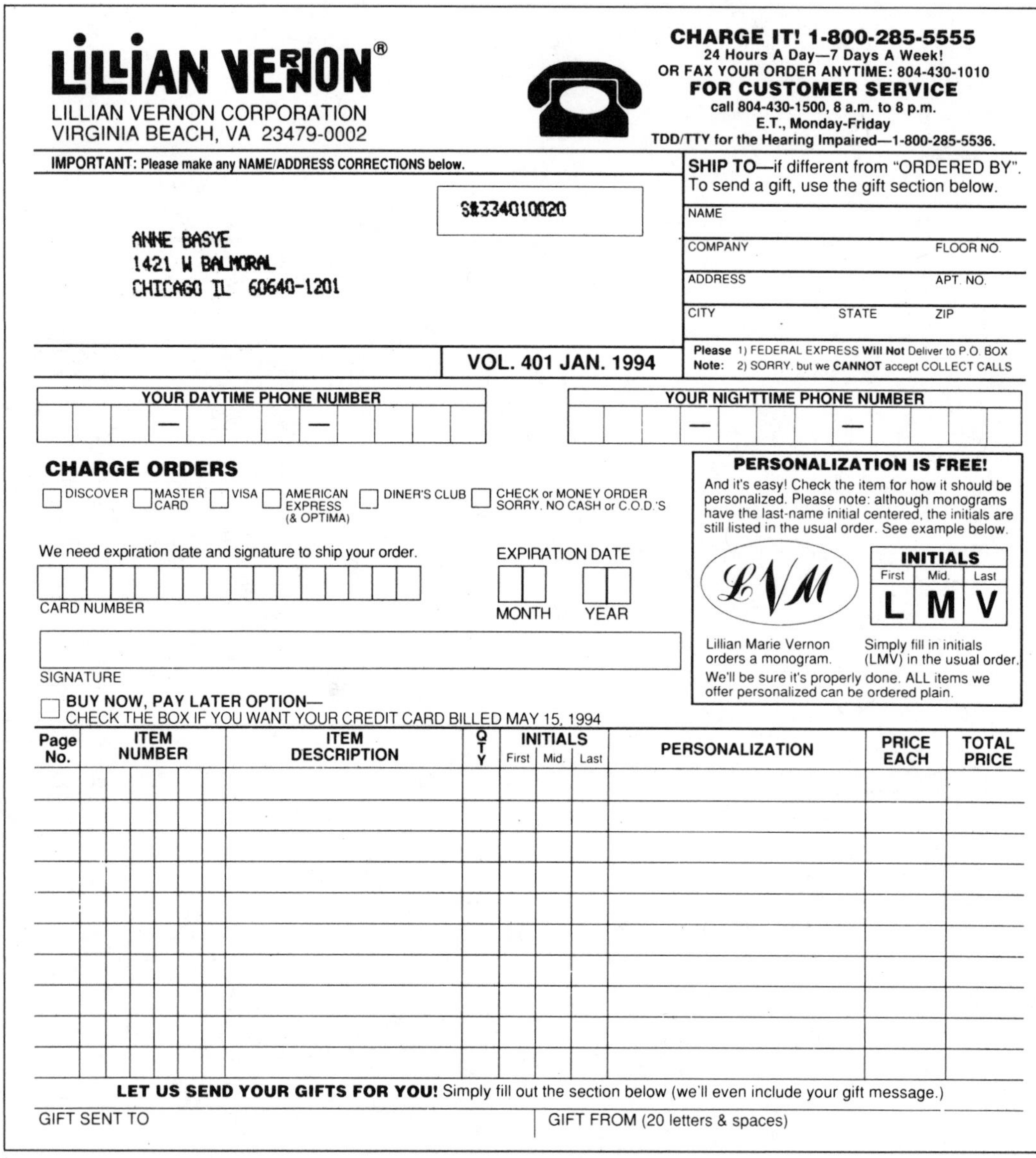

LILLIAN VERNON®
LILLIAN VERNON CORPORATION
VIRGINIA BEACH, VA 23479-0002

CHARGE IT! 1-800-285-5555
24 Hours A Day—7 Days A Week!
OR FAX YOUR ORDER ANYTIME: 804-430-1010
FOR CUSTOMER SERVICE
call 804-430-1500, 8 a.m. to 8 p.m.
E.T., Monday-Friday
TDD/TTY for the Hearing Impaired—1-800-285-5536.

IMPORTANT: Please make any NAME/ADDRESS CORRECTIONS below.

S‡334010020

ANNE BASYE
1421 W BALMORAL
CHICAGO IL 60640-1201

SHIP TO—if different from "ORDERED BY". To send a gift, use the gift section below.
NAME
COMPANY FLOOR NO.
ADDRESS APT. NO.
CITY STATE ZIP

VOL. 401 JAN. 1994

Please Note: 1) FEDERAL EXPRESS **Will Not** Deliver to P.O. BOX 2) SORRY, but we **CANNOT** accept COLLECT CALLS

YOUR DAYTIME PHONE NUMBER
YOUR NIGHTTIME PHONE NUMBER

CHARGE ORDERS
DISCOVER MASTER CARD VISA AMERICAN EXPRESS (& OPTIMA) DINER'S CLUB CHECK or MONEY ORDER SORRY, NO CASH or C.O.D.'S

We need expiration date and signature to ship your order.
CARD NUMBER
EXPIRATION DATE
MONTH YEAR
SIGNATURE

BUY NOW, PAY LATER OPTION—
CHECK THE BOX IF YOU WANT YOUR CREDIT CARD BILLED MAY 15, 1994

PERSONALIZATION IS FREE!
And it's easy! Check the item for how it should be personalized. Please note: although monograms have the last-name initial centered, the initials are still listed in the usual order. See example below.
INITIALS
First Mid. Last
L M V
Lillian Marie Vernon orders a monogram.
Simply fill in initials (LMV) in the usual order.
We'll be sure it's properly done. ALL items we offer personalized can be ordered plain.

Page No.	ITEM NUMBER	ITEM DESCRIPTION	QTY	INITIALS First	Mid.	Last	PERSONALIZATION	PRICE EACH	TOTAL PRICE

LET US SEND YOUR GIFTS FOR YOU! Simply fill out the section below (we'll even include your gift message.)
GIFT SENT TO
GIFT FROM (20 letters & spaces)

Figure 9.2 Lillian Vernon's order form

Spiegel keeps its order form simple by referencing the "How to Order" panel instead of squeezing a complicated delivery charge table onto the face of the order form (**Figure 9.3**). By designing its order form so sparely, Spiegel is able to include an application for its Spiegel FCNB Preferred Charge card. But it, too, lacks a thank you note.

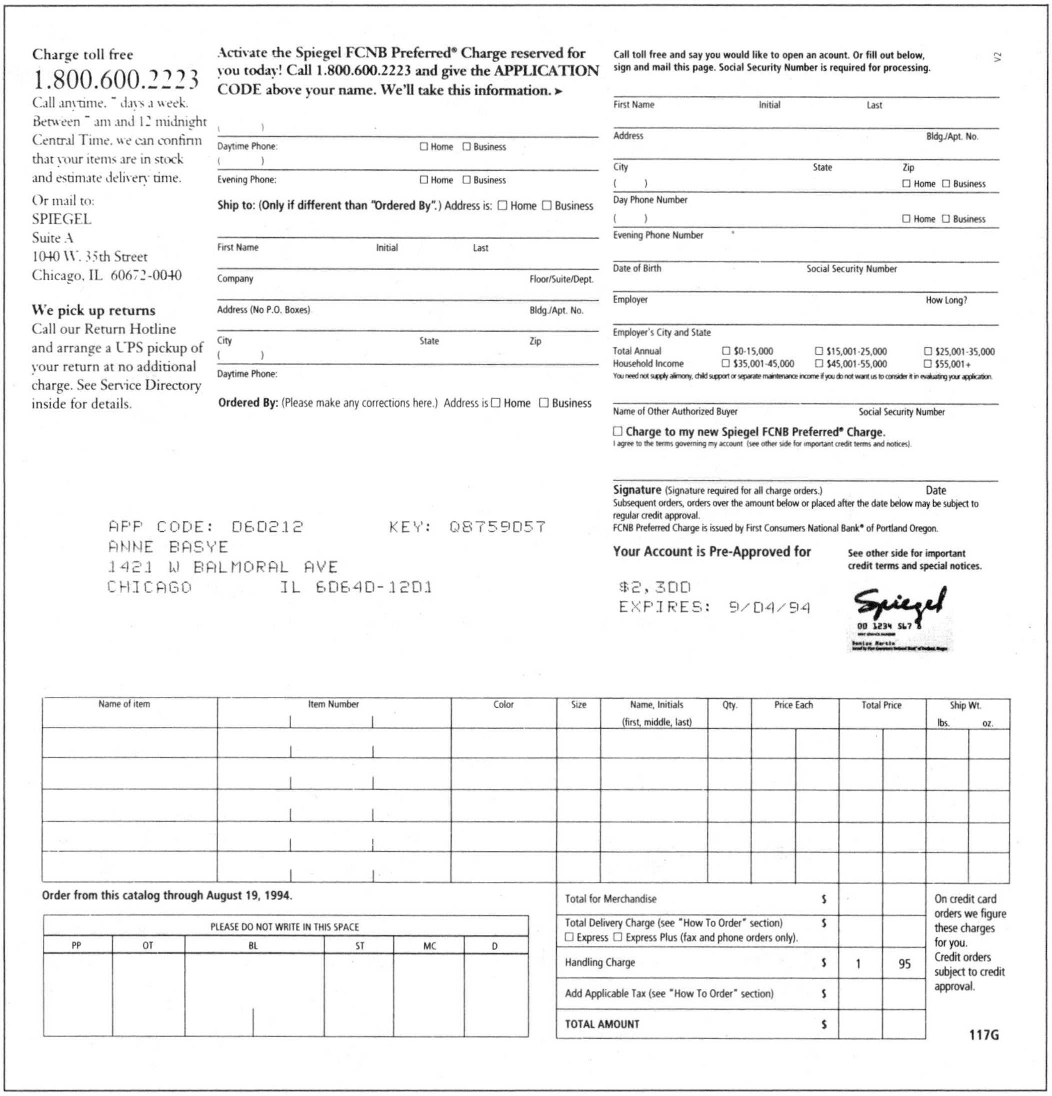
Charge toll free
1.800.600.2223
Call anytime, 7 days a week. Between 7 am and 12 midnight Central Time, we can confirm that your items are in stock and estimate delivery time.

Or mail to:
SPIEGEL
Suite A
1040 W. 35th Street
Chicago, IL 60672-0040

We pick up returns
Call our Return Hotline and arrange a UPS pickup of your return at no additional charge. See Service Directory inside for details.

Activate the Spiegel FCNB Preferred® Charge reserved for you today! Call 1.800.600.2223 and give the APPLICATION CODE above your name. We'll take this information. ➤

( )
Daytime Phone: ☐ Home ☐ Business
( )
Evening Phone: ☐ Home ☐ Business

Ship to: (Only if different than "Ordered By".) Address is: ☐ Home ☐ Business

First Name Initial Last
Company Floor/Suite/Dept.
Address (No P.O. Boxes) Bldg./Apt. No.
City State Zip
( )
Daytime Phone:

Ordered By: (Please make any corrections here.) Address is ☐ Home ☐ Business

APP CODE: 060212 KEY: 08759057
ANNE BASYE
1421 W BALMORAL AVE
CHICAGO IL 60640-1201

Call toll free and say you would like to open an acount. Or fill out below, sign and mail this page. Social Security Number is required for processing. V2

First Name Initial Last
Address Bldg./Apt. No.
City State Zip
( ) ☐ Home ☐ Business
Day Phone Number
( ) ☐ Home ☐ Business
Evening Phone Number
Date of Birth Social Security Number
Employer How Long?
Employer's City and State
Total Annual Household Income ☐ $0-15,000 ☐ $15,001-25,000 ☐ $25,001-35,000 ☐ $35,001-45,000 ☐ $45,001-55,000 ☐ $55,001+
You need not supply alimony, child support or separate maintenance income if you do not want us to consider it in evaluating your application.

Name of Other Authorized Buyer Social Security Number

☐ **Charge to my new Spiegel FCNB Preferred® Charge.**
I agree to the terms governing my account (see other side for important credit terms and notices).

Signature (Signature required for all charge orders.) Date
Subsequent orders, orders over the amount below or placed after the date below may be subject to regular credit approval.
FCNB Preferred Charge is issued by First Consumers National Bank® of Portland Oregon.

Your Account is Pre-Approved for
$2,300
EXPIRES: 9/04/94

See other side for important credit terms and special notices.

Spiegel
00 1234 567 8

Name of item	Item Number	Color	Size	Name, Initials (first, middle, last)	Qty.	Price Each	Total Price	Ship Wt. lbs.	oz.

Order from this catalog through August 19, 1994.

PLEASE DO NOT WRITE IN THIS SPACE					
PP	OT	BL	ST	MC	D

Total for Merchandise	$		
Total Delivery Charge (see "How To Order" section) ☐ Express ☐ Express Plus (fax and phone orders only).	$		
Handling Charge	$	1	95
Add Applicable Tax (see "How To Order" section)	$		
TOTAL AMOUNT	$		

On credit card orders we figure these charges for you. Credit orders subject to credit approval.

117G

Figure 9.3 Spiegel order form

Why is a thank you note so important? Because everyone likes to hear a word of thanks—especially as an order is being placed. Your customer service representatives will be able to offer a simple thank you to customers who order by phone, but a short note on your order form will acknowledge those who order by mail or facsimile machine.

The Information Panel

The information panel should discuss in detail every service you offer: toll-free ordering, fast delivery service, mail preference notification, return and exchange policies, and full guarantee declarations. Often a full panel of the order form plus the back of the ordering envelope is used for this information.

How much room is needed depends on your product line. If you sell clothing, a sizing chart, diagram, or other explanation might not only be appropriate but also help keep the return rate down. (This kind of information also instills customer confidence and encourages an order.) If you are a business-to-business cataloger, you may need to state your terms and conditions of sale, including product patent and copyright policies.

If your needs don't require use of a full panel of ordering information, you might include explanations of special offers, free gifts, or even merchandise you want to highlight.

Basic Facts to Tell Your Customer

1. Toll-free service. Explain your toll-free service. Promote the hours it is available, especially if you offer 800-number service around the clock and every day of the week. If you have more than one 800-number, explain what each is for.

2. Shipping information. Shipping information can be a very big benefit that can help close your sale. Tell your customer about the different shipping methods your company offers. Give the turnaround time for each. Heavily promote UPS or Federal Express delivery, or any other special delivery services you offer. Always promote your company's ability to promptly deliver its products.

Explain any special methods of shipping, and tell the charges for each. Are conditions for delivery outside the continental United States and for foreign delivery different? Be sure to say so.

3. Return policies. Should customers be dissatisfied or need to return the merchandise, it is beneficial to them to know how to return the goods. Do you have a preferred way you want the merchandise returned? Tell them how—insured and prepaid, original order included, special packaging for product protection. Letting the customer know merchandise can be returned (plus how to do it) strengthens customer confidence in the company.

4. Customer inquiries. You may have a special person or department assigned to this function, depending on your order volume and product line. If you do, tell the customer—this may be a big plus and something to promote heavily. For added friendliness, some companies even give the name of a particular person to call.

5. Guarantee. State your guarantee in full, whether it is only one sentence or several. Have you stated it elsewhere in the catalog? That's good—but be sure to state it again on the information panel. This is a very influential place, one referred to by most customers. The opportunity to build company credibility and instill customer confidence should be promoted here via your guarantee.

6. How-to-order basics. Telling customers how to order step-by-step, so they can easily check off the steps and place the order correctly, ensures proper order fulfillment and fast service—a big bonus for the customer. Number these steps to correspond with the steps needed on the order form, or give customers a check list to mark off for accuracy. Separate the requirements for ordering by mail and by phone—the phone customer needs additional information, such as telephone number and hours to place the order. Some companies encourage customers to fill in the order form before placing their phone order to ensure accuracy and speed of handling.

7. Mailing preference policy and service. Most catalog companies rent their lists to other catalog companies. By letting your customers know this and giving them the option of not receiving mailings from other companies, you help the mail order industry be its own watchdog. The more companies that comply, the less likely the federal government will become the watchdog.

Additional Information

As catalog order forms have grown, so has the amount of information they can provide. Consider adding these flourishes to help make your catalog stand out from the crowd.

1. Free catalog for a friend request and form. Personal referrals are wonderfully responsive names to add to your mailing list. The Serengeti Wildlife Apparel and Gift catalog introduces its message with the catchy phrase, "Hope You Had a Wild Time!" (**Figure 9.4**). Its position on the back of the order envelope makes it easy for the mail opening department to separate this information from order entry processing.

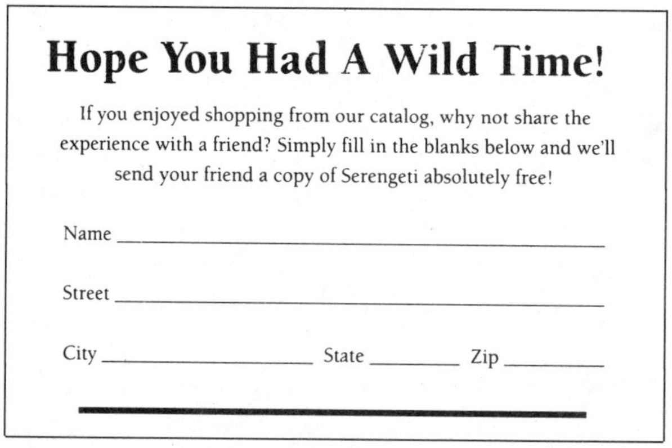
Hope You Had A Wild Time!

If you enjoyed shopping from our catalog, why not share the experience with a friend? Simply fill in the blanks below and we'll send your friend a copy of Serengeti absolutely free!

Name ____________________

Street ____________________

City ____________ State ________ Zip ________

Figure 9.4 Serengeti Wildlife Apparel and Gift order form

2. Gift service. Announcing this service is important, especially if your product line is conducive to gift-giving. If you offer a full gift wrapping and card enclosure service, an illustration is a nice touch but not absolutely necessary unless you offer different kinds of wrapping at different dollar costs. Because it is a gift catalog, Seasons (**Figure 9.5**) plays up its attractive wrapping service with a full-color illustration of its gift-box-and-paper combination.

3. Gift certificate opportunity. If you offer to send a gift certificate directly to the recipient, along with a catalog to aid in selection, you have a special service your customers will want to know about. Tell customers how to acquire a gift certificate, and in what dollar amounts it is available. Jackson & Perkins (**Figure 9.6**) not only offers step-by-step instructions on how to order a certificate, it includes a full-color illustration of its handsome certificate and enclosure.

Figure 9.5   Seasons order form

Figure 9.6   Jackson & Perkins order form

4. Gift selection service.   Helping the customer select gifts can be a big drawing card. In recent years many catalogs have offered bridal registry services. Ross-Simons devotes an entire panel to its bridal registry program offering solid benefits ("we can locate almost any pattern"; "gift selection is convenient for your guests") and a special telephone number to call to register (**Figure 9.7**). The copy does all it can to persuade the bride that ordering by telephone will be much easier for both bride and guests than visiting or ordering from a conventional department store.

The Ross-Simons Bridal Registry

A world of fine gifts and courteous service a phone call away. To register, just call 1-800-82-BRIDE, and provide us with your choice of china, flatware and crystal patterns. You needn't be limited to items featured in the Ross-Simons catalog. We carry most famous brands, and we can locate almost any pattern.

Registration is Easy!

Let us walk you through your bridal registry step-by-step. We'll mail you a confirmation of your choices, along with cards you can use to let your guests know you're registered with Ross-Simons. At your request, we'll mail catalogs to your guest list.

Gift Selection is Convenient For Your Guests

Your guests simply call Ross-Simons' toll-free order number. We'll help each guest select the perfect gift from your personal bridal registry! Of course, every gift carries our guarantee of satisfaction.

ON THIS VERY SPECIAL OCCASION, TREAT YOURSELF AND YOUR GUESTS TO FAMOUS ROSS-SIMONS QUALITY, SELECTION AND VALUE!

To Register, Call
1-800-82-BRIDE
(800-822-7433)

Figure 9.7   Ross-Simons order form

When you phone in your order, ask about our "Bumper Crop Specials."

We plan our stocks of plants several years in advance, because that's how long it takes to grow them. But each season brings its surprises, and they sometimes take the form of unexpected surpluses on which we are able to offer terrific discounts. When you call, be sure to ask your agent about any "Bumper Crop Specials" that are in effect that day. They change from week to week as sales and weather vary, but there's almost always a bargain or two to be had for the asking.

Figure 9.8   White Flower Farm order form

5. Delayed delivery service. This allows the customer to order now for delivery at a later specified time. An especially nice service for Christmas or Thanksgiving time, it allows the customer to place one order early for different people and different delivery times. Food and garden catalogs utilize delayed delivery most often. Plants, bulbs, trees, and shrubs must be shipped at specific times of the year, but are usually sent to the customer placing the order. In food catalogs, the percentage of gift orders is very high.

6. Telephone specials. It is smart telephone marketing to offer customers catalog specials when they call to place an order. Merchandise offers may be overstock or a special purchase. In either case, this type of offer is a big plus and deserves special promotion. Place the offer near your toll-free number for maximum exposure.

White Flower Farm offers "Bumper Crop Specials," a daily special on overstock plants and bulbs. **Figure 9.8** shows how the offer is promoted, next to the index of perennials and shrubs. The offer is mentioned again on the order panel, this time to secure permission for an outbound telephone sales call.

7. Product line aids. Some categories of merchandise benefit a great deal from extra attention. For product lines where personalization is a big factor, or for clothing, stationery, or metal products, you might want to include special instructions on how to order. Clothing is one obvious candidate for special attention since complaints run high and the customer naturally hesitates to place an order for fear of dissatisfaction. Charts telling how to determine one's correct size not only build customer confidence in placing an order, but also benefit the catalog company by cutting down on the number of refunds and exchanges. Size conversion tables can be helpful, as are simple instructions.

An apparel catalog that meets the challenge of keeping a low return factor while encouraging orders is Lands' End (**Figure 9.9**). Throughout its catalog, Lands' End does an exceptional job of explaining what materials are used and what features make their products superior. This measurement and conversion chart, which occupies the entire back of the order form, supports its message. The illustration shows how to measure for various types of clothing; a very extensive conversion chart relieves the customer's mind even more. A separate chart for children ensures that their clothes will fit perfectly, too. All these features act as insurance against returned goods.

The simplicity with which the chart is presented allows ease of interpretation, especially since the conversion chart tells what size to order for each article. The problem of size, which once was complex, deterred ordering, and produced a high return factor, now is solved so ordering becomes almost automatic.

The chart is not new or revolutionary, but it does accomplish two major goals. First, it encourages an order by putting the customer at ease about what size to order. Second, it decreases the percentage of returns due to improper size by assuring that customers will place more accurate orders. This is excellent use of an order form panel by an apparel company.

8. Credibility builders. The order form area is where the customer is going to place an order or consider placing an order. And building company credibility will certainly help make this decision a positive one. Hence the order form is an ideal place for customer testimonials, letters from the president, or information about retail locations.

L.L. Bean's information panel is loaded with elements to help the customer. **Figure 9.10** shows the importance placed on ordering by

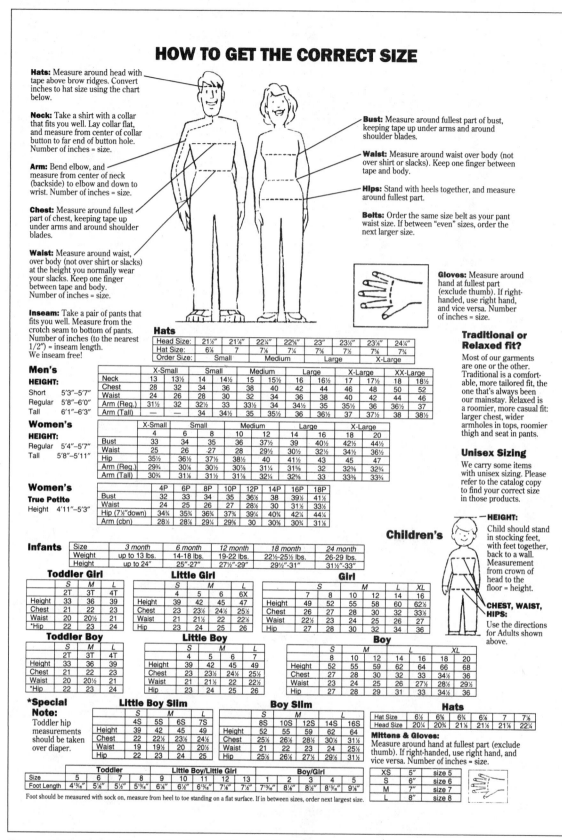

HOW TO GET THE CORRECT SIZE

Hats: Measure around head with tape above brow ridges. Convert inches to hat size using the chart below.

Neck: Take a shirt with a collar that fits you well. Lay collar flat, and measure from center of collar button to far end of button hole. Number of inches = size.

Arm: Bend elbow, and measure from center of neck (backside) to elbow and down to wrist. Number of inches = size.

Chest: Measure around fullest part of chest, keeping tape up under arms and around shoulder blades.

Waist: Measure around waist, over body (not over shirt or slacks) at the height you normally wear your slacks. Keep one finger between tape and body. Number of inches = size.

Inseam: Take a pair of pants that fits you well. Measure from the crotch seam to bottom of pants. Number of inches (to the nearest 1/2") = inseam length. We inseam free!

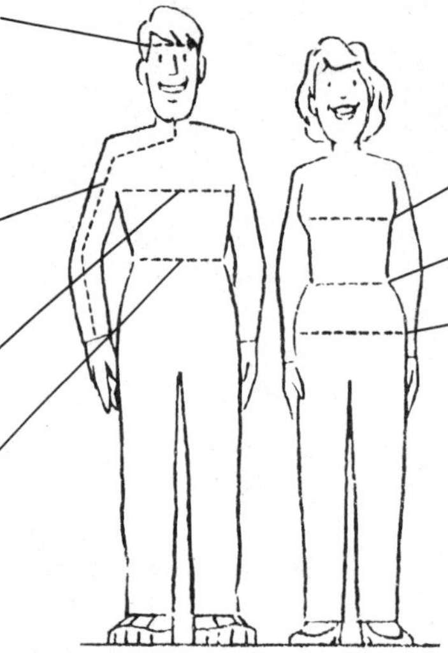

Bust: Measure around fullest part of bust, keeping tape up under arms and around shoulder blades.

Waist: Measure around waist over body (not over shirt or slacks). Keep one finger between tape and body.

Hips: Stand with heels together, and measure around fullest part.

Belts: Order the same size belt as your pant waist size. If between "even" sizes, order the next larger size.

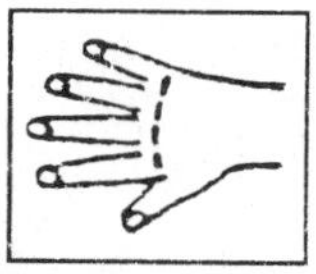

Gloves: Measure around hand at fullest part (exclude thumb). If right-handed, use right hand, and vice versa. Number of inches = size.

Hats

Head Size:	21½"	21⅞"	22¼"	22⅝"	23"	23½"	23⅞"	24¼"
Hat Size:	6⅞	7	7⅛	7¼	7⅜	7½	7⅝	7¾
Order Size:	Small		Medium		Large		X-Large	

Traditional or Relaxed fit?

Most of our garments are one or the other. Traditional is a comfortable, more tailored fit, the one that's always been our mainstay. Relaxed is a roomier, more casual fit: larger chest, wider armholes in tops, roomier thigh and seat in pants.

Unisex Sizing

We carry some items with unisex sizing. Please refer to the catalog copy to find your correct size in those products.

Men's

HEIGHT:
Short 5'3"–5'7"
Regular 5'8"–6'0"
Tall 6'1"–6'3"

	X-Small		Small		Medium		Large		X-Large		XX-Large	
Neck	13	13½	14	14½	15	15½	16	16½	17	17½	18	18½
Chest	28	32	34	36	38	40	42	44	46	48	50	52
Waist	24	26	28	30	32	34	36	38	40	42	44	46
Arm (Reg.)	31½	32	32½	33	33½	34	34½	35	35½	36	36½	37
Arm (Tall)	—	—	34	34½	35	35½	36	36½	37	37½	38	38½

Women's

HEIGHT:
Regular 5'4"–5'7"
Tall 5'8"–5'11"

	X-Small	Small		Medium		Large		X-Large	
	4	6	8	10	12	14	16	18	20
Bust	33	34	35	36	37½	39	40½	42½	44½
Waist	25	26	27	28	29½	30½	32½	34½	36½
Hip	35½	36½	37½	38½	40	41½	43	45	47
Arm (Reg.)	29¾	30⅛	30½	30⅞	31¼	31⅝	32	32⅜	32¾
Arm (Tall)	30¾	31⅛	31½	31⅞	32¼	32⅝	33	33⅜	33¾

Women's

True Petite
Height 4'11"–5'3"

	4P	6P	8P	10P	12P	14P	16P	18P
Bust	32	33	34	35	36½	38	39½	41½
Waist	24	25	26	27	28½	30	31½	33½
Hip (7½"down)	34¾	35¾	36¾	37¾	39¼	40¾	42¼	44¼
Arm (cbn)	28½	28⅞	29¼	29⅝	30	30⅜	30¾	31⅛

Children's

HEIGHT: Child should stand in stocking feet, with feet together, back to a wall. Measurement from crown of head to the floor = height.

CHEST, WAIST, HIPS: Use the directions for Adults shown above.

Infants

Size	3 month	6 month	12 month	18 month	24 month
Weight	up to 13 lbs.	14-18 lbs.	19-22 lbs.	22½-25½ lbs.	26-29 lbs.
Height	up to 24"	25"-27"	27½"-29"	29½"-31"	31½"-33"

Toddler Girl

	S	M	L
	2T	3T	4T
Height	33	36	39
Chest	21	22	23
Waist	20	20½	21
*Hip	22	23	24

Little Girl

	S	M		L
	4	5	6	6X
Height	39	42	45	47
Chest	23	23½	24½	25½
Waist	21	21½	22	22½
Hip	23	24	25	26

Girl

	S		M		L	XL
	7	8	10	12	14	16
Height	49	52	55	58	60	62½
Chest	26	27	28	30	32	33½
Waist	22½	23	24	25	26	27
Hip	27	28	30	32	34	36

Toddler Boy

	S	M	L
	2T	3T	4T
Height	33	36	39
Chest	21	22	23
Waist	20	20½	21
*Hip	22	23	24

Little Boy

	S	M		L
	4	5	6	7
Height	39	42	45	49
Chest	23	23½	24½	25½
Waist	21	21½	22	22½
Hip	23	24	25	26

Boy

	S	M		L		XL	
	8	10	12	14	16	18	20
Height	52	55	59	62	64	66	68
Chest	27	28	30	32	33	34½	36
Waist	23	24	25	26	27½	28½	29½
Hip	27	28	29	31	33	34½	36

***Special Note:**
Toddler hip measurements should be taken over diaper.

Little Boy Slim

	S	M		L
	4S	5S	6S	7S
Height	39	42	45	49
Chest	22	22½	23½	24½
Waist	19	19½	20	20½
Hip	22	23	24	25

Boy Slim

	S	M		L	
	8S	10S	12S	14S	16S
Height	52	55	59	62	64
Chest	25½	26½	28½	30½	31½
Waist	21	22	23	24	25½
Hip	25½	26½	27½	29½	31½

Hats

Hat Size	6½	6⅝	6¾	6⅞	7	7⅛
Head Size	20¼	20¾	21⅛	21½	21⅞	22¼

Mittens & Gloves:
Measure around hand at fullest part (exclude thumb). If right-handed, use right hand, and vice versa. Number of inches = size.

	Toddler				Little Boy/Little Girl					Boy/Girl				
Size	5	6	7	8	9	10	11	12	13	1	2	3	4	5
Foot Length	4 13/16"	5⅛"	5½"	5 13/16"	6⅛"	6½"	6 13/16"	7⅛"	7½"	7 13/16"	8⅛"	8½"	8 13/16"	9⅛"

Foot should be measured with sock on, measure from heel to toe standing on a flat surface. If in between sizes, order next largest size.

XS	5"	size 5
S	6"	size 6
M	7"	size 7
L	8"	size 8

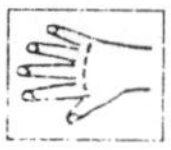

Figure 9.9 Lands' End order form. © Lands' End, Inc.

telephone and fax, with special assistance offered to the hearing impaired. Shipping information goes into the different types (even foreign) and includes a breakdown of the charges. Size guidelines plus a conversion chart, the mail preference policy, and the telephone number to call for assistance with returns are all referenced.

ORDER BY PHONE
U.S. and Canada—1-800-221-4221
International—207-865-3111
24 Hours a Day—7 Days a Week
For fastest service, please complete this order form and have your credit card handy.

ORDER BY MAIL
Please be sure to fill out your order form completely.

ORDER BY FAX
U.S.—207-797-8867
Canada and International—207-878-2104

TDD SERVICE 1-800-545-0090
We offer Telephone Device for the Deaf (TDD) for our hearing impaired customers.

CUSTOMER SERVICE
U.S. and Canada—1-800-341-4341
International—207-865-3161
We pride ourselves in superior customer service. We're here 24-hours a day to help with order status and repairs.

SHIPPING
Regular Shipping
We now ship most orders via Federal Express delivery service—for delivery in **2 to 5 business days** (depending on where you live) anywhere in the contiguous U.S. We charge $3.95 per address. Hawaii and Alaska orders are shipped via USPS Priority Service for $3.95; add $10.00 for FedEx delivery. APO/FPO P.O. Box orders are shipped via USPS.

Express Shipping
Federal Express* standard service–for delivery in **2 business days** anywhere in the U.S., add $9.00 per address in the contiguous U.S., $19.00 per address in Hawaii and Alaska.

Canadian and International Shipping
For shipping, duty and tax information, please call 1-800-341-4341 ext. 3736 in the U.S. and Canada. Outside the U.S. and Canada, please call 207-865-3161. Recipients may be responsible for paying Duties and Taxes for orders sent internationally.

Monogramming/Alterations
Please allow 1 to 2 extra days for delivery for orders containing monogramming and/or inseam alterations.
*Federal Express trademark used by permission.

RETURNS
If you need to return an item, please refer to your packing slip or call **1-800-341-4341** for assistance.

MAIL PREFERENCE SERVICE
Occasionally, we make a portion of our mailing list available to organizations whose products or services we think might be of interest to our customers—especially organizations that encourage responsible use of the outdoors. If you do not wish to receive such mailings, please copy your mailing label exactly as it appears on the back of the catalog and mail to: L.L. Bean, Inc., Dept. C.F.M, Freeport, Maine 04033-0001. Also, if you no longer wish to receive the L.L. Bean catalog, please include a note with a copy of your mailing label.

Please Help Us Conserve Our National Resources
If you are receiving more than one copy of the same catalog, please send us all of the mailing labels, showing us which one is correct.

Figure 9.10 L. L. Bean order form

 HOW TO ORDER
Order by mail
Use the order blank enclosed. Or write a letter giving product name, item number, and size or color. Send to Modern Farm, 1825 Big Horn Ave., Cody, WY 82414.
Order by telephone
Phone toll free 800-443-4934. Operators are on duty from 7:30-4:30 Mountain Time Monday-Friday. 7:30-Noon Saturday. After hours ordering service lets you order day and night. Dial direct and order with a charge to your VISA, Mastercard or Discover credit card.
Terms
Terms are payment-with-order. Please include your check, bank draft, money order or use your credit card. Sales tax must be added for the following states: Wyoming (4%), California (7-1/4%), and Texas (7-1/4%). Customer agrees to pay all bank charges for any checks which do not clear and all other costs of collection, including reasonable attorney's fees.
Shipping
We ship UPS wherever possible. If you prefer Parcel Post, please specify. On request we will ship your order by Air UPS Blue Label and bill you for the added cost.

 SHOP WITH CONFIDENCE
1. **Over 200,000 satisfied customers.**
   Modern Farm has over 200,000 customers who come to us year after year for all their ear tag and other ranch supply needs. They keep coming back because they know they'll get fair prices, great merchandise and excellent service!
2. **Only good quality offers.**
   With Modern Farm's guarantee, we only offer good quality merchandise. You must be satisfied.
3. **Lowest possible prices consistent with quality.**
   No seconds or inferior quality items are offered; so the value offered for the money is outstanding.
4. **Reliable product descriptions.**
   All of the products are described in this catalog in an honest, straightforward manner without exaggeration. Often you get much more information in the catalog than you could from a store clerk.
5. **Prompt shipments.**
   Items are often shipped from our building within 48 hours of receipt of your order. Some items are shipped from warehouses where fast service is their specialty. You will be notified of any unforeseen delay.
6. **Satisfaction guaranteed.**
   You must be completely satisfied with anything you order or return it immediately for a cheerful refund or replacement.
7. **Toll-free number to answer any questions.**
   Call our customer service department (toll free 800-443-4934) if you have any questions.

 CUSTOMER SERVICE
When phoning, please call (800-443-4934) between 7:30 a.m. and 4:30 p.m. Monday through Friday. Ask for Customer Service.

RETURNS AND EXCHANGES
Please fill out the information on the back of your packing slip and return it with your merchandise. We will handle your return the day we receive it.

CORRESPONDENCE
We appreciate any suggestions, comments or questions. Our customers are a vital part of our organization. Feel free to make any suggestions you see fit regarding our merchandise or service. Send to Customer Service Department.

MAILING LISTS
We occasionally make our customer list available to carefully screened companies whose products might be of interest to you. If you prefer not to receive such mailings, please copy your mailing label exactly and send to:

Modern Farm Mail Preference Service,
1825 Big Horn Ave., Cody, WY 82414.

Figure 9.11 Modern Farm order form

A business-to-business catalog that also packs its information panel full of elements to benefit and educate the customer is Modern Farm (**Figure 9.11**). An attractive line design of a barn acts as an attention-getter for the different subject areas. All-cap headlines complete the subject call-out. How to order, reasons to shop with confidence, and information about customer service, returns and exchanges, correspondence, and mailing lists all become special—each one declaring its own informational importance.

Modern Farm does an especially fine job of building company credibility and customer confidence with the "Shop with Confidence" section. Some good points can be gleaned by reviewing these seven reasons:

1. **Over 200,000 satisfied customers.** The headline alone tells customers and prospects that a lot of people believe in the company enough to purchase.

2. **Only good quality** is reinforced by the guarantee and tells the customer the company is proud of its products.

3. **Lowest possible prices** reminds customers that Modern Farm considers their pocketbooks, too.

4. **Reliable product descriptions** reinforces company credibility and belief in the company's products by truth-in-advertising. This also brings up a point that is very valid and influential in mail-order shopping: *"Often you get much more information in the catalog than you could from a store clerk."*

5. **Prompt shipments** tells customers the company cares about serving them quickly . . . "often within 48 hours of receipt of your order."

6. **Satisfaction guaranteed** emphasizes the desire to please the customer.

7. **Toll-free number to answer any questions** is yet another way of letting customers know the company backs up its products and truly cares about and welcomes customer interest.

Info panel can sell company

Most of these seven "reasons" have already been explained elsewhere on the page, but this is *promoting them—selling the product, service, delivery, dependability, and credibility.* It's space well used. And at the top of the page, three close-out products are offered at sale prices—the proceeds will no doubt pay for the order form.

In summary, the details given on the information panel will build customer confidence. In some cases this information allows the customer to try out vicariously the service or "try on" a product, thus eliminating fear of ordering. Clarifying the process of ordering will benefit the company, too, by allowing smoother order processing. And carefully worded information will help keep down refunds due to misunderstandings or to incorrect sizing or personalization.

Product Panel

Because the product panel has often been compared to a checkout line in a grocery or discount store where impulse items are sold, it is a popular area for sale merchandise and impulse products. Regular merchandise can be presented, too.

Once, the choice of product was determined by the number of ink colors used. Many products simply did not present well in one or two colors. But as more order forms are printed on four-color presses, these obstacles are vanishing.

Talbot's uses the front and back of the order form insert to display its popular cotton sweaters and linen jackets in full color (**Figure 9.12**). Williams-Sonoma (**Figure 9.13**) uses a two-panel foldout to picture five products for sale. The page layout follows that of the catalog for tight coordination and strong purchasing appeal.

If you use a black-and-white or two-color order form, you need to illustrate merchandise that can effectively be illustrated on these pages. Instead of promoting new computer software packages on its two-color

Figure 9.12   Talbots product panel

A The **Double Sink Mat Set** protects glasses and dishes from accidents. Set includes two 12" x 10¾" rubber grids for inside sinks, a 10¼" x 9" saddle for the ridge between sinks and a 12¾" x 15½" draining board grid. Made in Italy. Green or White. *The set* #46-684050 **$12.00** *Catalog only* ⊛

B **Folding Wire Dish Rack Set** includes a vinyl-coated steel rack and cutlery basket, with a polypropylene drainer mat. The white rack holds 23 plates and 10 cups or glasses; it measures 18¼" x 12½" x 9⅛" high when open (folds to 2⅛" deep). The utensil basket and 20" x 16" mat are available in Green, White or Blue. *The set* #46-631929 **$29.00** *Catalog only* ⊛

C These **Utensil Jars** keep favorite tools in easy reach. Choose crisp white or the peacock "eye" pattern in blue and brown. **White Utensil Jar** is made in China of porcelain. 5¼" diam., 6½" high. #46-660233 **$8.00** **Peacock Utensil Jar** is made in Poland of stoneware. 5¼" diam., 7" high. #46-685115 **$12.00**

A Encourage budding architects with our **Gingerbread House Mold**. One side forms a log cabin, the other a Victorian town house. Fill and bake either side of the mold twice to make four walls and a pitched roof for a complete house, then assemble with icing. Made of heavy cast iron with an Ironclad finish for a stick-resistant baking. Mold is 14" x 7"; makes a 5" x 4" x 4¾" high house. Instructions included. #46-136085 **$22.00** ⊛

B **Glazed Apricots** with the most marvelously concentrated aroma and flavor come from the Land Down Under! A favorite holiday gift, our Australian pitted whole apricots have a texture that is both tender and chewy. 2 lb., packed in a wooden box. #46-087874 **$26.00** ⊛

Order Toll-Free 24 Hours a Day
1 800 541 2233

Figure 9.13   Williams-Sonoma product panel

Figure 9.14   MacConnection product panel

product panel, MacConnection promotes upgrades of existing packages (**Figure 9.14**). Earth Care Paper uses its black-and-white panels to promote sale merchandise and a "grab bag" of merchandise ordered sight unseen (**Figure 9.15**).

By tipping an extra page to its order form, PaperDirect (**Figure 9.16**) creates a three-page section introducing two related products, a magazine and a spin-off catalog. To highlight the new magazine, PaperDirect even prints an additional, clip-out order form that can be inserted into an envelope addressed directly to Technique Magazine.

Figure 9.15   Earth Care Paper product panel

Figure 9.16   PaperDirect product panel

Ordering Envelope

In many cases, both the front or address side and the back of the envelope are used for customer education, imparting information, and selling products—and sometimes for special promotions such as a free gift or a bonus offer.

Should this area really be used for promotion and selling? Absolutely! The ordering envelope, like any other part of the catalog, should be expected to pay its way. Even though it is normally the carrier that brings the catalog customer orders, it can do more.

Front, Address Side

The most common function of the address side of the envelope is just what it says: the catalog company's name and address plus bar coding to be used by the post office for automatic sorting. Lines for the customer to fill in a return address are usually provided, too.

Figure 9.17 from Williams-Sonoma catalog shows the typical approach. General consumer catalogs indicate an area for customers to place their own stamp, while the majority of business-to-business catalogs provide a prepaid business reply envelope, as the Omaha Steaks envelope in **Figure 9.18** shows. The United States Post Office imposes specific design requirements on these envelopes; you can obtain them from your local post office.

A more attractive and certainly more profitable approach is to utilize the left area of the envelope for a design, message, function, or

Figure 9.17   Williams-Sonoma envelope

Figure 9.18   Omaha Steaks envelope

Figure 9.19   Omaha Steaks envelope

even for selling a product. **Figure 9.19,** again from Omaha Steaks, shows how effectively this area can be used for a "Rush this order!" message. The printing, in red ink, simulates a rubber stamp. This message indicates no expectation that the post office will deliver any faster; it just shows the customer that the company cares about receiving an order. An important addition is the message right below the return address area: "Check here if yours is a new address." If only twenty percent of the customers who really do have a new address check the box, it will save hours of time in data processing.

Back of the Envelope

The back of the envelope can and does bear more serious selling and promotion. There are no postal requirements for this space, so not to use it in some way is foolish. Williams-Sonoma uses the back of its envelope to promote two products with four-color illustrations and complete selling copy (**Figure 9.20**). And ample area is provided for the customer to fill in a friend's name to receive a Williams-Sonoma catalog.

Figure 9.21 from the Country Curtains catalog promotes phone ordering and provides space for two friends' names. L.L. Bean uses the back of the envelope for reinforcing customer confidence with its

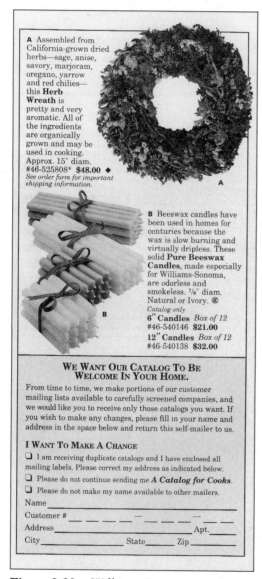

A Assembled from California-grown dried herbs—sage, anise, savory, marjoram, oregano, yarrow and red chilies—this **Herb Wreath** is pretty and very aromatic. All of the ingredients are organically grown and may be used in cooking. Approx. 15" diam. #46-525808* **$48.00** ◆ *See order form for important shipping information.*

B Beeswax candles have been used in homes for centuries because the wax is slow burning and virtually dripless. These solid **Pure Beeswax Candles**, made especially for Williams-Sonoma, are odorless and smokeless. ⅞" diam. Natural or Ivory. ®
Catalog only
6" Candles *Box of 12*
#46-540146 **$21.00**
12" Candles *Box of 12*
#46-540138 **$32.00**

WE WANT OUR CATALOG TO BE WELCOME IN YOUR HOME.

From time to time, we make portions of our customer mailing lists available to carefully screened companies, and we would like you to receive only those catalogs you want. If you wish to make any changes, please fill in your name and address in the space below and return this self-mailer to us.

I WANT TO MAKE A CHANGE

❑ I am receiving duplicate catalogs and I have enclosed all mailing labels. Please correct my address as indicated below.

❑ Please do not continue sending me *A Catalog for Cooks*.

❑ Please do not make my name available to other mailers.

Name _____
Customer # _ _ _ _ _ — _ _ _ _ — _ _ _
Address_____ Apt._____
City_____ State_____ Zip_____

Figure 9.20 Williams-Sonoma envelope

Country Curtains®...
Old-Fashioned Quality
and Conscientious Service

To Order by Phone:
Please call TOLL FREE 1-800-456-0321
24 hours, 7 days a week. MasterCard, VISA,
Discover Card or American Express.
For Customer Service:
Please call TOLL FREE 1-800-937-1237
Monday-Saturday 8:00 a.m. - 5:00 p.m. (EST)

From Outside the USA:
Please call 1-413-243-1300

To Reach Us By FAX:
Please dial 1-413-243-1067

**To Request a Catalog for
Yourself or a Friend:**
Please call TOLL FREE 1-800-876-6123,
Dept. KJAM

Dear Jane Fitzpatrick,
    Please send your **free** Country Curtains catalog to these friends:

NAME	KJAP
ADDRESS	
CITY	
STATE	ZIP

NAME	KJAQ
ADDRESS	
CITY	
STATE	ZIP

Please help us reduce paper waste in America. If you are receiving more than one Country Curtains catalog, please let us know by sending us your address labels marked "correct" and "incorrect." We'll be sure that you receive only one in the future. Thank you.

Figure 9.21 Country Curtains envelope

100 percent guarantee, promoting its toll-free telephone order service, and providing the customer with a final ordering checklist, and reminding the customer to include any address change (**Figure 9.22**). The panel also promotes L.L. Bean's gift service.

Omaha Steaks promotes its superior packaging to assure customers that the food they order will arrive safely. A diagram shows the packaging components very effectively (**Figure 9.23**). The copy strongly promotes such facts as "We're been shipping meat across the country and around the world for over 25 years," and states the company's emphatic guarantee. Because the insulated cooler box holding the frozen food is so sturdy, it is promoted as a picnic cooler and as a $4.00 value that is the customer's at no extra cost. This is smart promotion—something the customer can appreciate.

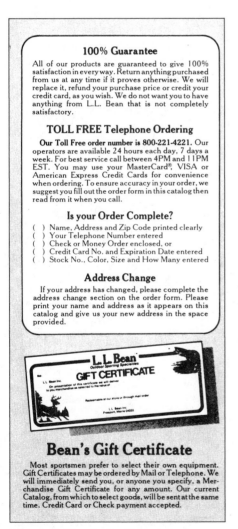

Figure 9.22   L. L. Bean envelope

Figure 9.23   Omaha Steaks envelope

Order Form Design

It is no small trick to design an order form that looks appealing, is logical for the customer to use, includes everything required by the type of products carried, and meets the internal needs of the catalog company. You will need to seek out an expert designer, and do a lot of upfront planning. As you work with your designer, let every step in the order-form design process be guided by these three words: simplicity, space, and logic.

Simplicity This is the most important characteristic of a successful order form. To keep your design clean and simple, minimize the requests or demands you make of your customer. Don't clutter your form with clever design elements that distract from the process of ordering. Keep the color scheme complementary and don't highlight or screen too many areas for emphasis. Ask only for information that is directly pertinent to the fulfillment of the order. If you do not preprint the customer's name and address, an area must be provided to accommodate this, too. Clearly state the method of payment, and include space for a ship-to address when someone besides the orderer will be receiving your goods.

Space Allow enough room on the ordering lines for the customer to comfortably write or print the necessary information. Many catalogs don't leave enough width and yet leave an extraordinary amount of heighth, which makes this area unsightly and difficult to use. Be sure there is enough room to write a name and address, if needed, for personalization. Make sure the boxes or lines for charge card numbers are large enough. Cramped space not only discourages action, but makes it difficult for your order entry department to decipher the numbers.

Logic Logic dictates the sequence in which you request information from your customer. Generally, customer information comes first, followed by ordering and payment information. If a conflict arises between the sequence that works best for your order entry department and the sequence that is most logical for the customer, choose the format that is best for the customer.

Although it is no longer being published, the sports gear cataloger Early Winters did an exceptional job of making its order form "user friendly" for its customers. (**Figure 9.24**). This order form separates the required information into three easy segments: shipping information, ordering information, and payment method information. In addition, the designer numbers each step in the natural sequence a customer would take when filling out the order form. The easy use of this form closes the sale!

Figure 9.25 shows how a business-to-business computer forms and business supplies catalog, NEBS, applies the same principles. Its "Fast Service Order Form" secures shipping information in steps one and two, ordering information in steps three, four, and five, and payment method information in an unnumbered box in the lower-right-hand

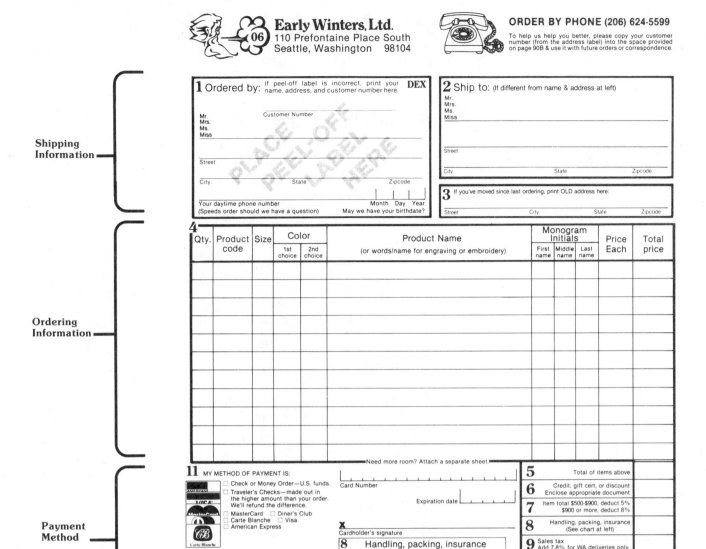

Figure 9.24 Early Winters order form

corner. What is hard to see here is the skilled use of a second color (blue) to accent the steps needed. Blue screened rules separate each area of the form, making the ordering process seem even simpler.

Closer examination of both examples reveals three very important features that make the order form appealing and easy to use: numbering the steps, allowing generous room to fill in information, and providing sectioned areas for charge card numbers.

1. The name and address area provides space for customer number, telephone number, and birthdate (account number recorded in company's records). Customers are encouraged to "Place peel-off label here"—a great aid to the order entry and record keeping departments. The unusual request for birthdate not only allows

➤ Phone TOLL FREE 1-800-225-9550, or FAX TOLL FREE 1-800-234-4324 • TEAR OUT HERE, FILL IN ORDER FORM AND ENCLOSE IN RETURN ENVELOPE ➤

1 FAST SERVICE ORDER FORM

(AREA CODE) PHONE NUMBER — FAX #

AUTHORIZED SIGNATURE — DATE

TYPE OF BUSINESS YOU ARE IN — Is this your first order? YES ☐ NO ☐

TO HELP US SEND YOU THE RIGHT PRODUCTS IN THE FUTURE, PLEASE TAKE A FEW SECONDS TO FILL OUT THESE SURVEY QUESTIONS.

WHAT KIND OF COMPUTER DO YOU OWN? ☐ APPLE ☐ TRS-80 ☐ IBM ☐ OTHER ______ MAKE/MODEL

WHAT KIND OF PRINTER DO YOU OWN? ☐ LASER/INK JET ☐ DOT MATRIX ☐ OTHER ______ NAME

WHAT TYPE OF SOFTWARE DO YOU USE FOR INVOICES & CHECKWRITING?

INVOICES:

CHECKWRITING:

2 BILL TO: Is mailing address correct? Make corrections here. DO NOT USE FOR PRODUCT IMPRINT INFORMATION.

FIRM NAME

ATTENTION

930-7D1-D91-979 D32
MAILCODE 82210

STREET ADDRESS

CARREERS INC
525D N BROADWAY ST #2DB

CITY STATE

CHICAGO IL 6D64D-2392

SHIP TO: Fill in only if different from billing address at left. For faster delivery, fill in street address instead of P.O. Box.

FIRM NAME

ATTENTION

STREET ADDRESS (For faster delivery, fill in street address instead of P.O. Box) — FLOOR, ROOM or STREET NUMBER

CITY — STATE — ZIP CODE

3 FORMS, SOFTWARE, SUPPLIES ORDER INFORMATION: Select options for each product as specified in catalog.

QUANTITY	PRODUCT NUMBER	NO. OF PARTS	DESCRIPTION	TO VERIFY COMPATIBILITY Please indicate Software used with form	CONSECUTIVE NUMBERING FORMS: (If you do not specify numbering will begin at 1001)	COLOR	TYPE STYLE	BUSINESS DESIGN NUMBER	UNIT PRICE	$ AMOUNT

4 CHECKS ORDER INFORMATION: To order checks by phone or FAX - see below for details.

QUANTITY	PRODUCT NUMBER	NO. OF PARTS	DESCRIPTION	TO VERIFY COMPATIBILITY Please indicate Software used with checks	CONSECUTIVE NUMBERING CHECKS: (You must specify starting number)	COLOR	TYPE STYLE	BUSINESS DESIGN NUMBER	UNIT PRICE	$ AMOUNT

5 IMPRINT INFORMATION: Send a printed sample or type or print wording below. For additional imprints or extra printing, please attach an extra piece of paper.

Imprint for Product Number(s) — Imprint for Product Number(s)

Phone numbers will not be imprinted on orders of Mailing Labels, Post Cards, Envelopes, unless checked here. ☐ (AREA CODE) PHONE NUMBER

Phone numbers will not be imprinted on orders of Mailing Labels, Post Cards, Envelopes, unless checked here. ☐ (AREA CODE) PHONE NUMBER

ORDER STATIONERY HERE: (LETTERHEADS, ENVELOPES, BUSINESS CARDS) (Be sure to fill in steps 1—5)

QUANTITY	PRODUCT	DESCRIPTION	LAYOUT	PAPER COLOR	PAPER FINISH Rippled, Laid, Smooth	INK* COLOR	INK* FINISH Raised Or Flat	TYPE STYLE	BUSINESS DESIGN	$ AMOUNT

* On 2 color stationery, 1st color is the imprint, the 2nd color is the logo and graphic line.

Imprinting for Letterhead, Envelopes and Business Cards

COMPANY NAME

DESCRIPTIVE LINE

ADDRESS

CITY/STATE/ZIP

PHONE

FAX

NOTE: You may add side copy for letterhead layout 5C (up to 5 lines). Please attach another sheet with this information.

For Letterhead, extra lines imprinted at bottom of letterhead ($6.00):

Line 1

Line 2

For Business Cards add:

EMPLOYEE NAME

EMPLOYEE TITLE

Attention Stationery Buyers! To ensure quality reproduction, your company logo must fit the space as noted below. (Note: Not all business designs fit in all layouts. Call for details.)

For Layouts 1C, 4C and 5C and 8L your logo or Business Design must fit within these dimensions.

1 ¼" × ⅝" Letterhead 8L, 5C

1 ¼" × ¾" Letterhead 4C, 1C

1" × ½" Business Card/Envelope — For all four

For Layouts 5L,6L your logo or Business Design must fit within these dimensions.

¾" × ¾" Letterhead

⅝" × ⅝" Business Card/ Envelope

CHECK ORDERS BY FAX OR PHONE:

HOW TO ORDER CHECKS AND DEPOSIT TICKETS

By FAX: Send your completed Order Form with a sample check marked "VOID."
FAX TOLL FREE, 1-800-234-4324.
By PHONE: 1. Before calling us at **1-800-225-9550, please have ready a check, or completed MICR specification sheet** for bank routing numbers and bank imprint information.
2. Find these symbols (⑆ ⑈) on your check and line them up with the boxes below.
3. Then simply copy all the numbers to the right of each symbol, leaving a blank box where there is a space. Substitute the letter C for the symbol (⑈), D for (⑉).
Have this available when speaking with our Sales Representatives.
Please Note: Any numbers to the left of this first symbol (⑆ ⑈) are not needed for processing your order. But be sure to specify consecutive numbering desired.

KEY: C= ⑈ D= ⑉ *You cannot use a deposit ticket to order checks.*

☐ **YOUR COMPANY LOGO:** First-time charge $25.00 minimum (Repeat use $5.00 per product)

☐ **EXTRA WORDING** for terms, etc., additional $6.00 charge per product.

SUB TOTAL

Residents of AZ, GA, MA, MO, TX, WI, please pay applicable sales tax. — TAX

Thank You! — TOTAL

Payment Method: Bill me — Check enclosed — VISA — MasterCard — American Express

Your order, plus shipping, will be charged to your credit card.

CARD NUMBER

Month / Year — Expiration Date

NAME

SIGNATURE

NEBS Computer Forms, Checks & Software
500 MAIN ST., GROTON, MA. 01471
TOLL FREE 1-800-225-9550

Figure 9.25 NEBS order form

the company a prime opportunity for individual promotion via special mailings and highly personalized letters, but it also provides the company with exacting information about the customer which will benefit overall customer profile analysis and product selection.

2. The address of the person the merchandise is to be shipped to assures the customer and the company of minimal error.

Step-by-step guidance

3. The address correction area allows the company to keep its record file current. The house list will remain credible and costs for postal handling and catalogs are kept down.

4. Product ordering information has been kept very simple, asking only for quantity, product code, product size and color choices, product name with desired personalizing information, price each, and total price. This is the minimum amount of information needed for a catalog carrying a large proportion of apparel. No extras such as page number or weight are asked for—the computer can be programmed to give the catalog company that information.

Steps 5, 6, 7, 8, 9, and 10 tally the business details. Two of the steps seem questionable for either the company's or the customer's benefit. Six, for example (credit, gift certificate, or discount), is a bookkeeping chore and constitutes a minimal number of total orders. Would this be better off on the information panel? The same is true for line seven. The percentage of orders totaling more than $500 is no doubt small compared with the total number of orders. Do these functions really act as incentives to increase orders, or are they just another line adding confusion to the process? Handling, packing and insurance, line eight, is nicely conveyed with a fee chart.

11. Method of payment is handled well—especially the area for the customer to fill in the numbers. A slight line indication is given each number box, acting as a guide for the customer to neatly fill in and making sure no numbers have been omitted.

NEBS also numbers the steps to be taken. Billing and shipping information is clearly designed for customer ease. Ample space is given for information to be filled in through a vertical format. Steps 3, 4, and 5 work hard to make sure that the customer supplies legible information that NEBS can use to manufacture accurately imprinted and numbered checks and forms.

The requests for typestyle selection, business design, and numbering requirements demand careful company handling and adequate space for the desired personalization. Again, the area is roomy, to encourage accuracy and multiple orders. What might look like excessive allowance for space only seems so because of exceptional design elements. The payment area is good, with individual boxes for charge card numbers— again assuring accuracy and also acting as a simple guide.

Both companies have been considerate by providing simplification of design and the progressive numbering system that guides the customer through the ordering steps.

Order Form Placement

Where to put the order form within your catalog is an important decision. Don't shortchange yourself by not giving it sufficient attention.

The pages of the catalog adjacent to the order form benefit from added sales. Because the catalog naturally opens up to the bound-in order form, it offers higher visibility for these pages, which are seen again when the customer places an order. Thus, these pages are one of the "contrived hot spots" discussed in Chapter 3.

An order form can appear in one of three positions: on a catalog page, in the middle of a catalog, and between catalog signatures.

Although increasing numbers of orders placed via facsimile and modem are convincing some business-to-business catalogs to print order forms on catalog pages, very few consumer catalogs do so. Customers hesitate to tear pages out of a consumer catalog, and catalogers hate to give up the "hot spots" that so naturally surround an order form.

Advantages Lower costs for printing and bindery; more than one order form easily included.	**Disadvantages** Loss of contrived hot spot and, therefore, loss of sales; customer must destroy catalog when using; writing surface "slick" because of coated stock used for catalog pages, so writing is more difficult; hard for customers to find.

The middle of the catalog has been the traditional place to locate the order form. Because the catalog parts naturally in the middle when collated and bound, it is the easiest spot in which to bind the order form. And depending on the number of pages in the catalog this can be the only space available to bind in the envelope. **Figure 9.26** illustrates the placement of the "middle" bind in.

Advantages Easy bindery function; order form easily found by customer; envelope and order form always together.	**Disadvantages** Loss of contrived hot spot (hot pages created when order form is bound between signatures) and, therefore, loss of sales.

The most advantageous positioning for an order form is between catalog signatures. And it is as easy as the middle binding position. A signature is the number of pages a press will print at one time. (See Chapter 10 for a full explanation.) If a press printed only 16 pages at one time and you had an 80-page catalog, there would be five signatures

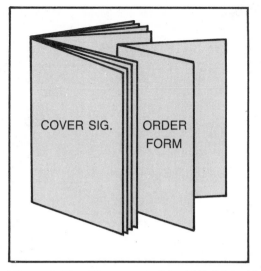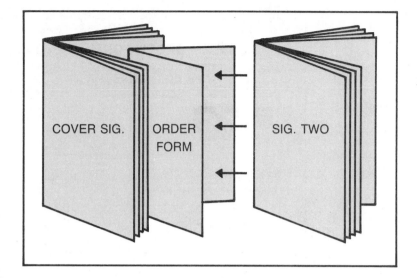

Figure 9.26   Placement of "middle" bind in

in the catalog and four opportunities to bind-in an order form.

Eliminating the middle binding spot, you would have three possibilities: between pages 8–9 and 72–73, 16–17 and 64–65, 24–25 and 56–57. The greatest problem is that the envelope might become separated from the order form, whereupon the irritated customer might decide against placing an order. However, a good designer and flexible envelope printer can get around this.

Advantages	Disadvantages
Creates two extra hot spots, meaning four pages of boosted sales; easy to bind; feasibility of two order forms and two envelopes.	Possible separation of envelope and order form.

Your Order Form Influences Ordering Channel Selection

Until recently, most catalogers included a bound-in order form and return envelope to give customers a convenient way to return their order. But as fewer orders arrive through the mail, some companies—primarily business-to-business catalogers—are turning to alternative methods of capturing orders—alternatives that steer customers into new ordering channels.

Quill Office Supply omits a traditional bound-in order form and return envelope (**Figure 9.27**). Instead, it includes several order form pages designed to be fax machine readable. Across the top, the form

Figure 9.27   Quill Office Supply order form

Ordering Worksheet
Please use as a guide before calling.

Quantity	Product Code	Description	Page	Unit Price	Total
2	40371	3261 NMS STANDALONE	9	$1,195	$2,390
2	98259	IMPLEMENTATION	9	$215	$430
2	98097	ADDIT. YR. UNIT EXCHG.	9	$84	$168

Prices: FOB origin. (Prices and product availability subject to change without notice.)
Normal Shipping terms: We ship to U.S. locations only.
Please note: Codex products are FCC approved for business use only.

All shipping is prepaid and added to your order. If your company has not established credit with Codex, please allow 24 hrs. for credit authorization before shipping.

*Protect your new equipment in transit. The small amount you spend ½ of one percent of total order) will guarantee that the equipment we ship to you will be protected against common transit casualties.

Sub-Total $ 2,988
Transit Insurance* (1/2 of one percent of sub-total) $ 11.95
Total before tax & shipping $ 2,999.95

Figure 9.28   Codex Express order form

reads "For quickest service, fax this order to (708) 634-0078." Fax orders are further encouraged by a complicated array of telephone numbers and mailing addresses for regional order centers where customers can place telephone and mail orders.

Follow Quill's lead if you want to encourage your customers to order by fax. You might also consider making the fax line an 800-number, offering a discount to fax users, and promising a special next-day return call or fax if there are any problems with a faxed order.

Codex Express, a catalog of computer network products designed for the business market, omits an order form altogether. Anticipating that all orders will either be called or faxed in, it includes only a sample, already-completed ordering worksheet to help customers organize orders (**Figure 9.28**). The copy above the worksheet details payment options and summarizes "Facts to have handy when you call"—but it leaves every step of organizing and communicating the information up to the customer!

Computer cataloger Unix Central offers its customers four ways to order: telephone, fax, mail, and electronic mail (**Figure 9.29**). The company's Internet address is shown on the order form (again, no envelope is included) and the back cover, and alternates with the 800-number on every other catalog page.

A handful of consumer catalogers have flirted with a supplemental order sheet showing bar codes for each product. Consumers with the appropriate hardware could then scan the bar codes and place an order via computer, without once speaking to a customer service rep or faxing in an order. Other, similar experiments will take place as the practice of online ordering through channels like Compuserve's Electronic Mall expands.

If you want to get more out of UNIX, get on the phone and call UNIX Central.

We offer the latest products with an unmatched level of service and support. We guarantee your satisfaction. If any product in this catalog isn't right for you – for any reason – just give us a call within 30 days. We offer quantity discounts for corporations on an ongoing basis, or for large purchases of a single product. No wonder so many companies have made us their sole supplier for UNIX products.

BILL TO:

Name

Company

Address

City   State   Zip

Phone

SHIP TO:

Name

Company

Address

City   State   Zip

Phone

QUANTITY	ITEM	USERS	FIXED/FLOATING	MEDIA	UNIT PRICE [1]	TOTAL

Subtotal	
Sales Tax [2]	
Shipping/Handling	$15.00 [3]
TOTAL	

HOW TO ORDER

By Phone
Just call 1-800-532-1771 between 6:00 a.m. and 6:00 p.m. Pacific Time, Monday through Friday. If you have questions about specific product features or compatibility requirement, our technical staff is ready to answer them. We're happy to accept corporate purchase orders by phone, subject to credit approval.

By Fax
Choose the products you want, then fill out the order form, put this page in your fax machine and dial 408-732-7335. If you're using a credit card, this is all you need to do. If you're using a purchase order, fax it with the order form.

By Mail
Just fill out the order form and pop it in the mail. Include your check, P.O. or fill in your credit card number. That's all there is to it.

By Electronic Mail
Just log onto Internet and send us the order information. Our E-mail address is:

sales@unixcentral.com

UNIX CENTRAL

474 Potrero Avenue, Sunnyvale, CA 94086-9406
Phone: 1-800-532-1771, Fax: 1-408-732-7335
E-mail: sales@unixcentral.com

METHOD OF PAYMENT

Except for check orders, all methods of payment are accepted by phone, fax, E-mail or mail.
Credit Card

☐ VISA   ☐ MasterCard   ☐ American Express

Credit Card Number

Expiration Date

Authorized Signature

Please Print Name

Check
Check Number Enclosed _____
Make your check payable to UNIX Central and mail to 474 Potrero Avenue, Sunnyvale, CA 94086. Checks must be cleared before shipment of your order.

Purchase Order
P.O. Number _____
You can fax your purchase order to us at 408-732-7335, or give it to us by E-mail or over the phone. We accept purchase orders from corporations, government agencies and educational institutions, subject to credit approval.

NOTES:

[1] We reserve the right to correct typographical errors. All prices subject to change without notice.

[2] California residents only, add applicable sales tax.

[3] Most items are shipped same-day via second-day air freight. The flat, $15 shipping/handling fee applies to all catalog products unless otherwise noted on product pages. Overnight delivery is also available for an additional charge.

Availability and freight charges on special-order (non-catalog) items may vary. Ask your sales representative for details.

Figure 9.29   Unix Central order form

While the method of transmitting an order may change, the information that must be captured is little short of eternal. No matter what the order form of the future looks like, its job will still be to encourage the customer to provide essential information in a manner that strikes the customer as simple, straightforward, and convenient.

Order Form Design Tips:

1. **Keep it clean.** Use lots of white space. Keep your form open and attractive. An order form that looks complicated IS complicated. This can result in missing or wrong information . . . or no order at all.

2. **Leave room to write.** Make your form easy to fill out. If necessary, increase the form's size to assure the order's legibility.

3. **Remember your order entry system.** The form should be compatible with your order entry system, especially if your system is computerized. A form with the same design as your computer format will speed order entry and fulfillment, while reducing input errors.

4. **Keep it simple.** Use of color can be confusing and distracting. Use basic black or some other dark color for important information. Colors should be used to highlight and enhance.

5. **Attract attention.** Use screens of black or second colors where you want to draw attention or create sections. Shade the areas you don't want filled in. Use screens sparingly.

6. **Color stripe your envelope.** If you get many kinds of mail, color stripe the edges of your return envelopes so rapid sorting can cut down your processing time.

7. **Don't confuse your customer.** Be consistent in layout and design. If you need to improve your order form, make changes that will present minimal confusion to customers.

8. **One step at a time.** Lead your customer step-by-step in filling out the order form. Doing so makes your form seem simple, even if you require lots of information. Consider numbering the steps.

Give Information:

1. **Explain your exchange policy.** Provide specifics on returns and exchanges, including postage. The Federal Trade Commission is becoming increasingly strict about this requirement.

2. **Reinforce your guarantee.** The order form is an ideal place to restate your guarantee, instilling confidence when the customer is about to place an order.

3. **Put postage charges on the order form.** Psychologically, including them in the price of the item or placing them next to the price raises the perceived cost. Put postage charges on the order form in a spot where they're seen after the customers have committed themselves to placing an order.

4. **Give your customer a mail preference option.** Offer not to extend use of the customer's name to other mailers.

5. **Tell customers how to pay.** If your company name is different from your catalog name, tell the customer so that checks can be made out properly. An alternative is to set up a system with your bank to accept checks made out both ways.

6. **Explain the minimum order on charge cards.** To assure that you cover costs, put a minimum on your charge orders.

7. **State delivery time.** This increases credibility by telling customers what you will do for them . . . and it reminds customers that you are concerned about fulfillment of the order.

8. **Date your prices and your catalog.** State when your catalog prices expire. "guaranteed until . . ." is better than "expire on . . . ." After that date, refer inquiries to your customer service department to ascertain the current price.

Ask for Information:

1. **Ask customers to use the label.** Remind people to affix mailing labels in the proper place on the order form; this is important for tracking codes. Try to reduce your costs by asking recipients of multiple catalogs to return the labels so you can eliminate duplicates from your lists. Of course, now that ink-jet printing of the customers name, address and other information on the order form is prevalent, this is not as important a concern as it once was.

2. **Ask for names for your mailing list.** Solicit the names of your customers' friends (they're likely to have similar interests). This is an excellent way to build your list of prospects at virtually no cost.

3. **Ask for a phone number.** Always ask for a way to contact the customer just in case there's a question about the order. Specify both a work and home number so you'll be able to reach the customer without delay.

4. **Ask for change of address information.** Also ask the customer to correct his address if necessary. Provide a separate box to write in a new address. Put old information in a nixy file to use for merge/purge purposes.

5. **Ask for a street address for UPS.** UPS will not deliver to a post office box. Without proper information, delivery is impossible.

6. Always find out where to ship the order. **Ask for "ship to" information or a gift address.**

And always thank customers for their orders!

Order Form Checklist:

☐ Gather information to include.
☐ Decide on position within the catalog.

Always:
1. Design with simplicity.
2. Keep customer uppermost in mind.
3. State information clearly and simply.
4. Include your company name and address.
5. Provide a phone number.
6. Allow ample room for customer to fill in information.
7. Thank the customer.

Strongly Consider:
1. Including guarantee on order form panel.
2. Taking the customer through the order steps via a numbering system.

CHAPTER 10

Production Planning

The difference between a catalog that lives up to your expectations and one that fails to meet them often lies in production planning. Its myriad details include selecting vendors to handle your prepress, printing, binding, and lettershop work; establishing a production schedule; selecting paper; approving color separations; and perhaps even supervising a press run.

Of these factors, scheduling is the most important. An intricate schedule is like a row of dominos. One missed date can set off an avalanche of missed deadlines that culminates in a delayed mailing date. And that can spell disaster during premium selling seasons—Christmas season, for example.

Before you set up a final production schedule, review the sample schedule shown in Chapter 2, Planning a Catalog. As you set your schedule, be realistic. Set deadlines that your creative staff and vendors can meet, and then stick to it—or you risk compromising your mailing date.

The Production Phase

These are three important steps in the final production phase of your catalog.

1. Choosing and working with a printer.

2. Choosing paper.

3. Choosing and working with a color separator.

4. Choosing a bindery and lettershop (if you are printing less than 25,000 catalogs and are working with a printer who does not offer complete binding and mailing services).

Choose Vendors As Soon As You Can

You should select key suppliers as soon as possible, so you can call upon them as you move through the creative process toward production. When you are reviewing final comps, for example, you may want to ask your printing sales representative to check them for potential printing problems. If a glitch is detected, you can make a design change early in the process, and avoid the trauma of discovering a printing problem on press.

A second reason to select vendors early is that you will get top priority within their plant. Catalogs are seasonal—summer, for example, is a busy time for producing Christmas catalogs. Every supplier is jammed during this time of year. Your book will only get top priority if you commit early.

Price, Quality, Service: Should You Expect All Three?

It's reasonable to want your catalog to be produced with the price, quality, and service you expect. But if you pressure your vendors to meet unreasonable dates, or supply materials that do not meet their specifications, you may only be able to meet two of these three objectives. When you select your vendors, consider the alternatives.

Price. If your main concern is to buy the job at a set price, you may preclude your supplier's ability to maintain quality. Or perhaps your quality standards can be met for the quoted price, but the supplier can not deliver the job on time.

On the other hand, you may select a supplier who meets your quality and service requirements, but is expensive. This supplier may take longer to okay a sheet, or might pull a job because of a bad plate. In this situation, you maintain price and quality, but put service at risk.

Quality. Insisting on quality may put your price and delivery dates in jeopardy. Let's say your catalog is on press when you discover that a photo of a sweater looks pink, when the copy describes it as "tomato red." If the color can't be corrected on press, you face the decision of going with what you have, or pulling the job—which will affect the price and possibly your delivery date.

Service. Say that you're locked into a mailing date. You've selected a supplier who can produce the job on time at the price you want, and you are confident that the quality will meet your standards. Knowing that your mail date is critical, your supplier will probably go to great lengths to handle emergencies—but you may have to pay extra or sacrifice quality to meet your date.

Step 1: Choosing and Working with a Printer

The lushness of your photographs, the quality of the color, the clarity of the type: everything you and your creative staff have labored to achieve can be polished to perfection by your printer. Or it can be just plain ruined.

A good printer will take your carefully designed, laid out, and photographed catalog and make it shine. A bad printer will take the same art materials and turn out a mediocre, lifeless book that will turn customers off.

How do you choose a good one?

First, ask your colleagues in the catalog industry, or look for printers who advertise in catalog industry journals. It is important to select a printer who specializes in catalogs and can make your catalog look its very best.

When you find likely candidates, ask for the following information.

1. Samples. Many sales people will not display poorly printed samples, but any samples can tell you a lot about the company. Ask how current the samples are. If many of them are a year or so old, it may mean there is a severe turnover in customers—and for a good reason.

Be sure to examine samples printed on the grade of paper you normally use. If yours is a low-ticket catalog, don't be swayed by a portfolio of high-fashion catalogs printed on quality sheets. You need to know if this printer can print well on commodity-grade paper. And if the wares displayed were all produced on commodity grades and you're looking for a "Rembrandt" . . . beware.

2. Proofs. If you are impressed with a particular sample that resembles your product, ask to see the proof. See how well the proof was matched on press. Perhaps talented press people were able to improve the quality.

3. References. Ask the salesperson for a list of catalogers he or she personally deals with, and call them up. Besides evaluating the printer, you need to make sure that the printer's liaison understands the catalog business and the printing business. You want to deal with someone who understands and satisfies your needs. Your colleagues in the industry can tell you how well the liaison meets their needs.

When you ask about the printer's equipment, find out about its mailing capabilities. Very big printing operations can print, bind, bundle, and bag your catalog into postal regions such as Sectional Center Facilities that can qualify you for a postal discount. You may prefer to deal with a large printer who can handle every step of production and lettershop, rather than splitting your work between a more modest printer and a separate mailing house.

It's a good idea to check up on your printer's financial strength. A company's financial condition goes up and down, just as the economy rises and falls. Avoid the trauma of having a printer falter while committed to producing your catalog. Weed out the undesirables in the beginning.

Finally, visit the plant. Talk to the people who make it happen. Walk through the press area and see what is running. Is the plant clean? Are the people busy but not panicked? Is the atmosphere businesslike? Do people seem alert and enthusiastic about their jobs? Are you received with a degree of excitement? Pay attention to your reactions. Your overall impression of the printing plant can say a lot about the kind of relationship you can establish with the vendor.

What You Should Tell Your Printers and Suppliers

Developing a good working relationship is a two-way street. Just as you need to know your printer's capabilities, your printer needs to know something about the way you and your company operate.

Take a moment to analyze your company's own culture. Do you typically meet your production schedules, or do you often run late because of late product deliveries, difficulties in getting approvals, or staff shortage? Your supplier must know your organization in order to give you the best possible service.

Your vendors will also want to know about your cash and payment policies. If your company is a slow payer, your supplier should know this up front. Otherwise you will fail to develop the kind of good, solid relationship that is necessary to produce a top-notch catalog.

How to Get Proper Bids on Your Printing Job

Whether you get bids on a per-catalog basis or on a yearly contract, you will want to have several printers bid on your project.

Prepare a bid sheet that asks all printers to estimate their prices based on identical specifications, so you can accurately compare each bid.

Besides asking printers to follow your bid sheet when making an estimate, ask them to give you a breakdown of costs in five categories: printing, paper, separations, binding, and freight. Asking for a breakdown will force them to be upfront with each item, and help you discover which printers low-bid a job, figuring they can make up the differences in author's alterations, or base their price on a lesser grade of paper.

Include the following information on your bid sheet.

1. **Title:** Give your job a name so you and your printer can call it by a common name.

2. **Unit:** Identify the type of job you are printing. Is this a catalog, an envelope, an order form?

3. **Quantity:** Have your job quoted in quantity breaks. Establish a starting point of so many thousands and request prices in various increments plus an "additional thousands" cost. For example, you might request quotes on printing 150,000, 175,000, 200,000, 225,000, and get an additional cost-per-thousand price. You'll see how dramatically the price per catalog will lower as the total quantity goes up. (Your mailing costs *increase* correspondingly, however!)

4. **Size:** Specify whether your catalog is 8-½" × 11", 6" × 9", a 6" × 10-⅞" "slim jim," 5-½" × 8-½", 11" × 11", or whatever trim size you want to use.

5. **Number of lots:** Are you printing more than one version? More than one cover? Identify the variations you want.

6. **Fold to:** Does the catalog fold to fit into an envelope?

7. **Number of pages:** Tell the printer whether your catalog is 24, 32, 64 pages, or more.

8. **Colors:** Indicate two, three, four, or however many colors you are using. Does the color print on one or both sides of the sheet?

9. **Bleed:** Does the ink run off the page? If your catalog pictures have no margins and ink runs to the edge of the page, your catalog bleeds. Bleeds usually cost more.

10. **Ink coverage:** A press sheet may have very light ink coverage (lots of white space, and 20% ink) or heavy ink coverage (75% to 85% ink, very little white space), which can influence how the art reproduces as well as how much the job will cost. Tell your printer how much ink there will be on a typical page. And, while you're at it, ask what kind of ink is used.

11. **Stock:** If you are providing the paper, tell the printer which one you are using. If the printer is to supply paper, ask for the name of the sheet, its grade, and its basis weight. Often, people think they are getting a great buy, only to discover that the printer has substituted an inferior grade of paper to lower the price. When recommending an alternate stock, the printer should specify the name and grade. Be sure to examine a printed sample!

12. **Art and preparation:** Specify how your art will be prepared. Will you supply mechanicals or a disk? If you supply a disk, will you send along a laser proof that shows color breaks and color position? Will the printer do the color separations, or will your separator provide film?

13. **Finishing and Binding:** Tell the printer whether your catalog will be perfect bound or saddle stitched. In the saddle stitch,

staples are bound in the spine of the catalog. In perfect binding, the catalog pages are collated, the left side ground off, and adhesive applied. Covers are glued on. Catalogers who expect their books to be kept over a period of time generally prefer this type of binding. Very large catalogs—those with more than 100 pages, such as office supply catalogs—have no choice but perfect binding. The least expensive and least used binding choice is the side-wire stitch, in which staples are inserted along the left front side of the catalog.

14. **Proofs:** If the printer is doing your color separations, how many proofs do you need? Will you accept prepress proofs, or do you want full-color press proofs? How many sets do you need?

15. **Packing:** If the printer is not mailing your catalog, specify how the printed material should be delivered to your lettershop. Should it be delivered in bulk, in cartons, or on skids? Keep in mind that delivering materials to another point before mailing them will add costs to your catalog.

16. **Destination:** If the printer is not mailing your catalog, where should it go?

17. **Delivery date:** Specify the date by which all material must arrive at the lettershop, or be in the mail.

If you prepare a proper bid sheet, all your printers will bid on the same specifications, and you will be able to make a valid comparison.

Printing Methods

There are three printing processes: *sheet-fed offset lithography*, *web offset lithography*, and *gravure*.

In both sheet-fed and web offset lithography, the image is transferred to the printed page via a blanket wrapped around a cylinder instead of directly from the original plate. (The blanket "offsets" the image from the cylinder to the paper.)

Offset presses are either sheet-fed or web-fed. In a sheet-fed press, separate sheets of paper are fed into the press, while a web press prints on rolls of paper that are trimmed after they have been printed on both sides ("perfected") and folded, gathered, and bound. Web presses operate at phenomenal speeds that are not economical for runs of less than about 50,000 catalogs. Hundreds of catalogs may have to be printed before color and registration are refined on a high-speed web press—an unacceptable amount of waste for a short-run catalog.

In gravure printing, ink is transferred to paper via "wells" that are etched by lasers into a cylinder. Although cylinders are expensive, the process starts to become economical for press runs of one million or more—which is also the life of the cylinder. This is a popular option for large mail-order companies who print millions of copies of one version of their catalog, but it is not a good choice for the cataloger who is printing multiple covers or otherwise "versioning" its catalog on press.

Gravure printing is in the forefront of *direct to cylinder* or *filmless* printing. In filmless printing, a cataloger producing a catalog with a desktop publishing system converts its files to the printer's prepress digital format. All images are converted to digital data, which then are used to etch the catalog pages onto the press cylinder. No film is involved in the engraving or proofing steps. Lands' End, Sears, and L.L. Bean are among the catalogers now producing catalogs direct to cylinder.

Filmless printing is in the works for offset printing, too. By the year 2000, you can expect to rely on filmless production techniques, whether you use offset or gravure printing.

Step 2: Choosing Paper

Paper should be selected carefully, because its weight and quality are elements that support your catalog's image. Coupled with its oversize format and lavish photography, the heavy, coated paper used by FAO Schwarz, for example, tells upscale customers that no expense was spared in the catalog's preparation. The simple newsprint chosen by Vermont Country Store conveys a message of old-fashioned value, while the recycled sheets used by Seventh Generation deliver a message of environmental consciousness.

If your company is large, the volume of paper you use may justify hiring a paper expert to purchase directly from the paper mill, saving you the commission a printer receives for purchasing paper for you. But most catalog companies ask the printer to negotiate and make long-term commitments to protect their paper supply and lock in prices.

Regardless of which method you use to purchase paper, you need to consider its properties when selecting the sheet you will use for your catalog. Finish, weight, bulk, grade, and grain are properties that affect price and print quality.

Finish refers to the feel and smoothness of the sheet. You can use paper as it comes from the driers of a paper machine, or you can buy paper that has been "calendared" or smoothed by being pressed through revolving rollers. Machine-calendared paper has a smooth finish; super-calendared paper is smoother still.

The smoothest finishes come with coated paper—paper that has been given a surface coating to provide a very smooth finish. Coated papers can reproduce finer halftone screens and provide crisper overall reproduction because they allow the ink to sit on the paper, rather than be absorbed into it (called *ink holdout*). Coated papers also offer higher capacity, because they minimize the likelihood that printing will "show through" from the back side of the sheet.

With few exceptions, paper is identified by basis *weight* in pounds of a ream (500 sheets) in its grade size. The main *grades* used for catalog printing are book grade paper, which comes in 25″ × 38″ sheets, and cover grade paper, which comes in 20″ × 26″ sheets. For example, one 500-sheet ream of 100-pound book paper weighs 100 pounds; five hundred sheets of 50-pound cover stock weighs 50 pounds.

Catalogers have traditionally preferred 60- or 70-pound paper, but, faced with mounting postal costs, many have shifted to 50- or even 45-pound sheets. A 24-page self-cover catalog in 60-pound stock would weigh 106 pounds per 1,000 catalogs. The same catalog printed on 45-pound stock would weigh 80 pounds per 1,000 catalogs—a savings of 25 percent. The reduced weight would allow you to include additional inserts or catalog pages, which in turn would increase your profit. If you decide to work with a lighter sheet, be sure to select a printer who can work well with lightweight paper. Not every printer can do so.

Heavier stocks are still used for catalog covers. While most consumer catalogs are self-covers (the cover is printed on the same stock as the interior pages), a catalog that is kept for a long time and referred to often (such as an office products catalog) may benefit from having a separate cover of heavier, sturdier stock.

When selecting the stock you're going to use, keep in mind that in addition to the weight of the sheet, you will want to know how much that sheet *bulks*. Bulk for book paper is expressed as the number of pages per inch for a given basis weight. For example, a 50-pound book stock can vary from 310 to 80 pages per inch. A very bulky stock might be chosen to give a small catalog (16 or 24 pages) the heft and feel of a larger catalog. A thin sheet would be chosen to make a very large catalog more manageable.

When ordering paper, keep in mind these three facts about *grain* direction:

1. Paper folds smoothly with the grain direction and roughens or cracks when folded across the grain.

2. Paper is stiffer in the grain direction.

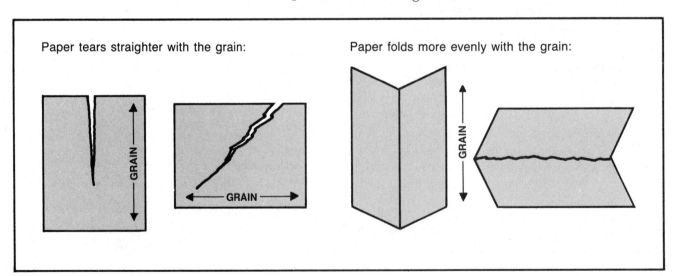

Figure 10.1   How Paper Tears and Folds

3. Paper expands or contracts more in the cross-grain direction when exposed to moisture changes. **Figure 10.1** shows a few simple tests that will illustrate how paper tears and folds.

Several other paper properties can affect the quality of your printed catalog.

- *Color* plays a large role in how your piece looks after it has been printed. Type is more easily read on a soft white, while process colors are more accurately reproduced on a neutral white.

- *Brightness* affects the contrast, brilliance, and snap of the printed subject. Artificial brighteners added to paper can affect reproduction because most are not neutral in color, but have excess blue reflectance.

- *Opacity* refers to the show-through of the printed image from the opposite side of the sheet or the adjoining sheet. Opacity is affected by the thickness of the sheet and the use of fillers, such as titanium dioxide.

- *Gloss* affects the appearance of the ink film on the paper.

- *Refractiveness* is light absorption in the surface of the paper, causing halftones to appear darker than they should.

When you are purchasing paper for a large run on a web press, make sure your printer and your paper supplier work closely to determine the exact specifications for your job. Because web shutdowns can be costly, rolls must be properly wound, protected, stored on end, and have good tensile strength to minimize tearing or breaking on the web. Paper should *always* be rolled with the grain direction paralleling the web. It should be uniform in thickness and free from scum, holes, spots, slitter dust, fiber picking, and lint. It should have a minimum of contraction and expansion, contain a minimum number of splices, and have sound cores for winding and delivery.

Coated Paper Finishes

All paper starts as wood pulp. In its initial stage, paper is brown; brighteners are added to make it white. The more brighteners are used, the whiter the sheet. The better-grade sheet is very white and has a high-gloss look. If you are producing a top-of-the-line catalog for fashions or valuable art, this is the sort of paper you should consider.

Matte-coated paper is fully coated paper with a nonglare finish. There is no off-the-paper-machines supercalendering or pressing through cylinders. This means that the mattes, as a group, are the bulkiest of the coated papers and have a somewhat grainy finishing, though they are still far superior to uncoated sheets in print quality.

Gloss-coated paper is double coated on both sides and supercalendered off the paper machine to heighten the gloss and reduce the sheet bulk. This process also reduces the sheet's brightness and opacity. The gloss-coated surface is smooth and sealed and is most suitable for true dot reproduction. There are five quality categories of gloss paper, with gloss, brightness, shade, and surface smoothness distinguishing between the categories and their price.

Dull-coated paper is also coated on both sides. It is also supercalendered as it comes off the machine, using a slightly different type of rollers. Steam is injected into the dull-coating process to retard gloss. The bulk loss is not as great as in a gloss paper, but the dull-coated surface is not as smooth as a gloss sheet, though it is smoother than a matte-grade sheet.

A relatively new entrant in the paper market is *non-glare paper*. This sheet is coated and very glossy, but does not give off a glare that might bother certain market segments such as older consumers.

At the other end of these high-quality coated papers (often called *free sheets*) is groundwood paper, which uses fewer brighteners and retains more of its pulpy quality. While coated groundwood paper does not have the brightness of the top-of-the-line sheets, it can be used very successfully for merchandise catalogs. It can also save you about 20 percent over the cost of a coated free sheet. About half of all catalog printing is done on coated groundwood sheets, with coated free sheets coming in second, and supercalendered uncoated sheets third.

Ink and Paper

Ink can play a very important part in the reproduction of artwork and photography. Ink is either transparent or opaque, but the bulk of your print job is done by processing printing and requires transparent ink.

Transparent ink modifies light by subtracting some colors from the light source and transmitting others. For example, look at something that appears to be green. That item subtracts red and some blue and shows you yellow and some blue to give your vision a shade of green. Opaque ink would reflect light and not allow you to see the underlying colors, thus eliminating the intermediate colors that create the effect and versatility of process printing.

Your paper stock becomes the reflecting light source for the ink placed on it. The paper is the immediate source of illumination for a transparent ink, and this is called *reflected illumination*. Because of the limitations of process inks, you may want to select a paper stock that is very white in order to show the colors in their purest form.

Paper can absorb some colors and reflect others. A sheet that absorbs and reflects colors equally is known as a *balanced sheet*. One that absorbs some colors and reflects others is known as an *unbalanced sheet*.

An unbalanced sheet always has a tint. For example, a sheet that absorbs more red and green will have a blue tint.

When you examine paper samples, remember that the area that remains unprinted will be the brightest portion of the overall page. The areas where ink has been applied will be less bright because the sheet has absorbed light (color). The most accurate color reproduction is obtained on papers that reflect the light that strikes them without changing its quality. In addition, the most brilliant color reproductions are obtained on papers with high, balanced reflectance.

What about Recycled Paper and Soy-Based Ink?

In an effort to reduce environmental impact and increase customer goodwill, many catalogers are using recycled paper for some portion of their printing.

Recycled paper is made up of post-consumer waste, pre-consumer de-inked paper, post-mill waste, mill waste paper and a small amount of virgin pulp. From an environmental point of view, sheets with the highest content of post-consumer waste are most desirable. But recycled papers are less bright than a comparable virgin sheet, and they do perform differently on press. For example, uncoated recycled paper is susceptible to *dot gain*—a situation in which images gain density as the "dots" in the halftone photographs spread. When dot gain occurs, shadows and midtone areas of photographs grow darker.

For best results, find a printer who has some experience printing with recycled sheets and can prevent problems that may arise on press. Tell your separator you plan to use a recycled sheet. By working together, your printer and separator can compensate for some of recycled paper's shortcomings.

An easy way to incorporate recycled paper into your catalog is to use it to print order forms and other bind-ins that have no halftones. If you do, be sure to tell your consumers that you are printing on recycled paper.

As consumers pay more attention to environmental practices, new "green" paper products are entering the market. Ask your printer or paper sales rep to keep you posted on developments like chlorine-free paper, and paper that uses no trees because it is made from wheat-straw pulp.

Another earth-friendly product is soy-based ink, which replaces some or all of the petroleum solvents in ink with soybean or other vegetable oils. But soy inks can slow down the printing process when coated paper is used, because soy does not dry as quickly as other inks. Your printer can tell how to get the best results from soy-based inks.

Choosing a Trim Size

The standard sizes for catalogs are 8-½" × 11", 5-½" × 8-½", 7-½" × 9-⅛" and 6" × 9". Catalogers seeking an especially lavish, high-end look occasionally print 11" × 11" catalogs.

Some catalogers are shaving trim sizes to save on paper and postal costs using the "slim jim" format (6-⅛" × 11-½"). Unfortunately, in some cases this format has also lowered response rates and reduced sales. Before you consider it, ask yourself first whether it fits your image. If you sell items, this may work for you. But if you sell a look or an image, this format is probably too constrained for you. And if you do choose a slim jim, your art director will have a hard time dealing with its tall, skinny page. If your products are horizontal, it may be completely incompatible!

Instead of choosing a format that may lower sales, try trimming a little more off a standard size. Reducing your 8-½" × 11" catalog to 8" × 10-¼" reduces only six percent of the size of your catalog yet can yield a 17 percent reduction in piece weight.

Step 3: Choosing And Working With A Color Separator

Your photographer took superb shots for your new catalog, but will your printed piece convey the full impact of those photographs and sell your products? It will if you get the right supplier to provide color separations and film to your printer.

Choosing a Separator

Your catalog printer may own a separation facility, or have separators with whom it works well. But if you need to find a separator yourself, keep these points in mind.

1. Look for a separator who handles catalogs like yours. If you're a high-fashion apparel catalog, you should consult with a sepa-

rator who does this type of work regularly. If you're producing an industrial book, you're wasting time with vendors who have a large color-corrections staff.

2. Visit the plant. Color separation is undergoing rapid technological change, and you want to be sure that your separator has up-to-date equipment that is arranged logically, not haphazardly. Look for the separator who places craftspeople in positions to coordinate efforts with an economical flow from one work station to the next. Or find one that is employing the "work cell" approach and has given small work teams exclusive responsibility for handling all prepress work on a given catalog. This approach can halve the time it takes to complete prepress work, and in most instances also increases the quality of the work.

3. Look for state-of-the-art equipment. Has this color separator invested in direct digital color proofing systems? These systems produce high-resolution color halftone proofs without using film—because they take digital information taken directly from a color electronic prepress system. They replace film-generated proofs such as Chromalins and Matchprints. These systems save time and money, and allow for additional color corrections.

If you use a color separator with a digital proofer, you can transmit your design and low-resolution art files from your desktop publishing system to your separator and get proofs almost on demand. (If you have a modem, you can do this over the phone.) The equipment lets you retouch, correct color, make silhouettes, resize, and match colors. Proofs will be available very quickly, and will accurately represent your final art.

4. Conduct the "white glove" test. A clean, environmentally sound plant will help guarantee a better product. Be certain there is a modern, efficient air conditioning system, with filters changed regularly to ensure dust and static control. If a stray speck of dust gets on your film, it will be on every catalog you print. Ask how the separator controls or prevents this problem.

5. Provide complete specifications. The more detailed they are, the fewer mistakes will be made. Tell the prospective separator

- The size of each page, and whether or not is should bleed.

- The kind of materials you will supply: reflective art such as photographs, drawings and other illustrative copy that is viewed and photographed by light reflected from its surface? Or transparencies, slides, and illustrative copy through which light must pass to be seen or reproduced?

- The kind of type reproduction: freestanding (black type), color, or knockout ("white" type reversed out of a color background).

Ask for a written estimate that details all aspects of the job. Your final bill should exactly coincide, the only exception being author's alterations and changes you made after the job was initiated.

6. Ask for references—and check them. Make sure the references are catalog companies like yours. Don't speak with Nieman Marcus or Tiffany if your catalog bears no resemblance to their books. Ask the references

- How long have you been doing business with XYZ color separators?

- Why did you select this firm?

- How has the firm lived up to your original expectations?

- During this period of time, have they worked with you to keep pace with current technology? How?

- Have there been any problems or emergency situations during the time you worked together? Please explain what happened.

- What was the firm's response when a problem arose?

- What's the worst situation you ever had with your present vendor? How did the vendor handle it?

By asking these questions and following these guidelines, you'll be on the road to finding the best color vendor for your catalog.

How Color Separations Are Made

To the separator's eye, all color is made up of just four basic process colors: magenta (process red), cyan (process blue), process yellow, and process black. Combinations of these four produce almost any color imaginable. The separator's job it to separate your artwork into four basic colors.

The computer techniques that have revolutionized the way catalog pages are designed, typeset, and composed have also affected the color separation industry. No longer is art masked, resized, and retouched manually. Today, computerized imaging systems let a system operator alter color, create and match tints, vignettes, and windows, and then cut fully assembled, one-piece film for printing. Image-processing systems can handle color separations, masking, retouching, dot etching, stripping, and proofing.

These systems allow you to manipulate art in ways that were unimaginable just a few years ago. They let you drop elements in a photo without scheduling a reshoot . . . make changes much closer to deadline . . . and include "for position only" proofs in your page layout, so you can get a better, earlier indication of what your final page will be.

With electronic scanning equipment, your color separator can scan artwork and store it on a computer disk. You receive a low-resolution version to insert on your page layout. When you send in your final page layout files, the separator can replace the low-resolution version with the very high-resolution image the printer will need for accurate reproduction.

For best results in turning over your page files to your color separator, make sure the files on your disks specify all type colors and background colors. Tell the engraver what halftone screen the printer will be using, and whether final film should be right-reading emulsion up, or emulsion down.

How to Proof Four-Color Work

There are two ways to proof separations: on prepress proofs, and on press proofs.

Prepress "dry proof" systems such as Chromalins and Matchprints are an extremely accurate way to judge how your separations will actually print—and are much less expensive than press proofs. The dry proof system puts simulated ink on paper much the same way the actual press does, and the result looks similar to a color print. The dry proof system can also incorporate press characteristics such a *dot gain* (when the dots take ink on press, getting "fatter" and making the color appear darker), which will make your separations look darker than you expected.

Dye-sublimation or "dye-sub" proofs that use heat to transfer the dot to the paper are somewhat less expensive than Chromalins, but also are less accurate.

Once the Cadillac of proofing methods, press proofs are rare today—due to their increasing expense and the increasing accuracy of pre-press proofs. A press proof will show you all of the actual printing characteristics and press problems that can be avoided, such as ink trap (when colors or screens of colors overlap and one color is "trapped" under another), dot gain, and sharpness. They are still sometimes used when a catalog is to be printed on a color stock instead of white—although Chromalin proofs can also be made on any paper stock.

For best results, press proofs should be run in positions, as they will run in the final catalog. They can be ganged together on one or two sheets and proofed together (called random proofing), but this approach does not guarantee quality reproduction. When the engraver pulls a four-color proof at random and not in the sequence in which individual illustrations will appear on the press (and in your catalog), you will have subjects of different intensities juxtaposed when actually running the job. Then adjustments will have to be made to compensate for this variation in color, and these adjustments will in turn affect all the other colors for the other products.

Figure 10.2 shows what a typical press proof sheet might look like once the artist has reviewed it and marked corrections. Let's take a look at what color corrections the artist has requested, starting at the top and going clockwise.

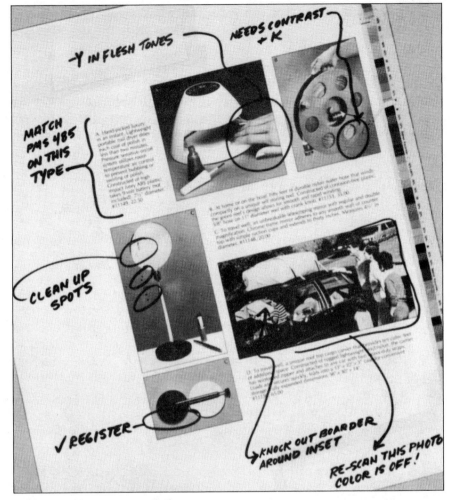

Figure 10.2 Press Proof Sheet

1. "Y in flesh tones." The flesh tones in the model's hands are off-color and would benefit from removing a little yellow.

2. "Needs contrast + K." The product is appearing flat and blending too much with the background—needs more black.

3. "Re-scan this photo, color is off!" The artist is asking that the photograph be scanned again for modification so the colors become correct.

4. "Knock out border around inset." The artist is asking that the inset be cleaned up by removing a partial border that was meant for size guidance only.

5. "Check register." The printing images seem to be out of alignment and need to be corrected.

6. "Clean up spots." Spots can be as harmless as pieces of dust the printer has overlooked (these are easily removed). Spots on the transparency could also have been overlooked and these, unfortunately, are on the plates and therefore much harder to correct.

7. "Match PMS 485 on this type." The artist is calling for a specific ink color in which the designated type is to appear.

On the right edge of the proof sheet you'll usually see a color bar. Color bars are as important as the color proof itself. Without the color bar, your printer will be in the dark as to how the film and proofs read across the sheet. If the readings vary during the press run, the color bars help your printer adjust the equipment to match the supplied proof. Your printer will use a densitometer to read and measure the optical density of your separations and the evenness of the color bars, and closely match the proof your separator supplies.

Art directors sometimes expect an exact reproduction on paper of the transparency as it appears when viewed on a light box. But light must flow through transparencies to show color brilliance. When that color is transferred to paper, some concession in color and brilliance must be made.

One art director uses an interesting technique to assess a proof's accuracy. He looks at the transparencies when the first proofs come in to see what the engravers have obtained and to know what to expect when the transparencies are transferred to paper. But from then on, he corrects proofs for what is pleasing to the eye. When something looks pleasing, it may not be necessary to duplicate the transparency that was shot. Those who insist that it be reproduced exactly will be sadly disappointed over and over again.

When it's your turn to proof color separations, examine them in a systematic manner.

1. Look at your proofs in a proper viewing area, with 5,000 degree Kelvin lighting. Your film supplier and your printer use this standard; to be consistent, you should, too.

2. Use a very good magnifying glass (at least 10-power magnification) and look at small detail areas on your proof. Look at tree limbs, eyelashes and fine areas and be sure that they are crystal clear. If they are not crisp and your original transparency was sharp, there is a problem in your separation. Return it to the separator.

3. Now look at the neutrals. Look at the whites and see that they are white. Check out the grays and see that they are a neutral gray and that the beiges are, in fact, a neutral beige. If they are tinged with any type of color (blue, pink, etc.) return these separations. You could end up with a printing problem if these are not corrected.

4. Finally, look at the overall color. If the separation is sharp and the neutrals are in balance, you will like the overall look of your color.

When your are unsure of your proof or feel that more could be done with a given subject, discuss it with your film supplier. He or she should be able to indicate whether additional work would produce the job you want—or trigger a problem on press.

Saving Money with a Two-Color Catalog

No one will say that two-color catalogs duplicate the brightness or attractiveness of four-color pieces or that sales for most product lines will be as great. But some product lines—wire, cement repair material, nuts and bolts, seminars, books—can do very well with two-color printing.

Consider, first, that the cost of separations is usually included in the printing price. Also, proofing a two-color catalog is much less time-consuming than proofing a four-color catalog.

When you print a two-color catalog with two signatures—say an 8-page and a 16-page signature—you can choose a separate PMS color for each signature. (PMS stands for Pantone Matching System—a standardized color designation system.) For instance, you can use black and PMS 485 (a red) on the 16 pages, and then black and PMS 124 (a mustard gold) on the 8 pages. When the 8 and 16 pages are combined, the illusion of a multi-color catalog is created.

You can also combine different percentages of your two colors to create a multi-colored effect on each page. But be careful which size of type you use. **Figure 10.3** shows that a 6-point italic type with thin serifs is not strong enough to stand out clearly against a tinted background. But a type with more weight, such as a gothic sans serif typeface or an 8-point sans serif, can be used with deeper tints.

TYPE FACE, WEIGHT AND SIZE; SCREEN SIZE AND PERCENTAGE AFFECT LEGIBILITY —

TYPE FACE, WEIGHT AND SIZE; SCREEN SIZE AND PERCENTAGE AFFECT LEGIBILITY —

Type face, weight and size; screen size and percentage affect legibility — affect legibility —

Type face, weight and size; screen size and percentage affect legibility — affect legibility —

TYPE FACE, WEIGHT AND SIZE; SCREEN SIZE AND PERCENTAGE AFFECT LEGIBILITY —

TYPE FACE, WEIGHT AND SIZE; SCREEN SIZE AND PERCENTAGE AFFECT LEGIBILITY — TYPE

Type face, weight and size; screen size and percentage affect legibility — affect legibility —

Type face, weight and size; screen size and percentage affect legibility — affect legibility — Type face,

| 10% | 20% | 30% | 40% | 50% | 60% | 70% | 80% | 90% | 100% |

Creating the Illusion of More Than Two Colors

Let's look at how a two-color print job can be aesthetically accomplished with a colorful look. In reality this is relatively simple to accomplish. Suppose you have an eight-page catalog you'd like to design on a low budget, but with a colorful effect. When you lay out the piece, side one will contain four pages: one, four, five, and eight. Side two will hold pages two, three, six, and seven.

Print side one in two-color. This means your front and back cover (pages one and eight) and centerspread (pages four and five) will print in single color. The layout form in **Figure 10.4** shows how this works to create a multi-color appearance.

Figure 10.4 Sample Layout

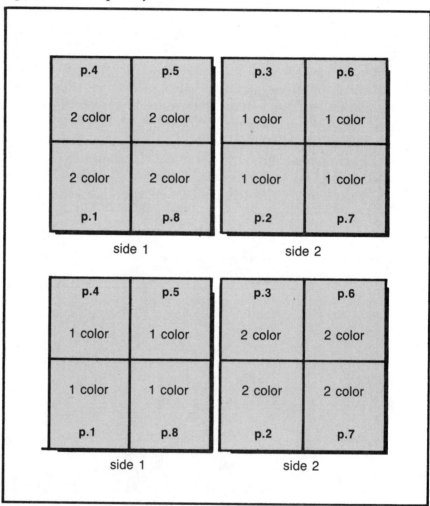

Figure 10.5 Sample Layout

When the catalog is assembled, you will create a *look* of more than two colors. Creativity plays a part in similar illusions. In addition to the layout just proposed, let us take another example.

Using the same format, the page layout now looks like the one shown in **Figure 10.5**. We have reversed the color format, using the single color on side one. What does this accomplish? Page one, your front cover, now can be designed with bold type or an illustration using the mezzotint technique advantageously in a single color.

Remember that black does not necessarily have to be used. Dark blues or grays work well. This technique allows you to print the first two inside facing pages (two and three) in two colors, further enhancing the illusion of more color in your book. Pages six and seven now are your two-color pages, which creates a problem: your centerspread (pages four and five) must appear in a single color.

One solution is a technique called a split fountain. This is a method by which you can add an additional color across the sheet by separating and dividing the ink fountain approximately in half, using two different colors across the page. The example in **Figure 10.6** explains what happens to pages one, four, five, and eight when they are kept in a single color, but with a split fountain.

As the ink fountain prints and moves over the side one form, the two different colors on the single color side are printed at the same time. In addition, if the proper colors are chosen on side two, you can blend the two colors to form a range of colors, such as blue, yellow, and a blend of the two which is green.

You can imagine what a catalog using this technique will look like. Also, not that your back cover, page eight, prints in a different color from your front cover, page one.

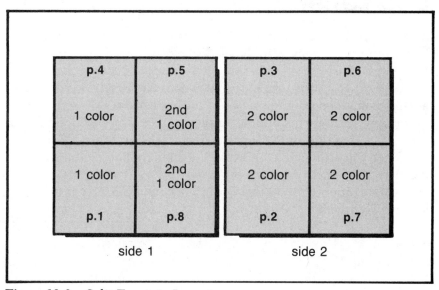

Figure 10.6   Split Fountain Layout

Color Separation Checklist

☐ Identify Method of Color Separation Needed.
☐ Establish Type of Proof Required.

Always:
1. Request a written estimate per job.
2. Furnish separator with a list of specifications.
3. Furnish a clean and complete mechanical to follow.
4. Furnish to-size artwork.
5. Identify desired special effects.

Strongly Consider:
Having the printer and color separator communicate directly to clarify the printer's needs.

Step 4: Choosing A Bindery and Lettershop

At one time, most catalogs were shipped from the printer/binder to a lettershop, where they were labeled, bagged, sorted, and transferred to the post office for efficient and cost-effective delivery.

Today, most large catalog printers can handle all the functions of a lettershop, rendering Step 4 the final part of Step 3. Using ink jet technology, printers can address catalogs, add source codes, bind, bundle, bag and tag catalogs by postal Sectional Center Facility.

When you are looking for printers, ask about their mailing capabilities. It will be easier and less expensive to have your printer prepare your catalog for mail than to pay to transfer your materials to another location for finishing.

No matter who handles your mailing, it's worth it to learn all you can about the U.S. Postal Service and its regulations. Get a copy of the *Domestic Mail Manual*, the agency's official guide to mail preparation and classification. Available as a book or on a floppy disk, the manual is updated frequently as postal rates and requirements change. Contact your local bulk mail facility for a copy.

Getting the Catalog from Bindery to Lettershop

If you do need to ship your catalog from a printer to a lettershop, pack it carefully! If material is to run smoothly and quickly, it must be in good condition when it is put on the machine. Your catalog must arrive at the lettershop flat, undamaged, and packed so that when it's opened, it won't slither down the aisle in a river of brightly printed coated paper. To ensure its safe transfer

- Find out how the lettershop wants the material packed, and work with your printer to follow instructions. Don't be afraid to arrange a three-way conversation. A brief conference call can save a series of two-party conversations.

- Make sure material is properly marked and identified.

- Make sure every shipment includes a detailed packing slip indicating the items, packing and quantity of everything delivered.

Figure 10.7 shows a simple outside identification label. Labels could be printed in different color stock or ink colors so a single color could be identified as a particular code. Imagine the printing on the label printed in red, the details filled in with handwriting. All fifty boxes of code 84 would be color-coded as well as identified with filled-in information. With just a little extra effort, a sample piece could be attached to each individual carton, too, for even more insurance against error. Specifics concerning mail date, type of labeling, and class of mail would be sent along separately with any other needed information.

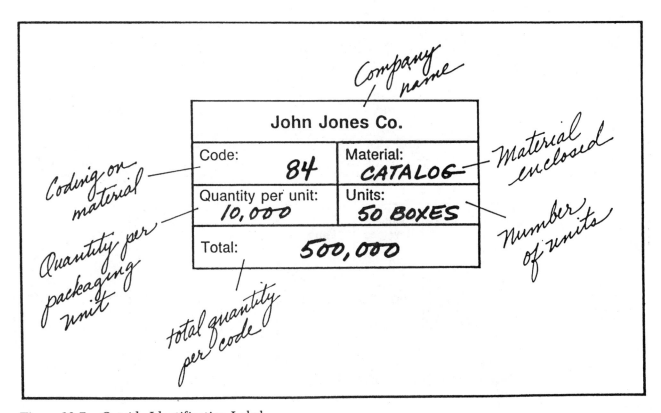

Figure 10.7 Outside Identification Label

Giving Instructions to Your Printer or Lettershop

Your printer or lettershop will need complete information about your *catalog configuration* and your *list configuration* to get it into the mail.

Catalog configuration includes the size, weight, and thickness of your catalog, plus any extras such as an outer envelope. List configuration can have the greatest effect on lettershop costs. A list of 50,000 names consisting of a single ZIP sequence may cost less per thousand to mail than a list of 100,000 names consisting of four segments of 25,000 each. A single list of 25,000 in a local area may cost less per thousand to mail than a list of 100,000 with national distribution.

By putting your instructions in writing, you will state your plans clearly, make sure your printer/lettershop acts on instructions exactly as you understand them, and allow your printer/lettershop to question any part of the mailing procedure that may not be clear. Written instructions also provide a reference point if a question arises later.

For a simple mailing, provide this information:

1. Title of mailing.

2. Drop dates (drop all material on one date, on a scheduled series of dates, within a time span, or as completed?).

3. Total pieces of mail to be dropped.

4. How to mail (first class, presorted first class, bulk third class, five-digit presorted bulk class, carrier route presorted first or third class?).

5. How to affix postage (permit imprint/indicia, meter, or postage stamps?).

6. Description of printed materials.

7. Description and expected arrival date of lists (sources of lists and any coding will be helpful in identifying lists).

For a complex mailing, a matrix is a handy way to describe in simple terms what would otherwise be a tedious and cumbersome set

Panel Piece	Outer Envelope	Letter	Catalog	Order Form	BRE	List
1-25,000	OA - 1	LA - 1	CA - 1	OFA - 1	RA - 1	A - 1
2- 5,000	OA - 1	LA - 2	CA - 1	OFA - 2	RA - 1	A - 2
3- 5,000	OA - 1	LA - 1	CA - 2	OFA - 3	RA - 1	A - 3
4- 5,000	OA - 2	LA - 1	CA - 1	OFA - 4	RA - 1	A - 4
4- 5,000	OA - 1	----	CA - 1	OFA - 5	RA - 1	A - 5
5- 5,000	OA - 1	LA - 1	CA - 1	OFA - 6	----	A - 6

Figure 10.8   Sample Small Mailing Matrix

of instructions. This substitutes for the list of enclosures and coding information of a simple mailing (but includes that information in a different format). A matrix for a small mailing might look like the sample in **Figure 10.8**. This tells the printer/lettershop what it needs to know to put the correct pieces in the correct envelope and to label with the correct list. Other matrix formats are used by many mailers. Just convey your intentions clearly!

Your written instructions should also tell the printer/lettershop what to do with overstock. If there are extra catalogs or order forms, should they be placed back in stock, destroyed, or shipped elsewhere?

Alternatives to Ink Jetting Addresses

Some small catalogs and start-up catalogs still affix labels to their address panels. There are four types of labels.

1. Plain paper or "Cheshire" labels that print in sheets and are affixed by cutting the labels apart, applying glue to the back, and placing them on the mailing piece. This is the least expensive type of label.

2. Gummed labels, backed with glue like that used on postage stamps or envelope flaps. They come on sheets or continuous forms that are perforated and can be applied by hand or by machine. Gummed label stock costs about four times as much as plain paper label stock.

3. Heat-activated adhesive labels, normally affixed by machine and made to adhere to just about any surface. They require a heating element for the labeling machine, can be expensive, and should be used only when demanded by a specific situation.

4. Pressure-sensitive labels (or Kleen-Stik labels), die-cut with a latex adhesive backing (similar to the back of cellophane tape) and placed on a waxy paper that allows their relatively easy removal. They can be affixed by removing the backing and applying them directly to the mailing piece. They also may be left on the backing. These labels cost about three times more than gummed or heat-activated labels, and the lettershop may charge slightly more to machine-affix them. But they do help capture important information, because the customer can remove the label and affix it to the order form, where the order entry department can read important source code and customer number information.

The physical characteristics of labels can affect their compatibility with printer/lettershop capability. It's wise to furnish your printer/lettershop with a list of these characteristics. That way, you can be sure the lettershop can accept any deviations from the norm.

	4-Up	5-Up
Width of printout paper:	14⁷⁄₈"	14⁷⁄₈"
Vertical distance between fanfolds:	11"	11"
Label width:	3.4"	2.6"
Number of labels across:	4	5
Maximum number of characters per line:	33	23
Minimum distance from labels to pinfeed holes:	0.3"	0.3"
Centering of labels on printout paper:	Yes	Yes
Label Height:	1"	1"
Number of lines per inch:	6 or 8	6 or 8
Maximum number of lines per label:	5 or 7	5 or 7
Whether labels print across fanfold "perf":	No	No
Sequence of labels in printout (NS or EW):	EW	EW

Information Needed by List Processor

If your list processing house will provide the lettershop or printer with bag tags—usually required if your list is to be carrier route or five-digit presorted—it is important to provide the list processor with the following information:

- Name, city, and state of your lettershop.

- Complete weight of your mailing piece.

- Size of your mailing piece.

- Maximum weight per mailing bag.

- Minimum number of pieces per bag.

Size and weight of the mailing piece must come from you. The other information usually is worked out between you, your printer or lettershop, and the list processing house. Establish size and weight from an actual sample of the mailing piece, or from an accurate dummy made of the same materials you'll print on. Lacking that, a fairly accurate estimate of weight can be made from the number of pages, page size, and basis weight. Take note if some pages are on a different weight stock.

How to Detect Mailing Errors

Sometimes, despite your best efforts, errors do occur—mostly in the area of lists, materials, or dates.

The best way to track your mailing and uncover errors is still to salt your name in every mailing list you use. This will show you what happened with each list: when you receive the piece in your mailbox, you'll know that the list, material, and mailing date were (or were not) as desired. You may want to use the names of others in your organization, as well as friends, relatives, and business associates. (As both a courtesy and a precaution, let everyone know what to expect, when to expect it, and what you want them to do.)

Another way to get samples of mailing pieces is to use the address correction service of the U.S. Postal Service. Since undeliverable pieces will be representative of the entire mailing, they'll provide useful information as to the material mailed and the approximate date it arrived at the destination post office. You'll also be able to use the information to clean your own lists.

You can get documentation of mailing dates by requiring postal receipts for all mailings. If the postage was paid by permit imprint, you should request Form 3062. This form is filled out by the mailer on the front and by the Postal Service on the reverse. The date filled in by the Postal Service is the date of acceptance not necessarily the date the mail was delivered to the post office.

If the postage was paid by stamps or meter, request Form 3606. This is filled in on one side only, with charges based on the number of pieces in each mailing. Copies of Form 3602 can be obtained after the mailing, but doing so requires a written request to the Postal Service and can take some time. Copies of Form 3606 cannot be requested after the mailing. These forms can also be used to check on quantities mailed and are especially useful if a separate form is used for each cell of a mailing, with a notation as to which cell each represents. Comparison with expected cell counts is useful.

Finally, you can detect mailing errors by reconciling materials on hand at the start of a mailing with materials used and inventory remaining at the end. Significant differences require explanation.

Great Communication Makes A Great Catalog

If you are serving as the catalog production manager, you should not only communicate with your suppliers—you should make sure they communicate with each other.

If they don't, the end result may be a poorly printed book for which no one accepts responsibility. Your color separator may blame your printer for the problem; your printer may blame the separator. To prevent this unhappy standoff, follow these guidelines.

1. To make sure your printer and separator communicate from the get go, set up a meeting with both to review your needs and point out what is important in your catalog. Show examples of previous catalogs if you can. Talk about your schedule and set realistic deadlines that all parties can meet. Write up a conference report of the meeting and send it to everyone who attended.

2. Ask the printer to send a specification sheet to the color separator so the separator can create film that runs well on the printer's press. The spec sheet should contain:

- Whom to contact: name, address, and telephone number of the printer's key customer service personnel and any other people related to the job who can furnish valuable information.

- Screen ruling for film prep.

- Film orientation.

- Ink density requirements.

- Type of ink and ink rotation—which order the colors will be run in.

- Sample of paper stock and any knowledge about the peculiarities of the paper.

- Proofing specifications: what type of proof is preferred; which others will be accepted (Chromalin, Matchprint, etc.).

- Type of press on which the job is running and particular characteristics of that press.

- Dot gain percentages for press/paper combinations.

- Any other detailed instructions as to how the film should be supplied.

3. Ask your color separator to send sample film to your printer far in advance of the final deadline. This way the printer can determine whether the film meets its specifications. It is the printer's responsibility to notify the separator immediately if there is a problem with it. Many printers also make their own proof from supplied film, to see that their proof matches that of the color separator. If the color separator runs proofs, ask to see proofs on the same paper stock you selected for the press run.

4. Schedule a day to review your materials with your printer and separator: page layouts, transparencies, and instructions—*especially* the transparencies. Your instructions should include:

- An overview of what is important, i. e. backgrounds, clothing colors, what you want to highlight.

- A photocopy of your final art.

- A bound sample of your current catalog.

- An outline by catalog page that lists, for each transparency its number; a description or its name; its size; its scan percentage; comments on color. Don't make your catalog a puzzle to be solved by your separator. Put your transparencies in a notebook and number them. Make sure the number matches your art board stat.

Following these steps will ensure that both vendors understand what is required to complete your book properly.

Checklist to Avoid Production Problems

Creative Production
1. Don't design in your own problems. Make sure what you are planning to do on pre-press and press is something your suppliers can do.
2. Hire a good photographer.
3. Use top-quality transparencies. Make sure you have the best product shots at the photo shoot. Don't expect the separator to fix your problem!
4. Evaluate all transparencies under proper lighting before you send them to the separator. A reshoot can be cheaper than time on the electronic imaging system.
5. Save your outtakes. Transparencies can be misplaced!

Desktop Publishing
1. Always submit a laser or thermal proof representing the latest version of your page file.
2. Make sure to list every font and every program (including version) for all the files on your disk.
3. Always send a test disk to your color prepress house before beginning full production. Make sure they are able to open your files.
4. Don't make color judgments from your color monitor. The color you see is RGB (red, green, blue) and you will need CMYX (cyan, magenta, yellow, black) to print.

Artboard Mechanicals
1. Never, ever use paper clips on your mechanicals.
2. Send clean artboards and mark bleeds and trim sizes.
3. Identify your transparencies with the scan percentage.
4. Photostat transparencies or reflective art to show exact cropping size.
5. Position your art with keys.
6. Indicate color breaks on tissue.
7. Paste up on a single artboard.
8. Identify key line positioning. Let the separator position the key line perfectly.
9. Proof your artboards. Hire a proofreader or read the copy out loud with at least one other person.
10. The best way to proof a phone number is to call it.
11. Don't overlook the obvious. Read everything out loud, even the name and address of your company.

Press Run
1. Know the factors of color on press: paper stock, quality, and density of inks used.
2. Go to the press run.
3. Keep your final product in mind during the press check.
4. Check out samples of bindery and ink jetting or labeling and review them with the printer. Make sure they meet postal regulations!

CHAPTER 11

Legal Matters

Industry self-regulation and governmental laws, regulations and restrictions may seem little more than unwelcome restraints on your mail-
order activities. But that's not the case.

Most laws and regulations are simply good business practice—and
when you adhere to them, you do your industry and your customers
a big favor. A company that uses ethical, honest business practices and
doesn't try to stretch the limits of state and federal regulations builds
customer confidence and a sound business order industry. A company
that operates on the margins of the law spoils things for everybody.

The public's favorable attitude toward mail-order companies is in-
fluenced by many factors. Fast delivery, truthful copy and illustrations,
strong guarantees fully stated and backed-up—all these influence the
positioning of mail order in the customer's mind, and mold the character
of the industry.

How can you help make the character positive? What statutes affect
your catalog? Where can you get help?

How to Create Successful Catalogs does not pretend to act as a legal
advisor. The next few pages will call your attention to the better-known
statutes you may need to comply with, as well as ethical matters of
growing concern to your customers.

Four Laws Affecting the Catalog Marketer

Four of the federal laws that target the mail-order industry are designed
to protect the consumer. All are found in the United States Code, which
lists pertinent amendments and judicial interpretations that can help
you determine whether you are in compliance.

Truth in Lending Regulation Z (passed 1969 and amended) deals with
all companies engaged in selling on credit to the consumer, including

property, money, or a service primarily for personal, household, or family use. The act runs more than 100 pages and even sets forth definitions of the goods and services and intended users. The Equal Credit Provisions prohibit discrimination. Familiarity with this act is essential in any sale on credit.

Fair Credit Billing Act This law provides a procedure to settle disputed billing.

Fair Credit Reporting Act Covered here are the consumer obligations of a user of credit information from credit agencies, including the rights and procedures for the consumer to examine those reports and correct inaccuracies.

As credit sales increase and consumer credit records grow more revealing, the extent to which this information may be accessed is being debated by courts, legislators, and consumers. While courts have ruled that using credit records to "prescreen" and target mail-order consumers for credit offers is a permissible use of a consumer credit report, you should keep an eye out for amendments that may restrict this use.

Fair Debt Collections Practices Act Although this act applies only to collection agencies and not to creditors, direct mailers should be aware of the prohibited abuses.

Federal Trade Commission Regulations

Numerous FTC regulations affect the direct-mail industry, among them the Magnuson-Moss Warranty Act dealing with the disclosure and use of a warranty, and rulings on the negative option mode of selling and guarantees and deceptive advertising. Copies of these regulations are available from the Federal Trade Commission, Office of Public Information, 6th and Pennsylvania Avenue NW, Washington DC 20580. The FTC also issues a complimentary weekly FTC News Summary— an essential tool for anyone wishing to stay abreast of new rulings. You an order the summary by writing to the FTC at this address.

The Mail or Telephone Order Merchandise Rule

The Mail Order Rule (also called the "30-day rule") was issued by the Federal Trade commission in 1971 following consumer complaints about mail-order companies who failed to:

- deliver merchandise on time;
- deliver merchandise at all;

- make prompt refunds;
- answer customer inquiries about delayed or lost orders.

Under the Rule, the cataloger must ship merchandise within a reasonable amount of time (30 days after receipt of order) unless otherwise stated in an advertisement. When there is a shipping delay, the Rule requires that you notify your customers of the delay and provide them with an option either to agree to the delay or to cancel the order and receive a prompt refund. For each additional delay, your customers must be notified that they must send you a signed consent to a further delay or a refund will be given.

Originally designed to cover only orders placed by mail, in 1994 the Rule was amended to include orders placed by telephone, fax machine, on-line transmission, and pre-recorded messages, and is now known as the Mail or Telephone Order Merchandise Rule.

The FTC publishes a handy reference called *A Business Guide to the Federal Trade Commission's Mail Order Rule*. It provides the complete text of the Rule along with explanations of how to comply with it.

Applying the 30-Day Rule

The 30 days in which you must ship merchandise are counted from the time a *properly completed* order is received. "Properly completed" means:

- where there is a credit sale and the buyer has not previously tendered partial payment, the time at which the seller charges the buyer's account;

- where the buyer tenders full or partial payment in the proper amount in the form of cash, check, or money order, the time at which the seller has received both said payment and an order from the buyer, containing all the information needed by the seller to process and ship the order.

The Rule provides that you may not solicit any order for the sale of merchandise through the mail unless, at the time of solicitation, you expect that you will be able to ship any ordered merchandise to the buyer:

1. Within that time clearly and conspicuously stated in any such solicitation (e.g., "four to six weeks"), or

2. If no time is clearly and conspicuously stated, within 30 days after receipt of a properly completed order from the buyer.

If, when a customer places a telephone order, your customer service person informs the customer that the ordered merchandise is not available for shipment, your disclosure is considered a newly negotiated shipping date and does not constitute a "delay notice" under the Rule.

The FTC rules provide that selling, shipping, or invoicing goods different from those ordered is an unfair and deceptive practice. The FTC has held that in connection with bicycles, for example, substituting merchandise not identical in all respects to the order, except with the consent of the customer, is a deceptive practice. A seller cannot substitute a like product for the original without the customer's permission.

How to Avoid Sending a "Delayed Merchandise" Shipment Notice

Rather than being concerned with what to do if you violate this ruling, *you should first be concerned with how to keep from making the violation*. Six distinctly different classifications of merchandise require six distinctively different approaches. Let's see what the classifications are and what approach is needed for each.

1. Merchandise warehoused by the catalog company. You should have a system to take care of problem products *before they are listed in your catalog*. Develop systems to assure that merchandise will be in your warehouse before you mail your catalog. The main steps to incorporate are:

- Notify suppliers of your intention to list the product and the approximate volume you expect to use.

- Ask suppliers to verify (preferably in writing) the availability of the product . . . and the supplier's ability to ship your quantity estimates when needed.

- Delete from the catalog any product that does not have availability and shipping dates that comply with your needs.

Monitor your drop shipping

2. Merchandise drop shipped. If you must rely on others to ship products for you (because of limitations or product completion needs such as personalization), you still should verify the supply . . . just as you do for the products you warehouse yourself. You should have a fulfillment contract with the drop-ship supplier stating a required shipping time. (You also should have a monitoring system to place decoy orders to make sure the drop shipper is complying.) State in your catalog the amount of time these products will take to ship . . . an additional two to four weeks is not unusual, depending on your order relay system to the drop shipper: for example, "Please allow six weeks for personalization." And smooth out your system of relaying orders, so that no time is wasted at *your* end.

3. Seasonal merchandise. Most plants, trees, bulbs, or shrubs need to be planted at different times of the year in different areas of the country. These items do not fall prey to the 30-day rule. Chocolate candy would melt if sent during the hot summer months. Many pastries and cakes would spoil. For products such as these, a catalog notice of availability is provided: for example, "Available for delivery until May 15 to all 50 states."

4. Delayed shipment by customer request.   Many people order gifts and wish the recipient to receive them at a specific time. Catalog companies set up a system internally to accommodate these wishes. Food catalogs thrive on this business and provide a special area on the order form for the customer to fill in the desired arrival date.

Delay notices

5. Made-to-order merchandise.   Products such as furniture and limited-edition pieces of art fall under this classification. A special piece of furniture may take as long as six months to be completed and shipped to the customer. The catalog must state this. A limited-edition bronze sculpture may not be in a casting production for several months after ordering. Copy should read something like this: "Shipment about the first of January 1996."

6. Search-and-send merchandise.   Replacement services, such as sterling silver flatware, and china and glass companies will often accept an order based on fulfillment when they locate the product. The advantage to the customer of placing a firm order for a hard-to-find product and paying for it when the order is placed is the privilege of ownership and receipt when the product is found. The catalog company must clearly state this procedure and provide for a signed document by the customer in order to operate safely in this manner.

These general guidelines will help you avoid sending costly delay notices. Knowing the FTC rules and having your lawyer inform you as to actions which may be exceptions are the best steps to take. Then you'll know how to comply with the law . . . and still avoid the expense of sending delay notices!

"Bait Advertising," a Trap to Avoid

The violation of FTC guidelines regarding "bait advertising" subjects the violator to federal fines and injunctive relief, as well as to possible fraud actions by victimized purchasers. Never jeopardize a good mail-order business with overtones of the old "bait and switch" scheme. In the long run, you will not only subject yourself to litigation and legal ramifications, but you will also find your business activities short-lived.

Bait advertising is defined in Federal Trade Commission guidelines as an alluring, but insincere, offer to sell a product or service which the advertiser, in truth, does not intend or want to sell. The primary goal is to switch consumers from buying the advertised merchandise in order to sell something else, usually at a higher price or on a basis more advantageous to the advertiser. Sometimes the real aim of a bait advertisement is to obtain leads on persons interested in buying merchandise similar to what was featured in a particular ad. The merchandiser may not send the same product as originally featured in the ad. The guideline on bait advertising clearly states that no advertisement should create a false impression of grade, quality, make, value, currency of a model, size, color, usability, or origin of the product offered, or which may otherwise misrepresent the product so that later, on disclosure of the true facts, the purchaser may be switched from the advertised product to another. Note that, even if the mail-order merchandiser makes known the true facts to the buyer at a subsequent time, the law is still violated if the first contact or interview is secured by deception.

The same regulation also covers the practice of trying to discourage the purchase of advertised merchandise in order to sell other merchandise. Practices that are considered by the FTC in determining whether or not the advertisement is a bona fide offer are:

1. Refusal to show, demonstrate, or sell the product offered in accordance with the terms of the offer, as well as failure to ship the product advertised (instead shipping a different product).

2. Disparagement of the advertised product by acts or words.

3. Failure to have available at all advertised outlets a sufficient quantity of the product to meet reasonable anticipated demands . . . unless it is clearly disclosed in the advertising that the supply is limited or available only at a designated location.

4. Refusal to take order for the advertised merchandise to be delivered within a reasonable period of time.

5. Showing or demonstrating a product that is defective, unusable, or impracticable for the purpose represented.

6. Use of compensation or penalization of salespeople, designed to prevent or discourage them from selling the advertised product.

In essence, the merchandiser should not pursue a practice of "unselling" with the intention of selling other merchandise in its place. The following practices constitute evidence of whether or not the initial sale was in good faith:

1. Accepting a deposit for the advertised product, then switching the purchaser to a higher-priced product.

2. Failure to either deliver the advertised product within a reasonable time or make refund.

3. Disparagement by acts or words of the advertised product, the guarantee, credit terms, service availability, repairs, or any other aspect of the product.

4. The delivery of an advertised product that is defective, unusable, or impracticable for the purpose represented or implied in the advertisement.

The guideline for "bait advertising" as adopted by the FTC is contained in 16 CFR 238 and was adopted on November 24, 1959.

Avoid Deceptive Advertising of Guarantees

One of the most popular methods of selling mail-order merchandise is to guarantee the product. The Federal Trade Commission, on April 26, 1960, adopted a rule regarding "Deceptive Advertising of Guarantees" (which can be found in 16 CFR 239). This federal regulation sets forth *what should be contained in a guarantee.*

In a general, any advertisement of a guarantee must clearly and conspicuously *disclose the nature and extent of the guarantee.* This means that the disclosure should contain:

1. What product or part of the product is guaranteed.

2. What characteristics or properties of the product or designated part thereof are covered by, or excluded from, the guarantee.

3. What is the duration of the guarantee.

4. What, if anything, anyone claiming under the guarantee must do before the guarantor will furnish the obligation under the guarantee (such as returning the product or paying for the services or labor charges).

In addition, the mail-order advertiser must clearly and conspicuously disclose the identity and manner in which the guarantor will perform, i.e., whether the guarantor will repair, replace, or refund. If the guarantee is on a pro rata basis (such as tires), the advertising should clearly disclose this fact, particularly the basis on which the article will be prorated (e.g., the time for which the guaranteed product has been used and any deductions made based on that issue). In addition, if the guarantees are to be adjusted on the basis of a price other than the price actually paid by the purchaser, this price should be clearly and conspicuously disclosed.

What to state in a guarantee

Such advertising comments as "satisfaction or your money back," "10-day free trial," or similar representations will be *construed as a guarantee* that the full purchase price will be refunded at the option of the purchaser. If this type of guarantee is subject to any conditions or limitations whatsoever, these conditions or limitations must be set forth. If the words "life," "lifetime," or the like are used in advertising to show the duration of the guarantee, and they relate to any life other than that of the purchaser or original user, the life referred to also must be clearly and conspicuously disclosed.

Some mail-order advertisers like to state in their ads "guaranteed to save you 50 percent," "guaranteed never to be undersold," or "guaranteed lowest prices in town." When these advertisements are made, they should include a clear and conspicuous disclosure of what the guarantor will do if the savings are not realized, together with any time or other limitations that the advertiser/guarantor may impose. Thus, if you use "guaranteed lowest price in town," you should accompany that ad with a disclosure such as, "If, within 30 days from the date you buy a Widge from me, you are not satisfied, I will refund your money." Also note that guaranteeing under a situation where the guarantor does not or cannot perform is also a violation of the FTC rules. Therefore, a mail-order seller may not advertise or represent that a product is guaranteed when said seller cannot or does not promptly and scrupulously fulfill all guarantee obligations. Don't advertise "satisfaction or your money back" when you cannot or do not intend promptly to make full refund upon request.

Shipment guaranteed

Realize that a guarantee can also be a *misrepresentation*, subjecting the representor to a possible fraud action. Therefore, if a mail order merchandiser runs an ad stating "guaranteed for 36 months," the merchandiser is representing that the product normally can be expected to last for 36 months. Such a guarantee should never be used on a product that cannot last for the period stated in the guarantee wording. A vivid example of this type of guarantee would be an ad stating "Guaranteed to grow hair or money back." This can be a *fraudulent* misrepresentation in and of itself, *even if money is returned*. The unhappy bald person could have an action for fraud to recover any actual damages suffered by the inability to grow hair, as well as for punitive damages that are permissible for recovery by the plaintiff in such fraud actions.

Stating a Shipping Time Can Be Legally Binding

The FTC has found that the failure to fill orders, or failure to fill them in the time promised, or within a reasonable time after acceptance of the order constitutes an unfair and deceptive practice.

Additionally, the FTC mail-order merchandise 30-day rule provides that it is an unfair or deceptive act for sellers to solicit any order for the sale of merchandise to be ordered by the buyer through the mail, unless the sellers have a reasonable expectation of being able to ship any order or merchandise to the buyer *within the time clearly and conspicuously stated in any such solicitation*. In other words, if shipment is guaranteed within 24 hours after recept of order, and shipment is not so made, the FTC may find that the seller has engaged in an unfair or deceptive practice.

Be Careful! Don't Suggest That a Product Is Made of Something It's Not

To regulate unfair and misleading practices, the Federal Trade Commission has developed certain rules that are intended to have the force of law. Such rules are set out and referred to as "Federal Trade Commission Guides and Policies." A violation can subject offenders to fines and injunctive remedies by the FTC, as well as to civil actions by purchasers who have been victims of wrongful advertising or a breach of these federal rules.

These misleading practices are covered by general acts, as well as very specific ones. Usually the specific situations have arisen because the FTC wishes to direct attention to a particular product area (such as shoes and slippers), or because of requests from specific businesses that wish to have something from the general acts clarified in their special area. One can gain insight regarding not only the letter of the law, but also its intention, by perusing the specific situations.

Such is the case with advertising shoes, for example. Say that a shoe or slipper is visually depicted in advertising with sufficient clarity to create the impression that the pictorially visible non-leather parts (exclusive of heels) are composed of leather or split leather (or that pictorially visible leather parts are composed of a different kind or type of leather than is the case). The advertising *must contain a statement* clearly and conspicuously disclosing that the visible part or parts are simulated or imitation leather, or the general nature of the visible part or parts must be depicted to show they are not leather or not the type of leather they seem.

It should also be noted by the mail-order merchandiser that the term "leather" or other terms suggestive of leather may be unqualifiedly used only when the shoes or slippers are composed in all *substantial* parts of top grain leather, exclusive of heels, stiffening, and ornamentation. If the shoe or slipper is substantially leather, such terms may be used, if immediately *qualified to show clearly* what parts are leather, provided no leather content shall be emphasized to exaggerate or otherwise deceptively represent the quantity, quality, or extent of leather present.

The federal rule prohibits the unqualified use of the term "leather" and any other terms suggestive of leather to describe shoes and slippers or parts thereof made from split leather or from ground, pulverized, or shredded leather. The term may be used only if qualified so as to provide an *accurate, non-deceptive description.*

Terms suggestive of leather to describe the appearance of a non-leather material must be immediately accompanied by a disclosure that the terms refer only to the appearance and that the material is not leather. An example of this would be "imitation alligator." Furthermore, no trade name, coin name, trademark, depiction symbol, or other words or terms may be used that would *convey the impression* that the shoes or slippers advertised are made with a certain kind of type of material when they are not. An example of such an identification would be the use of "Duraleather" or "Bark Hyde."

State true components

"Free." How to Use This Powerful Word Legally

The words "free" merchandise or service are promotional devices frequently used by mail-order merchandisers to attract customers. Because of the effect on the purchaser, *all such advertising must be pursued with extreme caution to avoid any possibility that the buyer will be misled or deceived.* The most common advertising language includes "free," "buy one—get one free," "two-for-one sale," "50% off with purchase of two," or "1 cent sale." Some related advertising gimmicks, including "Cents Off," "Half-Price Sale," "One-Half Off," may raise many of the same questions.

Be careful about "free"

One of the FTC guidelines is entitled *"Use of the Word 'Free' and Similar Representations,"* contained in 16 CFR 251; 36 Federal Register 21517. Under this guideline, the word "free" indicates that the purchaser is paying nothing for the article, or no more than the regular price for another article, where this is a condition of getting the free merchandise. The FTC feels a purchaser has a right to believe that a merchant will not directly and immediately recover, in whole or in part, the cost of the free merchandise or service by marking up the price of the article which must be purchased or by the substitution of inferior merchandise or service. The article to be purchased must be sold at its regular price, i.e., the price at which the seller has openly and actively sold the product, in the geographic market in which he is now making the "free" offer, in the most recent and regular course of his business, and for a reasonably substantial period of time. The FTC generally considers this period to be 30 days or more. Where consumer products or services fluctuate in price, the regular price is the lowest price of any substantial sales during the 30 days. Note that, except in the case of an introductory offer, if no substantial sales actually are made at the regular price, a "free" or similar offer would not be proper.

The merchandiser of a "free" offer should clearly state all terms, conditions, and obligations at the outset, leaving no reasonable probability that the terms of the offer might be misunderstood (subjecting the merchandiser to liability). A disclosure of terms in a footnote of an ad to which reference is made by an asterisk or other symbol *is not* regarded as making disclosure at the outset.

The FTC even carries the obligation for wrongful advertising of "free" to the supplier: if a supplier knows that a retailer is improperly advertising the word "free," it is improper for the supplier to continue offering the product to this retailer. The supplier should take appropriate action to bring an end to the description, including the withdrawal of the word "free" from the offer. The supplier is also required to offer the product as promoted to all competing retailers or resalers, under the same terms and conditions. If suppliers advertise the promotion, they should identify areas where the offer *is not available,* if the ad is likely to be seen in such areas. They should clearly state that it is available through participating resalers, indicating the extent of participation by using terms such as "some," "all," "a majority," or "a few," as the situation may dictate.

Introductory offers are covered by another rule. In essence, no "free" offer should occur when introducing a new product or service at a specified price unless the seller expects, in good faith, to discontinue the offer after a limited time. The merchandiser must intend to then sell the product minus the "free" offer, but at the same price at which it was promoted with the "free" offer.

A single size of product or single kind of service should not be advertised with a "free" offer in a trade area for more than six months in any twelve-month period, and at least 30 days should elapse before another such offer is promoted in the same trade area. No more than three such offers should be made in the same area in any twelve-month period. Furthermore, during this period, the merchandiser's sale of the product in the size promoted with a "free" offer (in that trade area) should not exceed 50 percent of the total volume of the merchandiser's sale of the product, in the same size, in that trade area.

Don't think you can skirt the law by substituting different words such as a "gift," "Given without charge," "bonus," or other words or terms that tend to convey the impression to the consumer public that an article of merchandise or service is "free." By following these FTC guidelines, you can not only help avoid governmental intervention and civil lawsuits, but you can also successfully conduct your sale.

What Trademarks Mean to Your Business

Frequently overlooked is the possibility of acquiring *one of the most valuable business assets* available under U.S. and international law—the exclusive protection of your right to business goodwill as reflected in a *registered trademark* or *service mark*. These are names and designs that describe products or services to form mental concepts or identification in purchasers' minds.

The primary function of any trademark or service mark is to identify the particular product or service of one business from that of another. This identification is called a trademark to identify a particular physical product, and a service mark to identify intangible actions or services. Unlike patents and copyrights, a *trademark can remain exclusive property in perpetuity* if the business does not abandon it by ceasing to use the mark—or through such conduct, including acts of omission or commission, which causes the mark to lose its significance as an indication of its origin. Substantial monies are spent in promoting the name of a product or service. So trademarks can develop into valuable business assets, even a major factor in the continued success of a particular marketing program.

The cardinal rule when choosing a trademark is that *registrable trademark or service mark words must be adjectives* and, therefore, must modify a noun that is a generic name of a product or service. For example, "Universal" is a registered trademark to identify the exercise equipment of a particular manufacturer. "Universal," the adjective, modifies "exercise equipment," the noun, and designates to the buying public that they should not just buy *any* exercise equipment, but should buy "*Universal* exercise equipment."

If the consuming public comes to treat the trademark as a noun or the name of a type of product or service, rather than as an adjective and a designation for one particular brand of product or service, the mark will no longer identify and distinguish the business' goods or services but may become a generic term. The Otis Elevator Company, after 50 years of use, lost a trademark on the word "escalator" by using it as a noun rather than referring to an "Escalator moving staircase."

Proper use of a trademark is such that if you eliminated the trademark from the advertising copy it would still give you a completed sentence. Example: "Build your body with Universal exercise equipment." Note the difference if you eliminate "Universal" from copy that reads "Build your body with Universal."

Privacy—The Consumer Issue of the 1990s

The sophisticated technology used to capture information about consumers is starting to make people nervous—and generating a backlash among consumers who fear that their privacy is vanishing.

As a result, the privacy issue is under intense scrutiny from the media and every level of government. Both Congress and the executive branch are examining the risks and benefits of data privacy, and hundreds of privacy bills are flooding state legislatures.

To stay in business, you need free and unrestricted access to information about your customers. But you can adhere to the highest ethical standards, and take steps to ensure that information you collect is not improperly or accidentally given to parties who may abuse it. Practicing this kind of "aggressive self-regulation," says the Direct Marketing Association, may help postpone or prevent restrictive legislation. Do your utmost to incorporate good business practices into your operation, and let your customers know and exercise their options.

Mail Preference Service and In-house Name Suppression

One of the best ways to allay your customers' fears about privacy is to tell them how they can keep their names from being rented out to other mailers.

The Mail Preference Service, established by the Direct Marketing Association in 1971, offers consumers the chance to add or remove their names from a mailing list. By contacting MPS, consumers can "opt out" of many lists by indicating they do not wish their names made available to outside sources for marketing purposes. Telephone Preference Service, established in 1985, offers the same service to consumers who do not wish to be contacted by telephone. Consumers can ask to have their names removed from specific lists, or from all lists altogether.

While some catalogs promote Mail Preference Service on their order forms, more choose to promote their own in-house suppression systems. The Exposures catalog uses a fairly standard mail preference message (**Figure 11.1**). It discloses its rental practices in general, saying "Occasionally we offer our customer names to other quality mailers." It then gives customers the option of not having their names rented: "If you would rather not receive such mailings, please send your mail label to . . ." The message is friendly and not offensive to the customer or to the company's rental practices.

The Pottery Barn catalog goes a step further, encouraging customers to communicate exactly how they want their name used (**Figure 11.2**). Under the reassuring headline, "We Want Our Catalogs to be Welcome

EW-6

ORDER TOLL FREE
1-800-222-4947

8 AM to MIDNIGHT (EST) – 7 Days A Week

CUSTOMER SERVICE/ORDER STATUS
For order status or additional information,
please write:

Customer Service Dept.,
1 Memory Lane, P.O. Box 3615
Oshkosh, WI 54903-3615
Or call 1-800-572-5750
Mon - Fri, 8 AM to 8 PM (EST)

SHIPPING
We ship all non-personalized items in stock within 48 hours by UPS or Parcel Post in the Continental U.S. Please use street address where possible. P.O. boxes may delay delivery. Delivery time will be about 1-2 weeks. For express service, see below.

MONOGRAMMING AND ENGRAVING*
Many items in this catalog can be personalized for an additional charge as noted. (Don't forget to add this charge to your total.) Please indicate engraving location where applicable, i.e., center, top, bottom, etc. Allow three weeks extra please (4-5 weeks total). Script or block available on engravable frames. Block type only for gold tooling on albums. Engraving will vary with size of frame.

RETURN POLICY
Follow the instructions on the back side of your packing slip. (Sorry, I can't accept C.O.D. shipments or refund original or return shipping costs.)

HELP PROTECT THE ENVIRONMENT
If you are receiving duplicate catalogs, please send us the labels with addresses that are being duplicated.

MAIL PREFERENCE SERVICE
Occasionally we offer our customer names to other quality mailers. If you would rather not receive such mailings, please send your mail label to:
EXPOSURES, Mail Preference Service, 1 Memory Lane, P.O. Box 3615, Oshkosh, WI 54903-3615

SPECIAL OFFER: SEE INSIDE

Figure 11.1 Exposures catalog

WE WANT OUR CATALOGS TO BE WELCOME IN YOUR HOME

From time to time, we make portions of our customer mailing lists available to carefully screened companies, and we would like to continue sending you only those catalogs you want to receive. If you want to make any changes, please copy your mailing label in the space provided below, tear on perforation and enclose in envelope.

Fold and tear on perforation and enclose in envelope.
I WANT TO MAKE A CHANGE:
☐ I am receiving duplicate catalogs.
Please change the enclosed mailing labels to the address below.
☐ Please do not send Pottery Barn.
☐ Please do not make my name available to other mailers.

Name _____
Customer Account # _____
Address _____ Apt. ____
City _____ State ____ Zip ____

Figure 11.2 Pottery Barn catalog

in Your Home," it offers the standard message but adds a checklist that lets customers indicate whether they want to end duplicate mailings, continue to receive Pottery Barn but not have their names rented, or stop receiving it altogether.

To make it easier for the customer, Pottery Barn suggests enclosing the tear-off form inside its envelope. (Exposures tells customers to send their label to the "Mail Preference Department," implying the need for an additional envelope.) And to underscore the upbeat tone and its promise of service, the opposite side of the coupon lets customers pass along the name of a friend who might enjoy receiving a catalog.

Send Your Friends A Catalog
Many of you get downright excited about our catalog, and get tired of having it borrowed all the time! Please give us the names of interested friends and we'll send them a free copy.

_____
Name

_____
Address

_____
City   State/Zip

*   *   *

_____
Name

_____
Address

_____
City   State/Zip

*Are You Getting Duplicate
or Unwanted Catalogs?*
If you receive multiple copies of our catalog, please send us all the mailing labels and then pass extra catalogs along to friends. If you prefer that we do not rent your name to other catalogs or environmental organizations, please send us your mailing label or call us at 1-800-762-7325 and let us know.

To further insure your privacy, you can ask to be on the Direct Marketing Association's Do Not Rent list. You can contact the *Direct Marketing Association at PO Box 3861, New York, NY 10163.*

For Credit Card Orders Call Toll-Free
1-800-762-7325
Printed on Recycled Paper (of course!)

Figure 11.3   Real Goods catalog

Customers of Real Goods, a catalog marketer of alternative energy products, can simply call an 800-number to remove their names from the list or opt out of list rental (See **Figure 11.3**). Real Goods takes the side of its customers by addressing the privacy issue directly. The phrase "To further insure your privacy . . ." introduces the DMA's Mail Preference Service address and tells customers what the service will provide.

An extremely simple approach is used by Rocky Mountain Computer Outfitters, which simply provides a box on the order form that customers can check if they prefer not to have their names shared. (See **Figure 11.4**). But this innovative company turns mailing list rentals into a consumer benefit. Computer enthusiasts are likely to answer "yes" to the question, "Do you like hearing about new computer products and services?"—and think twice about removing their name.

What's the worst that could happen by putting this type of message in your catalog? A customer (yours) could ask not to be sent any future catalogs. All this would do is save you money—for the printing of the catalog and postage—since this customer most likely would not purchase anyway. But chances are, your customers will stay with you and recommend you to their friends.

By offering name suppression options and promoting Mail Preference Service, you are lessening the possibility of mandatory federal legislation—a possibility that increases every day. And you are letting your customers know that you are sensitive to the privacy issues that may concern them.

Robert Ellis Smith of *The Privacy Journal* believes that privacy initiatives can be a real opportunity to direct marketers. He points out that consumers who ask to be removed from a list are sending you one of two messages: either "Don't waste your money on me," or "I want to do business with you, but don't rent my name." In an era in which information about customers is gold, this is valuable data.

Is this purchase for business or personal use? **Business** ☐ **Personal** ☐

METHOD OF PAYMENT – (DO NOT SEND CASH)

All Purchase Orders are subject to credit approval unless you have an account with Computer Outfitters. Please call first.

☐ Check/M.O. **Make check payable to Rocky Mountain Computer Outfitters.** Check or money order must be in U.S. funds. Checks must have your name preprinted on them. Returned checks are subject to a service charge of $15.

☐ VISA ☐ MasterCard ☐ American Express / OPTIMA ☐ Discover Card

Name as it appears on card:

Account #:

(Please include all numbers on your card.)

Expiration date: Signature:

THANK YOU FOR YOUR ORDER!

Shipping Charge		
Sub Total		
Ohio Residents Add 6% Sales Tax		
TOTAL		

Do you like hearing about new computer products and services? Occasionally we share your name with other companies when we think you might be interested. If you'd prefer **not to be included in these offers**, check here. ☐

Figure 11.4 Rocky Mountain Computer catalog

Keeping Your Customer List Secure

A second area of concern about privacy surrounds the information you gather about your customers during a transaction. The steps you take to guard its confidentiality are important, even though your customers may never know about them—unless something goes wrong.

You can protect your customers from unscrupulous marketers by carefully screening each potential renter of your house list. Watch out for prospective list customers who:

- make unclear offers or outlandish claims;

- make offers that are in bad taste;

- solicit credit offers using an 800-number only. (By omitting a street address, they may be attempting to circumvent the jurisdiction of the U.S. Postal Service.)

When in doubt, ask for a sample of the merchandise the renter is proposing to sell. And always, always seed your list with decoys so you know what exactly your customers are seeing. A fraudulent operation may secure your approval with one offer, but substitute another when your list is used. Decoys will let you detect and put an end to this kind of fraud.

If you suspect illegal or unethical operations, check out the company with the Better Business Bureau, local consumer agencies, or the United States Postal Inspection Service.

When you rent your customer list, be sure you are providing only those data that are appropriate for direct marketing purposes. The DMA cautions that

> information and selection criteria that may be considered to be personal and intimate in nature by all reasonable standards should not provide the basis for lists to be made available for rental, sale, or exchange when there is a reasonable expectation by the consumer that the information would be kept confidential.

The Direct Marketing Association's Guidelines for Mailing List Practices offers more steps you can take to keep your proprietary list—and your customers—from falling into the wrong hands.

Another important measure you can take to safeguard your customers is to ensure that the credit information they supply remains confidential and secure. In its *Fair Information Practices Checklist,* the Direct Marketing Association recommends these precautions:

- Make someone in your company responsible for list security.

- Establish restrictions on your employees to protect against unauthorized access to your list.

- Tell your employees that customer data is confidential and that misuse may result in personal or civil liability.

- Install security measures that prevent remote access to your list via computer.

- Make sure anyone who rents your list observes these same precautions.

Stress to your employees that these procedures must be followed because your company is committed to maintaining and protecting the privacy of your customers.

Consider telling your customers, too. In a world in which personal privacy is a growing concern, you're better off being their ally, not their foe.

APPENDIX

Choosing Type

Deciding which typestyles or sizes to use in your catalog is a decision as important as how to best present a product or how to best describe it.

You'll be safe if you always, always follow these two basic rules:

1. Keep it simple.

2. Make it easy to read.

Here are a few suggestions for observing these rules in your catalog.

- Keep body copy and headlines in a style that is easy to read. Use fancy typestyles only for your logo or occasionally to create an accent.

- Don't mix too many typeface families. You can design an attractive catalog with just one type family, such as Times.

- Use light weight type for body copy, medium weight for subheads, bold for heads. Save italic for accents.

- Serif type is generally easier to read than sans serif type. (For examples of each, see Figure 1)

SERIF	SANS-SERIF
Korinna	Avant Garde
Souvenir	Helvetica
Palatino	Optima
Times Roman	Serif Gothic

Figure 1

- When determining line spacing or leading (the amount of space between lines), use a distance that lets the eye travel over the page with little effort. Lines set too close together or too far apart produce poor readability and eye strain.

Proofreader's Marks and Meanings

Symbol	Meaning	Example	Corrected
e	Take out	This is easy ? *e*	This is easy
ē	Delete and close up	This is (not) easy. *ē*	This is easy.
#	Insert space (air)	This is̲easy. #	This is easy.
eq #	Equal Space	Thisiš easy *eq* #	This is easy.
⌒	Close up	This ⌒ is easy	This is easy.
⌣	Less space between words	This ⌣ is ⌣ easy.	This is easy.
tr	Transpose letters	Thissi/easy	This is easy
tr	Transpose words	is easy (This)	This is easy
wf	Wrong style of type	This (is easy.)	This is easy.
lc	Set in lower case	T(HIS)is easy. *lc*	This is easy.
ls	Letter space	This is e a s y.	This is easy.
caps	Set in caps	t̲h̲i̲s̲ is easy. *caps*	THIS is easy.
sc	Set in small caps	THIS is easy. *sc*	THIS IS EASY.
ital	Set in italic type	This is easy. *ital*	*This is easy.*
rom	Set in roman type	(*This is easy.*) *rom*	This is easy.
bf	Set in bold face	This is easy. *bf*	This **is** easy.
stet	Let it stand	This is (easy.) *stet*	This is easy.
sp	Spell out	This is (e-z.) *sp*	This is easy.
¶	Start paragraph	¶ This is easy.	This is easy.
no ¶	No paragraph	This is ⅃ easy.	This is easy.
|←	Flush left	|← This is easy.	This is easy.
⊓	Raise	This⌐is⌐easy.	This is easy.

Figure 2

- Avoid long line lengths. Don't set more than 40 to 60 characters on a line. When you use very short line lengths, use ragged right type instead of justifying type.

- Choose a type size that permits easy reading, preferably an 8- or 9-point type.

Symbol	Meaning	Example	Corrected
⊔	Lower	This⌊is⌋easy.	This is easy.
⊏	Move left	⊏ This is easy.	This is easy.
⊐	Move right	This is easy. ⊐	This is easy.
‖	Align type	This is easy. ‖	This is easy.
=	Straighten line	This is easy. =	This is easy.
⊙	Insert period	This is easy ⊙	This is easy.
⌾	Insert comma	This is easy ⌾	This is easy,
⊙	Insert colon	This is easy ⊙	This is easy:
⊙	Insert semicolon	This is easy ⊙	This is easy;
⌄	Insert apostrophe	Thiss easy.	This's easy.
⌄ ⌄	Insert quotation marks	⌄This is easy.⌄	"This is easy."
=/	Insert hyphen	This is easy =/	This is easy-
⌄	Insert exclamation mark	This is easy⌄	This is easy!
⌄	Insert question mark	This is easy⌄	This is easy?
?	Query for author	This is easy. ?	Oh yeah!
⊏/⊐	Insert brackets	⌈This is easy.⌉	[This is easy.]
(/)	Insert parenthesis	(/) This is easy. (/)	(This is easy.)
◻	Indent 1 em	◻This is easy.	This is easy.
◻◻	Indent 2 ems	◻◻This is easy.	This is easy.
✗	Broken type	✗ This is easy.	This is easy.
ok ʷ⁄c	OK "with corrections"		
ok ⁰⁄c	OK "as corrected"		

- Don't let your designer run small type against a navy blue, burgundy, dark grey, or other dark background. Thin type may fill in and will certainly be difficult to read. Black type on white paper is *still* the easiest of all to comprehend!

- Colored type can be attractive but may cause reading problems. Small, colored type may reproduce badly because the colors diminish the type's quality.

- Proof your copy carefully. Check for uniform style of punctuation, spelling, capitalization, indentation, and so on. Use the proofreading marks in Figure 2.

Glossary

Additive primaries In color reproduction, red, green, and blue.

Address correction requested (ACR) When printed in the upper left-hand corner of the address portion of the mailing piece (just below the return address), an ACR endorsement authorizes the U.S. Postal Service, for a fee, to furnish the known new address of a person no longer at the address on the mailing piece. Also, undeliverable and unforwardable mail is returned to the sender.

Advertising Any paid communication through various media by business firms, nonprofit organizations, or individuals who are generally identified in the message and who hope to inform or persuade members of a specific audience.

Against the grain Folding or feeding paper at right angles to (against) the grain of the paper.

Agate line A standard of measurement for depth of columns of advertising space. One column inch equals fourteen agate lines.

Airbrush In artwork, a small pressure gun shaped like a pencil that sprays watercolor pigment by means of compressed air. Used to correct and obtain tone or graduated tonal effects, especially on reflective art.

Antique finish Surface of the sheet that features a natural rough finish; usually used for cover papers.

Art Illustrations used in catalogs and advertising for the purpose of visually selling a product.

Basis size Wide variety of papers, each having specific dimensions—e.g., cover paper is 20 inches × 26 inches, bond paper is 17 inches × 22 inches.

Basis weight Weight in pounds of 500 sheets (a ream) of paper cut to certain standard sizes; which are 25 × 38, 20 × 26. This may be referred to as, "80 lb." stock, "60 lb." stock, and so on.

Bible paper Very lightweight, bright, strong, opaque paper, commonly made from rag pulp and mineral filler.

Black-and-white Originals or reproductions (photographs, printing) in single color, as distinguished from multicolor.

Bleed When the printed image extends to the trim edge of the sheet or page, hence "bleeding off the page."

Blister Blemish or bubble caused by too-sudden drying.

Blueprint A photoprint made from stripped-up negatives or positives, used as a proof to check position of all image elements (copy, photos, art).

Body copy The main wording of a selling message, not including the headlines.

Body type A type used for the main text of a catalog, as distinguished from the headings and headlines.

Boldface Type having thick, heavy face, used for emphasis.

Boldface type Type that is bold in line and heavier than the text type, which is light in line.

Bond paper A grade of writing or printing paper with the essentials of durability and strength; used on letterheads and business forms.

Book paper A general term for a group of papers made for the printing trade, excluding newsprint.

Book papers—premium High-cost papers. Their most important qualities are high opacity with low caliper.

Break for color To separate parts that are to be printed in different colors.

Brightness The degree of perceived whiteness of a pulp.

Bringing color up The task of improving the color once the job is on press, to meet the standards of an acceptable job.

Bulk The degree of thickness of paper.

Bulk mail A category of third-class mail specially processed for mailing before delivery to the post office. It consists of a large quantity of identical pieces, each addressed to a different name. The Postal Department's definition of bulk: nonpreferential second, third, and fourth-class mail. Includes parcel post, ordinary papers, and circulars.

Buyer One who orders merchandise or a service.

C/A Change of Address.

Calendering The smoothing of paper by cast-iron rollers that are attached at the end of the paper-making machines.

Calender rolls A set or stack of horizontal cast-iron rolls at the end of a paper machine. Paper is passed between the rolls to increase the smoothness and gloss of the paper's surface.

Caliper The thickness of paper, usually expressed in thousandths of an inch (mils).

Caps and small caps Two sizes of capital letters, made within one size and family of type.

Catalog buyer One who purchases merchandise or a service from a catalog.

CD-Rom catalog A catalog delivered on a compact, read-only memory disk.

Chemical pulp The treatment of groundwood chips with chemicals to remove impurities such as lignin, resins, and gums. The two primary chemicals are sulfite and sulfate.

Cheshire label Specially prepared paper to be mechanically affixed to a mailing piece. In rolls, fanfold, or accordion fold, the paper contains names and addresses printed by a computer in a special format—usually 4 across and 11 down, or 44 to a page—for processing on a Cheshire labeling machine.

Chrome An abbreviation of Ektachrome, Kodachrome, or any other transparency film. The trade name, "Chromalin," is a color proofing system by DuPont.

Chromalin A way of producing a color proof (less expensive than press proofs). It is color applied to a Kromekote stock (looks like clear plastic sheets) in 4 separate "sheets" one color at a time, which when overlaid, show what your 4-color will look like when run.

Coated book paper A paper that is coated on both sides, most often used for letterpress printing. Available in glossy and dull finish.

Coated offset A paper that is coated on both sides; used in offset printing. It has a high resistance to picking. Available in glossy and dull finish.

Coated paper Paper with a surface coating that produces a smooth finish.

Coding A group of letters and numbers used to identify certain characteristics of an address on a list. Also, a code used on reply devices to identify the source from which the address was obtained, such as a mailing list, magazine, or newspaper.

Collate To assemble the various elements of a mailing in sequence for insertion in a mailing envelope. Also, the combining of two or more ordered files to produce a single-ordered file. The same as merge, as in Merge-Purge.

Color bars Bars of the three primary colors plus black located at the edge of a printed sheet so that they can be read with a densitometer to determine ink density.

Color correction Any method, such as masking, dot-etching, re-etching, and scanning, used to improve color image.

Color print A inexpensive version of a Dye Transfer. It is shot photographically, and provides less quality.

Color separation The process of separating full-color originals into the primary printing colors in negative or positive form by photographic process. An artist can also make separations by manually making separate overlays for each color.

Composition Either the setting of type or the material set in type.

Comprehensive layout A detailed artist's rendition that indicates positioning of all elements.

Computer personalization The printing of a letter or other promotional communication by computer, using the recipient's name, address, and information based on data from one or more computer records in order to tailor the promotional message to that specific individual.

Condensed type A narrow or slender width type face.

Contact print A photographic print made from a negative or positive in contact with sensitized paper, film, or printing plate.

Contact screen A photographically-made halftone screen on film having a dot structure of graded density.

Continuous tone An unscreened photographic image containing variable tones from black to white.

Contrast Tonal gradation among the highlights, middle tones, and shadows.

Contrived hot spots Pages of the catalog to which the customer is specifically referred and which therefore tend to produce extra sales.

Copy Text, headlines, or manuscript used to explain a product or service.

Cover paper A term applied to a variety of papers used for the covers of catalogs; usually heavier than the inside pages.

Crop The removal of portions of a photograph or illustration as indicated by lines ("cropmarks") around the subject.

Cross direction The direction across the grain of paper.

Curl The distortion of a sheet due to differences in structure or coating from one side to the other. Also, the waving of paper due to the absorption of moisture.

Cyan One of the subtractive primaries used for one of the four-color process inks. It reflects blue and green light and absorbs red light.

Dandy roll A wire cylinder on a paper-making machine that adds wove or laid effects to the texture.

Deckle The width of the wet sheet as it comes off the wire of a paper machine.

Deckle edge The untrimmed, feathery edge of paper formed where the pulp flows against the deckle.

Densitometer A sensitive photoelectric instrument that measures the density of photographic images and colors.

Density A measure of the relative darkening or blackening of photographic images.

Digest-sized catalog Catalog measuring $5\frac{1}{2} \times 8\frac{1}{2}$ inches.

Digital direct-to-cylinder printing *See* filmless printing.

Digital photography Filmless photography that captures and digitizes images and transfers them directly to a Postscript catalog page.

Direct digital color proofing system Digital proofing system that quickly produces high-resolution color proofs from digital information taken directly from an electronic prepress system. Approval and Digital Matchprint are two such systems.

Direct Marketing Association (DMA) International trade association representing direct marketing. Founded in 1917.

Disk-based catalog A catalog produced on a computer disk or a CD-rom disk.

Display Type Type that is larger and generally fancier than text. Generally used for main headlines.

Domestic Mail Manual The U.S. Postal Service's official guide to mail preparation and classification.

Dot The individual element of a halftone.

Dot etching Chemical etching used to increase or reduce the amount of color to be printed. Dot etching negatives increases color; dot etching positives reduces color.

Drop-out Portions of originals that do not reproduce, especially colored lines or background areas (often on purpose).

Dull finish Low-gloss finish.

Dummy A preliminary layout showing the position of illustrations and text as they are to appear in the final catalog reproduction.

Duplex paper Paper with a different color or finish on each side.

Dye transfer A print of art (that looks like a color print) in which the four colors have been produced one color at a time to closely approximate the original art. Used as a vehicle for retouching, when retouching is necessary.

Em The square (area) of a type body.

Embossed finish Paper with a raised or depressed surface resembling wood, cloth, or other patterns.

En One-half the width of an em.

Enamel A term applied to a coated paper or to a coating material on a paper.

Enamel paper High-gloss polish paper, coated on one side.

English finish A grade of book paper with a smooth, uniform finish.

Engraver's proofs Proofs pulled on stock to show you what the chromes look like on paper.

Etch The production of an image on photographic plate by chemical or electrolytic action.

Face The printing surface of a piece of type.

Federal Trade Commission (FTC) Government regulatory bureau overseeing advertising claims and practices.

Felt side The smoother side of the paper.

Filmless printing A method of printing in which a catalog is produced on computer, its page files are converted to a digital format etched onto the press cylinder, so that no film is involved in the engraving or proofing steps. Also called digital direct-to-cylinder printing.

Filter In color separation photography, a colored piece of gelatin used over the lens or between lenses.

Fine paper Includes printing, writing, and cover papers.

Flush left (or right) In composition, type set to be aligned along the left (or right) edge.

Focus Defines the sharpness of a photograph. To the separator and printer, focus delineates the percentage scale of the original to the final image reproduced in print; i.e., focus at 50 percent (half size).

Foil Paper coated with either aluminum or bronze powder finish or leaf finish.

Folio The page number.

Font The complete assortment of type of one size and face.

Format The size, style, type, margins, printing requirements, etc. of a printed piece.

Four-color process Use of four printing plates—magenta, yellow, cyan, plus black—to reproduce a full-color printed piece.

Free sheet Paper free of mechanical wood pulp.

Friend-of-a-friend (friend recommendation) The name of an prospective customer sent to a catalog company by an established customer so the "friend" will receive a catalog. Generally derived by specific request or a specific program. A third-party inquiry; a referral name.

Fuzz Fibers projecting from the surface of paper.

Gate fold, gate flap An extension of a page in an order form or in any printed piece that is folded so it swings out gatewise when unfolded for reading.

Generation Each succeeding stage in reproduction from the original copy.

Gloss Surface quality that reflects light.

Grade A means of ranking various kinds of paper by quality.

Grain In papermaking, the direction in which most fibers lie (corresponds with the direction the paper is made on paper machine).

Grain long When paper grain (fibers) runs parallel to the long direction of the sheet.

Grain short When paper grain (fibers) runs parallel to the short direction of the sheet.

Grammage A metric term for expressing the basis width of paper.

Groundwood pulp A mechanically-prepared wood pulp used in the manufacture of newsprint and publication papers.

Guarantee The pledge of satisfaction made by seller to buyer that specifies the terms by which the seller will honor his pledge.

Gutter The blank space, after printing area, or inner (center) margin of catalog.

Hard copy Typewritten copy reproduced simultaneously from magnetic, paper, or perforated tape.

High contrast A reproduction in which the difference in darkness (density) between neighboring areas is greater than in the original.

High finish A smooth finish.

Highlight The lightest or whitest parts in a photograph represented in a halftone reproduction by the finest dots or the absence of all dots in a specific portion of a photograph.

Hot spot An area of a catalog that naturally produces added sales such as: front cover, back cover, pages two and three, middle pages.

Imposition Laying out pages in a press form so that they will be in the correct order after the printed sheet is folded.

Impression The pressure of type, plate or blanket or the effect of that pressure as it comes in contact with the paper.

Impression cylinder The cylinder on a printing press against which the paper picks up the impression.

Ink density The ability of ink to absorb light. Can be measured by densitometer.

Ink fountain The device that stores ink and supplies it to the inking rollers of a press.

Ink jet A non-impact printing process that places droplets of ink on paper using information supplied in magnetic tape form. Used to address and personalize catalogs and order forms.

Insert A printed piece placed (inserted) into a catalog or another printed piece.

Italic The style of letters that slope forward as opposed to the upright or roman; often used when indicating a quote or for words requiring emphasis.

Justify To align both right and left margins or to indicate the exact number of characters to fit a given space.

Key To code copy to a dummy by means of symbols or letters. Also, a number or group of numbers that identifies a specific item.

Keyline A mechanical outline used to indicate the exact shape, position, and size of artwork elements such as halftones, line sketches, copy.

Kodachromes A specific brand name of the Eastman Kodak Company; their transparencies and/or reproduction of same. Often used in reference to color transparencies.

Kraft A paper or board containing unbleached wood pulp (brown in color).

Kromekote Coated paper rolled under pressure against a polished, heated cylinder to produce a highly glossed enamel finish. A brand name.

Kromolite Method of producing drop-out halftones photographically through use of filters and combination of line and halftone negatives.

Label A piece of paper with the name and address of the recipient to be affixed to a mailing.

Lacquer A clear coating, usually glossy, applied to a printed sheet for protection or effect.

Laid paper Paper with parallel lines on the surface, giving a ribbed effect.

Laminate proofs A proof that simulates the look of a final printed piece by providing single-sheet proofs made from film negatives or positives. Known as Chromalin or Matchprint.

Laser An intense light beam with very narrow band width that can produce images by electronic impulses. It makes possible imaging by remote control from computers or facsimile transmission.

Laser platemaking The use of lasers for scanning pasteups and/or exposing plates in the same or remote locations.

Leaders Rows of dashes or dots used to guide the eye across the page.

Letterpress Any printing that is done direct from type. The term is used in contrast to printing done by the offset process.

Letterset (dry offset) The printing process that uses a blanket (like conventional offset) for transferring the image from plate to paper.

Lettershop A company that handles the mechanical details of mailing, addressing, imprinting, collating, inserting.

Letterspacing The placing of additional space between each letter of a word.

Lightface A description given to type having a face with thin lines that prints a light tone, as opposed to bold or black-face type.

Line copy Any copy suitable for reproduction without using a halftone screen.

Line drawings Artwork with solid black lines that can be reproduced without using halftone screens.

Lithography A printing process that prints from plates made from photographs. Offset lithography is usually called simply "offset."

Machine coated Paper that is coated on one or two sides on the paper machine.

Machine finish (M.F.) Any finish produced on papermaking machines.

Machine glazed (M.G.) High-gloss finish produced mechanically on papermaking machines.

Mail date(s) Date(s) on which a company mails a specific promotion. If rented lists are used, the date(s) on which a list user, by prior arrangement with list owner, is obligated to mail a specific list. No other date is acceptable without express approval of the list owner.

Mailer An advertiser who uses the mail to promote a product or service. A direct mail advertising piece. A wrapper, tube, or a folding carton used to protect materials in the mail.

Mail order A method of conducting business wherein merchandise is offered by mail; orders are received by mail, by telephone, or electronically; and/or merchandise is shipped by mail.

Mail oriented The characteristic of responding to mail order offers.

Mail Preference Service (MPS) A service of the Direct Marketing Association by which consumers can request to have their names removed from or added to mailing lists. The names are made available to both association members and nonmembers.

Make ready Material used on a printing press to bring all type matter and illustrations to the point of reproductive quality. Also the process of preparing material on the press.

Make ready sheets Sheets used in getting reproductive quality when starting a production press run. These sheets are generally waste.

Makeup The arrangement of lines of type and illustrations into pages.

Market A group of people having both purchasing power and the willingness to spend to meet either needs or desires.

Marketing Those business activities that direct the flow of goods and services from the producer to the consumer.

Marketing mix The manipulation of marketing variables into a suitable marketing program for a particular firm. Includes product, package, price, distribution, channels, personal selling, advertising, and sales promotions.

Marketing plan A formal, written "blueprint" for an organization's entire marketing program.

Marketing research The systematic gathering, recording, and analyzing of data about problems concerning the marketing of goods and services. Includes the study of size, structure, composition, disposable income, and other factors of a particular segment of the broader market.

Market profile Description of the demographics and psychographics of a target market. Notes the sex, age, income, and other characteristics of persons making up a specific market.

Market segmentation The division of the total market into homogeneous subsets. This marketing strategy makes it possible for each subset to be addressed most appropriately.

Market share That percentage of a market controlled by a particular company or product line.

Market test The controlled testing of a limited but carefully chosen sector of a market in order to predict sales or profits of one or several marketing actions, either in absolute or relative terms.

Matte finish Dull paper finish without gloss or luster.

Matte print Photoprint having a dull finish.

Measure (type) The length, usually expressed in picas or ems, of a single line of type.

Mechanical A term for a camera-ready pasteup of artwork. It includes type, photos, and line art, all on one artboard.

Mechanical pulp Groundwood pulp produced by mechanically grinding wood chips.

Mechanical screen The dot or line pattern used by a photoengraver for reproducing an illustration.

Mechanical separations Art prepared with separate overlays for each color to be used in printing.

Middle tones The tonal range between highlights and shadows of a photograph or reproduction.

Moire Undesirable pattern that results when a cut is made from the print of a halftone or certain other types of printed illustrations; i.e., by photographing a printed illustration.

Mylar In offset preparation, a polyester film made by DuPont and, because of its mechanical strength and dimensional stability, specially suited for shipping positives.

Name-removal service Part of the Mail Preference Service of the Direct Marketing Association providing a form that a consumer can fill out and return, requesting that his name be removed from all mailing lists used by participating members of the Association and other direct mail users.

Negative Film containing an image in which the values of the original are reversed so that the dark areas appear light and vice versa.

Newsprint Paper made mostly from groundwood pulp and small amounts of chemical pulp.

North/south labels Reading from top to bottom, these mailing labels are designed to be affixed with Cheshire equipment.

Odd page Right-hand pages, which carry odd folios (3, 5, 7, etc.).

Off color Paper or ink that does not match a specified sample.

Offset Printing process using an intermediate blanket cylinder to transfer an image from the image carrier to the substrate. Short for offset lithography.

O.K. A/C Proofreader's mark to indicate a proof is without error.

O.K'd sheet A sheet signed to indicate the job is okayed and can be printed.

O.K. W/C Proof is okay except for indicated corrections.

Opacity That property of paper that minimizes the "show-through" of printing from the back side or the next sheet.

Opaque In photoengraving and offset lithography, to paint out areas on a negative not wanted on the plate. In paper, the property that makes it less transparent.

Opaque ink An ink that conceals all color beneath it.

Optical character recognition (OCR) The use of light-sensitive devices for the machine identification of printed characters.

Optical scanner A device that optically scans printed data and converts each character into an electronic equivalent for processing.

Order blank envelopes Business reply envelopes with an order form printed on one side of a sheet and the address reply form on the other. Recipient fills in order, folds and seals envelope for mailing.

Order card A reply card—often a self-mailer—to be filled out, checked or initialed by prospect or customer, and mailed back to the advertiser for the purpose of initiating a reply or order.

Out of register When color plates are out of alignment or are not printed in perfect relationship for accurate reproduction.

Overlay A transparent covering over artwork where color break, instructions, or corrections are marked.

Overrun That printing which is in excess of the amount specified—up to 10 percent usually acceptable.

Page makeup Assembly of all elements to make up a page. Desktop publishing systems electronically assemble page elements to compose a complete page with all elements in place.

Page proof Typesetting proof that shows type in its position on the page.

Pagination Arranging pages in proper sequence.

Paper grain Grain of paper runs parallel with length of paper as it is received from the mill.

Peel-off-label A self-adhesive label on a backing sheet that is attached to a mailing piece. Designed to be removed and placed on order blank or card.

Perfect binding Machine binding method wherein the back folds are cut off, leaf edges roughed, glue applied, and a cover then attached without the use of binding wire or sewing.

Perfecting press Rotary printing two sides of paper during one operation.

Personalizing Individualizing direct mail pieces by adding the name of the recipient.

Photo-composing The assembly of separate elements into an integrated page layout.

Photolettering Display type lines created by photographically printing individual characters on photosensitive paper or film.

Photomechanical Any platemaking process using photographic negatives or positives exposed onto plates or cylinders covered with photosensitive coating.

Photostat A positive reproduction of a piece of art on paper. A trade name.

Pick The small particles of paper that loosen from the surface during printing.

Picking The lifting of the paper surface during printing. It occurs when pulling force (tack) of ink is greater than surface strength of paper.

Piggy-back An offer riding along with another offer at no charge.

Pigment In printing inks, the fine solid particles used to give color, body, or opacity.

Pinpoint dot The finest halftone dot used in photoengravings.

Pin register The use of accurately positioned holes and special pins on copy, film, plates and presses to insure proper register or fit of colors.

Platen Flat surface upon which paper rests when it comes in contact with printing surfaces. Also short for platen press.

Platen press Any press that gives a printed impression by bringing together two flat surfaces, one of which is called a bed and the other a platen.

Plates Flat, smooth pieces of metal that have been treated to create a printing surface.

Plough/fold A special piece of equipment attached to web presses that allows a printed piece to be folded while a job is running, thus reducing costs.

Plugging A condition in which the nonprint area between dots fills in with ink so that it is solid black.

PMS colors Refers to Pantone Matching System, an established color system that gives the percentage of (red) Cyan, Blue, Black, and Yellow needed to match a color sample. Colors are designated as PMS 265, for example.

Point size Standardized measurement system for type. There are twelve points (approximately 1/72 inch) to a pica and six picas to an inch.

Positive In photography, film containing an image in which the dark and light values are the same as in the original.

Prepress proofs In color reproduction, proofs that approximate the look of the printed art before it is printed.

Press proofs In color reproduction, a proof of color from a proof press, in advance of the production run.

Press sheet The printed sheet.

Pressure-sensitive paper Material with an adhesive coating, protected by a backing sheet until used, and which will stick without moistening.

Primary letters Lower-case characters that have no ascenders or descenders.

Print quality The properties of paper that affect its appearance and the quality of printing reproduction.

Process colors In printing, the subtractive primaries: yellow, magenta, and cyan, plus black in four-color process printing.

Process four-color printing The use of yellow, red, blue, and black positives for reproducing almost any color.

Process plates Color plates, two or more, used in combination with each other to produce other colors and shades.

Process printing Use of primary colors printed over each other with nonopaque inks to produce a variety of tints and hues.

Product positioning Communication techniques to develop a marketing strategy insuring that a product or service is viewed and understood by potential customers as what the seller wants it to represent.

Progressive proofs A set of proofs separated into color sequence starting with black, blue, red, and ending with yellow. Each set will show what the single color looks like when separated out of a four-color chrome. As each color is overlayed on top of another, the printer finally arrives at the four-color appearance. Progressives are extremely helpful in determining any color corrections.

Proofing Denotes the operation of pulling proofs of plates for proofreading, revising, trial, approval of illustration, and other purposes prior to printing.

Proof press A small printing press, usually hand-operated, for pulling proofs.

Prove To pull a proof.

Psychographics Statistical description of a group of consumers based on characteristics of interests, lifestyles, or attitudes.

Pull sheets Sheets removed from the run after every press stop. They are considered good sheets.

Pulling a proof Printer's term for making a copy of a cut or type matter on a proof press.

Pulp Papermaking material existing in a disintegrated fibrous wet or dry state.

Qualified leads Truly interested prospects as distinguished from the merely curious. Individuals who have taken some type of positive action in their inquiries about a given product or service, such as sending a small fee for a catalog.

Rag book High-quality book with longevity, made from rag content paper.

Rag content paper Bond and ledger papers containing from 25 percent to 100 percent rag fibers.

Ream Five hundred sheets of paper.

Ream weight The weight of one ream of paper (also called basis weight).

Reduction Decreasing the density or opacity of a negative by removing some of the metallic silver forming the image.

Reflection copy (reflective art) An illustration that is viewed and must be photographed by light reflected from its surface, such as photographs, drawings.

Register In printing, fitting of two or more printing images on the same paper in exact alignment with each other.

Register marks Crosses, lines, or other devices applied to original copy prior to photography; used for positioning negatives in register, or for register of two or more colors in process printing.

Reproduction proof A reproducible copy of an illustration or type pulled on a special proof press; used for camera ready art to be photographed for offset reproduction or engraving. Commonly called "Repro".

Retouching A process that adds or takes away color to improve the printing reproduction of artwork.

Return postage guaranteed Legend that should be imprinted on the address face of envelopes or other mailing pieces if the mailer wishes the Postal Service to return undeliverable third class bulk mail. There is a charge equivalent to the single piece third class rate for each such piece returned.

Rotary press Letterpress in which paper fed from a continuous roll is printed as it passes between an impression cylinder and a curved printing plate.

Rotogravure paper A specially finished paper used for rotogravure printing.

Rough A loose layout in sketchy form generally used in the planning stages of product presentation or catalog page layout.

Run-around In composition, the term describing a type area set in line lengths that are adjusted to fit around a picture or another element of the design.

Saddle stitching A method of binding, with wire staples fastened through the back fold, enabling a catalog to open out flat.

Saddle wire The fastening of a booklet by wire through the middle fold of the sheets (saddle stitch).

Sans serif Letters without serifs (or shoulders).

Satin finish A special smooth paper finish suggesting satin.

Scaling Determining the proper size of a printed image by reducing or enlarging the original.

Scanner An electronic device used to correct and separate color.

Score To impress a mark with a string or rule in the paper to make folding easier.

Screen A pattern consisting of the number of dots per square inch in a halftone.

Secondary color Violet, orange, green produced by mixing two primary colors.

Self-mailer A direct mail piece that needs no outer envelope or special wrapper.

Separation negative A negative made from any single color of a multicolor illustration.

Serif The short cross-lines (also called shoulders) at the ends of the main strokes of many letters in some type faces.

Shadow The darkest parts in a photograph, represented in a halftone by the largest dots.

Sheet fed Gravure printing produced on separate sheets of paper (in contrast to rotogravure, which is done on a continuous web or roll of paper).

Short grain paper Paper made with the machine direction in the shortest sheet dimension.

Show-through The printing of text or illustrations that can be seen through the sheet on the reverse side under normal lighting conditions.

Side-stitching A binding method with wire staples driven through the far left side of a catalog, entering from the cover and fastening on the back cover. Also Side Wire.

Side-wire In binding, to wire the pages or signatures of a catalog on the left side front near the backbone.

Signature A section of printed sheets in 8, 12, 16, or 32 pages made by folding a single printed sheet.

Silhouette An illustration from which the background of the image has been cut or etched away (dropped out).

Silverprint A photocopy used as a proof.

Skid A platform support for a pile of cut sheets, boxes, or catalogs.

Slim jim A catalog with a 6" × 11" trim size that qualifies for bulk letter rates if it weighs no more than 3.3067 ounces.

Slitting Cutting printed paper into two or more sections by means of cutting wheels on a press or folder.

Small caps An alphabet of smaller capital letters approximately the size of the lower case letters.

Soft dot In photography, a dot whose halation or fringe is excessive. Conversely, when the fringe is so slight as to be barely noticeable and the dot is very sharp, it is called 'hard.'

Solid (type) Type matter set with no added leading.

Solids One hundred percent tones or colors that have no dots in them when printed.

Source code An identifier, usually four to six characters in length assigned to a prospect or customer record and appearing on the printed label. It enables the client to track the performance of lists and catalogs when responses come back.

Soy-based ink Ink in which petroleum oil is partially replaced by soybean oil.

Spacing Separation between characters or groups of characters in type. Letterspacing between individual characters. Wordspacing between words. Linespacing between lines.

Spectrum The complete range of colors in the rainbow, from short wavelengths (blue) to long wavelengths (red).

Spine Backbone of a catalog or book.

Splice The joining of two webs of paper.

Spot glue Glue added to a printed piece or envelope in a "spot" that allows another piece to be attached to it, or which allows a position to be maintained.

Square halftone A finishing style in which the halftone screen runs to the edge of the printing plate, which is trimmed straight both vertically and horizontally.

Step-and-repeat The procedure of reproducing the same image from one negative or positive any number of times on a printing plate.

Stet A proofreader's mark, written in the margin, signifying that the original copy, marked for corrections, should remain unchanged.

Stitch The number of staples used in the spine of a catalog—usually two.

Stock Paper or other material to be printed.

Stock photo Photographs by professional photographers on a variety of subjects available for reproduction commercially for a determined fee. Users choose an appropriate photograph for a fee rather than commissioning a specific shot.

Strip-in To insert additional material into a photographic negative or positive used for platemaking.

Stripping In offset-lithography, the positioning of negatives (or positives) on a flat (goldenrod) prior to platemaking.

Studio A commercial organization that prepares artwork or photography for advertising.

Supercalender stock A paper stock with a high glossy finish, produced by calendering.

Tack The pulling power of separation force of ink. A tacky ink has high separation forces and can cause surface picking or splitting of weak papers.

Tensile strength Resistance to force parallel to the plane of a specific size sheet of paper.

Text The body matter (editorial) of a page or book, as distinguished from the headings.

Third class mail Non-personalized mail with delayed handling. Most direct mail advertising is sent third class.

Three-color process The reproduction of a full-color original by using three colors, usually red, yellow, and blue.

Tints Various even tone areas (strengths) of a solid color.

Tone The shade or degree of a color. A quality or value of a color.

Tone value Intensity of a color or a mass of type, as compared to black, white, and gray.

Translucency Ability to transmit light without being transparent.

Transparency A photographic image on film that allows images to be seen through a sheet. Black and white and four-color.

Transpose To exchange the positions of a letter, word, or line with that of another letter, word, or line.

Trim The maximum width of finished paper that can be made by a particular machine.

Type gauge A printer's tool calibrated in picas and used for type measurement.

Typographic error Mistake made when type is set.

Typography The process of setting material in type for printing.

U.C. Upper-case or capital letters.

U&LC Upper and Lower case. Capital and small letters.

Unbleached Paper not treated by bleaching; has a light brown hue.

Undercoat A clear coating sometimes applied to foil during printing, but before laying on ink. Frequently used under white ink to emphasize white ink color.

Underlay Pieces of paper pasted under type or cut to bring it to the proper level for printing.

Unit In multicolor presses, refers to the combination of inking, plate and impression operations to print each color. A four-color press has four printing units, each with its own inking, plate, and impression functions.

-up In printing, two-up, three-up, etc., refers to imposition of material to be printed on a larger size sheet to take advantage of full press capacity.

UPS United Parcel Service.

USPS United States Postal Service.

Vellum finish In papermaking, a toothy finish that is relatively absorbent for fast ink penetration.

Velox An engraver's halftone print of a photograph. Used for placement or reproduction, and also for retouching.

Vignette An illustration in which the background gradually fades away, in contrast to a silhouette or an illustration with a full background. Also, a halftone in which the tone of the engraving blends into the white of the paper.

Warm color In printing, a color that has a yellowish or reddish cast.

Wash A drawing done in a wet medium as opposed to a line drawing.

Wash drawing Drawing in which a water-soluble color is applied as a wash.

Whiteness The extent to which a paper approaches ideal white.

White envelope Envelope having a die-cut window on the front, exposing address printed on enclosure. Window may be open or covered with transparent material. Also called window envelope or die-cut envelope.

White mail An order or reply that is not on coded order form sent out by advertiser, making it difficult or impossible to trace which promotional piece prompted response. Refers also to all mail other than orders and payments.

Wire stitching The fastening together (binding) of pages with wire staples.

With the grain Folding or feeding paper into a press parallel to the grain of the paper.

Woodcut Printing plate made by carving nonprinting areas out of a type-high block of wood.

Wove paper Paper having a uniform, unlined surface and a soft, smooth finish.

Yellow One of the subtractive primaries, the hue of which is used for one of the four-color process inks. It reflects red and green light and absorbs blue light.

Index

Manufacturer's information, for
    product work sessions, 81–86, 92
Marketer, 7
Markets, new, 4
Master grid. *See* Grid layout
Merchandiser, 7
    and product work sessions, 86–87
Mixed product format, 52–54
    alphabetical organization and, 54
    color and, 52–53
Multiple covers, 38

Non-print alternatives, 4–5

On-line catalogs, 4–5
Order form, 271–304
    checklist for, 304
    credibility and, 281–283
    design of, 292–295, 301
    envelope for, 288–291
    improvement techniques, 276
    information given and requested on,
        302–303
    information panel and, 276–284
    ordering channel impact of, 297–301
    panel for, 272–27
    placement of, 296–297
    positioning of, 264–265
    product panel and, 285–287

Packaging, guarantee of, 250–251
Page layout, 54–62. *See also* Layout
    asymmetrical, 58–62, 63
    symmetrical, 55–57, 63
Panel
    information, 276–284
    order form, 272–276
    product, 285–287
Paper
    choosing, 311–316
    finishes for, 313–314
    ink and, 314–315
    trim size of, 316
Personality, of catalog, 166
Photographer, 7
    directing, 98–99, 111–113
    finding, 95–98
Photography, 11, 95–104. *See also* Art;
        Page layout
    vs. art, 151–158
    art combined with, 158–162
    back cover, 107–111
    basic techniques of, 113–119
    captions for, 230, 241–242
    end-benefit shot, 136–140

ensuring good reproduction, 162–163
    headlines for, 230, 237–241
    inside product, 111–113
    in-use shot, 130–136
    layouts and, 119–139, 140–141
    propped shot, 123–129
    stock photos, 102–104
    straight shot, 119–123
    studio shooting, 99–100
Planning, 9–26
    production, 305–334
PMS colors, 323
Positioning, in product presentation,
        146, 147
Press preparation, 12
Press run, 334
Price, guarantee of, 251, 258–259
Price lines, 204–206
Print, non-print alternatives to, 4–5
Printing, 12. *See also* Production
        planning
    bids for, 308–310
    bindery and lettershop selection, 326–
        331
    choosing and working with printer,
        307–311
    color separation and, 317–323
    costs and, 306
    methods of, 310–311
    paper for, 311–316
    press run and, 334
Privacy, legal guidelines and, 346–351
Privacy Journal, The, 349
Product(s). *See also* Focus
    art used to enhance, 156–157
    comparative presentations of, 145–149
    deceptive advertising about, 342–343
    guarantee of, 250
    selection of, 87
    test results and, 83, 92
Product body copy. *See* Copywriting
Product category format, 49–50
Product changes, 22–24
Product formats, customer reading
        patterns and, 53. *See also* Formats
Production
    creative, 333
    quality of, 3
    schedule for, 13, 15–21
    steps in, 14–15
Production manager, 7
Production planning, 305–334
    bindery and lettershop selection, 326–
        331
    checklist for, 333–334

color separator and, 317–323
    paper and ink selection, 311–316
    price, quality, service, and, 306
    printer and, 307–311
    vendor selection, 306
Production samples, 82
Production team, 7
Product panel, on order form, 285–287
Product photography, 111–113. *See also*
        Art; Photography
Product review, 10–11
Product work sessions, 81–94
    art and copy clippings for, 82–83
    concluding, 92–93
    conducting, 87–92
    defined, 81
    manufacturer's information for, 83–86
    merchandiser's notes for, 86–87
    session requirements, 81–87
Promotion, 3
    and envelope, 288–291
Proofing
    of copy. *See* Copywriting
    of four-color work, 320–323
Proportion. *See* Page layout
Prototypes, 82

Reading patterns, of customers, 53
Regulations. *See* Legal guidelines
Regulation Z. *See* Truth in Lending
Research, image and, 27

Sales history, 88
Sales promotion
    on back cover, 40–43
    on front cover, 34–35
Schedule (creative)
    production, 13, 15–21
    setting up and maintaining, 12
    steps in, 14–15
    twenty-one week countdown and, 15–21
Search-and-send merchandise, 339
Seasonal merchandise, 338–339
Segmentation, 2
Selling, and envelope, 288–291
Separator. *See* Color separation
Service, guarantee of, 250
Shipping
    delayed merchandise shipment notice
        and, 338–339
    legality of time statements, 342
Single product category catalog, 35–38
Size, art showing, 152–154. *See also*
        Layout
Smith, Robert Ellis, 349

MAXWELL SROGE COMPANY, INC.
522 Forest Avenue
Evanston, Illinois 60602
Tel: (708) 866-1890
FAX: (708) 866-1899

Consulting

For more than 20 years, Maxwell Sroge Company has specialized in mail order and catalog consulting. During the time, the company has worked with large, mid-sized and small businesses, helping them start new businesses, build and improve existing businesses as well as buy and sell businesses. Clients include IBM; AT&T; General Foods; Swiss Colony; Mars; Spiegel; Quaker Oats; Gillette; Otto Versand, and RCA, among others.

Catalog Design

Working with top firms such as Barclay Haggin Kartomen & Reese/MORENOW, Maxwell Sroge company offers assistance with consumer and business-to-business catalogs, providing clients with creative services, photography and state-of-the-art computer publishing capabilities.

Publishing

Maxwell Sroge Publishing produces two bi-weekly newsletters:
Non-Store Marketing Report monitors the entire non-store market for management executives. Vital, expert analysis of up-to-the-minute news, facts and trends. A must for inside information and predictions in this challenging industry. Includes two Company Profiles in each issue and a quarterly Trendwatch financial report.
The Catalog Marketer, the "how-to" newsletter on creating and producing catalogs. Industry experts share proven ideas and advice on every area of cataloging from design to art, copy, lists, printing, merchandise, telemarketing, cost controls, analysis and more.

International Catalog Consulting and Production

In partnership with experts in the United States and abroad, Maxwell Sroge Company has formed Trans Atlantic Catalogue Corporation (TRACC). TRACC offers assistance to U.S. catalog companies who wish to launch their catalog businesses in the United Kingdom and Europe. In addition to turnkey management support, these international partners offer market research, catalog marketing expertise and experience in conducting business outside the United States.